IN DEFENSE OF CHRISTIAN HUNGARY

IN DEFENSE OF CHRISTIAN HUNGARY

Religion, Nationalism, and Antisemitism, 1890–1944

Paul A. Hanebrink

CORNELL UNIVERSITY PRESS

Ithaca and London

Cornell University Press gratefully acknowledges receipt of
a grant from Rutgers, the State University of New Jersey,
which aided in the publication of this book.

First published 2006 by Cornell University Press
Printed in the United States of America

Library of Congress Cataloging-in-Publication Data

Hanebrink, Paul A.
    In defense of Christian Hungary : religion, nationalism, and antisemitism, 1890–1944 /
Paul A. Hanebrink.
        p. cm.
    Includes bibliographical references and index.
    ISBN-13: 978-0-8014-4485-2 (cloth : alk. paper)
    ISBN-10: 0-8014-4485-3 (cloth : alk. paper)
    1. Hungary—Politics and government—1918–1945. 2. Christianity and
politics—Hungary—History—20th century. 3. Nationalism—Hungary—History—
20th century. 4. Nationalism—Religious aspects—Christianity—History—20th
century. 5. Christianity and antisemitism—Hungary—History—20th century.
6. Antisemitism—Political aspects—Hungary—History—20th century. I. Title.
    DB955.H34 2006
    943.9'043—dc22   2006006041

Cornell University Press strives to use environmentally responsible
suppliers and materials to the fullest extent possible in the publishing
of its books. Such materials include vegetable-based, low-VOC inks
and acid-free papers that are recycled, totally chlorine-free, or partly
composed of nonwood fibers. For further information, visit our website
at www.cornellpress.cornell.edu.

Cloth printing   10 9 8 7 6 5 4 3 2 1

Contents

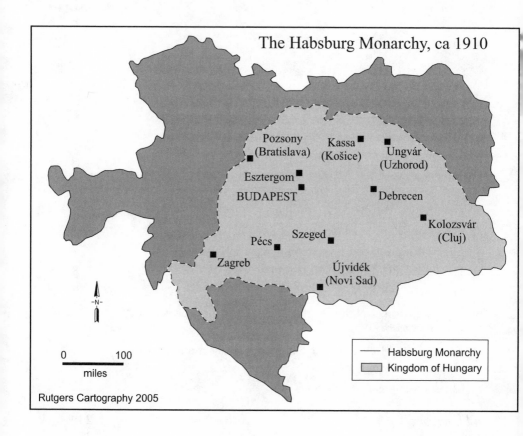

The Habsburg Monarchy, ca 1910

Pozsony
(Bratislava)

Kassa
(Košice)

Ungvár
(Uzhorod)

Esztergom

BUDAPEST

Debrecen

Kolozsvár
(Cluj)

Pécs

Szeged

Zagreb

Újvidék
(Novi Sad)

-N-

0   100
miles

Habsburg Monarchy
Kingdom of Hungary

Rutgers Cartography 2005

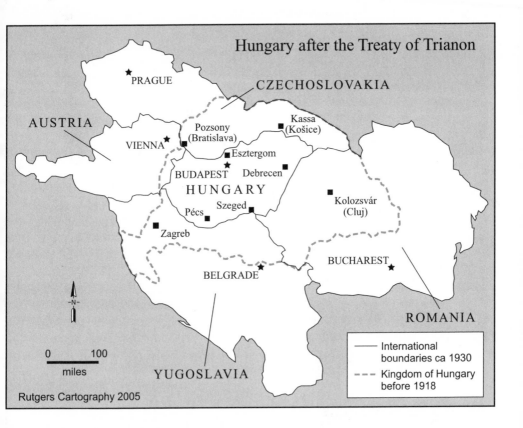

Hungary after the Treaty of Trianon

PRAGUE

CZECHOSLOVAKIA

AUSTRIA

VIENNA

Pozsony
(Bratislava)

Kassa
(Košice)

Esztergom

BUDAPEST

Debrecen

HUNGARY

Pécs

Szeged

Kolozsvár
(Cluj)

Zagreb

BUCHAREST

BELGRADE

ROMANIA

—N—

0   100

miles

YUGOSLAVIA

—— International
boundaries ca 1930

– – – Kingdom of Hungary
before 1918

Rutgers Cartography 2005

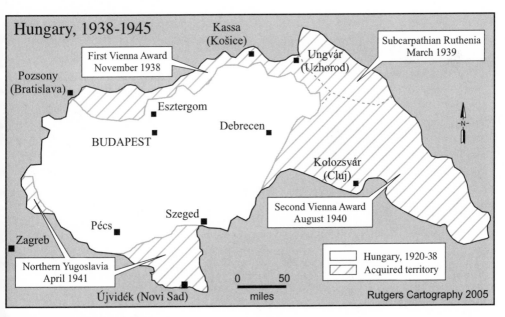

Hungary, 1938-1945

Kassa
(Košice)

First Vienna Award
November 1938

Ungvár
(Uzhorod)

Subcarpathian Ruthenia
March 1939

Pozsony
(Bratislava)

Esztergom

Debrecen

BUDAPEST

Kolozsvár
(Cluj)

—N—

Szeged

Second Vienna Award
August 1940

Pécs

Zagreb

Hungary, 1920-38

Acquired territory

Northern Yugoslavia
April 1941

0   50

miles

Újvidék (Novi Sad)

Rutgers Cartography 2005

Acknowledgments

I began working on Christian nationalism in Hungary at the University of Chicago. Michael Geyer and John W. Boyer advised me on the project from its very beginnings and taught me to think broadly about Central Europe and Hungary's place within it. I am fortunate to count them as teachers and friends. At Chicago, Susan Gal also gave me invaluable suggestions. My interest in the history of Hungary and of the former Habsburg lands developed first as an undergraduate in the seminars of Professor István Deák at Columbia University. István has remained a generous adviser and friend. At Cornell University Press, Roger Haydon has answered all my questions and concerns with attentiveness and good humor. I also thank Teresa Jesionowski for her help with the manuscript. I am grateful to the two anonymous readers for the press who offered invaluable suggestions for the final version. Of course, any errors in what follows are my own.

In writing this book, I have made several research trips to Hungary and accumulated debts that I am happy to acknowledge here. First, I thank Dr. Attila Pók of the Institute of History of the Hungarian Academy of Sciences for first orienting me in Budapest, introducing me to so many people, and being generous with his time and advice. András Gerő, Jenő Gergely, Dániel Szabó, and Margit Balogh were kind enough to speak with me at early stages in this project and offer their views. András Hegedűs and his colleagues at the Primatial Archive in Esztergom and Edit Nagy and her colleagues at the Ráday Archive of the Danubian Reformed Church District made research in those places a true intellectual pleasure. Mrs. Sándor Uray kindly gave permission to examine the papers of her father, László Ravasz, which are kept in the Ráday Archive. On my briefer forays into the Hungarian National Archives and the Lutheran (Evangélikus) National Archive, the archivists welcomed me and helped find my way through their collections. The entire staff of the Hungarian National Library was unfailingly gracious as they helped me track down references and periodicals. I also thank the Hungarian National Museum and the Historical Photo Archive there for permission to use the photograph that adorns the jacket of this book. Thanks also to Mrs. Gyula Stemmler and her colleagues in the Photo Archive for helping me locate the photo. Mike Siegel patiently negotiated the complexities of East-Central European politics and geography to create the maps.

Research requires money and a number of grant-giving institutions have given generous support. A Fulbright/IIE grant made it possible to spend a rewarding year in Hungary. A CASPIC grant from the University of Chicago allowed me to devote the next year to thinking and writing about what I had gathered. In the fall of 1999, the United States Holocaust Memorial Museum also offered me a place to work on the problem of Christian nationalism in a truly stimulating environment. Rutgers University has helped to support research and publication of this book. Through the generosity of an ACLS-Eastern Europe grant, I had the luxury of a year of leave to write and revise and the happy possibility of spending that time in Charlotte, North Carolina.

I am grateful to Jim Bjork, David Frey, Eagle Glassheim, Paul Steege, Christine Haynes, Árpád von Klimó, Samuel Moyn, Cindy Paces, and Mark Wilson for long discussions, helpful research suggestions, and above all, for friendship. No one could ask for a more welcoming intellectual environment than the one I found when I came to Rutgers. Belinda Davis, John Gillis, Matt Matsuda, Jim Masschaele, and Bonnie Smith all read parts of this work and helped me shape its arguments more forcefully. As I was preparing this manuscript, the Kennebunkport Circle was formed. It is a marvelous forum for discussing work in progress in absolutely idyllic surroundings, and I can only hope it continues.

My greatest debts are to those closest to me. I have my interest in history from my parents, Wayne and Anneliese Hanebrink, who have always encouraged me in my study of it. Their love and support have been constant and continue to sustain me. Finally, I cannot imagine this book without Melissa Feinberg. She has read, talked about, and listened to many versions of this work, even as she was writing a book of her own. With her keen eye for what is essential, she has always kept me focused on the bigger picture when I threatened to lose myself in the details. Since I have known her, I have been inspired by the passion, spirit, and critical engagement that she brings to her own work. Her example has changed how I think about writing history. For her love and intellectual companionship, I am profoundly grateful.

P.A.H.

IN DEFENSE OF CHRISTIAN HUNGARY

Introduction

When Cardinal Eugenio Pacelli, state secretary at the Vatican but soon to
be Pope Pius XII, came to Budapest for the Thirty-fourth International Eucharistic Congress in May 1938, he arrived in a country that was celebrat-
ing nearly a millennium of Christian history. For five days, public life was
filled with events proclaiming the close relationship between the Hungarian state and the Roman Catholic Church. Tens of thousands of pilgrims
from around the world joined Hungarian Catholics in worship, conferences, and parades. The high point of the Congress was a celebration of
mass by Cardinal Pacelli at a special altar erected in Budapest's Heroes'
Square. With statues of some of Hungary's greatest historical figures forming a backdrop, Cardinal Pacelli praised the country for serving as a bastion of Christendom in the past and the present. The ceremony was attended by Hungary's leading politicians, both Catholic and Protestant.
Even after the Congress had ended, and the visitors had returned home,
Hungary continued to celebrate its historic place in Christendom. 1938
was the nine hundredth anniversary of the death of Hungary's patron
saint, St. István, the king who had converted his country to Christianity at
the turn of the second millennium. Throughout the year, Catholic leaders
and state officials arranged numerous festivities including the exhibition
of holy relics such as the holy right hand of St. István, pilgrimages, banquets, and academic conferences. All this glorified the king who was cred-
ited with founding the Hungarian state and making Hungary a Christian
nation.

These were not isolated events in Hungary after 1919, nor was the celebration of Hungary's Christian past and present exclusively the province
of the Roman Catholic Church. After World War I, Hungary was de-

feated, humiliated by a short-lived but disruptive Bolshevik revolution, and occupied by neighboring states that had laid claim to some two-thirds of the country's territory. Faced with these catastrophes, politicians and public figures called for the defense of "Christian values" in public life with a zeal absolutely unknown before 1914. Through the nineteenth century, Hungary's political elite had been liberal, confessionally tolerant, and in favor of keeping the church out of public politics. Now, after the war, in a much reduced state where an admiral, Miklós Horthy, served as regent and where the political elite worried how to contain the effects of war and revolution, public figures of all Christian confessions repeatedly proclaimed Hungary's essential identity as a Christian nation. They also embraced antisemitic stereotypes, something the country's political elite had largely resisted in the decades before the war. After 1919, fears of a destructive "Jewish" influence became commonplace. Religious and secular leaders often disagreed about what exactly this meant, and what sort of means should be used to combat it. Throughout the period between the two world wars, they debated whether Christianity marked a religious, cultural, or racial identity. But all could agree that some kind of antisemitic policy was necessary. In postwar Christian Hungary, the new religious nationalism went hand-in-hand with a more exclusionary vision of nationhood. In the months following the 1919 Bolshevik revolution, this consensus could often be deadly for Hungary's Jews. In 1944, when Hungary was occupied by Nazi Germany, its consequences were catastrophic.

Historians of nationalism in Eastern Europe have generally understood the turn toward illiberal and antisemitic politics in the region as a transformation or radicalization of secular nationalism.[1] Scholars of the Hungarian case typically depict Christian national ideology in interwar Hungary as another example of this phenomenon. Acknowledging the dominance of liberal nationalism in pre-1914 Hungary, they have debated exactly how the country's political culture could be transformed into something so different in such a short time. Many emphasize the reaction to war, revolution, and partition in 1918–20 as a shock that convinced many Hungarians that liberalism had no future. Others find that this sudden shift had a significant prehistory beginning at least in the 1880s, when the economic upheavals of industrialization led many Hungarians to blame liberalism for their own uncertain social status. In both interpretations, however, religion is marginal to the political drama that unfolded. Consequently, scholars generally describe the history of Hungary between 1919 and 1944 as a thoroughly secular struggle between radical or fascist

---

1. See, e.g., Brian Porter, *When Nationalism Began to Hate: Imagining Politics in Nineteenth Century Poland* (New York: Oxford University Press, 2000).

nationalists and conservative opponents who continued to practice a more moderate brand of nationalist politics.[2] Both groups declared themselves Christian nationalists, but historians generally see their Christianity as purely symbolic and interpret their use of Christian sacred symbols as a strategy for legitimizing the use of power. In general, many historians agree that talk of Christian nationalism in Hungary amounted to little more than an antisemitic code.

In this book, I argue against this interpretation. At a time when social commentators commonly speak about "culture wars" or even a "new cold war" between secular and religious worldviews,[3] it is necessary to take seriously the Christianity within Christian nationalist ideology in Hungary. In this book, I present the case of interwar Christian Hungary as a significant opportunity to examine the role that religion can play in remaking modern nation-states and promoting or undermining tolerant and pluralistic societies. I take this approach for several reasons. First, scholars of nationalisms in places as diverse as Poland and India have shown that religious symbols and narratives are powerful means for the expression and definition of national identities.[4] This was certainly the case in Hungary, where religious and secular figures alike found in Hungary's Christian religious traditions the material with which they could fashion a new (though putatively ancient) sense of what it meant to be Hungarian. New symbolic practices, new holidays, and above all new narratives of Hungarian history all served to mark the break with the liberal past and to create the reality in political and intellectual life of the "Christian Hungarian" nation. But religion is also more than a set of historical memories that inspire people to take political action. A growing body of theoretical literature has proposed that the interaction between religious people and secular politicians determine the form and content of a nation's public sphere.[5] In this book, I try to bring a sustained investigation of a particular historical case to these theoretical inquiries. To combat what they perceived as

2. István Deák, "Hungary," in *The European Right: A Historical Profile*, ed. Hans Rogger and Eugen Weber (Berkeley: University of California Press, 1966), 364–407.

3. See, e.g., Mark Juergensmeyer, *The New Cold War? Religious Nationalism Confronts the Secular State* (Berkeley: University of California Press, 1993).

4. Peter van der Veer, *Religious Nationalism: Hindus and Muslims in India* (Berkeley: University of California Press, 1994). In the East-Central European context, see Cynthia J. Paces, "The Czech Nation Must Be Catholic! An Alternative Version of Czech Nationalism during the First Republic," *Nationalities Papers* 27, no. 3 (1999): 407–28, and Brian Porter, "The Catholic Nation: Religion, Identity, and the Narratives of Polish History," *Slavic and East European Journal* 45, no. 2 (March 2001): 259–99.

5. Peter van der Veer, *Imperial Encounters: Religion and Modernity in India and Britain* (Princeton: Princeton University Press, 2001), 14–29. Talal Asad, "Secularism, Nation-State, Religion," in *Formations of the Secular: Christianity, Islam, Modernity*, ed. Talal Asad (Stanford: Stanford University Press, 2003), 181–204.

"anti-Christian politics," Hungarian Catholics and Protestants alike began to imagine a more vigorous role for religion within national society. Religion, they maintained, could also be a modern worldview, a set of moral absolutes that guided an individual to act publicly in a hostile secular world. After 1918, no one imagined that postwar Hungary should be a medieval theocracy in which church and state were one, or that only priests and pastors could run the country. But religious and secular nationalists alike insisted, in a way that resonates in our own contemporary world, that in a time of national crisis the state could not be neutral when it came to questions of political morality or public mores. They demanded a national society in which the public sphere was defined as a Christian space. Eliminating destructive "anti-Christian" forces thus became an axiom of political life in interwar Christian Hungary.

Secular nationalism alone did not make Hungary into an intolerant society after 1918. Religion was central to the process. Together religious Christians and secular nationalists pushed antisemitism to the center of public life in Hungary. But a word or two of caution is in order. First, this book argues that there is absolutely no straight line from Christianity as a religion to political antisemitism in Hungary or anywhere else. In recent years, books on "Hitler's pope" and the Vatican, the anti-Jewish legacy in Christian doctrine, or the enthusiasm with which Christian clergymen in various places embraced antisemitism and even murder, have drawn renewed attention to the responsibility of Europe's Christian churches for explicitly or tacitly condoning mass murder.[6] For some, this scholarship serves to justify calls for new thinking within Christianity (and especially within the Catholic Church) today. Others join a tradition established by earlier scholars of antisemitism as they highlight the legacy of anti-Jewish thinking that Christianity bequeathed to European culture from its earliest days up until the modern age. Clearly, there are many excellent reasons for theologians, scholars of religion, and people of faith to debate Christian-Jewish relations and the place of Jews within Christian thought. But this book takes the position that historians who search through the epistles of Paul to explain the origins of anti-Jewish persecution in 1930s and 1940s Europe will find that the exercise yields meager results. The history of Hungary between 1890 and 1944 is filled with many religious

6. Among the most prominent recent works on this much-debated topic are: Michael Phayer, *The Catholic Church and the Holocaust, 1930–1965* (Bloomington: Indiana University Press, 2000); David I. Kertzer, *The Popes Against the Jews: The Vatican's Role in the Rise of Modern Anti-Semitism* (New York: Alfred A. Knopf, 2001); James Carroll, *Constantine's Sword: The Church and the Jews. A History* (Boston: Houghton Mifflin, 2001); John Cornwell, *Hitler's Pope: The Secret History of Pius XII* (New York: Viking, 1999); Daniel Jonah Goldhagen, *A Moral Reckoning: The Role of the Catholic Church in the Holocaust and Its Unfulfilled Duty of Repair* (New York: Alfred A. Knopf, 2002).

Christians who justified antisemitic politics by referring to scripture or theology. But there are also examples such as the Calvinist bishop Dezső Baltazár, the Catholic nun Margit Slachta, or the Lutheran pastor Gábor Sztéhló whose faith led them to draw very different conclusions about Christian-Jewish relations. Each of these figures publicly denounced the rise of political antisemitism in Hungary as a threat to the liberties of Jews and Christians alike; the latter two courageously sheltered Jews during the terrible months of fascist rule in Budapest in 1944–45. Theirs were minority voices within their churches. Even so, their stories should remind us that persecution is an historically complex phenomenon, one that cannot be reduced to the premises suggested by religious texts.

Second, by itself, the redemptive promise of religion is not the spring that sets off mass murder. Regardless of their particular faith, religious fanatics everywhere have justified horrific acts of violence by declaring that redemption in the next world can only come by exterminating evil in this one.[7] In the current age of global terrorism, a number of scholars have examined the apocalyptic potential within religious zeal, drawing attention to the "cosmic war" between good and evil that so many different religions share.[8] Others have found the categories of "religion" and "violence" to be useful in thinking about the ways in which communities in many times and places have homogenized themselves and others into hostile camps of believers and unbelievers.[9] More generally, political philosophers since the Enlightenment have often contrasted rational secular politics to the "irrationality" of religious faith. This assumption has inspired latter-day students of nationalism and fascism to compare "irrational" and illiberal politics to religion, creating analytic hybrids like "political religion" or describing nationalism as a "secular religion."[10] Thinking about religion in this way can sometimes be conceptually useful. Still, it is important to remember again that historical religions cannot be reduced to the passions or totalizing visions of cosmic war that they sometimes inspire or sanction. Religion can be an important element of violent nation-

7. Norman Cohn, *Cosmos, Chaos, and the World to Come: The Ancient Roots of Apocalyptic Faith* (New Haven: Yale University Press, 2001); Eugen Weber, *Apocalypses: Prophecies, Cults, and Millennial Beliefs through the Ages* (Cambridge: Harvard University Press, 1999).

8. Mark Juergensmeyer, *Terror in the Mind of God: The Global Rise of Religious Violence* (Berkeley: University of California Press, 2000).

9. Hent de Vries, *Religion and Violence: Philosophical Perspectives from Kant to Derrida* (Baltimore: Johns Hopkins University Press, 2002).

10. Emilio Gentile, *The Sacralization of Politics in Fascist Italy* (Cambridge: Harvard University Press, 1996); George L. Mosse, *The Nationalization of the Masses: Political Symbolism and Mass Movements in Germany from the Napoleonic Wars through the Third Reich* (New York: H. Fertig, 1975).

alism, as it was in the former Yugoslavia in the 1990s.[11] But it need not be. There are numerous examples of historical contexts where different religions and religious institutions have coexisted peacefully, if at times uneasily or unequally, in Europe and around the world. Even when coexistence has turned violent, the bloodshed does not always explode into exterminatory genocide.[12]

These caveats should not, however, lull historians of antisemitism into drawing too sharp a distinction between religious and secular ideologies of persecution. Historians of anti-Jewish stereotypes often distinguish between secular modern and religious premodern forms of anti-Jewish hatred.[13] Before the Enlightenment, theology (Jews as "Christ-killers") and religious superstitions like blood libel inspired Christians to persecute Jews. In the modern era, however, people hostile to Jews have grounded their dislike in nationalist or racial ideologies, coining a new word—antisemitism—to signal the modernity of their hatred. Among its merits, this approach clearly demonstrates the political, social, and cultural differences between medieval pogroms and the genocide of Jews in the twentieth century. Conflating both into one history of the "longest hatred" does little to explain either.[14] However, certain weaknesses inevitably accompany every attempt at conceptual clarity. Because they distinguish between modern genocide and premodern persecution, historians of antisemitism focus most closely on secular ideologies of nationalism and racism to explain the origins of the Holocaust. When historians do examine the responsibility of Europe's Christian churches for genocide, they most often invoke untheorized notions of "political climate" or "political atmosphere," arguing, for example, that religious leaders contributed to a persecuting "climate" or poisoned a tolerant "atmosphere" by preaching ancient religious prejudices against Jews. Yet conceptually distinct forms of antisemitism can and do exist simultaneously. It is the task of the historian to analyze their interaction within a given historical context.[15] By distinguishing so sharply between different kinds of antisemitism, historians of

11. Michael A. Sells, *The Bridge Betrayed: Religion and Genocide in Bosnia* (Berkeley: University of California Press, 1996).
12. David Nirenberg, *Communities of Violence: Persecution of Minorities in the Middle Ages* (Princeton: Princeton University Press, 1996).
13. Jacob Katz, *From Prejudice to Destruction: Anti-Semitism, 1700–1933* (Cambridge: Harvard University Press, 1980).
14. Robert S. Wistrich, *Antisemitism: The Longest Hatred* (New York: Methuen, 1991).
15. See, e.g., Kertzer, *The Popes against the Jews*; also Christhard Hoffmann, "Christlicher Antijudaismus und moderner Antisemitismus. Zusammenhänge und Differenzen als Problem der historischen Antisemitismusforschung," in *Christlicher Antijudaismus und Antisemitismus: Theologische und kirchliche Programme Deutscher Christen*, ed. Leonore Siegele-Wenschkewitz (Frankfurt a.M.: Haag und Hercken, 1994), 293–317.

the Holocaust too often obscure the role of the Christian churches and religious leaders in sustaining antisemitic politics in an age of genocide.

Throughout this book, I examine the ways in which competing visions of "Christian Hungary" and the threat that Jews posed to it can both oppose, but also paradoxically reinforce, each other, paying particular attention in later chapters to the ways in which "converts" and "Jewish conversion" were imagined, discussed, and deployed within political debate. Despite certain attempts by some political leaders and even some churchmen to reconcile race with religion,[16] most of Europe's Christian churches remained doctrinally opposed to theories of racial hierarchy, maintaining that Christian salvation was open to all. When many European states began to pass anti-Jewish laws, Christian religious leaders tried to secure exemptions for converts, arguing that they were no longer Jews despite the fantasies of racial biologists. These protests may have been weak and too often ineffective, but they do demonstrate the differences in principle between race and religion. But to those who were persecuted and murdered as Jews, what mattered was the stark and often deadly reality of exclusion.[17] All forms of antisemitism—whether religious, cultural, or racial—invariably amounted to the same thing for Jews in 1930s and 1940s Europe: exclusion from the national community.[18] Throughout the interwar years, Hungarians debated what it meant to say that Hungary was a Christian nation. Their disagreements became increasingly vitriolic by the late 1930s, often turning on the differences between race and religion. At the same time, all parties—radicals and conservatives, secular politicians and religious leaders—agreed that some form of exclusionary policy was necessary. Until 1944, Hungarian Jews experienced this competition as a process of dissimilation, rapid at some times and imperceptibly slow at others.[19] For years, it seemed that Regent Miklós Horthy and his supporters among the ruling conservative oligarchy might ultimately control or tame this process. In March 1944, however, German occupiers removed these checks. Within days and weeks, all the symbols and narratives of Christian nationalism became conflated into a single reality. Jews were pariahs, a people marked and set apart, morally and spatially, from the

16. Richard Steigmann-Gall, *The Holy Reich: Nazi Conceptions of Christianity, 1919–1945* (New York: Cambridge University Press, 2003); Doris L. Bergen, *Twisted Cross: The German Christian Movement in the Third Reich* (Chapel Hill: University of North Carolina Press, 1996).

17. Moshe Y. Herczl, *Christianity and the Holocaust of Hungarian Jewry*, trans. Joel Lerner (New York: New York University Press, 1993).

18. Hannah Arendt, *The Origins of Totalitarianism* (New York, 1973), 267–302.

19. Rolf Fischer, *Entwicklungsstufen des Antisemitismus in Ungarn, 1867–1939. Die Zerstörung der magyarisch-jüdischen Symbiose* (Munich: R. Oldenbourg, 1988).

Hungarian nation. Ultimately, the competition between secular and religious nationalists to define the nation had the effect of linking different kinds of antisemitism—secular and religious, modern and premodern—simultaneously. These linkages robbed the churches, as public institutions, of any effective way to oppose the force of radical antisemitic politics. Christianity should not be confused with biological racism. But the Christian churches are still bound up inextricably in the violent exclusion of Jews from Hungarian national society.

This book describes the attempts of religious and secular nationalists to imagine their nation in opposition to Jews. It tells a story of exclusion, not of how that exclusion was experienced. At this point, it is fair to ask if this approach is not one-sided. Should there be greater focus on the victims of persecution? By focusing on the process of exclusion, does this book risk replicating, in the guise of history, the ideology of exclusion it seeks to study? In this book, I argue that a critical history of Christian nationalist ideology is both possible and necessary in its own right. To place exclusionary politics in an historical or analytical context is not to condone, excuse, or "explain away" the violence that followed. It is not enough for the historian to write a chronicle of hateful acts, establishing the exclusion of Jewish Hungarians from national society as a matter of record. Even as historians begin to write the history of Jewish life in Hungary between the two world wars,[20] we must still ask how and why a society came apart in the way that it did. As will be shown in the pages that follow, many Hungarians found that thinking of their nation as "Christian" led them to reshape fundamental aspects of the polity in which they lived. What line should separate religion from secular life in a "Christian state?" What role should religious leaders play in nationalist politics? How did one ensure that public mores were demonstrably "Christian?" As religious and secular nationalists found new and competing answers to these questions, they introduced a logic of exclusion into public life that came to have catastrophic consequences. Taking the measure of these developments requires paying close attention to the competition to define what it meant to be Christian in Christian Hungary. This book is an attempt to do exactly that.

One further observation is in order. This book presents the competition

20. One recent effort is Zsuzsanna Ozsváth, *In the Footsteps of Orpheus: The Life and Times of Miklós Radnóti* (Bloomington: Indiana University Press, 2000). Exemplary studies of the German context suggest how this approach might be developed for Hungary: Saul Friedländer, *Nazi Germany and the Jews*, vol. 1 (New York: HarperCollins, 1997); Marion A. Kaplan, *Between Dignity and Despair: Jewish Life in Nazi Germany* (New York: Oxford University Press, 1998); Till van Rahden, *Juden und andere Breslauer: Die Beziehungen zwischen Juden, Protestanten, und Katholiken in einer deutschen Grossstadt* (Göttingen: Vandenhoeck u. Ruprecht, 2000).

to create an explicitly religious nationalism as a contest by and large between Catholics and Calvinists. Hungary's Reformed or Calvinist Church
was the largest of Hungary's Protestant churches, embracing roughly 20
percent of the population. (This was still many fewer than the 64 percent
of Hungarians who were baptized into the Roman Catholic Church.) But
it was not the only one. During the interwar era, some 6 percent of Hungarians were Lutheran; there were also approximately six thousand Unitarians and perhaps a similar number of Baptists. Of these other Protestant confessions, the Lutheran Church was clearly the most important,
socially and historically. After all, Lajos Kossuth, the great revolutionary
of 1848, had been baptized Lutheran. Some of the best high schools in the
country, educating many of the leading talents of interwar Hungary, were
run by the Lutheran Church. Despite this, I focus almost exclusively on
debates between Hungary's Catholics and Calvinists to understand the development of Christian nationalism. There are several reasons for this.
First, the large and politically powerful Catholic Church always saw
Calvinism as its most important rival. For decades, the Calvinist Church
played a leading role in the struggle for independence from the Catholic
Habsburg dynasty, something I discuss in chapter 1. In addition, the
Calvinist Church prided itself on being composed almost exclusively of
ethnic Magyars. The Lutheran Church, in contrast, had ethnic Germans
and Slovaks among its members. Although the church was overwhelmingly Hungarian after the partition of Hungary, it had been roughly evenly
divided between these three ethnic groups before World War I. For this
reason, Calvinists tended to think of theirs as the ethnic "Magyar religion" and to link their faith to an explicitly ethnic nationalism in ways
that became tremendously important during the interwar era. Throughout
this book, I pay close attention to this fusion of religion and ethnicity, contrasting it with Catholic attempts to tie Christian nationalism more clearly
to the Hungarian state. In these debates, a wide variety of public intellectuals, some of them with close ties to a particular church and some with
none, invoked Catholicism and Calvinism to justify their support for
state-based or ethnic nationalism. Many also invoked these two churches
as symbols for a nation located on the cultural divide between East and
West and forced to choose between them. The Lutheran Church figured
much less prominently in these debates. When I discuss Protestants in this
book generally, I do so only when Hungary's Calvinist and Lutheran religious leaders had the same view of the issue at hand. In all other cases, I
have clearly identified individuals by their confessional affiliation as
Catholics, Calvinists, or Lutherans.

1

The Origins of Christian Nationalism, 1890–1914

Before 1914, Hungary was a kingdom within the Habsburg Monarchy. Though the Kingdom of Hungary had been a sovereign state throughout the Middle Ages, invading Ottoman Turkish armies broke Hungary apart in 1526. For more than one hundred fifty years, Hungary was divided into three parts: Transylvania in the East, where Hungarian princes enjoyed political autonomy; an area in the West, controlled by the Habsburg dynasty; and a region in the center under direct Ottoman control. As the Habsburg army began to push the Ottomans from Central Europe in the 1680s, they also began to extend their control over the whole Kingdom of Hungary. In 1687, the Hungarian Diet granted the Habsburgs the right of male succession, formally making Hungary a part of the Habsburg realm. But not all were reconciled to the new order. Especially in eastern Hungary, where the nobility had exercised substantial independence during the years of Ottoman rule, the new political reality was particularly galling. This intransigence produced a decade long rebellion against the Habsburgs in the early 1700s. It failed. Undeterred, many gentry nobles embraced liberalism in the first decades of the nineteenth century as a way of asserting their independence in a different way. Inspired by the dream of national self-determination, liberal revolutionaries launched an ill-fated revolution in 1848. Though their revolt was crushed, Hungary's political elite soon negotiated a substantial amount of political autonomy from the dynasty. The Compromise of 1867 transformed the Habsburg Empire into a Dual Monarchy (the Austro-Hungarian Monarchy) and gave Hungary's liberal gentry oligarchs the chance to chart their own path in domestic affairs for the first time in centuries.

"All Hungarian citizens," the framers of Hungary's first Dualist Era laws declared in 1868, "constitute a nation in the political sense, the one and indivisible Hungarian nation."[1] Despite this optimism, Hungary's citizens were deeply divided by nationality, religion, and class. Slightly less than half (41.6 percent of the population, according to one 1880 estimate) of them were Hungarian-speaking ethnic Magyars. The rest described themselves to census takers as members of more than a dozen other nationalities. By the middle of the nineteenth century, many of these non-Magyar ethnic groups had nationalist leaders of their own, all of them eager to secure political rights for their peoples. Even among those who declared Hungarian to be their primary language of communication, there was disunity. Roman Catholics were the most numerous by far. A 1910 census that excluded Croatia-Slavonia showed that almost half (49.3 percent) of all people living in Hungary were Roman Catholics. Of these, 65 percent were ethnic Magyars. Hungarian speakers overwhelmingly dominated the Reformed (Calvinist) Church (only 14.3 percent of the total population, but of these, 98.4 percent were ethnic Magyars). Other Christian confessions also included Hungarian speakers: 32 percent of the country's Lutherans (7 percent of the total population) and 15 percent of Greek Catholics (11 percent of the total population) were Magyars. Three-quarters (76.89 percent) of the country's Jews (5 percent of the total population) also declared Hungarian their primary language of communication by 1910.[2] Finally, no amount of patriotic rhetoric could conceal the fact that the vast majority of Hungary's citizens were disenfranchised. Voting regulations barred women, the growing industrial working class in Hungary's larger cities, and most of the country's peasants from voting. Even among those who could vote, the system was gerrymandered after 1867 in such a way as to ensure a parliamentary majority of ethnic Magyar liberals who supported the 1867 Compromise and strenuously resisted any attempt to reform or change the country's political structure.

Overcoming these divisions was the first task of Hungary's liberal elite after 1867. Religious equality, they firmly believed, contributed to these goals. Among their first actions were laws passed in 1868 that granted equal status to Protestantism and civic equality to Jews. With these measures, they aimed to counteract the effects of the Habsburg dynasty's long-standing policies on religion. For much of the time that the Habsburgs ruled Hungary, the ruling house had allied itself with the Roman Catholic

1. This is the text of Law XLIV of 1868, a foundational law of Dualist-era Hungary.
2. Margit Balogh and Jenő Gergely, *Egyházak az újkori Magyarországon, 1790–1992: Adattár* (Budapest: História. MTA Történettudományi Intézete, 1996), 162–63. The figures from 1910 exclude Croatia-Slavonia, which was almost exclusively divided amongst Roman Catholics (71.6 percent) and Orthodox Christians (24.9 percent). See ibid., 162. Ethnic Magyars were, of course, a small minority in this region.

Church. In the seventeenth and eighteenth centuries, Habsburg rulers had supported the Counterreformation in Central Europe as a way of crushing political dissent. The dynasty renewed its alliance with the church after the failed Hungarian revolution in 1848, concluding a concordat with the Vatican that confirmed the Catholic Church's extensive rights and privileges in Hungary. Both strategies were calculated assaults on Protestantism in Hungary, many of whose leading adherents were gentry nobles renowned for their anti-Habsburg sentiment. Though there had been periods of expanded toleration, during the reign of Joseph II in the 1780s for example, the Habsburg dynasty had generally supported Roman Catholicism as the only state religion. When the 1867 Compromise gave Hungary's liberal nationalist elite a chance to expand religious equality and thereby promote a national identity opposed to Catholic Habsburg dominion, they seized the opportunity with both hands. By making religious difference a purely private matter, all Hungarian citizens could embrace a common public allegiance to the Hungarian state. Nationalism, they hoped, would be a "national secular religion," a faith in Hungarian supremacy that transcended confessional and regional divides.[3]

Political reality fell far short of these ideals. Because the imperial dynasty in Vienna still controlled or exerted tremendous influence in important aspects of Hungarian public life, Hungary's liberal elite could only go so far in asserting their independence. For example, Hungarians still had to serve in a joint imperial-royal army. They also had to accept financial decisions made by imperial-royal banks in Vienna. Religion was another area in which there were definite limits on Hungary's freedom of action. Although the Habsburg ruler, Francis Joseph I, recognized the right of all religions to a basic level of tolerance, he insisted that the Roman Catholic Church remain preeminent throughout all his lands, including Hungary. To him (and to the Vatican), the Catholic Church remained what it had been for centuries, a pillar of authority and order and a crucial ally to secular rulers. It could never be simply a free and private association of individuals within civil society. Recognizing that their hands were tied, Hungary's liberal oligarchs backed away from separating church and state. Instead, they erected a "hierarchy of privileges" that embraced all Hungary's organized religions.[4] Some faiths, like the Reformed (Calvinist), the Lutheran, the Unitarian, and the Orthodox (both Serbian and Romanian) churches, were labeled "received" churches. In effect, they became "state

3. Cited in Paul Lendvai, *The Hungarians: A Thousand Years of Victory in Defeat* (Princeton: Princeton University Press, 2003), 304.

4. László Péter, "Hungarian Liberals and Church-State Relations (1867–1900)," in *Hungary and European Civilization*, ed. György Ránki and Attila Pók (Budapest: Akadémiai Kiadó, 1989), 119.

churches" equivalent to the Roman Catholic Church before the law. Other faiths, like Hungary's tiny Baptist and Muslim communities, were labeled "recognized" religions, and consequently enjoyed a secondary status. Until 1895, Judaism was only a "recognized" religion, even if Hungarian Jews, as individuals, enjoyed full civic equality. By spreading out legal privileges in this way, Hungary's liberal oligarchs aimed to dilute the authority of the Catholic Church. From this confused legal jumble, many hoped that something resembling religious equality in public life might result.

The "hierarchy of privilege" that Hungary's liberals adopted only ensured that religion would continue to be a divisive public issue. Without separation of church and state, there could be no civil marriage. When confessionally mixed couples had children, each child had to be assigned to a particular confessional community. Parents could not simply choose a faith for their child. Instead, a series of ministerial directives classified all children according to their sex and their parents' confession: sons followed fathers, and daughters were baptized into their mother's church. But these measures had no teeth and eager clergymen sometimes disregarded them in their zeal to bring new souls into the flock. Allegedly, it was Catholic parish priests who broke the law most often, baptizing newborns "away" from their legally stipulated confession and into the Catholic Church.[5] Protestants complained bitterly about this practice, arguing that it only demonstrated what power the Catholic Church still exercised in society. By dint of centuries of tradition and political preferment, they noted, the Roman Catholic Church had far greater wealth, in landed property especially, than did the Protestant churches, as well as a much more extensive system of schools, seminaries, universities, and social-welfare foundations. Until there was a true separation of church and state, the Catholic Church would always remain first among equals in the eyes of any Hungarian government and could therefore afford to flout government directives with impunity.

Hungary's Jews felt these inequalities even more acutely. After receiving civil equality in 1868, many Jews found new social and economic opportunities open to them in the dynamic and growing Hungarian economy. Within a generation, Jews had risen to prominence in many professions, especially in business, finance, and the free professions of law and medicine. Many embraced Neolog Judaism, especially those living in Hungary's cities, and above all those in the capital city, Budapest. Seeing in Hungarian nationalism an ideology of emancipation and toleration that promised to put Christian-Jewish conflict firmly in the past, these liberal

---

5. Moritz Csáky, *Der Kulturkampf in Ungarn: Die kirchenpolitische Gesetzgebung der Jahre 1894/95* (Graz: Böhlau, 1967), 33.

Jews adopted a Hungarian national identity without hesitation. Because of their social success, Hungary's liberal Jewish community leaders resented the second-class status of Judaism under law. As members of a religion that was only "recognized," Hungary's Jewish communities did not receive the same level of state support as the "received" Christian confessions did. Schools and institutions of charity run by the Jewish community leaders relied largely on donations from wealthy benefactors to meet their operating expenses. Even more galling, Jews could not describe their nationality as Hungarian in the same way that Hungarians of other faiths could. Though a Hungarian-speaking Protestant could list himself on the census as, say, a "Hungarian of the Lutheran faith," Jews who spoke Hungarian, embraced Hungarian nationalism without question, and felt themselves to be Hungarian in every way could not call themselves "Hungarians of the Israelite faith." Instead, they were members of a separate Jewish nation, just as if their mother tongue and cultural identification were Slovak or German. For all these reasons, "reception," or equal status with Hungary's Christian churches, acquired powerful symbolic meaning for Hungary's large and powerful liberal Jewish community. As Lajos Szabolcsi, son of the editor-in-chief of Hungary's most important Reformed Jewish newspaper, recalled in his memoirs: "Reception . . . as a slogan and a symbol was just as much an expression of the religious politics of Hungarian Jews as the menorah was of our faith."[6] Without reception, emancipation was incomplete.

Hungary's liberal political elite approached these problems cautiously. No one wanted a "culture war" (*Kulturkampf*) of the sort that had inflamed German society in the 1870s. There, state authorities attempted an outright assault on the position of the Catholic Church in society, hoping to compel the clergy to recognize the supremacy of the new German nation-state. At the height of the struggle, German authorities had hundreds of recalcitrant priests and several bishops in jail for civil disobedience. Nor did Hungary's liberals find any inspiration in the violently anticlerical tradition of the French revolution. No one in Hungary imagined for an instant that religion should be replaced by an enlightened cult of some Supreme Being, or that Catholic priests should be forced to swear an oath of allegiance to the Hungarian state. Instead, Hungary's nationalist liberals imagined a "free church" in a "free state," a vaguely worded but moderate solution that recognized the importance and power of religion in society while asserting the supremacy of civil law. Despite their caution, however, Hungary's political elite deeply resented the idea that Hungary's

---

6. Lajos Szabolcsi, *Két emberöltő: Az Egyenlőség évtizedei (1881–1931). Emlékezések, dokumentumok* (Budapest: MTA Judaisztikai Kutatócsoport, 1993), 54.

clergy could openly disregard laws and ordinances issued by government officials. Minister of Religion and Education Albin Csáky, expressed the feelings of many when he criticized those who ignored the law: "One thing is incontrovertible: the law of 1868 [widening religious equality] was not promulgated only to be disobeyed."[7] In 1890, Minister Csáky proposed a revised set of ordinances, ordering clergymen to make disputed baptismal records public and stipulating a stiff fine should they fail to comply. But many Catholic priests, supported by the Vatican, were no more inclined to heed the new regulations than they had been to obey the older ones. Faced with opposition, the Hungarian government began to discuss more drastic measures.

The Illusion of Religious Neutrality: Protestants, Jews, and Anticlericalism

Having had to abandon a clear separation of church and state in favor of a murkier and less principled "hierarchy of privileges," many liberal nationalists in Hungary were outraged that the Catholic Church continued to flout even a moderate regulation of civil religious matters. When Catholic clergy rejected Minister Csáky's 1890 ordinances, the Hungarian government moved to assert their supremacy in a more decisive fashion. In 1892, it brought several bills before Parliament for deliberation. In addition to a law authorizing secular authorities to take over birth and marriage registries from the churches, Hungary's political leaders also proposed establishing civil marriage in Hungary, as well as raising Judaism once and for all to the status of a "received" religion alongside the Catholic and Protestant churches. With these measures, they hoped finally to dismantle the barriers that divided Hungarian citizens in law and thereby assert the nation's unity decisively.

In his speech to Parliament in favor of civil marriage, Dezső Szilágyi, the minister of justice, explained his government's purpose in no uncertain terms. "In such a divided nation as ours, legal institutions must not be factors of differentiation and separation, but instead the interest of the state exists in the fact that the legal order of the state shall be an assimilating factor and that it help raise the political unity of the nation through its social cohesion." The state, Szilágyi explained, could not tolerate marriage laws that erected "dividing walls" between citizens. All Hungarians must be equal before the law.[8] Hungary's liberal Jewish leaders made the very

7. Cited in Csáky, *Kulturkampf*, 43.
8. Speech of 2 December 1893, in *Szilágyi Dezső beszédei*, ed. Béla Vihar (Budapest: Athenaeum, 1909), 291.

same argument in favor of "reception." In their drive to draft a bill authorizing the legal "reception" of Judaism, Reformed Jewish leaders argued forcefully that Jewish reception solidified the unity of the state.[9] As the prominent liberal politician Vilmos Vázsonyi put it in a petition to the Hungarian parliament from a national conference of Hungarian Jews, the Hungarian state was a "confessionless community," defined by the 1868 religious laws as a polity in which Christians and Jews alike were equally free to order their religious affairs. This freedom helped all Hungarians to put aside their differences and unite against the nation's enemies. In a time when the Hungarian state was joined in battle against "clericalism" and the "discordant activities" of the non-Magyar nationalities, Hungary required social unity, a goal that Jewish "reception" could only further.[10] Hungary's liberals were agreed. Only in a state absolutely neutral toward confession would the Hungarian nation truly achieve the unity it so desperately sought.

Did this conflict "over the place of religion in a modern polity" amount to a "culture war?"[11] Mindful of the vitriolic state-church conflict in Germany, Italy, Spain, and elsewhere, Hungary's liberal leaders did their best to reassure Hungarian Catholics and leaders in the Catholic Church that, in this case, it did not. In parliament, Minister Dezső Szilágyi insisted that religious reforms like civil marriage should not be understood as a sign of religious persecution. "[This law] would only injure religious principles if the law commanded a person to do something that his religious convictions forbade, or if the law forbade something that a person's religious beliefs commanded." In private, Szilágyi insisted, Hungary's citizens might hold whatever religious views they chose. In the "sphere of personal conviction," the law would always allow for the free expression of religious beliefs. But more was at stake than a simple legal question. The Catholic Church, doggedly defending its vast privileges against any attempt at reform, remained a significant obstacle preventing Hungary's liberals from realizing their political ideals. When Dezső Szilágyi described the civil marriage bill before the Hungarian parliament as a legal instrument by

9. Anikó Prepuk, "Miért éppen recepció? Az izraelita vallás egyenjogúsítása az 1890–es években," in *Emlékkönyv L. Nagy Zsuzsa 70. születésnapjára*, ed. János Angi (Debrecen: Multiplex Media-DUP, 2000), 263–81.

10. "Kérvény a magyar országgyűléshez," in *Vázsonyi Vilmos beszédei és írásai*, 2 vols., ed. Hugó Csergó and József Balassa (Budapest: Az Országos Vázsonyi-Emlékbizottság kiadása, 1927), vol. 1, 50–54.

11. Christopher Clark and Wolfram Kaiser, "The European Culture Wars," in *Culture Wars: Secular-Catholic Conflict in Nineteenth-Century Europe*, ed. Christopher Clark and Wolfram Kaiser (Cambridge: Cambridge University Press, 2003), 1. Also Robert Nemes, "The Uncivil Origins of Civil Marriage: Hungary," in *Culture Wars*, ed. Clark and Kaiser, 314–15 and 363–64.

which the state might further the "strengthening of the political unity of the nation" and the "blending-together" of the "nation's different foundational elements," it was clear (if unstated) that opposition to the law was an antinational act.[12] Hungary's liberals may not have indulged in the vulgar depiction of priests as gluttons and depraved sexual predators that were sometimes a feature of secular-Catholic conflict elsewhere in Europe at this time.[13] But they most strenuously objected to the ways in which the Catholic Church continued to oppose their political vision. These objections raised an important question: if the leaders of some faiths—Protestantism and liberal Judaism—supported the secular ambitions of the government while those of others—Roman Catholicism—did not, would it really be possible for Hungary's liberals to stick to the principle of religious neutrality that Szilágyi had outlined?

After all, Hungary's Protestant churches had embraced liberal nationalism without reservation. Many of Hungary's most prominent liberals were Protestants. Dezső Szilágyi, for example, was not only minister of justice, he was also a lay leader in Hungary's Reformed (Calvinist) Church. In addition, Hungary's Protestant leaders had zealously supported every attempt to expand religious equality and limit the material and social dominance of the Catholic Church in Hungary.[14] Many had fully and openly embraced the idea of Jewish religious equality as a principle befitting a modern, tolerant, and progressive nation.[15] This support for the government's reforms sometimes tipped over into clearly anti-Catholic invective. At one assembly held in 1892, the Calvinist bishop of the Transdanubian Church District, Gábor Pap, himself a member of the Liberal Party and an intransigent veteran of the 1848 revolutionary war against the Habsburgs, transformed a gathering of religious and lay leaders into a militantly anti-Catholic demonstration.[16] Though some speakers at the meeting, including the former prime minister, Kálmán Tisza, tried to frame their criticism of the Catholic Church in moderate tones, Pap straightforwardly declared Catholicism to be "hostile to freedom and reactionary." In absolutist tones, Bishop Pap declared himself unable to believe that "at the end of the nineteenth century, the Hungarian state would be willing to relinquish its authority in favor of any confession at all, or that Mankind is now tak-

---

12. *Szilágyi Dezső beszédei,* ed. Vihár, 290, 295ff.

13. Wolfram Kaiser, " 'Clericalism—That Is Our Enemy!' European Anticlericalism and the Culture Wars," in *Culture Wars,* ed. Clark and Kaiser, 47–76.

14. László Kósa, "A református egyház az egyházpolitikai küzdelmek idején," *Protestáns Szemle* (1996/1): 52–62.

15. See, e.g., Farkas Szőts, "A zsidó vallás recepciója," *Protestáns Egyházi és Iskolai Lap* 36, no. 4 (26 January 1893): 49–50.

16. Unlike other Presbyterian churches, Hungary's Reformed Church had and has a titular bishop as well as a general curator (lay president) at the head of each church district.

ing steps backward, instead of striding forward." The nation's best hope, he maintained, lay with Protestantism and "freedom, progress, and modern civilization."[17]

Many other Hungarian Protestants shared Bishop Pap's conviction that religious toleration was a sign of their country's modern and civilized character. In a state where the forces of progress reigned, unity and concord in the civic affairs of the nation could only be strengthened when every individual had the right to heed his own conscience in religious matters. One 1910 treatise on Protestantism's role in the development of the Hungarian state shows how Protestants linked these concepts: "Protestantism's idea of the individual gave birth to the national idea, as one that directs the selfish elements of society into the service of the public interest and that revives culture again, making it internal, effective, and, in truth, national."[18] Protestantism was thus a "political principle, which discovered its past program in the independent, constitutional, and national state." Hungary's Protestants firmly believed they had led the nation's struggle for independence both by defending their own right to free worship, as well as by giving their compatriots the moral courage to defend their other political rights against absolutist tyranny. This had helped to make Hungary a modern society, one which "stood on a national basis, . . . [was] constitutional in its organization, and this constitution is democratic. . . . In it, the universal role of Roman Catholicism, so characteristic of the middle ages, has finally ended . . . and, . . . every church has descended to the status of a subordinate society."[19] Now, political representatives of the people, not potentates of the church, had the power to craft laws determining the moral and social obligations of individuals to society. In their modern state, Hungarians, as a unified nation, could indeed hope to chart their own political future.

In turn, Hungary's liberal politicians attached the same significance to the Protestant churches. For many, it was an article of faith that Protestantism in Hungary was more "national" than Catholicism could ever be. In a pamphlet from the 1880s urging liberals to take a harder course of action against Catholic opposition, the liberal publicist and politician Gusztáv Beksics asked "which Church: the Catholic or the Protestant Church has the greater value for the country (*haza*) . . . ? . . . The answer cannot be in doubt."[20] "If Protestantism," he argued, "had not gained

17. PAAA, Öst. 92/Bd.2.A7715. Clipping from *Pester Lloyd*, attached to Report from Vienna. 7 September 1892. See also Nemes, "Uncivil Origins," 322–24.

18. József Pokoly, *A protestantizmus hatása a magyar állami életre* (Budapest: Magyar Protestáns Irodalmi Társaság, 1910), 131.

19. Ibid., 521–23.

20. Timoleon (Gusztáv Beksics), *Legújabb politikai divat* (Budapest: Zilahy Sámuel, 1884), 27.

ground in Hungary, and more to the point, had not touched the specific
Magyar race, the Magyar nation would have undergone far greater trials.
And perhaps it would not have survived those trials." Popular history
echoed the views of theoreticians like Beksics.[21] The most widely read histories in Dualist-era Hungary dealt with the early-eighteenth-century rebellions against Habsburg absolutism. The heroes of these histories were
always the Protestant, mainly Calvinist, yeoman farmers—the *kuruc* in
Hungarian—who fought bitterly to defend their political and religious liberties.[22] *Kuruc* warriors figured prominently as metaphors for patriotism
in the political vocabulary of the day; one historian (also a Liberal politician) even invented *kuruc* camp songs to compensate for the small number
of sources describing the daily life of these implacable freedom fighters.[23]
More concretely, the great revolutionary leader, Lajos Kossuth, himself a
Lutheran, had stood in the pulpit of the Calvinist Great Church in Debrecen when he finally declared independence from Austria in the heady
spring of 1849. As recently as the late 1850s and early 1860s, during the
controversy of the so-called "Protestant patent," the imperial house had
tried to interfere in the internal government of the Protestant churches, in
an ultimately unsuccessful attempt to reduce the power in the church districts of the gentry noble lay leaders.[24] The move was widely read as a
transparent attack on the public visibility of prominent Magyar nationalists. To Protestants, all this proved that they, and not their Catholic compatriots, had acted first, suffered the worst, and done the most, in the
name of liberty.

Many Jewish Hungarians, especially those sympathetic to Enlightenment reform in Judaism, drew connections between religious equality and
national progress with similar vigor. Their support relied less on centuries-
old historical ties between their faith and the national project. Although
there was evidence of some Jewish presence within the Kingdom of Hungary since the early middle ages, the vast majority of Jewish Hungarians
traced their roots in Hungary to immigrants who had come from Moravia
and elsewhere beginning in the late 1700s.[25] But a great number of Hun-

21. An intellectual biography of Beksics is Zsuzsa L. Nagy, "A nemzeti állam eszméje Beksics Gusztávnál," *Századok* 97, no. 6 (1963): 1243–77.
22. István Deák, "Historiography of the Countries of Eastern Europe: Hungary," *American Historical Review* 97, no. 4 (October 1992): 1041–1063, esp. 1047. Also Steven Bela
Vardy, *Modern Hungarian Historiography* (Boulder, CO: East European Quarterly, 1976).
23. The historian was Kálmán Thaly. On his importance to the historiographical culture
of Dualist-era Hungary, see Ágnes R. Várkonyi, *Thaly Kálmán és történetírása* (Budapest:
Akadémiai Kiadó, 1961)
24. Friedrich Gottas, *Die Frage der Protestanten in Ungarn in der Ära des Neoabsolutismus* (Munich: Oldenbourg, 1965).
25. Lajos Venetianer, *A magyar zsidóság története a honfoglalástól a világháborúkitöréséig: Különös tekintettel gazdasági és művelődési fejlődésére* (Budapest: Fővárosi
könyvkiadó, 1922).

gary's Jews embraced and identified with the revolutionary war of 1848 as enthusiastically as did Hungarian Protestants, seeing it as an emancipatory struggle for the entire nation without distinction.[26] In that year, Hungary's "lawful revolutionaries" had extended the prospect of religious and civic equality to Jewish and Christian citizens alike.[27] These same liberal ideals motivated the country's political elite in 1868, almost as soon as the Compromise of 1867 had come into effect, to seek a more equitable place for Hungary's Jews within civil and constitutional law. To be sure, Jewish Hungarians were divided amongst themselves over how best to respond to these overtures of equality and toleration. Neolog Jews, hopeful to reform their faith in the spirit of Enlightenment, planned to work closely with government officials to create some kind of institution that could represent all Jews under law. This, they maintained, would ensure the continued assimilation of Jewish Hungarians into the nation's legal and social life. Orthodox Jews, on the other hand, resisted efforts to create any kind of centralized, churchlike, Jewish religious body, fearing that it would undermine the interpretive authority of individual rabbis in questions of faith. These divisions between Neolog and Orthodox Jews in Hungary only deepened over time.[28] Nevertheless, it was clear to even the most skeptical that the liberal and secular nationalism of Hungary's gentry noble elite was far more open to Jewish religious equality than the Catholic Church ever would be.

Encouraged by strong governmental support for Jewish emancipation and assimilation, Hungary's Neolog communities entered confidently into the religious-political disputes of the 1890s. Clearly, Neolog leaders favored Jewish "reception" under Hungarian law as the necessary completion of a process begun in 1867, even if they recognized that "reception" was not the same as separation of church and state. Prominent legal talents, like the liberal politician Vilmos Vázsonyi, laid out the arguments for Jewish reception. In an 1892 petition to Parliament written by Vázsonyi and signed by a number of prominent Neolog figures, Vázsonyi argued that legal equality and social equality went hand-in-hand: "So long as Jews are not raised to the same level of equality with other confessions, the interests of democracy and of Jewry are closely inter-related. The current situation of the Jewish confession is a serious injury to the principle of true democracy. . . . Anyone who takes democracy seriously must recognize

26. Béla Bernstein, *A negyvennyolcas magyar szabadságharc és a zsidók: A zsidó honvédek négy névjegyzékével* (Budapest: Múlt és Jövő Kiadó, 1998).

27. István Deák, *The Lawful Revolution: Louis Kossuth and the Hungarians, 1848–1849* (New York: Columbia University Press, 1979).

28. Jacob Katz, *A végzetes szakadás: Az ortodoxia kiválása a zsidóhitközségekből Magyarországon és Németországban* (Budapest: Múlt és Jövő Kiadó, 1999)

that today there can hardly be any greater present task than the improvement of the fate of Jewry." By extending reception to Hungary's Jews, and thus completing the work of emancipation begun over two decades previously, the Hungarian state would seal the loyalty of a committed and patriotic community within the nation—Hungarian Jews, for whom "state and nation were always sacred."[29]

At the same time, however, Neolog leaders were anxious to demonstrate that they did not favor the supremacy of civil over religious law simply because it would be "good" for Hungary's Jews. They also strongly supported the other pieces of legislation, such as the civil marriage law, that Hungary's liberal nationalist elite had proposed. In an article in the leading Neolog newspaper, *Equality*, Vilmos Vázsonyi pointed out that civil marriage might well make it possible for more Jews to leave their faith by marrying out of Judaism. In no way could this be considered any sort of boon for the Hungarian Jewish community; in fact, Orthodox Jews remained deeply suspicious of the new civil marriage law precisely because of the very real possibility of easier intermarriage that it raised. Nevertheless, Vázsonyi asserted that Jewish Hungarians strongly favored any legislation that made possible the free expression of religious beliefs under law. "Among us there is no one who only considers himself Jewish and thus liberalism and Hungarian nationalism always raise a barrier against the excesses of confessionalism." It was a matter of "great state and social interest" that there be civil marriage in Hungary—Vázsonyi described it in one place as the "crowning of individual equality in law"—and so no Hungarian Jew ought to raise any objection to any part of the government's drive to establish the supremacy of civil over religious law.[30]

As Neolog leaders, led by Vázsonyi, declared their support for the government's religious policy, they also repeatedly denounced the Catholic Church for its opposition. In a tone much the same as that taken by non-Jewish liberal politicians like Gusztáv Beksics, liberal Jewish leaders described "clericalism" as one of the greatest threats to national unity, rivaling the nationalist politics of Hungary's minorities in its dangerous potential. The "Hungarian state," declared Vilmos Vázsonyi, was engaged in a "war with clericalism and with divisive nationalist activities on the field of church politics." To men like Vázsonyi, it was clear that the interests of democracy and national autonomy demanded that a truly confessionless state not sit back and adopt a neutral position toward all faiths. It had to level the playing field, restraining some and supporting others until

---

29. "Kérvény a magyar országgyűléshez," dated 6 January 1892, in *Vázsonyi Vilmos beszédei és írásai.*
30. Vilmos Vázsonyi, "A polgári házasság," *Egyenlőség,* 3 November 1893.

true equality was achieved. Reception and civil marriage were essential. Without them, the Hungarian state could not "tear the weapon from the hand of intolerant clericals."[31] Thus, Hungary's liberal Jewish leaders took a position on religious equality already well-established by Protestant nationalists. Progress and unity demanded that the government assert the primacy of secular civil law over religious tradition. Inevitably, the Catholic Church came to be seen as an enemy.

Of course, simplistic reductions of Catholicism to antinational "clericalism" became difficult to sustain the more closely one examined them. The national-liberal consensus that inspired so many Hungarian lawmakers to demand civil marriage and religious equality clearly cut across confessional lines. This consensus grew out of the experience of the 1848 revolution and the decades of liberal reform that had preceded it, in which Hungarians of all religious backgrounds had fought for the cause of national independence. Catholics had most certainly taken part in this struggle. Although the episcopate of the Catholic Church had stood beside the Austrian army in 1848, many Hungarian Catholics, including a fair number of parish priests, had not. After 1867, some of Hungary's leading statesmen were nationally minded liberal Catholics. Indeed, the minister whose ordinance touched off the church-political crisis of the 1890s, Albin Csáky, followed a long line of liberal Catholics who had been ministers of education and religion. From József Eötvös, creator of the 1868 church-state law, to Csáky, Hungary's liberal Catholic politicians sought to balance religious equality with their desire as nationalists for the maximum attainable independence for Hungary. Even the most intransigent nationalists were forced to admit that Catholicism, in certain eras, had demonstrated a laudable national spirit. With evident unwillingness, Gusztáv Beksics admitted that Catholicism had "at times defended [the Hungarian state], though only weakly and in a lukewarm way."[32]

Nevertheless, it was clear that Hungary's Protestants and their Neolog Jewish allies supported the government's strongly secularist agenda without reservation. Repeatedly, Hungarian liberal nationalists wondered aloud if the Catholic Church could be trusted as a national ally in the same way. They were certainly not alone. The conflicts between liberals and the Catholic Church that had flared up all over Europe, from France and England, to Germany, to Italy and Spain, made "clericalism" and "ultramontanism" into slogans for all that liberals disliked about the Catholic Church.[33] Everywhere, societies were embracing national integration as

31. Ibid.
32. Timoleon [Beksics], *Legújabb politikai divat*, 21.
33. Kaiser, "Clericalism—That Is Our Enemy!"

the mark of modern civilization. In such a world, the historical traditions and privileges that bound Catholics to each other across national borders could only seem reactionary. Hungary's liberal oligarchs were careful to avoid any drastic assault on the church. But even this could not prevent many Hungarian Catholics from hearing a sharp edge in their criticism of "clerical" politics and seeing clear preference in their treatment of Protestants and Jews. For this reason, the state secretary of the Vatican in the 1890s, Cardinal Mariano Rampolla, urged Hungary's episcopate to stiffen its resolve and resist the liberal and secularizing vision of religious equality in Hungary. After having fought similar culture wars in several other European countries in the last decades of the nineteenth century, the church could not "hand over the apostolic kingdom of St. Stephan to the Calvinists and the Jews without a fight."[34]

Secular Society and Its Discontents: Catholics and the Christian State

As Hungarian liberals tried to expand the scope of secular civil law, they energized Hungarian Catholics into a vigorous opposition. Encouraged by the Vatican, clergy and lay Catholics together organized a fierce public campaign against the laws on civil marriage and Jewish "reception." Their mass public demonstrations, which resulted in 1895 in a new Catholic political party, as well as the lively journalistic and pamphlet literature they printed in hitherto unimagined numbers, constitute the beginnings of political Catholicism in Hungary.[35] Though none of this could, in the end, prevent passage of the despised liberal religious laws, this opposition raised concerns about the place (or rather, the absence) of religion in the public sphere and in national society in ways that remained powerful long after the immediate excitement had faded.

A fragile, but potentially powerful, alliance between Hungary's lay Catholic magnates, the lower clergy, and the Catholic intelligentsia led the opposition. Catholic aristocrats worried that any assault on historical privileges would ultimately undermine their own position as an elite caste within society. To defend their social position, these magnates developed a surprising taste for modern party politics. Hungary's lower clergy also played a prominent role in shaping the emerging Catholic politics in Hun-

34. Cited in Árpád von Klimó, *Nation, Konfession, Geschichte: Zur nationalen Geschichtskultur Ungarns im europäischen Kontext (1860–1948)* (Munich: R. Oldenbourg, 2003), 92.
35. Dániel Szabó, "A néppárt megalakulása," *Történelmi Szemle* 20, no. 2 (1977), 169–208. See also Jenő Gergely, *A politikai katolicizmus Magyarországon, 1890–1950* (Budapest: Kossuth, 1977).

gary. One priest in particular, János Molnár of Komárom, became known
to Catholics all over Hungary as an icon of principled intransigence in the
face of a hostile state.[36] In this, the clergy shared a common position with
prominent Catholic laity. Members of the Catholic "middle class"—low-
to mid-level civil servants, professionals, and teachers—expressed their
opposition to the ministerial directive in the pages of the *Hungarian State*,
a newspaper close to, but not funded by, the Catholic Church. This paper
repeatedly urged Hungary's bishops to defend the faith against "godless
liberalism" without regard for the consequences.[37] Thus important groups
within Hungarian Catholic society urged the hierarchy to resist any state
intervention into the church's affairs.

Officials in the Vatican, seeing the church under attack in so many other
countries in Europe, publicly supported Catholic opposition in Hungary.
The committee of cardinals hastily convened to study the issue directed
Hungary's priests not to surrender baptismal records to Protestants for
fear of delivering up innocent souls to heretics.[38] Instead, the Vatican's
state secretary and head of this committee, Cardinal Mariano Rampolla
suggested that the directive might simply be annulled or, even better, that
the 1868 law itself might be revised to the greater advantage of the church.
Hungary's lower clergy and ultramontane lay leaders took heart from this
uncompromising stance, especially after the official texts of Rampolla's secret reply to the cardinal-primate were made public in the pages of the
Hungarian State. As Hungary's Catholic middle class, along with a significant part of the clergy, became ever more militant in its resistance to ministerial policy, they pulled the Hungarian episcopate, sometimes against
its will, into a more oppositional stance. At the height of the political
furor, the Vatican even issued a papal encyclical encouraging Hungarian
Catholics in their defense of the faith.[39]

The newly emergent Catholic public worried above all about the consequences of removing religion from the laws and institutions of the state. In
meetings of lay and religious leaders, prominent Catholics argued that this
was simply impossible. Religion was a kind of worldview that linked private to public life. At one of the first Catholic Congresses held in Hungary, meetings designed to bring clergy and laity together in public gath-
erings of the Catholic community, Lajos Rajner, canon at Esztergom,
spoke for all present when he accused Hungary's liberals of dividing each
of its citizens in two. "Look where the dualism of liberals leads! Two con-

36. Nemes, "The Uncivil Origins."
37. On the Catholic press in general, and *Hungarian State* in particular, see Tamás Dersi,
A századvég katolikus sajtója (Budapest: Akadémiai Kiadó, 1973), 82–93.
38. Csáky, *Kulturkampf*, 49–59.
39. The encyclical was titled *Constanti Hungarorum* and was issued 2 September 1893.

sciences in one person, two gods in one world: one in heaven for the private person, another on earth for the social person!" Divisions between private piety and public life, which liberals assumed so readily, were completely artificial. "We Catholics," Rajner proclaimed, "believe there is only one conscience," a conscience that shaped an individual's actions in public as well as in private. To maintain otherwise was indeed a form of religious persecution: "If the state is to be independent of God, then there will exist an atmosphere in which the authority of God cannot spread." Separating society neatly into secular and religious space was simply a fiction, an artifice that Catholics like Lajos Rajner argued would have grievous consequences.[40]

To Hungary's Catholic opposition, the idea that secular civil equality would somehow strengthen the nation, seemed both a vain hope and a dangerous proposition. Catholic speakers often struck a note reminiscent of Edmund Burke, arguing that every society rested on national traditions formed organically over the course of centuries. Hungary, these Catholics argued, was historically a Christian state, a fact that liberals denied at their peril. In his opening address to the 1894 Catholic Congress, one of the leaders of the new Catholic People's Party, Count Miklós Mór Esterházy, argued forcefully that a "Christian spirit" was the "spiritual source of our state institutions and the foundation of our cultural development."[41] In Parliament, Bishop Lőrinc Schlauch made a similar argument, decrying the impending civil marriage law that promised to "shake the entire moral foundation, on which the Hungarian people have lived to this point." He went on: "I would consider it a mistake if the Hungarian nation, turning from its noble calling, would either declare it a goal to force an equality in religious matters, or else to divorce itself from those factors [i.e. of religion] with which it is bound by thousands upon thousands of ties."[42] Societies, Schlauch argued, rested on certain moral foundations and drew their strength from these values. These foundations could not be shuffled at will, nor could they be constructed according to the latest philosophical prescription. A nation cut loose from ties of tradition, bound together only by wholly theoretical civic bonds, would weaken, becoming in the end a hollow shell that would certainly break into pieces in the first storm.

40. From the speech of Lajos Rajner, canon at Esztergom, held at the Catholic Congress in Budapest on 16 January 1894. "Beszéd a katholikusok kötelmeiről a magán- és közéletben," in *A katolikus nagygyűlés Budapesten 1894: Január 16–ikán* (Budapest: Athenaeum, 1894), 43ff.

41. Speech of Count Miklós Mór Esterházy, given at the Budapest Catholic Congress on 16 January 1894. *A katolikus nagygyűlés,* 23.

42. Speech to the Upper House of Parliament of 9 May 1893. "Az egyhazpolitikai kérdésekről," in *Schlauch Lőrinc bíbornok-püspök beszédei és dolgozatai,* vol. 4 (Budapest: Franklin, 1899), 61ff.

Catholics also wondered whether a secular, "confessionless" state could even preserve, let alone create, any kind of social unity. Without a clear moral vision guiding lawmakers, a vision to be had only from religion, it seemed to them that a nation must surely fall apart. Again, Bishop (after 1893, Cardinal) Schlauch was among the most eloquent, making a series of speeches on religious political questions in the Upper House of Hungary's Parliament. On one of these occasions, Schlauch argued forcefully that any state that took it upon itself to be simply a kind of neutral arbiter between religions or value systems was doomed to fragment. A state had to rest on some common positive truths or moral precepts to enjoy any measure of social cohesion: "In general, states are established and exist as positive factors; negative factors can only become corrupted. But the principle which is the point of departure for confessionlessness is negative in nature, because it denies the basis on which society and thus the state must rest. The world has not yet seen an atheistic state, yet the principle with which such a dangerous experiment is made leads straight in that direction."[43] Catholics like Schlauch were especially concerned that a confessionally "neutral" state would leave a kind of vacuum, a moral free-for-all in which other values, deeply alien to Hungarian custom and tradition, might take hold. A Hungary that was no longer Christian left the door wide open, in Schlauch's words, for "the triumphant entry march of cosmopolitanism. . . . The destruction of the Christian framework of Hungarian society opens a free path to the invasion of non-Christian elements."[44] A state had ultimately to proclaim its allegiance to a particular set of moral values, which could be derived in the Hungarian context only from Christianity. Without such a foundation, an insidious moral relativism would prevail and the liberal dream of a secular, confessionally neutral state would prove to be nothing more than the first step toward a self-destructive surrender to the forces of anarchy.

As Bishop Schlauch's admonitions against "cosmopolitanism" might suggest, anxieties about secularism often blended easily with antisemitic language. This had become clear already in the early 1880s, when Hungary's liberal government had tried unsuccessfully to pass a law allowing Christian-Jewish intermarriage. In opposing the government, politically active priests in parliament and in meetings throughout the country had regularly condemned intermarriage as a Jewish plot to establish greater

43. Speech to the Upper House of the Hungarian Parliament of 22 March 1895. "A felekezetnélküliségről," in *Schlauch Lőrinc beszédei*, vol. 4, 130ff.

44. Speech to the Upper House of the Hungarian Parliament of 3 October 1894. "A vallás szabad gyakorlatáról," in *Schlauch Lőrinc beszédei*, vol. 4, 111.

power over Christian society in Hungary.[45] Of course, the episcopate generally shied away from the most inflammatory variations of this rhetoric. In drafting a response to the proposed religious-political laws in late February 1893, Hungary's bishops briefly considered issuing a statement describing Jews as a separate nation within Hungary, bound by traditions at once religious and national that made conversion from Christianity to Judaism (or vice versa) a question of national belonging. However, outrage in the liberal press, which vehemently defended the right of Hungary's Jews as Hungarians, showed the episcopal bench the political risks of that position. When finally released to the public, the bishops' statement made no mention of Jews as a separate nationality and confined objections to Jewish "reception" to purely theological concerns.[46] Others were less cautious. One rising young star, Ottokár Prohászka, in the 1890s still a theological instructor in Esztergom but destined to be named bishop of Székesfehérvár in 1905, was more willing than Bishop Schlauch had been to describe the "non-Christian elements" making their way into Hungarian society. To Prohászka, Hungary was clearly besieged by a secular and anti-Christian "Jewish spirit." In a lengthy article written to oppose Jewish "reception," Prohászka argued that Jews were driven by a worldview entirely their own, a moral vision antithetical in every way to Christianity. To establish a secular state, a polity in which the law was confessionally neutral and all faiths were equal, was to open the gates to a Trojan horse. "Jewish morality is the real curse of Christian civilization, a curse that will ruin Christian culture without fail if it does not cast out the poison from itself; thus Christian states cannot receive Jewry, but must defend themselves against it."[47] Confining religion to private life and reducing it to simple expressions of personal piety could only lead to "Jewish" domination in Hungarian society and a complete distortion of those traditional Christian values so necessary for the preservation of social order.

In the Hungary of the 1890s, however, militant calls for a "culture war" were largely rhetorical. Neither Hungary's government nor, when pressed, Hungary's episcopate were really eager for a showdown. Despite Catholic

45. Miklós Szabó, *Az újkonzervativizmus és a jobboldali radikalizmus története (1867–1918)* (Budapest: Új Mandátum, 2003), 110. More generally, Dániel Szabó, "A néppárt megalakulása," 181–83.
46. The Catholic historian Gábor Salacz describes the affair in Gábor Salacz, *A magyar kultúrharc története, 1890–1895* (Pécs: Dunántúl Pécsi Egyetemi Könyvkiadó, 1938), 235. Understandably, Jewish liberals were especially outraged. See Vilmos Vázsonyi, "Pax," *Egyenlőség*, 3 March 1893, 1–4.
47. This essay first appeared in the Catholic newspaper, *Magyar Sion*, in 1893. "A zsidó recepció a morális szempontból" has been reprinted in *Prohászka Ottokár: Kultúra és terror*, ed. Rezső Szíj (Budapest: Szenci Molnár Társaság, 1997), 15–33; quote taken from 15–16.

opposition, it was clear to everyone that Hungary's liberals, as the largest party in the country, held the upper hand. The emperor-king in Vienna, Francis Joseph I, could defy their policy only so long, before placing all aspects of the 1867 Dualist arrangement in jeopardy. Other issues crucial to the monarchy's survival, like important legislation regarding the Imperial and Royal Army, were also at stake. Under these political pressures, Francis Joseph ultimately signaled his acceptance of the religious reforms. All but the most intransigent of Catholic parliamentarians soon fell into line and voted in favor. Civil marriage received royal approval on 9 December 1894; Jewish reception on 16 October 1895. With this, the church-political struggles of the 1890s seemed to be ended. However, fears of a crumbling social unity, and the specter of political and moral chaos that Catholic leaders had warned would come from excluding religion from the public life of the state, refused to disappear. Nor did the association of secularism with "Jewish" values. In the years after the turn of the century, these things became part of a renewed and much more broadly defined "culture war."

A New Right and a New Left: The Disintegration of the Liberal Consensus

One year after parliament passed laws on civil marriage and Jewish "reception," liberal nationalism seemed to dominate Hungarian politics unchallenged. In 1896, Hungarians celebrated their millennium, a year-long series of parades and ceremonial banquets designed to commemorate one thousand years (more or less) of a Hungarian presence in Europe. The festivities also allowed Hungary's liberal oligarchs to celebrate themselves. By linking their own political vision to the earliest Hungarians, they made Hungary's current political system seem to be the natural result of all that had gone before it. For most, the "culture war" of the previous years was a distant memory, one that could be sanguinely contemplated in a multi-volume commemorative *History of the Hungarian Nation* as an "interesting conflict," one that had been "filled with mistakes," but which had in the end led to "great results."[48] However, this moment of confidence proved to be the high-water mark of liberalism in Hungary, not the beginning of a new golden age. In the years that followed, Hungary's liberal oligarchs continued to debate the question of constitutional autonomy as if the nineteenth century struggle between monarchs and a liberal nobility

---

48. Sándor Márki and Gusztáv Beksics, *A Modern Magyarország (1848–1896)*, vol. 10 of *A magyar nemzet története*, ed. Sándor Szilágyi (Budapest: Athenaeum, 1898), 766.

would never end. Meanwhile the industrial society developing outside the walls of Parliament had begun to change Hungarian society in countless unforeseen ways. Some Hungarian historians have described this willful blindness toward their changing society as the hallmark of an "age of decline," an era in which an ossified liberalism laid the seeds of later tragedy.[49] Others have argued that, in these years, liberalism in Hungary became a "static-defensive conservative ideology."[50] In these years, many began to search for a new political vision that could meet the challenges of an age of upheaval more effectively than liberalism. As the liberal nationalist consensus crumbled, the outlines of a "new Right" and a "new Left" began to emerge. For the adherents of these new political trends, the central issues in the "culture war" of the early 1890s were not dead or merely "interesting." As the nineteenth century gave way to the twentieth, growing ideological conflict between a "new Right" and a "new Left" breathed life into the "culture war" in Hungary.

The impetus for a new kind of right-wing or conservative politics came from a surprising quarter: the very same ethnic Hungarian gentry nobles who had carried the torch of liberal reform for so long. From their county seats, these lesser nobles had defended their constitutional prerogatives against Habsburg encroachment, leading Hungary into its "lawful revolution" in 1848 and supporting the Compromise of 1867 that gave Hungary its substantial autonomy.[51] They had also welcomed the country's economic modernization, financing infrastructural improvements that made the first stirrings of industrial production possible in Hungary. By the end of the century, however, the unquestioned place of this class at the head of the nation (and of the Hungarian state) was rapidly eroding, and with it the liberal sympathies of many of its members. Increasingly, Hungary's ethnic minorities challenged ethnic Magyar hegemony, demanding substantive minority rights and a real sharing of political power. In response, many of Hungary's political elite, among them Gusztáv Beksics, grew obsessed with ethnic conflict, devising linguistic and educational policies to guarantee Magyar supremacy and resorting easily to repression when legal instruments failed. In Budapest, too, the liberal elite faced opposition, as the new industrial working class demanded the rights to vote and organize. Here, too, political protest was met with repressive force. Finally, economic development began to erode the gentry's social position in the countryside where it was rooted. Gentry landowners soon found that the

---

49. Gyula Szekfű, *Három nemzedék és ami utána következik* (Budapest: AKV-Maecenas, 1989), 265–71 and ff.
50. Miklós Szabó, *Az újkonzervativizmus*, 222–25.
51. Deák, *Lawful Revolution*.

competition in international grain markets wielded a ruthless price scissors, leaving landowners under the threat of bankruptcy. Though Hungary's political elite generally still adhered to their liberal principles before World War I, many increasingly found themselves taking up or at least contemplating a more conservative kind of politics.

One of these was István Bernát, a leading agrarian politician (and also a Calvinist lay leader). In a pamphlet entitled *Mortgaged Hungary*, Bernát tried to understand Hungary's shifting social and economic structure. Like many, he saw economic change at the root of all other upheavals in Hungarian society. Bernát was hard pressed to identify the dangerous "domestic enemies" by name. The forces at work on Hungarian society seemed to transcend individual actors. Bernát knew only that social values, chief among them land, were quickly becoming little more than goods for purchase or sale. As a result, "indebted land, stripped of its stability, also loses its entire ethical character, its political and social weight. . . . The basis on which our nation developed itself . . . vanishes into dust."[52] Hungarian society, he argued, had once rested on a common set of values and social mores—values embodied in landed estates and in the unquestioned right of the gentry nobility to exercise political power because of it. Without this foundation, political power was simply a commodity, up for sale to the highest bidder and cut loose from any ties to Hungarian culture or history. Without land and the political privileges that accompanied it, the gentry faced inevitable irrelevance. Many feared the Hungarian nation would not survive such a loss.

In his pamphlet, István Bernát had described a new threat to national sovereignty, one posed not by the Habsburgs but by "plutocrats" and "lords of mobile capital," or an even more disembodied force like "Capital" itself. By 1896, when his pamphlet first appeared, these shapeless phantoms had become familiar elements in what was commonly called "the Jewish question" all over Europe.[53] At the end of the nineteenth century, Jews were widely assumed to be responsible for all the social upheaval European society was experiencing. Jewish existence in diaspora, perceived as ingrained rootlessness, seemed to prefigure the fate of all Europeans, as traditional social identities dissolved. Hungarians pondered a similar "Jewish question" in their own country. Many of the beleaguered landowners dabbled in antisemitic politics or looked on approvingly. Some even had ties to Hungary's first antisemitic party, a motley assort-

52. István Bernát, *Das verpfändete Ungarn* (Budapest: Patria, 1896), 15.

53. Shulamit Volkov, "Antisemitism as a Cultural Code: Reflections on the History and Historiography of Antisemitism in Imperial Germany," *Leo Baeck Yearbook* 23 (1978): 25–46.

ment of political adventurers led by Győző Istóczy in the early 1880s.[54] Istóczy's greatest political success had come in 1883, when he worked zealously to transform a young girl's mysterious death in the village of Tiszaeszlár into an explosive blood libel trial that became a sensation throughout Europe.[55] Hungary's antisemites lost that trial, but Istóczy capitalized on his fame in the next elections, winning seventeen seats for his National Antisemitic Party.

In nineteenth-century Hungary, the liberal political establishment in Hungary was still willing to prevent a party devoted exclusively to hating Jews from enjoying anything more than a brief success. Soon after his triumphs, Istóczy's star began to fade, and his party began to disintegrate. However, the furor over the Tiszaeszlár affair, and the initial success of the Antisemitic Party proved that antisemitism could be a potent political force. By the 1890s, many Hungarian gentry, eager like István Bernát for some political initiative designed so that "sovereignty returns into the hands of the nation,"[56] had adopted antisemitic positions. Many believed that Jewish investors were eagerly buying up property from bankrupt gentry at an alarming rate. To counter this, they formed credit cooperatives, lending offices designed to offer loans at rates more favorable than those to be had from "Jewish capital." István Bernát was himself an attorney for the largest of these, the League of Hungarian Landholders.

Within Hungary's political structure, these pressure groups could never become true political parties. The country's entire political system was rigged to produce election results in which only politicians who supported the Compromise of 1867 without reservation could ever hope to govern.[57] Suffrage laws and electoral districting combined to prevent any reform movement from ever having success at the ballot box. However, electoral politics were by no means the only kind of political action. The credit unions and cooperative leagues that comprised agrarian politics in Hungary promised a new vision of national society. In their rhetoric, the constitutional and political threat posed by the Habsburgs simply vanished. These "new conservatives," as the historian Miklós Szabó has called them, focused instead on inchoate socioeconomic threats, developing a broad cultural critique into a profoundly antiliberal ideological convic-

54. Andrew Handler, *An Early Blueprint for Zionism: Győző Istóczy's Political Anti-Semitism* (Boulder, CO: East European Monographs, 1989); Judit Kubinszky, *Politikai antiszemitizmus Magyarországon, 1875–1890* (Budapest: Kossuth, 1976).
55. Andrew Handler, *Blood Libel at Tiszaeszlár* (Boulder, CO: East European Monographs, 1980).
56. Bernát, *Das verpfändete Ungarn*, 42.
57. András Gerő, *The Hungarian Parliament, 1867–1918: A Mirage of Power*, trans. James Patterson and Eniko Koncz (Boulder, CO: Social Science Monographs, 1997).

tion.[58] Casting off liberal-national political traditions, they became a new Right, energized by their opposition to an alien "Jewish spirit" and the destructive "progress" it threatened to bring to the true and "Christian" Hungary.

This new Right fed, and in turn was fed by, a similar transformation on the Left of Hungary's political spectrum. Here too, one time liberals had begun to find by the turn of the century that Hungary's traditional liberal nationalism was an insufficient response to a rapidly changing society. Even as Hungary's gentry searched for ways to preserve their social and political hegemony, democratic reformers laid the blame for mounting social troubles squarely at their feet. Hungary's political structure, they observed, ensured that few of the workers in the new industrial districts on the outskirts of Budapest and almost none of the millions of peasants working on Hungary's landed estates had any political voice. The country's restive nationalities, many felt, justly demanded some concession to their linguistic and cultural differences. Most important, Hungary's political elite had to abandon its rigid insistence that an outdated political and social structure was the only form that Hungarian nationhood might take. Like the "neoconservatives," whom they bitterly opposed, this emerging New Left had little patience for constitutional questions of Habsburg-Hungarian relations. To them, as well, a much greater battle was brewing over the cultural and moral foundations of Hungarian society. And like the new Right, they too focused their broad and loosely linked hopes and beliefs around a slogan designed to encapsulate the gist of their ideological convictions. If the Right imagined a "Christian Hungary," then the new Left, by the beginning of the twentieth century, was beginning to imagine a "progressive Hungary."

Who made up Hungary's new "progressive Left?" A wide variety of individuals and social groups, urban-based and drawn mainly from the ranks of labor leaders, the intelligentsia, white-collar workers in the private sector, artists, and journalists, formed an alternative political culture united loosely around the idea of "progress." No one political party or organization served as the focus for these reformist trends. Just as the new forms of conservative politics began in pressure groups outside the formal party structure, so too did efforts at democratic reform. Because the existing political parties resisted redirection from within, members of the new urban middle classes sympathetic to ideas of reform transformed other organizations and social spaces into locations for progressive politics. Some

---

58. See Szabó's seminal article: Miklós Szabó, "Új vonások a századfordulói magyar konzervatív politikai gondolkodásban," *Századok* 108, no. 1 (1974): 3–65. His posthumously published synthesis of right-wing politics in the Dualist Era sums up a lifetime's research into this problem. Szabó, *Az újkonzervativizmus.*

found a new political home in Masonic lodges. Important centers of liberal associational life, these had been active in Hungary since the eighteenth century and had played an important role in the pre–March 1848 decades of reform politics. After 1900, some lodges, especially those in Budapest, took on a new role as important centers of critical debate aimed at transforming the sterile liberal consensus that dominated public life in Hungary as well as the social system on which it rested.[59] Soon these were joined by academic societies, such as the Society for Social Science, founded by radical democrats in 1900 for the purpose of submitting all of Hungarian life to sociological analysis. The society's journal, *Twentieth Century*, became a leading forum for progressive thought, as did university student associations, like the Galileo Circle in Budapest. In the pages of these journals and in the meeting rooms of these circles, members debated the nationality question, argued for universal suffrage, including women's suffrage, and called for the complete separation of church and state. Such efforts focused support for Hungary's small, but important, Social Democratic Party; it also stimulated leading reformers to found new political parties. By 1914, there was also a small Radical Democratic Party in Hungary, based largely in Budapest.

Other reformers turned to journalism or to art; in fin-de-siècle Budapest, as the historian Péter Hanák has argued, modernist artistic circles and critical literary or scholarly reviews served as "workshops" of sorts in which a new generation of Hungarian intellectuals tried to imagine a society different from the one in which the gentry ruled.[60] Some were poets, like the extremely influential Endre Ady whose verse galvanized a whole generation with its radical calls for social change as well as its revolutionary use of language. Others, like the young György (Georg) Lukács and his colleagues, aimed more generally at establishing a new and critical voice in Hungarian philosophy and letters, one that linked their intellectual work to a program of social reform.[61] Still others, like the composer Béla Bartók, challenged mainstream Hungarian culture simply by choosing new materials and forms for their artistic expression.[62] In the tense world of fin-de-siècle Budapest, this too had political repercussions. Some were sympathetic to some sort of socialism; others preferred to think of themselves as radical bourgeois democrats.

59. Miklós Szabó, *Az újkonzervativizmus*, 226–27.
60. Péter Hanák, "The Garden and the Workshop: Reflections on Fin-de-Siècle Culture in Vienna and Budapest," in *The Garden and the Workshop. Essays on the Cultural History of Vienna and Budapest* (Princeton: Princeton University Press, 1998), 63–97.
61. Mary Gluck, *Georg Lukács and His Generation, 1900–1918* (Cambridge, MA: Harvard University Press, 1985).
62. Judit Frigyesi, *Béla Bartók and Turn-of-the-Century Budapest* (Berkeley: University of California Press, 1998).

A great many of the most prominent critical intellectuals in fin-de-siècle Budapest, like their counterparts in Vienna and Prague, came from Hungary's assimilated Jewish bourgeoisie.[63] Historians have speculated that their role in an undeniable golden age of cultural production in Hungary and in Central Europe derives from their ambiguous position as a generation both accepted within Hungarian society but also subtly marginalized by Hungary's gentry noble "taste-setters." Of course, not every progressive intellectual in Hungary was Jewish; some of the most important were not. Nor is it true to say that Hungary's Jewish communities stood behind all these reformist projects. Even within Budapest, the majority of the city's Jewish middle class had little interest in cultural revolt; nor did their support for progressive politics necessarily extend to support for those who proclaimed themselves socialists or who advocated radical economic transformation. The history of national and religious identities within the more Orthodox communities of provincial Hungary remains to be written, but here too there was little connection to the progressive political circles of Budapest. Even so, the fact that so many of those active in progressive intellectual circles were Jewish made the cause of "Progress" seem a decidedly "Jewish" endeavor, especially to those on the Right.

In sum, progressive politics in Hungary at the end of the Dualist Era resembled more a crazy quilt of intellectual ferment than a sociologically identifiable group, a community of moral and political sentiment best described as a "counter-culture" with its own "value-system," its own "inner democracy," and its own "separate institutions."[64] Lacking mass-based workers' parties of the sort that could be found in Austria or Germany or the expanded suffrage laws necessary to build them, there was no public space in which this new Left could build a mass movement unified around a common and coherent political program.[65] Instead, Hungarian progressives, gathering in a variety of circles and clubs as often at odds with one another as in alliance, were bound together solely by their unshakeable conviction that contemporary Hungarian society was both unjust and undemocratic. The "Progress" they demanded was a call for a more open society, a polity in which new voices might be heard, and new, more democratic ways of governing across class and ethnic lines might be imagined.

63. See, e.g., Steven Beller, *Vienna and the Jews, 1867–1938: A Cultural History* (Cambridge: Cambridge University Press, 1989); Scott Spector, *Prague Territories: National Conflict and Cultural Innovation in Franz Kafka's Fin-de-Siècle* (Berkeley: University of California Press, 2000).

64. György Litván, " 'Magyar gondolat—szabad gondolat' Nacionalizmus és progresszió a század eleji Magyarországon," in György Litván, *Októberek üzenete* (Budapest: Osiris, 1996), 43.

65. Mary Gluck, "In Search of 'That Semi-Mythical Waif: Hungarian Liberalism': The Culture of Political Radicalism in 1918–1919," *Austrian History Yearbook* 22 (1991): 108.

As Hungary entered the twentieth century, these radical reformers, like the neoconservatives who were their nemesis, knew with certainty that their country's destiny would be determined, not by further wrangling with the Habsburg dynasty, but by the looming, Europeanwide conflict between the forces of Progress and Reaction themselves.[66]

"The Black Flag": Christian Politics and the Catholic Church

Catholic critics of a secular society found that their cultural fears had much in common with the "neoconservative" or new Right opposition to the "Jewish spirit" at work in Hungary. This mutual sense that Hungary's Christian culture was under siege only increased after the turn of the century, as Hungary's progressive movement called more loudly and more persistently for the nation's moral and cultural renewal. Already in 1890, Bishop Prohászka had declared his anxieties about secularism in explicitly antisemitic language, declaring that "the Jewish worldview has stood, since the beginning, in a war with the Christian conception."[67] By 1903, Prohászka devoted a whole book to the question of religion in society, describing Catholicism as the "triumphant worldview" in his work of the same name. Throughout the book, Prohászka contrasted Catholicism to progressive movements, and to socialism in particular, concluding that only the Catholic faith formed a system of values that might truly make an individual feel at home in the modern world.[68] Described by one historian of Hungarian Catholicism as a "forerunner of the second Vatican council," Prohászka become known outside Hungary as well as one of the leading advocates of modern Catholicism, a faith aware of contemporary intellectual developments and open to the good that scientific and technological advances might bring, while ever critical of materialist ideologies that led to the erosion of faith.[69] To some in the Catholic Church, Prohászka's wide-ranging familiarity with the thought of contemporary philosophers (for example, Henri Bergson) went too far; in 1911, three of Prohászka's writings were judged to be contrary to the teachings of the

66. Szabó, *Az újkonzervativizmus*, 227.

67. *Prohászka Ottokár: Kultúra és terror*, "A zsidó recepció," 28.

68. Ottokár Prohászka, *A diadalmas világnézet*, in *Prohászka Ottokár összegyüjtött munkái*, ed. Antal Schütz (Budapest: St. István Társulat kiadása, 1927).

69. Ferenc Szabó, S.J., *Keresztény gondolkodók a XX. században* (Szeged: Agapé, 2004), 410–448, citation on 413. There is a substantial literature on Prohászka's modernism. In addition to the works of Ferenc Szabó, S.J., see Jenő Gergely, *Prohászka Ottokár: "A napbaöltözött ember"* (Budapest: Gondolat, 1994), including the bibliography, 246–48.

church and placed on the Index.[70] Nevertheless, Prohászka remained a towering figure in fin-de-siècle Hungarian Catholicism, symbol of a new generation of Catholics eager to fight the emerging "culture war" by bringing a reinvigorated faith into the public sphere.[71]

Elsewhere, the rhetoric proclaiming a Christian society embattled by alien forces was becoming heated. This was especially true on university campuses. In 1900, vandals tore a cross off the national coat of arms in a newly constructed building at the university in Budapest. Right-wing students immediately concluded that the vandals, who never were identified, were Jewish, and called for a vigorous action against "growing pan-Judaism" on campus. At the start of the 1901 academic year, these same students demanded that crosses be hung in every classroom to mark the Christian character of the university. They marched through campus, placed crosses in lecture halls, and published letters and pamphlets in sympathetic newspapers to publicize their cause. University administrators, adhering to their nineteenth-century liberal ethos, would have none of it, restating the university's commitment to secular education, ordering the crosses removed, and issuing stern warnings to the students involved.[72] Nevertheless, the affair demonstrated the continued potency of Christian antisemitic rhetoric at the start of the new century.

Not everyone understood the same thing by "Christian society," however, a fact that troubled the new generation of politically engaged Catholic leaders. Few of the conservative students hanging crosses in the lecture halls of Budapest's university in 1901 were moved by religious zeal.[73] Most understood the "Jewish spirit" primarily as a threat to their post-graduation job prospects, especially in the free professions of law and medicine where bourgeois Jewish graduates were especially prominent. Similarly, Hungary's Catholic press devoted increasing space to Hungary's "Jewish question" in all its economic, cultural, and political variations.[74] But writers in these papers expressed their antiliberal cultural criticism, for all their virulence, in the most general of terms. Specific confessional refer-

70. The context in which three of Prohászka's writings were placed on the Index is explored in *Catholicism Contending with Modernity: Roman Catholic Modernism and Anti-Modernism in Historical Context*, ed. Darrel Jodock (Cambridge: Cambridge University Press, 2000).

71. Zoltán Nyisztor, *Ötven esztendő: Századunk magyar katolikus megújhodása* (Vienna: Opus mystici corporis, 1962).

72. Citation taken from Mary Gluck's summary of the "cross movement." Gluck, *Georg Lukács*, 60–61. Miklós Szabó offers a more detailed analysis in *Az újkonzervativizmus*, 184–97.

73. Miklós Szabó, *Az újkonzervativizmus*, 197.

74. Dániel Szabó, "A Néppárt megalakulása," 207–8.

ences rarely entered into their invective. In the so-called Christian press, the enemy was always a vaguely defined "atheism," "religious indifference," "moral relativism," or "bourgeois democracy" as such.[75] This gave Christian politics a clear antiliberal "worldview." But it also meant that Catholicism tended to be pushed to the side in favor of "Christian" and anti-Jewish rhetoric with broader appeal. Looking back at the fin-de-siècle rhetoric of Christian defense from the vantage point of 1917, Béla Bangha, a prominent Jesuit and a leader in the effort to create a truly Catholic press in Hungary, summed up Catholic concerns neatly: "In principle, the concentration of Christians against unbelief and Jewish excesses sounds very fine; but in practice such a concentration has . . . never succeeded."[76] Sooner or later, the Christianity in such a nationalist politics became so watered down that it lost its power to transform society.

Concerned about the direction of Christian nationalist politics, politically engaged Catholics worked to imagine the moral renewal of Hungarian society on explicitly Catholic terms. They did this, however, without a mass political party to support them in their efforts. Although the People's Party, founded in 1895, was supposed to have played this role, a number of factors combined to prevent it, as well as the reformist Christian Social movement founded some years later, from becoming mass political parties along the lines of the Christian Social Party in Vienna or the German Center Party. Most important, Hungary had a highly restrictive suffrage law, confining political life to the world of social elites throughout the nineteenth century. Moreover, a good part of the Magyar-dominated counties of Hungary (favored under Hungary's system of suffrage) had Protestant majorities unlikely to support a confessionally Catholic party. Nor could Hungarian Catholics unequivocally embrace a confessional political identity in the way that German Catholics had done with such success. In the face of restive national minorities that included the predominantly Catholic Slovaks, Magyars of all confessions were always forced to consider the consequences of choosing religion over nation. In any case, the magnate landholders who were the party's parliamentary leadership had no intention of extending significant rights to minorities or even to disenfranchised Magyars, certainly not the right to vote. Their deep concern for a traditional social order made them extremely reluctant to respond in any meaningful way to economic grievances, preventing the People's Party or any other Catholic political organization in Hungary from becoming a

---

75. Miklós Szabó, *Az újkonzervativizmus*, 197.

76. "Father Bangha's report about the Catholic press question," Esztergomi Prímási Levéltár (EPL), Cat. 44: 3078/1920.

mass political organization that addressed and managed socioeconomic protest.[77] Indeed, party leaders personally assured Pope Leo XIII that their party would not become an entity like Vienna's Christian Social Party.[78]

Without a mass political party to champion their cause in the rough and tumble of open electoral politics, religious activists in the clergy and the laity poured their efforts in the press and public debate to define the rhetorical battles between "progress" and "reaction" for themselves, sharpening these conflicts with the intensity of their interventions. No one did more in this regard than the Jesuit father, Béla Bangha. Revered during the interwar years as the father of the Catholic press, Bangha began in the last years of the Dual Monarchy to organize self-consciously Catholic newspapers and journals that might replace the more generally "Christian" and antiliberal papers that had hitherto been the main forum for Hungarian Catholicism.[79] To Bangha, this was critical, since only a truly Catholic public voice could offer a sustained and compelling alternative to the liberal and progressive "Jewish press" that he felt made up the mainstream of Hungarian public opinion. Such an ideological alternative, he believed, might win away Hungary's urban bourgeoisie from the blandishments of the progressive radical press, creating instead a solidly conservative Christian middle class under the tutelage of the Catholic Church. With financial support from the episcopate, Bangha soon established a number of journals with a respectable readership among Hungary's Catholics.[80]

These rhetorical strategies allowed Catholic activists to remain at the forefront of the emerging "culture war," defining the moral stakes of the battle of worldviews for conservatives. Through the efforts of men like Father Bangha, but also through the more vaguely "Christian" alliances between Catholics and others, Catholicism became indelibly associated with the new conservative politics. Nowhere was this more true than in liberal-progressive circles. In the years before World War I, Hungary's socialists and bourgeois-radicals took up the banner of anticlericalism, calling for absolute separation of church and state, especially in matters of education, where they considered religious instruction to be poisonous to the minds of impressionable young democrats. Moreover, Hungarian progressives

---

77. The contrast with Vienna is stark. See John W. Boyer, *Political Radicalism in Late Imperial Vienna: Origins of the Christian Social Movement, 1848–1897* (Chicago: University of Chicago Press, 1981).

78. Dániel Szabó, "A Néppárt az 1896. évi országgyűlési választásokon," *Századok* 112, no. 4 (1978): 732.

79. See, e.g., Zoltán Nyisztor, *Bangha Béla élete és műve* (Budapest: Pázmány Péter Irodalmi Társaság, 1941).

80. Miklós Szabó, *Az újkonzervativizmus*, 255–60. See also Jenő Gergely, *A politikai katolicizmus Magyarországon.*

refused to make any distinctions between religious forms of Christian politics and their more secular alternatives. Although religious activists formed only one group within Hungary's new conservative "Christian" politics, progressives took Catholic activists as symbol of everything they opposed. In feuilletons and public speeches, poets like Ady attacked clergy like Bishop Ottokár Prohászka or Béla Bangha by name, associating them and their church with all that was reactionary in Hungary.[81] To the Right, the language of "Christian nationalism" might have admitted of many different interpretations. On the Left, however, the standard of Christian Hungary flew like a "black flag,"[82] energizing progressive reformers to take up the cause of secular society and attack the church as the embodiment of all reactionary forces in the country. The Catholic Church stood at the center of a deepening ideological divide.

Calvinism between Scylla and Charybdis

As the "culture war" heated up, Hungary's Calvinists were especially concerned about their place between the emerging new Right and new Left. Theirs had been the church from whose pulpits generations of pastors had thundered against the iniquities of the Catholic Habsburgs. Now some Calvinists feared that this invective had become clichéd from overuse and wondered how they could make their faith relevant again in public life. Dezső Szabó, a radical intellectual who took particular pride in his Calvinist upbringing, wrote about this cultural shift in a polemical article entitled "The Problem of Hungarian Protestantism," published in the modernist journal *West*. "As the principles of social democracy take the place of national liberalism and as the now so-called radical trends appear in the economic, moral, and social arenas, a saddening crisis threatens Protestantism: that of falling between two chairs."[83] In his estimation, Catholicism and socialism were the only two comprehensive worldviews viable in contemporary Hungary. In 1848, liberal nationalism had stood for progress. Now socialists had usurped their role, naming all their endeavors "progressive" and "radical" as Kossuth and his allies once had done. Liberal politicians, mired in a political structure that looked only to the past, had nothing new to offer. Only Catholicism had the philosophical scope

---

81. Lee Congdon, "Endre Ady's Summons to National Regeneration in Hungary, 1900–1919," *Slavic Review* 33, no. 2 (1974): 302–22.
82. The phrase is Endre Ady's. See "A fekete lobogó a falukon," which first appeared in *Nagyváradi Napló*, 20 August 1903.
83. Dezső Szabó, "A magyar protestantizmus problémái," *Nyugat*, 16 July 1913, 118–21, quote taken from 118.

to be a feasible intellectual alternative. Protestants would have to choose, Szabó believed, or else fall into the widening chasm between them.

Dezső Szabó, whose writings would be so influential among the populist Right in interwar Hungary, himself argued in this essay that "Protestantism can only survive if it is the organ of continuous progress."[84] The two respondents to Szabó's article, the prominent intellectuals Endre Ady and Zsigmond Móricz, themselves also self-acknowledged products of a Calvinist upbringing, agreed that much with Szabó, though they criticized other aspects of his argument. For example, Endre Ady, towering figure among progressive intellectuals, disagreed with Szabó that opposition to the Habsburgs had lost all meaning. In his writing, he tried to reinvigorate the old Protestant opposition to the Habsburgs with new cultural resonance. As he put it, the monarchy stood for "clerical Catholicism" and once again "Protestant negation" was the "old, tried, and true weapon." But negation, he agreed with Szabó, had to be progressive in nature, for Hungarian Protestantism meant nothing less than "eternal objection and outrage against any kind of chains, and a solidarity of those who don't want to belong anywhere where the sheep-pen is more important than the flock."[85] In another, earlier article, Ady put his view more clearly still: "Protestantism embraced liberalism as its child; it will do the same with social democracy. . . . This will mean nothing less than: a purified liberalism. A purified Protestantism. A purified Christianity."[86] In the battle against reaction, Protestantism, for Ady and many of his readers, was the indispensable ally of a progressive Hungary.

A growing number of Calvinists refused, however, to assume any natural connection between their confession and Hungary's progressive forces. One of them, a rising star among Budapest's Calvinist theologians named Jenő Sebestyén,[87] argued in a number of essays published in the immediate pre- and postwar years, that Protestant liberalism had always been a conservative liberalism. True "liberalism," he argued, was very different from the progressive "libertinism of modern world views, operating without God, and permitting anarchic, radical, in short, the most egregious excesses."[88] This fine distinction betrayed a nagging concern among Hun-

---

84. Ibid.
85. Endre Ady, "Egy probléma: Kettő," in Ady Endre összes prózai művei. Újságcikkek, tanulmányok. Vol. 11 (Budapest: Akadémiai Kiadó, 1955–82), 415–17. The article first appeared in Nyugat, 16 August 1913.
86. Endre Ady, "Protestantizmus és szocializmus," in Ady Endre összes prózai művei, 3:344–45. The article first appeared in Nagyváradi Napló, 21 December 1902.
87. For a brief biography, see Sándor Ladányi, "Sebestyén Jenő," in Emlékkönyv Sebestyén Jenő születésének 100. évfordulójára, ed. Sándor Ladányi (Budapest: Református Egyház Zsinati Irodájának Sajtóosztálya, 1984), 10–22.
88. Jenő Sebestyén, "A protestáns liberálizmus kérdése," Protestáns Egyházi és Iskolai Lap 55, no. 14 (7 April 1912): 210–12, esp. 210.

gary's conservative Calvinists. Although they recognized the obvious similarities between their own distaste for Hungary's progressive Left and that of their Catholic counterparts, they worried about being engulfed in a general "Christian" politics so dominated by Catholic voices. During the war, Sebestyén looked back again on this dilemma, remembering that in those years, "the situation of Protestantism became difficult. Its liberalism and anticlericalism drew it to the free thinkers (*szabadszelleműek*); its Christianity, however, gave it common cause with Roman Catholicism. . . . What should we do?"[89] Sebestyén's answer was to imagine Calvinism as its own worldview, a third option between socialism and Catholicism that solved the "problem of Hungarian Protestantism" perceived by Dezső Szabó and others. "We have a different position. . . . We are joining neither the ultramontanes nor the socialists, because we, by standing on the basis of a separate and independent worldview, want to be a separate and independent factor in Hungarian society."[90]

In this, Sebestyén took his inspiration from the Dutch Calvinist theologian Abraham Kuyper.[91] Believing that Dutch Calvinism had become sterile and diluted through its long association with liberal politics, Kuyper asserted throughout his life that Calvinism ought to be a worldview, or as he put it, a "life-system," in its own right, a holistic faith that could never be compartmentalized into certain areas or roles as liberalism demanded.[92] Because of these beliefs, Kuyper championed state support for religious education, pushing for the establishment of an explicitly Protestant university free from government control. He also founded an antiliberal Calvinist political movement and then led it into coalition government with a Catholic party, serving as prime minister of the Netherlands from 1901–5. Kuyper's belief in Calvinism as a modern worldview exerted tremendous influence outside the Netherlands, not least in Hungary where Jenő Sebestyén became the most prominent champion of Calvinism as a worldview on the model of Kuyper. To Sebestyén and others, Kuyper's critique of liberal Protestantism was equally relevant in Hungary, where the Protestant churches seemingly had little to say in the emerging "culture war." Here too the vision of a reinvigorated Calvinism, able to be its own "worldview" in a shifting and uncertain cultural landscape was attrac-

---

89. Jenő Sebestyén, "Keresztyén konczentráció," *Protestáns Egyházi és Iskolai Lap* 60, no. 14 (8 April 1917): 154.

90. Sebestyén, "A debreczeni liberálizmus," *Protestáns Egyházi és Iskolai Lap* 55, no. 16 (21 April 1912): 244.

91. Frank Vandenburg, *Abraham Kuyper* (Grand Rapids: Eerdmans, 1960).

92. See, e.g., Nicholas Wolterstorff, "Abraham Kuyper's Model of a Democratic Polity for Societies with a Religiously Diverse Citizenry," in *Kuyper Reconsidered: Aspects of His Life and Work*, ed. Cornelis van der Kooi and Jan de Bruijn (Amsterdam: VU Uitgeverij, 1999), 190–205; Peter Heslam, *Creating a Christian Worldview: Abraham Kuyper's Lectures on Calvinism* (Grand Rapids: Eerdmans, 1998), esp. 85–112.

tive.[93] Indeed, Abraham Kuyper's political activities offered a solution to the dilemma posed by Dezső Szabó: how to maneuver between the twin dangers of Catholicism and secularism. Invoking Kuyper, Sebestyén proposed in 1913 a "Christian concentration" with Catholics against secular liberalism: "Kuyper thus did exactly what Calvin had announced in his time. . . . If one must, better to hold with the Catholics than with the faithless."[94]

Like no other, the question of Freemasonry epitomized these dilemmas and revealed the deep divisions between Hungarian Protestants over the place of their church in the emerging ideological clash. Liberal Protestants had joined Masonic lodges in great numbers during the nineteenth century. The lodges themselves had been important centers of enlightened reformist political discussion in the decades before 1848; after the 1867 Compromise, membership was almost essential for a successful career in liberal nationalist politics. Yet, István Bernát, agrarian leader and prominent lay leader in the Reformed Church, pointedly denounced the new role that freemasonic lodges were playing in Hungary's progressive politics and asked, in a series of articles in a prominent Protestant journal, whether any true Protestant could remain a Mason in these ideologically divided times. Soon, he argued, his readers would have to choose between "revolution and the maintenance of social order."[95] Bernát, joined by others, went on to single out particular supporters of Freemasonry who also held positions within the Reformed Church and were thus guilty of an especially awful betrayal.[96] Conservative Calvinists like Bernát and Sebestyén also invoked the specter of Freemasonry to justify the efforts they made to expand their contacts with antiliberal Protestants around Europe and especially with Dutch Calvinists close to Abraham Kuyper. All this, as Sebestyén argued time and again, was necessary to reclaim true Protestantism from the progressive radicals who were debasing it.

Invoking the evils of Freemasonry to justify a significant reorientation within their church angered many liberal Calvinists, who accused men like Bernát and Sebestyén of importing a crypto-Catholic dogmatism into

93. Sebestyén addressed the place of Calvinism in an age of cultural crisis in an extended essay contrasting Calvinism to the radical nihilism of Friedrich Nietzsche: Jenő Sebestyén, *Kálvin és Nietzsche* (Budapest: Kókai, 1917)

94. Jenő Sebestyén, "Még egy válasz Akárkinek," *Lelkészegyesület* 6, no. 1 (4 January 1913): 6–8, see 7.

95. István Bernát, "Felelet a válaszra," *Protestáns Egyházi és Iskolai Lap* 56, no. 31 (3 August 1913): 480–81. See also his earlier article "Hitünk jövőjéért," *Protestáns Egyházi és Iskolai Lap* 56, no. 26 (29 June 1913): 405–6

96. See, e.g., the opprobrium with which conservative Protestants read Gáspár Aczél, *A szabadkőművesség titkai* (Budapest: Márkus S. Könyvnyomda, 1911). For their outrage, see, in addition to Bernát's "Hitünk jövőjéért," Gyula Mezey, "Protestáns hitünk védelme és a szabadkőművesség," *Protestáns Szemle* (1913): 582–91.

Hungarian Protestant thought.[97] Beyond this, however, many liberals within the Reformed Church clung to the traditions of liberal progress that Freemasonry had represented in Hungary for so long. As one wrote to the editor of *Protestant Review*,

> I know that, of all the confessions, the activities and opinion of Protestants best approach the activities and opinion of freemasons; and I know that freemasonry considers Protestantism the religion most compatible with the progress of humanity. . . . These attacks [against freemasonry] bind Protestants unwittingly as comrades-in-arms with clericalism, the greatest enemy of Protestantism, against which freemasonry fights with the greatest energy.[98]

Some Calvinists turned to the very newspapers so associated with Freemasonry in Hungary to express their anger; one referred to Bernát and his allies as "Calvinist Jesuits" and lamented the threat to intellectual freedom that, he felt, inspired the antifreemasonic attacks.[99] Naturally, the editors of radical anticlerical papers were only too eager to print these letters, adding their own editorial leaders in support.[100] Other Calvinists confined their dissatisfaction to the Protestant press, but were no less critical of the attacks on Hungary's liberal Protestant traditions.[101] Despite disagreements about what "progress" might mean, and how much of it was good, liberal Protestants could agree nobody—not Catholics and not the Protestants who seemed to be echoing them—had the right to destroy in broad strokes an institution and a tradition so vital to liberty in Hungary.

Not surprisingly, the issues at stake in debates about Freemasonry—moral certainty versus free intellectual inquiry and social order versus unfettered "progress"—sometimes overlapped with debates about the "Jewish question." Elsewhere in Europe, since at least the time of the French Revolution, Jews and Freemasons had figured prominently in anxieties about a collapsing social order.[102] These associations were slow to take root in Hungarian Protestant circles, but in the last years of the Dual Monarchy, some had begun to link the spread of moral uncertainty to "Jewish" cultural in-

97. Akárki, "A Kálvin Szövetség aknamunkája," *Lelkészegyesület* 5, no. 50 (14 December 1912), 1003, and "Még egyszer a Kálvin-szövetség aknamunkája," *Lelkészegyesület* 5, no. 52 (28 December 1912): 1046–48.
98. Ráday Levéltár (RL): C./141, Papers of László Ravasz, 14. doboz. Gusztáv Kádár to László Ravasz, 21 December 1913.
99. See, e.g., Dr. Pál Kovács, "Kálvinista Jezsuiták," *Világ* (10 August 1913), 11.
100. "Válaszúton," *Világ* (23 July 1913), 1.
101. See, e.g., Benő Haypál, "Tanítsatok minden népet," *Protestáns Egyházi és Iskolai Lap* 56, no. 29 (20 July 1913): 448–50.
102. Johannes Rogalla von Bieberstein, *Die These von der Verschwörung, 1776–1945: Philosophen, Freimaurer, Juden, Liberale und Sozialisten als Verschwörer gegen die Sozialordnung* (Bern: Herbert Lang and P. Lang, 1976).

fluence and so to question their church's traditional support for Jewish integration in language that echoed the debates about Freemasonry, progress, and moral order. In 1917, a rising young star in the Hungarian Calvinist Church named László Ravasz, who would become the leading figure in his church after 1918, submitted an essay to the sociological journal *Twentieth Century* as part of an open forum on the "Jewish Question" in Hungary. Ravasz asserted that there was, indeed, a "Jewish Question" and then proceeded to analyze it at length. After a long discussion of its origins in ancient times, Ravasz turned to the present-day. Ravasz sharply criticized those who were so beholden to Enlightenment ideas about individual liberty that they had come to romanticize Jewish emancipation as the hallmark of a just society. Jews as a people, he claimed, inclined much more than non-Jews to certain characteristics; among these were "Utilitarianism (*Utilismus*), Hedonism, the dissolution of the legal framework, and a lack of history." These "Jewish" traits found their expression in the ailments of modern society. They were, in a sense, "industrial illnesses of the Jewish psyche." As solution, Ravasz could only pose the complete elimination of everything that made Jews Jews: "language, name, tradition, and when the time is right, religion." Salvation lay only with the "world-conquering truths of the Christian life- and worldview."[103]

Of course, others rejected Ravasz's arguments. In the same special issue of *Twentieth Century*, the pastor Benő Haypál, who had written in defense of the Masonic lodges a few years earlier, dismissed antisemitism as a Catholic "clericalist" stratagem and suggested that the "people of Moses and those of Jesus" could easily find common moral ground in a battle against hate. Others took a more sociological approach, finding the cause of the "Jewish question" in the narrowness of the Hungarian middle class.[104] The most outspoken of all, however, stood by his church's traditional defense of religious equality without compromise. In an article published in 1917 in the journal *Equality*, printed by Hungary's Neolog Jewish community, the Calvinist bishop of the Transtibiscan Church District, Dezső Baltazár reflected on the historic significance of Jewish emancipation to Hungarian society. The laws that had granted equal rights to Jews had been, he argued, part of a larger vision for a liberal and inclusive national society, one where the rule of law guaranteed individual freedoms.

103. Contribution of Dr. László Ravasz, *A zsidókérdés Magyarországon: A Huszadik Század körkérdése* (Budapest: Társadalomtudományi Társaság kiadása, 1917), 126–29, see esp. 127–28.
104. Cited in Ladislaus Martin Pákozdy, "Juden und Christen in Ungarn nach 1526," in *Kirche und Synagoge: Handbuch zur Geschichte von Christen und Juden*, ed. Karl-Heinrich Rengstorff and Siegfried v. Kortzfleisch (Stuttgart: Ernst Klett Verlag, 1970), 569–605. See here 594–96.

"This truth," he wrote, "must be defended with solicitous care . . . because if the truth of the law should become obscured regarding the Jews, then this shadow could easily extend to the interest of [other] confessions."[105] Jewish civil rights were thus a kind of benchmark for the respect of all civil liberties in Hungary. Discriminating against Jews, Baltazár suggested, could lead a government to contemplate curtailing the rights of others as well, including Protestants. It was thus incumbent on Hungary's Protestants to safeguard their nation's liberal traditions.

The very different positions taken by Bishop Baltazár and László Ravasz on the "Jewish Question" were emblematic in many ways of the larger anxieties among Hungarian Protestants in the last years of the Habsburg monarchy. Some, like Baltazár, clung stubbornly to a liberal faith, seeing any deviation as an abandonment of their Protestant identity. In a letter to Ravasz, the bishop felt it necessary to recall the principled traditions that had given Protestantism its moral vigor. "So long as it remains liberal (*szabadelvű*), Protestantism has justification in this world. If this property ends, it would be much more correct for it to dissolve back to where it broke away from."[106] In other words, an illiberal Protestantism was essentially Catholicism. Yet Ravasz was among those who worried about the consequences of allowing society to entertain any and all moral values without discrimination. In his memoirs written decades later, Ravasz recalled the prewar years as a time in which a general struggle between belief and unbelief had convulsed Hungarian society: "This war was at its strongest in the first decades of the century. In this war, one had to defend such defensive, protective factors like religion, the church, morality, nation, history, and tradition." With this culture war in mind, Ravasz's embrace of his church's liberal past was much more circumscribed: "It was only possible to go so far on the road of radical progress, but one could not support the diabolical world destruction of godlessness."[107] For Ravasz and conservative Protestants like him, there were simply some beliefs and values that society could not tolerate in its midst. Their fears, and the mutual hostility between their allies on Hungary's new Right and their opponents on the progressive Left, would only intensify during the crisis of world war.

———

The years before 1914 were an age of cultural anxiety in Hungary, as they were everywhere else in Europe. Though old debates about relations

105. Dezső Baltazár, "Az 1848: XX t.-c. és a zsidóság," *Egyenlőség* 36, no. 45 (17 November 1917): 2.

106. RL: C./141, Papers of László Ravasz , 13. doboz. Dezső Baltazár to László Ravasz, 6 March 1914, 1–2.

107. László Ravasz, *Emlékezéseim* (Budapest: Református Egyház Zsinati Irodájának Sajtóosztálya, 1992), 122–23.

with the Habsburg dynasty continued to dominate parliamentary debates, figures on the new Right increasingly wondered whether the greatest threat to national sovereignty was not constitutional, but rather cultural— the spread of complex and seemingly incomprehensible ideas and practices that had begun to undermine Hungary's traditional social order. These concerns influenced, and in turn were influenced by, worries shared by Catholic and Protestant leaders in Hungary about the spread of secularism and the rise of moral disorder. In different ways, and in keeping with their different theological traditions, leading figures in Hungary's Roman Catholic and Calvinist churches began to imagine ways to arrest these dangerous trends by asserting religion more vigorously in the rough-and-tumble of modern public life. In so doing, they inevitably engaged in Hungary's Jewish question, shaping it and sometimes propelling it by placing a more traditional, theological anti-Judaism into a thoroughly modern debate about "Jewish values" in society. Of course, it must be emphasized that, before 1914, Hungary's ruling liberal elite resisted the spread of antisemitic politics on principle. Prominent political leaders openly condemned anti-Jewish rhetoric as destructive of national unity and continued to embrace Jewish assimilation as a desirable social project. Even so, a vision of Christian Hungary had been created, one that fused religious and secular concerns about Jews and their responsibility for unsettling social and cultural changes. These anxieties did not disappear. When the Dual Monarchy began to collapse under the pressures of modern war, they gained even greater power.

2

A War of Belief,
1918–1919

In 1914, the liberal nationalist consensus that had governed political life in Hungary throughout the nineteenth century still held. Hungary remained ruled by a liberal oligarchy that derived its electoral mandate from only a tiny percentage of the citizenry. Despite constant criticism from the Left, no serious effort to reform the arcane system of gerrymandering, legal restrictions, corruption, and outright repression that determined suffrage rights in Hungary had ever been attempted. The nation's political leaders continued to defend the country's liberal heritage, much to the chagrin of the neoconservative Right. Hungary also remained a state dominated by ethnic Hungarians, though this too came at the price of a good deal of repression. Even if almost all leaders of any note among Hungary's ethnic minorities still called for rights and autonomy within Hungary, rather than secession or independence, the nation's ruling elite refused to consider any substantive reform in this area either, maintaining that Hungarians must instead shoulder their historic mission to play a leading role of uplift in the region. No one embodied this combination of "liberal vision" and "conservative statecraft" that characterized Hungarian political culture in these last prewar decades better than the prime minister himself, István Tisza.[1] Though Tisza, as boss of the ruling liberal Party of Work, spoke openly and sincerely about the centrality of liberal thought to Hungarian life, he increasingly turned to strong-arm tactics to keep the state together and the Dualist arrangement of 1867 intact.

As everywhere else in Europe, crowds in Budapest and throughout Hun-

---

1. Gábor Vermes, *István Tisza: The Liberal Vision and Conservative Statecraft of a Magyar Nationalist* (Boulder: East European Monographs, 1985).

gary greeted the declaration of war in 1914 with excitement and jubilation. Political leaders called for national unity in the face of the awesome responsibilities of war, a kind of *Burgfrieden* respected even by those politicians most critical of the political order. Despite horrific losses in the initial campaigns—the armies of the monarchy suffered nearly 800,000 casualties on the eastern front in the autumn of 1914 and a further 800,000 in the first months of 1915—this political truce held for the first two years of the war. By 1916, however, the Habsburg monarchy's situation had become precarious. In the summer of 1916, a massive Russian offensive shattered the military effectiveness of the monarchy's army. Only decisive German intervention halted the Russian advance and enabled Austro-Hungarian forces to recapture their former positions on the eastern front. Though Austro-Hungarian forces remained in the field until the collapse in 1918, "in the last two years of the war, the Monarchy's army was vegetating."[2] This obvious weakness encouraged the Romanian government to abandon its position of neutrality, lay claim to Hungarian territory, and declare war on the Habsburg monarchy. As Romanian troops advanced on Transylvania, a region in which ethnic Romanians outnumbered ethnic Magyars in many places, Hungarians began to fear a looming ethnic war. Again, this threat could only be turned by pleading with German military officials for reinforcements along Hungary's border and elsewhere in the southeastern theater. By the end of 1916, the government of István Tisza found that, to preserve Hungary's traditional ethnic and political order, it had hostaged the nation to the fate of the German military. To a political class fiercely jealous of its independence, this turn of events was humiliating.[3] The prospect of a Hungary dependent on Germany for its survival energized the Hungarian Left, inspiring the most serious challenge to the liberal nationalist status quo since the war began.

Visions of a New Hungary: The Renewal of Democratic Politics in 1918

In July 1916, a loose coalition of progressive democrats and the most fiercely independence-minded nationalists formed a new political party around Count Mihály Károlyi, a maverick aristocrat with many ties to Hungary's progressive intellectual circles. These strange political bedfellows agreed on a number of issues: the need for independence from the Habsburg dynasty and a separate peace between Hungary and the Allies;

2. József Galántai, *Hungary in the First World War*, trans. Éva Grusz and Judit Pokoly (Budapest: Akadémiai Kiadó, 1989), 182.
3. Ibid., 182. More generally, 93–95; 180–92.

a widening of the franchise to include, in the minds of most, universal male suffrage; and some economic reform, including especially land reform. Károlyi's party, as it was commonly called, grew in strength during the last two years of the war; eventually, this alliance of progressives and bourgeois nationalists would become the nucleus of Hungary's first postwar government.[4] At the same time, its platform reinvigorated prewar debates about the democratization of Hungary. Attendance in the debating circles and university societies, those venues so central to "progressive Hungary" since the turn of the century, rose dramatically toward the end of the war, giving the intellectuals who argued there for political, social, and moral reform even greater public prominence.[5]

Worsening conditions on the home front also energized Hungary's small Social Democratic Party. In the last two years of the war, prices for basic goods skyrocketed, decimating the real wages of those middle- and lower-middle-class Hungarians living on fixed salaries. By 1917, wages were worth less than half what they had been in 1914. In response, a growing number of clerks, engineers, and civil servants found their way into socialist trade unions, formerly the province of Hungary's small, but well-organized working class. Drawn by union successes in defending wage levels, the number of dues-paying union members increased sevenfold between 1915 and 1918. The added strength inspired the leaders of Hungary's Social Democratic Party to more militant demands, including higher wages, better working conditions, and, most important, an immediate cease-fire without annexations.[6]

For Hungary's governing class, however, any thought of reform was unacceptable. To them, the crisis of war demanded that they hew closely to the tenets of the traditional liberal nationalist consensus in Hungary: trust in parliamentary government, zealous defense of Magyar hegemony in Hungary, and a belief that a liberal elite could best speak for a nation largely without political voice. For this reason, neither the liberal politicians who made up Prime Minister István Tisza's ruling Party of Work nor the vast majority of the parliamentary opposition were willing to consider any substantial suffrage or land reform, or to contemplate a peace that did not involve a clear victory. This political class also rejected out of hand any concessions to Hungary's ethnic minorities. Instead, they placed their

4. István Deák, "The Decline and Fall of Habsburg Hungary, 1914–1918," in *Hungary in Revolution, 1918–19: Nine Essays*, ed. Iván Völgyes (Lincoln: University of Nebraska Press, 1971), 23. Also, Gábor Vermes, "Hungarian Politics and Society on the Eve of Revolution," in *Revolutions and Interventions in Hungary and Its Neighbor States, 1918–19*, ed. Peter Pastor (Boulder: Social Science Monographs, 1988), 107–23, see 110–11.
5. Deák, "The Decline and Fall," 27; see also Gluck, *Georg Lukács*, 182.
6. Deák, "The Decline and Fall," 25–26.

hopes in a decisive German victory in the East, an arrangement that would reduce rival Romania and Serbia to weak neighbors, shatter the hopes of minorities within Hungary, and permit ethnic Hungarians, guided as ever by the ruling liberal oligarchy, to retain hegemony without change or compromise. Prime Minister Tisza himself, an iron-willed strong man, coerced members of his ruling party to support him without question. Even after Tisza was forced from office by political rivals in 1917, he remained the dominant figure in Hungarian politics, overshadowing his weaker successors and ensuring that nothing but the most minimal suffrage reform passed in the Hungarian parliament. Of course, his success in shaping policy out of office depended in great measure on the willingness of Hungary's parliamentarians to agree in principle with his views. Despite signs of a looming crisis in 1917 and 1918, "normality" prevailed in Hungarian politics. "The forms of constitutional life went on," and the great majority in Hungary's governing establishment continued to act until the end of the war and the collapse of the monarchy as though the political structure of prewar Hungary could and would emerge intact and unaltered in any respect.[7]

Condemning this intransigence as reactionary and backward, the Hungarian Left insisted that the emergence of a new and modern Hungary after the war depended on several issues. Even if there was no shared vision of what the "new Hungary" would be, everyone on the Left could agree that it would only arise within a democratic political system. Hungary, they demanded, could not continue to be ruled by a government elected by some 8 percent of the country's population. All groups demanded universal male suffrage; some even went further to push women's right to vote as well.[8] Nationalities policy—the "neuralgic point"[9] of Hungary's democratic opposition—was even more contentious. Opponents of democratic reform in the government insisted that universal suffrage and minority rights made up a common threat to the essential nature of the Hungarian state. If non-Magyars enjoyed the right to vote without exception or qualification, the entire edifice would crumble, leaving the Hungarian nation weakened and exposed; one intellectual close to István Tisza, the former prime minister, put it this way: "Universal suffrage would endanger Hungary's territorial integrity. . . . The optimists say that,

7. Vermes, "Hungarian Politics and Society," 113, more generally, 109–16. Also Deák, "The Decline and Fall," 26–27.

8. On the question of women's suffrage, see Susan Zimmermann, Die bessere Hälfte? Frauenbewegungen und Frauenbestrebungen im Ungarn der Habsburgermonarchie 1848 bis 1918 (Vienna: Promedia, 1999).

9. György Litván, " 'Magyar gondolat—szabad gondolat': Nacionalizmus és progresszió a század eleji Magyarországon," in György Litván, Októberek üzenete, 82; more generally, 82–87.

if we treat the ethnic minorities well, they will love their country. But . . . what they imagine their country to be is incompatible with the Hungarian conception of the state."[10] Even within Károlyi's party, many members tried to imagine ways to balance universal suffrage with a clear vision of Magyar hegemony within Hungary. In opposition to this, progressives personally close to Károlyi argued that democracy and minority rights were inseparable and that both were necessary for a modern and just society. This vision soon became Károlyi's as well. Led by Oszkár Jászi, the foremost advocate of minority rights in Hungary, progressive democrats proposed transforming Hungary into a confederation of nations, a kind of "Switzerland of the East" in which each nation would enjoy substantial autonomy within a common political framework.

Jászi's belief that Hungary must be democratic and tolerant in its ethnic policy to be a truly modern nation was typical of a certain strain of radical thought within the Hungarian Left. Within the Károlyi party, there were almost as many ideas about what the "new Hungary" might look like as there were members. Even so, an important core of progressive politicians and intellectuals stood out for their public prominence. These young radicals, a group that included men like Oszkár Jászi, grounded their views of social change and democratic ideals firmly in sociological theory.[11] In Masonic lodges, university circles, and debating societies like the Society for Social Science, these progressive thinkers sharpened a vision of Hungary's future by proposing and then debating the existence of knowable and identifiable laws that governed a society's modernization. Sociology, they declared, demonstrated irrefutably that Hungary lagged behind the West by any marker of modernization one might choose. Above all, these radicals "diagnosed the underlying problem of Hungarian society as one of philosophic backwardness."[12] In progressive circles, it was clear that Hungary had failed to keep pace with the West primarily because its politicians, economists, and policymakers adhered to a "reactionary world view," defined by outdated and semifeudal beliefs in the nature of man and of society. For these young social theorists, possessed of a faith in the prescriptive power of sociology, democracy would not be simply a pluralist conversation of voices that included those hitherto silenced by an oligarchic regime. Instead, it would be a new society, in which Enlightenment ideals of reason, secularism, and science—in short, everything that was modern—triumphed in its centuries-old struggle against obscurantism and reaction.

10. The intellectual was Ferenc Herczeg, as cited by Gábor Vermes, in "Hungarian Politics and Society," 116.
11. Gluck, *Georg Lukács*, 88ff.
12. Ibid., 89.

Hungary's progressive radicals believed that religion had no place in the public life of a modern and progressive society if believers could not reconcile their faith to the rational and secular laws of social progress.[13] Though they shared a belief with Hungary's nineteenth-century liberal elite in the desirability of separating church and state, they had none of the instinct for pragmatic compromise in religious matters that had guided men like Albin Csáky or József Eötvös. Instead, they insisted on principle that the nation's salvation lay in the triumph of "free thought" over religious obscurantism. At a 1909 meeting of the freemasonic Martinovics lodge, Oszkár Jászi proclaimed his opposition to any form of public religion that contradicted the laws of progress as determined by rational inquiry. Though he held the principle of freedom of conscience in the highest regard, it was the duty of all progressively minded Hungarians to "oppose religion where it appears as a feudal, reactionary institution, as a shackle on the freedom of conscience."[14] Others took an even more vitriolic tone. Oszkár Fáber, a leading exponent of anticlerical thought in Hungary and the future minister for the liquidation of religious matters during the 1919 Bolshevik regime of Béla Kun, pronounced religion a deception in one prewar tract[15] and "clericalism" a "nation-destroying danger" in another.[16] Zsigmond Kunfi, who would also serve in the Kun regime as minister of religious and public education, admiringly followed the French Third Republic's assault on the Catholic Church and the separation of church and state in that country in 1905 in a series of articles for *Twentieth Century*, the most prestigious forum for sociological inquiry in Hungary.[17] For progressives who understood "philosophical backwardness" to be at the core of Hungary's political life, such views were logical consequences. Jászi announced that the pages of his journal *Twentieth Century* would "remain closed to one, and only one, tendency. Every explicit or implicit . . . expression of the reactionary worldview will be banished. And this does not contradict our strongly held belief in the freedom of speech, because reactionary political theory cannot be, by definition, scientific theory."[18] It followed that individuals might practice whatever faith they chose in private. However, religion could have no place in the public sphere. As the clerical ideology of reaction, it was anathema to progress.

13. Gyula Mérei, *Polgári radikalizmus Magyarországon, 1900–1919* (Budapest: Karpinszky Aladár könyvnyomda, 1947), 47–50.

14. Cited in László Heverdle, "A Martinovics-páholy antiklerikális sajtópolitikája," *Magyar Könyvszemle* 99, no. 2 (1983): 139.

15. Oszkár Fáber, *A keresztényszocializmus* (Budapest: Népszava, 1907).

16. Heverdle, "A Martinovics-páholy," 142.

17. Zsigmond Kunfi, "A franczia kultúrharcz," *Huszadik Század* (1905): 185ff, 292ff, 423ff, 492ff.

18. Gluck, *Georg Lukács*, 90.

Despite this vision of a clear struggle between progress and reaction, the network of intellectuals, left-liberal politicians, socialists, and artists who comprised the Left in Hungary did not imagine an imminent revolution. Certainly, Hungary's Social Democratic Party became more outspoken in their opposition to the regime in the wake of the Russian Revolution. Party leaders organized mass demonstrations on behalf of suffrage reform, and in January, and again in June 1918, a massive wave of strikes halted production for days throughout Hungary. However, party leaders, comfortable in their role as opposition party and convinced, despite their rhetoric, that the time had not yet come for revolution, eagerly accepted vague (and unfulfilled) promises of reform and soon called an end to the strikes. This did not prevent wildcat strikes from breaking out spontaneously throughout Hungary on numerous occasions in 1918; barracks revolts also erupted in several places in these months, inspired perhaps by revolutionary events, but again in no way linked to the actions of Hungarian Social Democrats.[19] Party leaders were also powerless to dissuade radicals from breaking with the party to form syndicalist groups more appreciative of Bolshevik achievements in Russia. These self-named "revolutionary socialists," with roots in the most radical circles of Hungary's debating societies, called for workers' councils outside of the control of mainstream party leaders. Despite a good deal of public attention, including the trial of some of them for sedition, these dissidents by themselves were unable to force a split within the party rank and file; nor could they push party leaders to take a more radical line. On the eve of the monarchy's collapse, Hungary's Social Democrats, like all the other groups making up the Left in Hungary, were strong in number, and ardent in their rhetoric, but by no means resolved on a revolutionary course.[20]

The collapse of the monarchy, when it came in late October 1918, surprised the radical democrats and socialists who comprised the Hungarian Left as much as it did everyone else in Hungary. Despite fervent hopes for the democratization of Hungary, no one could imagine a Hungarian state that did not encompass the entire historic Kingdom of Hungary; German military observers scoffed at the "magical belief" they found in all Hungarians that enemy armies would somehow stop at the "red-white-green frontier posts."[21] Even more significantly, the progressive intellectuals who imagined a more democratic Hungary had no experience at all with mass political mobilization. Theirs had been a counterculture formed in editorial offices, coffee-houses, and debating societies, a milieu that inspired

19. Deák, "The Decline and Fall," 25–8.
20. Rudolf L. Tőkés, *Béla Kun and the Hungarian Soviet Republic: The Origins and Role of the Communist Party of Hungary in the Revolutions of 1918–1919* (New York: Praeger, 1967), 33–47.
21. Vermes, "Hungarian Politics and Society," 119.

impressive and truly daring theories about the nature of democratic government within a multiethnic and multicultural society. However, they had no more connection to the popular discontent over declining living standards, lower wages, and general war-weariness than did the liberal regime they so bitterly opposed.[22] By October 1918, it would certainly be true to say that power passed into the streets, and that popular unrest had become a force that no political power could ignore. But it was not an unrest that anyone on the Left commanded or led. In the last days of October 1918, power essentially fell into the laps of the progressive nationalist coalition around Count Mihály Károlyi. As Ferenc Göndör, a prominent socialist, later remarked: "The Revolution arrived as a hurricane, no one prepared it, and no one arranged it; it broke out by its own irresistible momentum."[23]

A War of Belief: Christian Hungary and the "Other Hungary"

Though the progressive and socialist opposition had been completely unable to force Hungary's Parliament to pass any substantive reform, the "new Right" in Hungary saw nothing but menace in leftist rhetoric. Since the turn-of-the-century, religious and secular neoconservatives had understood the disparate initiatives of the Left to be a coherent and insidious worldview, one alien to Hungarian national traditions. Though this leftist opposition had no tangible political gains to show for all its imaginative theoretical work, Hungary's "new Right" nonetheless perceived the ideological threat to national traditions to be even greater now that their country was at war. Between the regime in power and the leftist opposition, there was of course no political choice for them. As István Milotay, a radical right-wing publicist soon to take a prominent role in counterrevolutionary politics, warned: the only alternative to the conservative status quo was "Hungarian bolshevism."[24] His views were general; Béla Bangha, the Jesuit publicist who worked tirelessly for the creation of a Hungarian Catholic press, described Hungarian socialism as a "state within a state," a political power with interests contrary to those of social order.[25] None of this meant, however, that the "new Right" had abandoned its trenchant

22. Mary Gluck, "In Search of 'That Semi-Mythical Waif," 108.
23. As cited in Gábor Vermes, "The October Revolution in Hungary: From Károlyi to Kun," in Hungary in Revolution, ed. Iván Völgyes, 31.
24. Cited in Gábor Vermes, "Hungarian Politics and Society," 116.
25. B[éla] B[angha], "A szocializmus mint állam az államban," Magyar Kultúra 6, no. 13–14 (1918): 66–70.

criticism of the nineteenth-century liberal nationalist politics that continued, despite all the upheavals of the war, to dominate Hungarian political life. For Hungarian "neoconservatives," fears of the menace that liberalism posed to society had proven all too prescient. The dissolution of social bonds, the questioning of all values, and above all, the rise of radically progressive politics that threatened to transform Hungary completely—all these catastrophes were now visited on the nation. As troops still fought and died on the front, the Right saw new lines of battle forming at home. The "culture war" had turned terrifyingly real.

Many described this clash as a struggle between two Hungaries: "Christian Hungary" and an "other Hungary." During the last months of the war, *New Generation*, a paper partially financed by a Catholic publishing firm but one decidedly secular in tone, ran a series entitled "words from the front." Ostensibly letters from "real" soldiers and officers at the front, each contribution in the series excoriated the cowardice and lack of national faith the author claimed to find at home. One letter, from a regimental commander, is typical in its description of the "other Hungary":

> that other Hungary . . . , which rose up during the war back at home and made the world of greed, selfishness, . . . spiritual and intellectual decay master at home. It was this other Hungary that brought deep disgust, inner discord, . . . between us. Often we have felt that if we have fought for this Hungary, or if this Hungary has been the fruit of our battles to this point, then all our suffering and every sacrifice has been for nothing.[26]

One should, of course, remember that at the same time the editors of *New Generation* were publishing such sentiments, war-weary soldiers were deserting from the ranks in droves. But deserting soldiers did not read *New Generation*, nor did the editors have them uppermost in their thoughts, however much they might have deplored their actions. Instead the editors were speaking to the Right, warning of the imminent and real danger, and urging all nationally minded Hungarians to zealous resistance. In the first letter in the series in late August 1918, the editors described the role they would play as simply one of recording a fury already roused: "We would be transmitters of those views, aspirations, actions, we might say, of that worldview, which is boiling over in the souls of Hungarians (*magyarság*), fighting and bleeding" on the front.[27]

They were not alone in seeing a real war of belief forming before their eyes. In the last two years of the war, religious figures, both Protestant and Catholic, also argued that the clash of worldviews they had identified by

26. "A frontok szava," *Új Nemzedék* 5, no. 29 (22 August 1918): 3–4.
27. Ibid.

the turn of the century had become manifest in the current national crisis. The Calvinist theologian, Jenő Sebestyén, took aim at a hostile "concentration of freethinkers" in one 1917 article. The atheists, freemasons, and Jews comprising this anti-Christian "concentration" had, in his assessment, become an "organized" worldview, mobilized in a quasi-"battlefield situation" to threaten the moral fabric of Hungary.[28] Catholic writers outlined the coming battle of beliefs even more clearly. Father Bangha, for example, called for war bonds to raise money for a Christian press established to check the power of the "Jewish media."[29] Another, in an article in the Jesuit-run magazine, *Hungarian Culture*, described an "international radical assault," fueled by ideas and "foreign aspirations" that Jews had brought to Hungary, fighting for social upheaval and internal turmoil. "We believe," he went on, "that in this clash the head of the freemasonic viper will be crushed. . . . We trust chiefly in the heroism of the Hungarians returning from the front, who demand retributive justice."[30] A latter-day war of belief, one could infer here as well, had already been joined.

In arguing that the cultural and moral threat posed by the Hungarian Left was now imminent, Hungary's "new Right" placed long established antisemitic arguments into a new and more radicalized context. If Hungarian neoconservatives had worried already before the war about the role that Jews were playing in the nation's cultural and economic life, they now warned the reading public that this role might well become a question of national defense. No one put this issue in starker terms than the Catholic bishop of Székesfehérvár, Ottokár Prohászka. In the late spring of 1918, Bishop Prohászka accused Hungary's Jews of shirking military service.[31] On the front lines, he maintained, one found Hungary's Christians in arms, fighting for their nation; the farther one got behind the lines, the more one found the Jews of Hungary, filling safe positions in the professions or cultural life. This trend, he warned, prefigured Hungary's doom, for it was precisely these "Jewish shirkers," whom the bishop described as "degenerate," who would shape the cultural life of postwar Hungary. "Culture," the Bishop argued, was the true war aim; "we have fought and conquered on the battlefields in vain," if others took control of Hungarian culture. Some three months later, he returned to these arguments in even more pointed fashion: would "the Hungarian Christian na-

---

28. Jenő Sebestyén, "Kerestyén konczentráczió," *Protestáns Egyházi és Iskolai Lap* 60, no. 14 (8 April 1917): 154.

29. Lajos Szabolcsi, *Két emberöltő*, 224.

30. Károly Burján, "Forradalmárok készenlétben," *Magyar Kultúra* 6, no. 20 (1918): 305–8.

31. Ottokár Prohászka,"Pro juventute catholica," *Alkotmány* (26 May 1918): 1–2.

tion maintain its hegemony in Hungary?" Did Hungary's Jews want Hungary to be Hungarian, or did they want a "Jewish country" (*Zsidóország*)?[32] In his articles, Bishop Prohászka described the crisis facing Hungary in deliberately apocalyptic terms. Christian Hungarians must act so that "world war did not become national devastation and heroism did not become slavery."[33] Faced with these questions of national destiny, Prohászka said flatly that his words were not antisemitic; they were simply "national self-defense."

As Lajos Szabolcsi, son of the editor of the Neolog Jewish newspaper *Equality*, remarked in his memoirs, the "Jewish question" became a "trumpet call" for the Right in the second half of the war.[34] Bishop Prohászka's charge that Jews were shirking military service was only one of the many ways in which Hungarians debated the place of Jews within a nation at war.[35] Of course, Jewish politicians, religious leaders, and public intellectuals made speech after speech, and filled the pages of newspapers throughout 1918, refuting Prohászka's charge with the most reliable data. No less an icon of the liberal nationalist order than former prime minister István Tisza spoke vehemently in parliament, denouncing antisemitism as unworthy of Hungary's political traditions and arguing that "everyone should be judged on his own merit, and not on the basis of his religion or race."[36] Still, the new Right remained undeterred, persistently identifying Jews as a threat both to social order and the nation's security. Fears of price-gouging, speculation, and black marketeering fueled some of this; in an economy of stagnant wages and rising prices, many wanted scapegoats for their misery. At the same time, increasing numbers of Jewish refugees from war-torn regions of Galicia also focused attention on the so-called "Jewish question." Right-wing papers seized on these stateless Jews as proof that an alien menace had come across the borders and penetrated to the center of Hungary. By 1918, then, the "Jewish question," long used by the Hungarian Right as a cultural code for illiberal and antimodernist politics, had come to symbolize vividly the web of threats to "Christian Hungary" that linked the outer and inner fronts of war.

These suspicions begged the question, of course, of how exactly to fight this internal enemy. All agreed that, in the face of domestic threats such as labor unrest, suffrage movements, and unbridgeable divisions with the

---

32. Ottokár Prohászka, "Elég volt-e?" in *Prohászka Ottokár összegyűjtött munkái*, 22:189–94. The article first appeared in *Alkotmány* (11 September 1918).
33. Prohászka, "Pro juventute catholica."
34. Lajos Szabolcsi, *Két emberöltő*, 183
35. See, e.g., *A zsidókérdés Magyarországon: A Huszadik Század körkérdése.*
36. Cited in Vermes, "Hungarian Politics and Society," 117.

country's ethnic minorities, Christian Hungarians must "concentrate" their power. "Christian concentration" would transcend party and confession. As Count József Károlyi, brother of the progressive Mihály Károlyi but himself a conservative nationalist, put it in an important 1917 speech, a "Christian concentration" would encompass all who "were faithful out of conviction to the Christian worldview, who together would employ this Christian worldview as a tool and as a weapon." It would "eliminate all the many differences which exist between parties, because the Christian word includes in it a decent and thoughtful conservatism and the most modern social ideas."[37] What form such a "concentration" was to take remained unclear. Many imagined policies to curb democratic aspirations, restrain social reform, and curtail the civil liberties of suspected "Jewish" traitors. Politically active Catholics believed that the coming postwar circumstances would thrust Hungary's weak Christian Socialist movement into the center of political attention. Still others found the nation's best hope outside politics. In an article printed in the Jesuit-run journal, *Hungarian Culture*, the conservative sociologist István Weis proposed the civil service as the best rallying point for a Christian "organization of forces." Hungary's political life, he argued, was irredeemably compromised by the agitation of alien democratic reformers and rabble-rousing socialists. Only the civil service, loyal to Hungary but untainted by political compromise, offered patriots the best chance to take back their state from those who threatened to hijack it.[38]

Still others believed that chaotic times called for stronger measures. Perhaps a "Christian concentration" should mobilize for battle in the literal sense of the word, bringing violence to bear on the "other Hungary?" The situation demanded a "settling of accounts," in the words of Károly Huszár, a prominent Christian Socialist politician, not a defeatist "transition" to some kind of peace-time compromise with the nation's enemies.[39] Huszár understood that a "settling of accounts" would be violent. In a speech to parliament in mid October, Huszár called for Hungary's national guard (*honvéd*) units to be pulled back from the front to combat the enemy at home. Others made similar demands. At a meeting called by the Catholic Press Association in the last days of October 1918 to discuss the most effective counterrevolutionary propaganda, one Catholic priest argued: "The question is whether or not we can organize 2,000 rifles, and with that, 2,000 men, who dared to fire in a given situation to keep the

37. Cited in Szabó, *Az újkonzervativizmus*, 329.
38. István Weis, "Az erők szervezése," *Magyar Kultúra* (20 February 1918): 145–54.
39. Károly Huszár, "A keresztényszocializmus, mint a jövő magyar politikai fejlődésének iránya," *Magyar Kultúra* (20 October 1918). Cited in Szabó, *Az újkonzervativizmus*, 336.

revolutionaries from us."[40] Such ideas found favor within military circles, increasingly desperate to preserve order behind the lines; Archduke József, commander of imperial-royal forces on the southern front in Tyrol and a figure in whom many on the Hungarian right confided in the last days of the war, talked to Emperor-King Karl about military repression, arguing that "the sabotage, already leading to catastrophe, must be put down, with military force if necessary."[41]

Nothing came of these plans for a "preventive counterrevolution." Events in October 1918 were simply moving too fast; in November 1918, Hungary was declared a republic. Even so, the emergence of an ideological "Christian nationalism" in the last months of the war, a view that understood Hungary at war also at home, would have significant repercussions. By October 1918, "Christian Hungary" had become a slogan embracing a variety of responses to Hungary's national emergency, a fusion of secular political concerns and religious rhetoric that suggested a politics of national redemption. In the emerging "Christian-nationalism," Christianity represented an antidemocratic moral vision. It also stood for a nation united against its enemies everywhere. By setting "Christian Hungary" against the "other Hungary," Christian nationalists could identify Jews with an inchoate but menacing threat to national security that transcended the internal and external theaters of war. As the monarchy crumbled, and hostile armies prepared to occupy Hungarian territory, the Right linked every challenge to their authority, finding in every threat the signs of an imminent civil war of belief.

A New Hungary: The Revolution
of November 1918

In late October 1918, the Habsburg monarchy collapsed. Institutions that had held together the multinational dynastic state vanished nearly overnight; soldiers of some fifteen nationalities streamed home from the fronts on which Austria-Hungary had been waging war for four long years. Throughout the monarchy, national councils sprang up to replace the rapidly crumbling authority of the dynasty. On 25 October, Count Mihály Károlyi, joined by Oszkár Jászi's Radical Party, and the Social Democrats, formed a National Council in Hungary as well. With crowds

40. Cited in Szabo, *Az újkonzervativizmus*, 339
41. Diary entry of 29 September 1918. Archduke József of Habsburg, *A világháború amilyennek én láttam*, vol. 7, *Tirol védelme és összeomlás* (Budapest: Magyar Tudományos Akadémia,1934), 387.

demonstrating in the streets for peace, democracy, and better living conditions, the council began work creating a new government. For some days, the attitude of the army was uncertain. However, the forces of the old order were stunned by the rapid disintegration and saw no choice but to turn power over to Károlyi and the council. On 31 October, Emperor-King Karl asked Károlyi to form a provisional government, consisting of the parties in the National Council, and to preserve what remained of social order. The next day, he released Hungary from its oath to the Habsburg crown; Károlyi and his government declared Hungary a republic two weeks later. The Dual Monarchy had ceased to exist.

The new Republic of Hungary was a state teetering on the brink of disintegration. Crowds in the streets had enthusiastically supported the declaration of the republic; yet, no party or leader had controlled those crowds. No one could say how fickle the democratic enthusiasms in the street were, nor what circumstances might push those same crowds to throw their support behind something or someone else. Moreover, the economic deprivations that had pushed many into the streets only worsened with the collapse of the monarchy. As the government's control of Hungary's border provinces weakened, the established transportation and trade networks began to crumble as well. Prices continued to rise, and standards of living continued to fall. However, the greatest threat to the new republic came from its new neighbors.

While Károlyi and his closest advisors placed their hopes for a just peace in the fair-mindedness of the Allied powers, the new states of Czechoslovakia and Yugoslavia, as well as the newly emboldened Kingdom of Romania, began to stake claims on Hungarian territory. Distrusting the military's political sympathies, the new Hungarian regime chose to demobilize the army, rather than immediately to create a new Hungarian Republican force. As Hungarian troops streamed home, the armies of the successor states, supported by the victorious Allied powers (and, especially, by the French) began to occupy parts of Hungary. To Hungarians everywhere, used to thinking of the integrity and inviolability of the historic Hungarian state as the highest national good, the occupations came as a profound shock. Many ethnic Hungarians living in the occupied regions, especially middle-class civil servants and state employees whose futures under a foreign government were particularly uncertain, fled their homes for Budapest, adding a refugee crisis to the already formidable list of challenges facing the new regime.

Despite these considerable pressures, Károlyi's new democratic government enjoyed a certain popular support in November 1918, if only because no one could imagine an alternative. Many hoped that Károlyi's diplomatic policy would somehow prove itself right in the end, and that he would be able to persuade the Allied powers to consider Hungary more favorably. The count, who had been active during the war in the international peace movement, had many personal contacts in the West; if anyone could exert influence in Paris, Washington, or London, many Hungarians reasoned, then that person was Mihály Károlyi. Others preferred the stability of any government to anarchy. Leaders of the major Christian churches swore allegiance to the new government and called for the preservation of public order. Hungary's Christian Socialist party soon joined the National Council; even those politically active Catholics most ideologically opposed to seeing the Left in power accepted the reality of the new government and abandoned (temporarily) their counterrevolutionary activities.[42] Prominent members of the old political parties tried to find their bearing in the new political landscape. Some retreated into private life, uncertain of the future, but hesitant to oppose the new regime; others offered their assistance to the Károlyi regime for a time, even though they opposed much of what it stood for.[43] Ardent nationalists of the "new Right" like István Milotay, a publicist who had excoriated the now ascendant "other Hungary" throughout 1918, conceded grudgingly that Hungary now had its independence and hoped that Hungarians might reinvigorate their national pride within the new state form.[44] All agreed that a new world had been born; as one article in the Catholic journal *Hungarian Culture* put it: "We must also take active part in the work . . . of reconstruction. . . . We cannot be absent where the pillars of a new Hungary are being laid, we cannot deny our support to those who are working to restore order."[45] None of this could be taken to indicate a sudden conversion to the dreams shared by those on Hungary's Left. Still, it did suggest that the Károlyi regime might have some room for maneuver in the autumn of 1918.

Nevertheless, many of those now professing their support for the new democratic republic had bitterly opposed any hint of such a thing only weeks earlier. Though conservatives now accepted the republic as the best option given the circumstances, no one could pretend that their gestures amounted to a committed embrace of the new regime. The Károlyi government thus faced a problem common to east-central Europe in 1918: how to generate and maintain support for democratic republics where

42. Jenő Gergely, "Keresztényszocialisták az 1918–as magyarországi polgári demokratikus forradalomban," *Történelmi Szemle* 12, no. 1–2 (1969): 37.
43. Ignác Romsics, *István Bethlen: A Great Conservative Statesman of Hungary, 1874–1946*, trans. Mario D. Fenyo (Boulder, CO: Social Science Monographs, 1995), 87.
44. István Milotay, "Forradalom után," *Új Nemzedék* (9 November 1918). Reprinted in *Álmok és tények: Magyar írók a demokráciáról és a nemzeti kérdésről a monarchia felbomlása idején*, ed. Farkas József (Budapest: Argumentum, 2001), 64–7.
45. Cited in Gergely, "Keresztényszocialisták," 38.

none had existed before.[46] In some new states, this question seemed, at least initially, to be less problematic: there was nearly unanimous support for constitutional democracy among Czechs, for example, even if understandings of what this might mean were more varied than any one cared to admit.[47] The Czechs, however, could see themselves as "victors" of the war; the circumstances that created the new Hungarian republic were much less auspicious. As in Germany, where many were deeply suspicious of the new Weimar Republic, or in the new Republic of Austria, "the state that nobody wanted,"[48] enthusiasm was much more restrained. Were these states doomed from their inception, if one half of society viewed their government as a poor substitute for what had gone before? Did a young democracy depend for its stability on the "whole moral and intellectual condition of a people," on customs and mores shared by all and not just some?[49] If it did, could these customs and mores be created and instilled in those who had hitherto resisted them? The future of the democratic republic in Hungary rested on this hopeful, but fragile, reed.

In Search of Consensus: Secularism and
Civic Allegiance

Though the government struggled to cope with mounting internal and external pressures until it collapsed in March 1919, observers could discern even in the first days of November a few of the principles that would guide Károlyi and his ministers in the months to come. The "new Hungary," so long anticipated by the Left, would be democratic, with universal suffrage granted to all. There would be an extensive program of land redistribution that would reduce the dominance of the landed nobility and improve the lot of Hungary's poor agricultural workers. And the government would ultimately abolish the "hierarchy of privileges" that had regulated religion in Hungarian society. Henceforth, public life would be unambiguously secular. But nagging doubts persisted. Each of these propositions had provoked intense opposition in the decades before 1914. The country's ruling elite had emphatically rejected any kind of voting or land reform; similarly, the Catholic Church had declared that any attempt to remove reli-

46. I am especially grateful to Melissa Feinberg and Samuel Moyn for many conversations that have helped me formulate the argument here.

47. Melissa Feinberg, *Elusive Equality: Gender, Citizenship, and the Limits of Democracy in Czechoslovakia, 1918–1950* (Pittsburgh: University of Pittsburgh Press, 2006), see esp. 11–40.

48. Hellmut Andics, *Der Staat, den keiner wollte: Österreich 1918–1938* (Vienna: Herder, 1962)

49. Alexis de Tocqueville, *Democracy in America* (New York: Knopf, 1956), 299.

gion from public life was immoral and dangerous. Many on the Left feared that these groups had already begun to subvert the republican regime's social and political agenda. A lead article in one of the most prominent radical newspapers warned that opposition to the revolution had not vanished overnight in the early days of November. "Moles . . . in the dark," they maintained, were "getting into the woodworks and gnawing through the structure of the republic not even half finished." Counterrevolutionaries, the newspaper's editors concluded darkly, might yet force the government, against its will, into a just but terrible "republican intolerance."[50] Would Hungary's revolutionaries feel compelled to follow the example of Maximilien Robespierre, using terror to force Hungarians into accepting republican and progressive virtue as the Jacobins had once done? In a famous essay on Bolshevism as a moral problem, the young György Lukács asked precisely this: If "the majority of men . . . do not want this world order," would it be necessary "to bring about freedom through oppression?"[51]

The example of the French revolution suggested that the Catholic Church would be one of the most implacable opponents of the new order. In 1789, French revolutionaries had found the Catholic Church squarely opposed to the liberties they proclaimed and had embarked on a radical and sometimes violent campaign to seize religious property and force priests to swear allegiance to the revolutionary government.[52] One hundred and thirty years later, many Hungarian progressives worried that Hungary's churches, if unreformed, would be a similarly intransigent obstacle to democracy. Their calls for the separation of church and state were indeed couched in aggressive tones.[53] Jenő Zoványi, a Calvinist theological instructor and church historian at the university in Debrecen, was one of these. Before the war, Zoványi had been the foremost champion of intellectual freedom at Calvinist seminaries and theological faculties, arguing that theological instructors had the absolute right to teach anything their consciences dictated—"agnosticism, pantheism, materialism, or monism"—without fear of church censure.[54] After the old order had col-

50. "Ellenforradalom?," Originally in *Világ* (6 December 1918). Reprinted in *Álmok és tények*, 144–47.

51. György Lukács, "A bolsevizmus mint erkölcsi probléma," Originally in *Szabadgondolat* (December 1918). Reprinted in *Álmok és tények*, 234. See also Gluck, *Georg Lukács*, 203–12.

52. Arno J. Mayer, *The Furies: Violence and Terror in the French and Russian Revolutions* (Princeton: Princeton University Press, 2000), 413–48.

53. Tibor Hajdu, *Az 1918–as magyarországi polgári demokratikus forradalom* (Budapest: Kossuth, 1968), 295.

54. Jenő Zoványi, "Hittudomány és tanszabadság," *Nyugat* 11, no. 11 (1 June 1918): 971, 973.

lapsed, and the Károlyi regime had taken power, Zoványi attracted attention by calling on several occasions for the absolute separation of church and state and the exclusion of religion from public education. Religion when tied to the state, he maintained, only fostered intolerance; "Every religion," he argued, "is intolerant towards others and is unable to see the fellow man in another person, [it sees] only someone of an opposing conviction." In a certain sense, then, religion was a "set of chains" from which "the spirit of youth" and, one might infer, the nation more generally, must be free.[55] In an article written for the progressive (and freemasonic) newspaper *World*, Zoványi took an even sharper tone:

> It is impossible for any unprejudiced and disinterested thinking person not to see that every assistance of a state founded on progressive and democratic principles must be withdrawn from the church—it is completely irrelevant to ask from which—from that serpent's nest of thirst for power, of retrograde tendencies, and of moral fever—the sooner the better; every act of defense must be taken against the possibility that this common spirit of the churches does not continue to radiate infection to a state finally longing for healthy development.[56]

To foster a pluralist and equal respect for all faiths as well as for those who had none, a democratic state had to confine to the private sphere those systems of belief it identified as undemocratic or intolerant. For Zoványi, still a theological instructor, religions of all kinds might have merit as private systems of ethics. In public, however, the civic bonds tying all citizens to each other depended on a common set of "progressive and democratic principles" informing political life.

Zoványi's assertions touched a nerve with parishioners and church leaders alike. One woman wrote to him, demanding to know what he would teach the youth if not religious principles: "Tell me, sir! Would you have the youth taught twisted Bolshevism?"[57] Conservative Protestants, long exasperated by Zoványi's radical embrace of "free thought" within Protestantism, viewed this latest outburst as only one more reason to view him with distaste.[58] Catholics also denounced separation of church and state, in more general but similar terms. Bishop Ottokár Prohászka, for example, worried what moral values the new state would publicly favor, if it were truly secular. In an article in the Catholic daily *Constitution* in early March 1919, the bishop compared the state to a despot setting up new

55. "Zoványi tanár az iskolai vallástanítás ellen," *Az Est* (25 December 1918).
56. Jenő Zoványi, "Politikai gyűlölködés az egyházban," *Világ* (14 January 1919): 7.
57. RL: C./101, Papers of Jenő Zoványi, Box 22. Margit Mária to Jenő Zoványi, 31 December 1918. NB: the letters are unordered.
58. See, e.g., Jenő Sebestyén, "Zoványi felolvasása," *Protestáns Egyházi és Iskolai Lap* 61, no. 15 (14 April 1918): 138–39.

idols.[59] In so doing, it arrogated to itself a right it did not have: namely, the right to "choose among different kinds of philosophical systems . . . to fling away the pure worldview and put in its place a materialist system, [and] make laws for the defense of this chosen direction of thought." To Prohászka, it was clearly "hypocrisy" as well as "tyranny" to speak of "freedom of thought," even as the state passed laws "making materialism compulsory in public education." Not only did this make freedom of conscience into a "caricature of itself," it also showed how completely the new regime misunderstood the power and role of religion in the life of the individual. Rather than creating a new culture, as the bishop put it in a series of articles collected in book form in the autumn of 1918 under the title *Culture and Terror*, the new regime—latter-day Jacobins—was simply instituting a reign of terror, a war of belief in which "anything that might ensure victory was permitted."[60] Such anticlerical zeal would surely produce its martyrs in due course.

Admonitions like these only provoked many on the Left to take an even firmer stand against counterrevolutionary enemies, both real and suspected. Only months earlier, many recalled, figures like Bishop Prohászka had written or published vicious denunciations of the "other Hungary" in implacable opposition to "Christian Hungary." Indeed, even in urging his flock to support the new order, Bishop Prohászka still cast the danger to the nation in clearly antisemitic terms, warning believers "not to listen to the words of pushy and destructive elements . . . —believe instead the blood of your blood, believe instead the leaders who live with you and suffer with you, rather than rootless, alien peddlers."[61] Moreover, the Catholic Church still enjoyed tremendous social and cultural power. What guarantee was there that it would not use its schools, printing presses, civic associations, and social institutions to spread views hostile to the republic? For these reasons, many on the Left reacted scornfully when Catholic religious leaders claimed discrimination or oppression. Religion, one socialist argued in a prominent newspaper of the Left, had done nothing but incite the ignorant to hatred and intolerance. Throughout history, priests had lied, preaching love and charity, while making distinctions between people based on faith and moving men to bestial acts. Better to have done with religion once and for all and to look instead to a secular utopia. He concluded with a credo more suited to a modern and egalitarian society: "We believe in the world transfiguring power of socialism and, turning

59. Ottokár Prohászka, "Vallásoktatás és modern szabadság," *Alkotmány* (6 March 1919): 1.
60. Ottokár Prohászka, *Kultúra és terror: A társadalmi kérdés*, vol. 11 in *Prohászka Ottokár összegyüjtött munkái*, 264–65.
61. "Prohászka püspök szózata," *Alkotmány* (6 November 1918): 9.

from the past with hatred, we march . . . determined and with heads high into a more beautiful and happier future."[62]

Thus, anticlericalism—a determination rooted in rational inquiry to separate politics from religion and reduce the power of the churches—came to symbolize the progress that everyone on the Hungarian Left embraced. Where supporters of the revolution saw an opportunity to create a new system of public mores that might govern political life, religious leaders saw intolerance and blatant disregard for the validity of their own most fundamental values. This in turn only spurred progressives—divided on so much else, from the future of private property to the proper place of the Communist Party—to denounce "clericalism" as the ideology of backwardness and counterrevolution, to be resisted at all costs in a Hungary on the road at last to modernity. The new regime, it seemed, might turn a blind eye to the varied systems of belief that its citizens professed in private. It could not, however, remain indifferent when religious figures, long known as opponents of progressive politics in Hungary, publicly propagated beliefs which everyone on the Left, from socialist to radical democrat, understood to be illiberal, antimodern, and undemocratic. Such views must be opposed, even attacked, lest they undermine the ongoing project of strengthening a new and fragile democracy. Exactly how they should be opposed, and precisely how coercive the new state might allow itself to be in this struggle of ideas, remained, however, open questions.

National Apocalypse and the Promise of Rebirth

In the wake of the November revolution, the Károlyi government also appealed to feelings of patriotism and national unity in their search for common ground on which to govern. Though the progressive politicians and intellectuals now in or close to the government had repeatedly been accused of antinational beliefs and un-Hungarian activities, all but the most committed socialists continued to hope that progress and nationalism need not be mutually exclusive and would not be in a new and modern Hungarian nation-state.[63] The Revolution of 1848, they argued, had held a promise of independence and liberty that the nation had cherished through the long decades of Dualist compromise. Now, Hungarians might once again embrace openly this tradition of democratic and progressive nationalism. To give concrete and public reality to this stance, the republi-

---

62. Ferenc Göndör, "Válasz Bangha páternek," originally in *Az Ember* (18 February 1919). Reprinted in Farkas József, *Álmok és tények*, 373–78.
63. Litván, " 'Magyar gondolat—szabad gondolat.' "

can government in Hungary renamed streets and squares in the name of the republic, tore down some of the most disliked statues commemorating Habsburg rule, adopted symbols of the revolution of 1848–49 (such as the coat of arms) as the public face of the new regime, and deliberately invoked the legacy of Lajos Kossuth in posters and public proclamations.[64] As elsewhere in Central Europe in 1918, these efforts all aimed at establishing the new republic as a presence in peoples' everyday life, forging legitimacy for Hungary's republican experiment by encouraging Hungarians to find their own national identity in the narrative of national history favored by the new regime.[65] If 1848 had been a revolution defeated, then 1918 could be the nation's redemption, a second chance to establish a modern society that might now renew and fulfill the aspirations of the Hungarian people for democratic self-government.

Invocations of Lajos Kossuth and the 1848 revolution notwithstanding, there was still good reason to doubt that the national consensus enjoyed by the National Council and the democratic republic it represented would be long-lived. The Károlyi regime lacked financial resources, domestic stability, and above all, international security. Even as the new government appealed to the revolutionary legacy of 1848, Czechoslovak, Yugoslav, and Romanian troops, with the support of the Allied Powers and particularly of the French, began to occupy portions of the historic Kingdom of Hungary, claiming pieces of Hungary as their own national territory in advance of any international settlement. Despite the efforts of Count Károlyi, Oszkár Jászi, and many other Hungarian politicians with international contacts, the regime's diplomatic pleas fell on deaf ears in Paris, London, and Washington. Outraged by the Károlyi government's reluctance to defend the country's borders with military force, and seeing in this a sign of the new regime's misplaced sympathies, many Hungarians, especially those on the Right, turned to an alternative vision of national history, one that promised the nation's rebirth from the ashes of defeat.

Themes of national death and resurrection were well established in Hungarian cultural, especially literary, traditions. At least since the sixteenth century, when parts of Hungary had been occupied by the Ottoman Turks, Hungarian poets had responded to national catastrophe by "veering from rational hopelessness to irrational confidence," alternating bleak

64. Klimó, *Nation, Konfession, Geschichte*, 187–201.

65. *Staging the Past: The Politics of Commemoration in Habsburg Central Europe, 1848 to the Present*, ed. Maria Bucur and Nancy M. Wingfield (West Lafayette, IN: Purdue University Press, 2001). See esp. the contribution in this volume by Cynthia J. Paces, "Religious Heroes for a Secular State: Commemorating Jan Hus and Saint Wenceslas in 1920s Czechoslovakia," 209–35.

despair in the face of annihilation and fervent hope for self-liberation and the nation's rebirth.[66] In part, Hungarian poets were making sense of a history marked by shattering defeats. Rebirth after national catastrophe—after 1849; after 1526 (the defeat at Mohács in which the advancing Ottoman Turkish army shattered Renaissance Hungary and subjected the nation to 150 years of foreign occupation); and even earlier, after 1241 (when invading Mongols annihilated the first medieval Hungarian kingdom)—was a central theme in the nation's historical culture. More general fears of the nation's dissolution in a sea of German and Slavic cultures also inspired preoccupation with the nation's death and its renewal.[67] Thus, a language of death and rebirth, invoked either as heroic persistence in the face of "cosmic loneliness" and the "death of civilization"[68] or as historical memory of renewal from defeat, was a prominent feature in the Hungarian literary canon, familiar (and deeply felt) for all educated readers of the late nineteenth and early twentieth centuries. This rich poetic tradition could be material for the most varied aesthetic and political projects. Endre Ady had, for example, famously described prewar Hungary as a "fallow land," a barren place in which he could yet find hope that Hungarians might embrace progress and so bring forth life out of death. This "and yet morality," as Péter Hanák and others have described it, inspired a whole generation of the Hungarian Left to imagine a new and democratic Hungary.[69] In 1918, however, it was the Right who laid the strongest claims to these mythic themes and called most clearly for the nation's resurrection.[70]

Clearly, these themes derived their power from the Christian religious tradition of sacrifice and resurrection. However, conservative nationalists also explicitly associated these themes with the language of Christian Hungary as it had developed in the last decades of the nineteenth century. Though Hungary's territorial catastrophe was entirely the creation of international politics, national myths of rebirth amidst devastation compelled Hungarians in the present, just as it had those of the past, to seek redemption above all within themselves.[71] For right-wing nationalists, this

66. Lendvai, *The Hungarians*, 132–34, Citation from the Hungarian literary critic Antal Szerb on 132. See also Zsuzsanna Ozsváth's remarks on "heroic memory" in Zsuzsanna Ozsváth, *In the Footsteps of Orpheus*, 49–52.

67. Frigyesi, *Béla Bartók*, 66–7.

68. Ibid.

69. Péter Hanák, "The Start of Endre Ady's Literary Career (1903–1905)," in *The Garden and the Workshop*, 132–34. Also Frigyesi, *Béla Bartók*, 75ff.

70. Michael Geyer discusses the centrality of myth-histories of death, defeat, and redemption to national identity in the postwar German context. See Michael Geyer, "Insurrectionary Warfare: The German Debate about a *Levée en Masse* in October 1918," *Journal of Modern History* 73 (September 2001): esp. 508–27.

71. Lendvai, *The Hungarians*, 132–33.

meant breaking with the liberal past, since liberalism had led inexorably to the moral and political free-for-all that they now perceived around them. One of the leaders of an important counterrevolutionary organization that called itself the Association of Awakening Magyars later recalled that this group formed not simply to oppose revolution, but "reached back to the past, looking for and finding the basis for the dissolution of Christian society and the collapse of Hungary in the decades of liberalism."[72] Similar language could be heard in the most right-wing of Catholic circles. "Christians! Awake!" thundered one writer in the newspaper *Christian Socialism*, mouthpiece for the most nationalist and antisemitic of politically active Catholics. Here too one could find Hungary described again as a Christian state. "We cannot dissemble, we say it openly: we will not bear it that a small element in our country spreads propaganda against us. We cannot bear that it provokes us with money, perversion, false slogans. . . . We are a Christian state, and we demand that we stay that way. . . . Christianity has always defended our home."[73] Generated in the very different political circumstances of the late nineteenth century, the language of Christian nationalism nevertheless captured exactly the sense of apocalypse and hope for regeneration shared across the Hungarian Right.

By December 1918, several groups, including the Association of Awakening Magyars (ÉME) and the Hungarian National Defense Association (MOVE), composed primarily of former officers, as well as prominent politicians of the old regime, had gathered in counterrevolutionary groups, dedicating themselves to national defense on the borders as well as at home. Many middle-class refugees from Transylvania and other occupied regions were also increasingly hostile to the republican government. Civil servants and professionals, these displaced former pillars of communities throughout the historic Kingdom of Hungary were desperate to recover their former homes and lives and outraged at the government's unwillingness to sacrifice everything in the name of national defense. Their bitterness made them fertile ground for the spread of irredentist politics. Across Hungary's resurgent nationalist Right, there was a common belief that long-suspected threats to national sovereignty inside and outside the nation had become real, and that the loss of territory on the borders was linked to the democrats aiming to transform Hungarian society as one unified, real, and very present threat to national security. The "other"—Jewish and progressive—Hungary was not only a scapegoat for Hungary's

72. Tibor Zinner, *Az ébredők fénykora, 1919–1923* (Budapest: Akadémiai Kiadó, 1989), 15.
73. J. Bognár, "Keresztények!, ébredjetek!," *Keresztény Szocializmus* 2, no. 48 (15 December 1918): 2.

miseries; it was, in the eyes of the Right, the cause of them as well, an enemy sapping the nation's will to embark on a crusade of self-liberation. "We have awoken," the Awakening Magyars declared, "to the fact that when we are subdued at home as well, our Christian Hungarian race will die. We have awoken to the fact that . . . a new imperialism, holding Christian Hungarians in slavery, is forming, that an oppressive re-enslavement will take place here, against which we . . . stand!"[74] Though Romanian, Czechoslovak, and Yugoslav troops were responsible for the (in 1918, still only de facto) partition of the country, the right worried, just as Bishop Prohászka had done in the summer of 1918, that if Christian Hungarians abandoned their most deeply felt national values in favor of an alien Jewish worldview, then their nation might indeed face a death after which no rebirth could come. In the face of this apocalypse, Christian nationalists could only appeal to their countrymen for a desperate struggle amidst despair: "Onward Hungarians, Christians! . . . Let our ideological enemies see that there are indeed still Hungarians in this nation!"[75]

This potent mix of Christianity, nationalism, and antisemitism only fueled demands on the Left for a radical social transformation that might eliminate the danger of a vicious and brutal counterrevolution once and for all. Progressive voices denounced the logic that ran: "We demand territorial integrity—down with the Jews!" warning that it would not be the "Jews who reply to the announcers of pogroms. Spartacus will answer them."[76] The spiral of invective was fatal for Hungary's fragile democracy. Right wing demands for a more vigorous territorial defense in the name of a regenerated Christian Hungary made it increasingly difficult for Prime Minister Károlyi to hold together a coalition that included left-wing Christian Socialists, moderate nationalists, bourgeois democrats, and socialists. Though Károlyi and Jászi, the minister of nationalities affairs, tried desperately to negotiate more favorable terms with Allied diplomats and occupation authorities, their efforts proved fruitless. The revolutionary government simply had no cards to play with the victorious Allies, whose decisions, ratified later in the 1920 Treaty of Trianon, to back the Czechoslovak, Romanian, and Yugoslav governments were decisive. This did not, however, prevent the Right from blaming Károlyi and his ministers for betraying their nation and selling out the fortunes of their countrymen in Transylvania, Slovakia, and elsewhere. By the end of 1918,

74. The pamphlet was reprinted in the paper Keresztény Szocializmus. "Mit akarnak az Ébredő Magyarok?," Keresztény Szocializmus 3, no. 9 (2 March 1919).

75. Dr. Kálmán Tóth, "Magyarok, keresztények előre!," Keresztény Szocializmus 2, no. 48 (15 December 1918): XX–XX.

76. Lajos Biró, "Jelszavak," originally in Világ (21 January 1919). Reprinted in Farkas József, Álmok és tények, 293–94.

Károlyi had lost the right wing of his government, as a number of bourgeois politicians resigned their positions.

In the aftermath, all efforts to create a broad consensus around the fragile republican democracy were doomed. Károlyi was forced to choose between moves to the left or the right to secure a governing majority. He chose the left, citing later the threat of counterrevolution: "I chose the politics of socialism, not only out of conviction, but because if I would have allowed it then, a bourgeois cabinet, if successful, would have become the instrument of the (right-radical) MOVE within two months."[77] However, Hungary's Social Democrats were themselves under pressure. Led by men returned from Moscow with experience of revolution, Hungary's Communist Party had become a powerful political force almost overnight. Party propagandists promised release from poverty in a workers' state and suggested, however vaguely, that the imminent partition of the country would somehow be unnecessary if revolution could spread from Russia to the rest of Europe. Many heard such a message with enthusiasm, transforming the Communist Party from a small coterie of revolutionaries into the only viable non-Rightist alternative to the government. When the Entente powers demanded that Hungarian troops evacuate large sections of Transylvania, a province of historic Hungary, and allow an international force to serve as neutral peacekeepers, the republican government found its situation hopeless and resigned. On 21 March, Hungary's Communists, allied with left-wing socialists, took power and proclaimed a Republic of Soviets.

Red Terror: The Bolshevik Revolution in Hungary

Only two weeks after Béla Kun and the Hungarian Bolsheviks took power, the artist Béla Uitz published an article in the Communist daily paper calling for a true dictatorship in art, society, indeed in all aspects of life. Only a dictatorship, Uitz argue, could safeguard the revolution in this time of transition. Hungary's transformation depended on the clear worldview that those with power would practice: "We must have a worldview, and we must have revolution—for only the consuming flames of these two can annihilate compromise, spinelessness, and unethical behavior."[78]

---

77. György Litván, "Az 1918–1919-es demokrácia két tűz között," in *Októberek üzenete*, 275.

78. Béla Uitz, "We Need a Dictatorship!" originally in *Vörös Újság* (10 April 1919). Translated and reprinted in *Between Worlds: A Sourcebook of Central European Avant-Gardes, 1910–1930*, ed. Timothy O. Benson and Éva Forgács (Cambridge: MIT Press, 2002), 225–27.

Uitz's logic was persuasive to many who supported this new revolutionary regime. György Lukács, who had posed the question of repressive means and just ends in his searching essay on "Bolshevism as a Moral Problem" found a similar answer, seeing in Communism the only sure guarantee against the return of an unjust and immoral political system. He joined the party shortly before it came to power. Kun's government also shared this sense of ideological embattlement, banning newspapers and organizations deemed oppositional and counterrevolutionary. Middle-class and aristocratic politicians were forced to choose between exile in Vienna or arrest in Hungary; the most fortunate retreated into private life. Especially in Budapest, party cadres, some filled by their zeal to nationalize property and others undoubtedly driven by more venal motives, often forced their way into homes of the bourgeoisie, confiscating what they could find in the name of the revolution and terrorizing the inhabitants as class enemies. In addition, a small group of thugs calling itself the "Lenin Boys" traveled throughout the country, seizing hostages for ransom and beating and sometimes killing individuals accused of counterrevolutionary tendencies. Contemporary assessments tallied some 590 victims of the Red Terror.[79]

The new Bolshevik regime had grandiose plans for Hungary. Almost immediately, Hungary's commissars began to nationalize the country's industries, banks, and agricultural estates. They also laid out a number of progressive reforms designed to transform Hungary into a socialist utopia, introducing laws to guarantee gender equality, to outlaw child labor, and to place all schools and institutions of higher learning under state control, to name a few. The Bolsheviks placed special emphasis on cultural transformation, since, like Uitz, they believed that public culture would be decisive in creating the new men and new women of Hungary's revolutionary future. In many respects, their cultural policy was similar in principle to that of the republican government that had preceded them.[80] Like the progressive democrats around Károlyi, the Bolsheviks also saw themselves locked in a battle with backward elements for the modernization of Hungary. However, Oszkár Jászi, for example, remained convinced that "no individual or class in society is justified in imposing a dictatorship on others."[81] The Bolsheviks had no such scruples about using the coercive powers of the state to impose their vision of modernity on society.

79. Recent research suggests that some included in this number were combat deaths in occupied territories which may or may not have had anything to do with ideological combat between Reds and counterrevolutionary Whites. For a discussion of this figure, and the historical controversy around it, see Eliza Ablovatski Johnson, "'Cleansing the Red Nest': Counterrevolution and White Terror in Munich and Budapest, 1919," Ph.D. diss., Columbia University, 2004, 76ff. For a more polemical account, see Albert Váry, A vörös uralom áldozatai Magyarországon, 3d ed. (Szeged: Szegedi Nyomda, 1993).

80. Tibor Hajdu, A magyarországi tanácsköztársaság (Budapest: Kossuth, 1969), 398–99.

81. Citation in Gluck, Georg Lukács, 202.

Almost as soon as they took power, Hungary's Communists determined to separate church from state with a thoroughness and force far in excess of anything that their democratic predecessors had contemplated. From the first, Kun and his fellow Bolsheviks insisted that the new workers' state would be strictly neutral toward religious belief. Everyone could believe in whatever God he or she wanted. However, the Hungarian Communist Party made a strict and absolute distinction between religion and church. The former might be tolerated, but the latter had to be eliminated from all areas of public life. Areas in which Hungary's churches had played a prominent social function, like education and social welfare, were now to be entirely the province of secular state authorities. For this reason, the Communist government banned all religious associations or movements from public life, and established an Office for the Liquidation of Religious Matters to oversee the elimination of religious publishing houses and printing presses. This office also oversaw the removal of nationalized property from churches and religious institutions. Without question, the new regime considered the Catholic Church its greatest rival. Although the Office for the Liquidation of Religious Matters did issue orders for state authorities to seize some buildings and assets from the Protestant churches, it concentrated its greatest energies on stripping the Catholic Church of its wealth. As administrators began to convert schools, seminaries, and convents into places for secular public use (cultural centers, nonreligious schools, etc.), many religious personnel found themselves without livelihoods and sometimes even without homes. Some were forced to find work in lay occupations. The image of nuns living in squalid rented rooms and working as charwomen remained powerful long after the Bolshevik regime collapsed. Others lived off the furtive kindnesses of their parishioners.[82]

Communist officials tried to assure the public that the new government did not oppose private individual faith. To this end, the People's Commissar for Education, Zsigmond Kunfi, issued a public statement during Easter week 1919, asserting that the state would not use churches for profane purposes. He also did his best to combat widespread rumors that the Communists were poised to outlaw marriage and sanction the wildest excesses of immorality. However, the party's own ideologues undermined these attempts at reasoned persuasion. With regularity, readers of the party's *Red Newspaper* could learn that all church doctrine was nothing

---

82. On Communist policy toward religion, see Leslie Laszlo, "The Church in the Storm of the Revolutions of 1918–1919 in Hungary," in *Revolutions and Interventions in Hungary*, ed. Peter Pastor, 189–97; Frank Eckelt, "The Internal Policies of the Hungarian Soviet Republic," in *Hungary in Revolution*, ed. Völgyes, 69–70; János Lieber, "A kommunista egyházüldözés Magyarországon," in *A proletárdiktatúra Magyarországon*, ed. Károly Huszár (Budapest: Újságüzem könyvkiadó és nyomda rt., 1920), 151–62.

more than counterrevolutionary propaganda. Inspired by this rhetoric, party cadres conducted the secularizing campaign with true anticlerical zeal in many places. In the course of nationalizing property, some did not hesitate to desecrate church buildings as well. Party strongmen sometimes disrupted religious services and processions also, shouting antireligious slogans and roughing up participants and bystanders. In some cases, they assaulted priests, pastors, and nuns. In a few cases, they even lynched priests or beat them to death. To opponents of the revolution, these men and women of the Christian churches became martyrs, and the stories of their persecution would become the stuff of counterrevolutionary propaganda after the Kun regime fell.[83]

Though the Bolshevik regime did enjoy a large measure of support, especially in Budapest, when they took power in late March 1919, their popularity soon faded. Many had been willing to suspend their political judgment, if the new regime could defend the country's territorial integrity more aggressively than the Károlyi government had. For this reason, many patriots with little sympathy for socialism heard what they wanted to hear when Béla Kun denounced the successor states claiming pieces of Hungarian territory as agents of bourgeois capitalist reaction, and called for a new Red Army to drive these exploiters from Hungarian soil in the name of world revolution. Among those willing to serve was a former colonel of the general staff, now chief of staff of the Red Army, Aurél Stromfeld. In this way, Communist internationalism briefly enjoyed nationalist support in Hungary. However, the Red Army faced a hopeless military situation; though it achieved some initial victories in northern Hungary/Slovakia, none of the Allied powers was willing to countenance a resurgent Hungary, let alone a Bolshevik Hungary. When the Entente issued an ultimatum, threatening escalating military action if the Hungarian troops did not withdraw, Kun pulled the army back. The retreat demoralized the army and convinced its most capable officers, like Stromfeld, to resign. Despite subsequent attempts to rally the troops, Kun and the Bolsheviks never regained their advantage. The army fell into disarray. By 4 August 1919, the Romanian army had entered Budapest, forcing Kun and most of the other Bolshevik leaders to flee to Austria.

Even as this military drama was playing out, the Bolsheviks had squandered their initial support in other ways as well. Plans to nationalize land, for example, were particularly unpopular, since they often left Hungary's landless peasants working for their old landlords under Communist Party supervision. Though the poverty of the millions of landless agricultural laborers in Hungary might have inclined them to support radical reformist

83. Lieber, "A kommunista egyházüldözés."

policies, the vast majority hoped only for a plot of land to call their own. To Kun and his fellow doctrinaire Communists, these desires were simply retrograde, indicating a tragic want of revolutionary consciousness in a class still hypnotized by petit bourgeois dreams of private property. A chasm widened between Budapest and the surrounding countryside that the Communist regime could never bridge.[84] Indeed, many rural Hungarians took Communist religious policy as proof that those in power simply had no respect for their deeply felt cultural traditions and ways of life; taking crucifixes from schools, dealing roughly with the local priest, and threatening to turn the village church into a movie theater or put it to some other secular use, only antagonized the majority of Hungary's peasants. By the time the Romanian army reached Budapest, the ruling Bolsheviks were themselves increasingly isolated within the capital city.

As support for the Bolshevik regime eroded, opponents began to plot a counterrevolution. Some conservative politicians had fled the country after March 1919, most no farther than Vienna, from which vantage point they could watch and wait, hatching innumerable schemes in the coffeehouses of the former imperial capital. Others had gathered in the southern Hungarian town of Szeged, in a region on the border with the new state of Yugoslavia under the military administration of the French. In Szeged, just out of reach of the Bolsheviks in Budapest, a second group of counterrevolutionaries could also begin to plan for the reconquest of their nation from the alien occupiers in Budapest and on the borders. Many of these were military officers, soldiers who had served on the monarchy's several fronts during the war as well as those who had been stationed behind the lines. In the summer of 1919, these officers joined the former National Army, a loosely organized military force stationed in Szeged and commanded by the former imperial and royal admiral, Miklós Horthy. All of them bitterly resented the dismantling of their country by neighboring states. But they too understood the threat to their nation's security in terms that transcended distinctions between external and internal enemies. These men in Szeged saw their country teetering on the precipice of an irredeemable apocalypse. As Béla Kun and his comrades fled the country in the early days of August 1919, they prepared at long last to fight a battle with their enemies that might bring to their nation redemption amidst ruin.

As Hungary's prewar liberal regime collapsed along with the Habsburg monarchy in November 1918, the socialists and radical democrats around

84. István Deák, "Budapest and the Hungarian Revolutions of 1918–1919," *Slavonic and East European Review* 46 (1968): 129–40.

Count Mihály Károlyi who found themselves replacing it worried about the system of public mores that ought to animate the new republican regime. To Hungary's progressive political elite, it was clear that church and state must be radically and decisively separated: religion, both as a symbol and as a crucial facet of social life, was too closely tied to all the "backward" aspects of the old regime that they were so eager to change. Unconstrained by the constitutional complexities of the now-vanished Habsburg monarchy, Hungary's new political leaders could advance these propositions boldly. Catholic and conservative Protestant religious leaders responded with anger, however, insisting that religion could never simply be exchanged for another more politically desirable worldview and arguing that removing Christianity from the public life of a nation could only lead to anarchy. Their dismay was part of a broader conservative resistance to the new republic, whose political leaders, it was believed among the nationalist Right, were inspired by alien, internationalist, and indeed "Jewish" visions without any roots in Hungarian life. The formation of a Bolshevik government was understood as the final indignity to be suffered by a prostrate nation, even if progressive democrats like Oszkár Jászi insisted with much justification then and later that Bolshevism was every bit as much a threat to their dream of a republican Hungary as was right-wing nationalism. Outraged by the social and cultural policies of the Kun regime, and eager to take revenge against the men who had carried them out, the Christian nationalist right began to prepare the rebirth of Christian Hungary.

3

The Redemption of Christian Hungary, 1919–1921

On 15 November 1919, Admiral Horthy, mounted on a splendid white horse, led his troops into Budapest. The procession did not exactly mark a military victory. Béla Kun had fled Hungary already on 1 August, and the succession of feeble cabinets which had governed in the months since had all done their best to reverse the achievements of the short-lived Bolshevik Revolution. Through all this, Horthy's army, formed during the months of Bolshevik rule in the southern Hungarian city of Szeged, had not fought a single military engagement. Indeed, the admiral had carefully timed his victory parade down Budapest's main avenues, waiting until the Romanian army of occupation, the main reason for the Bolshevik collapse, had withdrawn from the capital. Nor was it a proper army in the strictest military sense. Szeged, in the French zone of occupation and thus beyond the reach of Béla Kun's Communist regime, had been a haven for officers of the now vanished imperial and royal army. In the irregular ranks of those following Horthy through the streets of Budapest on that dreary November day, there were few enlisted soldiers. Captains and majors predominated. All of them had bitterly opposed the revolution and the "other Hungary" they blamed for it, and all of them now hoped for vengeance against the enemies who had inflicted such misery on their nation. For them, Budapest, the capital of that "other Hungary," was a center of insurrection that needed to be taught a lesson. Speaking to a huge crowd assembled before the imposing Parliament building, the admiral chastised the city:

> When we were still far from here. . . . I will be frank—we hated and cursed Budapest, because we did not see in it those who suffered, those who be-

came martyrs, but rather the filth of the nation all converging here. We loved, we called fondly to this city which became the corrupter of the nation in the last year. . . . This city denied its thousand year history, this city defamed its crown, its national colors and clothed itself in rags of red.[1]

In a word, Budapest was a "sinful city," (the *bűnös város*) a community which had to be punished for its crimes before it could return to its accustomed place at the head of the Hungarian nation.

Historians of Hungary have generally understood such invective against Budapest, the Communist party, and above all, Hungary's Jewish citizens, as a clear example of scapegoating. All Hungarian governments—progressive, revolutionary, or reactionary—were powerless to alter the nation's international circumstances. The Romanian army that had marched into Budapest to topple the Bolshevik regime withdrew in November, but to a point well within the borders of what had been historic Hungary. Internationally, the French were eager to fashion the newly independent states of Czechoslovakia, Yugoslavia, and an enlarged Romania into a Little Entente that would guarantee the dissolution of the Habsburg monarchy and preserve a balance of power in the region. As a result, each state annexed sections of what had been Hungarian territory, gaining a restive Hungarian minority in the process. Both the British and the American governments acquiesced in this, only too happy to wash their hands of this problematic corner of Europe and turn inward to pressing domestic concerns. Despite months of desperate lobbying in Paris, Hungary's representatives were unable to alter what had become a *fait accompli*; the Treaty of Trianon, signed on 4 June 1920, wrote the partition of Hungary into international law. As the nation literally adopted a public attitude of mourning, as refugees continued to pour into Budapest from the occupied cities (often to find no better accommodation than boxcars in the city's train stations), and as the state, burdened by a bureaucracy now too big for the territory it controlled, tried to find its economic footing, many looked for someone to blame for their misfortune. Budapest, the whole Hungarian Left, and above all, Jews, were ready targets for this rage. All those political and social groups associated with an antinational "Jewish spirit" could be found in greatest number in Budapest. Socialist and radical democratic parties were strongest there; the country's banks and largest industries were located in the capital; and Hungary's progressive intelligentsia gathered in the city's coffeehouses to discuss the nation's reform. Most important, Budapest was home to the one of the largest Jewish communities in Hungary, an assimilated group comprising some 20 percent of the city's

1. An excerpt of this speech is reproduced in *Források Budapest történetéhez, 1919–1945*, ed. József Szekeres (Budapest: Budapest Főváros Levéltára, 1971), 21.

population but whose participation in certain social and cultural circles was more prominent even than that. Decades of public debate about the "Jewish question" had fixed public attention on the achievements and upward social mobility of Hungary's Jews. Now the very success of their social and economic integration worked as a goad to those who found their national society turned upside down.

The antisemitic politics of Admiral Horthy's address to the citizens of Budapest in mid November 1919 was not simply a substitute for military action against neighboring states too powerful and too well-supported to challenge. Even before the war had ended, and Hungary had admitted defeat in 1918, the Right in Hungary had linked the war at the borders and fears for the nation's territorial integrity to concerns about internal order. As the revolutionary government had moved inexorably to the Left in 1918–19, and as neighboring states occupied vast sections of historic Hungary, many on the Right believed that their fears had been justified. After March 1919, from their exile in Szeged or in Vienna, the Hungarian Right, conservative and radical, monarchist and populist alike, had condemned the Bolshevik regime as the nadir in a long national decline. To those on the Right, a society devastated by the loss of sovereignty and beset within by internal enemies demanded redemption. First, however, it had to atone for its sins. Expiation and retribution, the national imperatives announced by Miklós Horthy on the steps of Parliament on a cold mid November day in 1919, soon dominated public life. The counterrevolution had begun.

The Christian-National Consensus

Writing in the revolutionary months of 1918 and 1919, the historian Gyula Szekfű began an historical essay that might make sense of the calamities that had befallen his country. A devout Catholic as well as a master of historical synthesis, Szekfű had already made a name for himself with a revisionist biography of the early-eighteenth-century Hungarian prince Ferenc Rakóczi II, a work that took issue with the national-liberal myths surrounding that anti-Habsburg noble. A 1918 study of the Hungarian state also betrayed the young historian's skepticism toward ideas of liberal progress. In his long essay written in exile, Szekfű again placed liberalism in Hungary at the center of his analysis. The result was *Three Generations and What Came Afterward*, a book that quickly became one of the most influential books in interwar Hungary when it appeared in 1920. He took as his point of departure the revolutions that followed the collapse of the Habsburg Monarchy, as well as the country's dismemberment in the postwar peace talks. In the preface to *Three Generations*, Szekfű presented these catastrophes as a consequence of Hungary's prewar political development, claiming "everyone must agree that the recent liberal past was an age of deviation, from which we can only raise ourselves with organized work, and through the building of true national traditions."[2] Szekfű argued that Hungarians had to do more than simply reject Béla Kun's short-lived 1919 Bolshevik regime or express their outrage at the partition of Hungary's historic lands. National renewal required a thorough rejection of the liberal political traditions that had dominated public life in the decades before the war. These had been fundamentally alien to Hungary's traditional political culture. Through three generations of political life in Hungary, their spread had seduced the nation's traditional gentry ruling class into irresponsible and self-interested shortsightedness and allowed an assimilating Jewish middle class to usurp their economic and cultural leadership. Their rise foreshadowed the end of historic Hungary. The nation's hope lay in reclaiming its traditional and historical role within the "Christian-Germanic cultural community," an entity that Szekfű understood in contrast to the secular and liberal heritage of republican France. Szekfű devoted much of this historical essay to describing the "true national traditions" that had existed in Hungary before the advent of liberalism. In his book, the historian identified an antinational "Jewish spirit" as one important cause of this cultural decline and suggested that a return to the political course envisioned by Hungary's pre-1848 conservative reformers could correct many of the ills that had arisen from Hungary's disastrous path into the modern age. The implications were clear, and many in Hungary's political elite drew them: the nation could be redeemed if it rejected not only the revolutionary excesses of the radicals and the Bolsheviks, but also the alien liberalism that had spawned them.

Szekfű's analysis was the product of years of reflection on the trajectory of Hungarian history, and was written in a scholarly, if essayistic and more popular tone. This did not, however, prevent older, more liberal colleagues in the historical profession from denouncing the work as a foray into "political waters."[3] In a sense, these critics were absolutely correct, since *Three Generations* expressed in a scholarly genre the view of Hungary's recent past that dominated public thought about the nation's circumstances in the aftermath of the Bolshevik revolution and for many years afterward. On 4 December 1919, for example, representatives of

2. Gyula Szekfű, *Három nemzedék és ami utána következik* (Budapest: ÁKV-Maecenas Reprint, 1989), 6.

3. This was the view of the liberal historian Henrik Marczali. See *Szekfű Gyula: Nép, nemzet, állam. Válogatott tanulmányok,* ed. Vilmos Erős (Budapest: Osiris, 2002), 730.

Hungary's three major Protestant confessions (Calvinist, Lutheran, and Unitarian) held a conference in Budapest to call for Christian unity in the face of the national emergency. In the resolution produced after a day of speeches, the delegates assessed the nation's plight in terms stronger in tone, but not much different in substance from Szekfű's analysis: "The country's incomparable military, economic, and moral catastrophe has been caused by the spread of a destructive spiritual campaign consciously directed against the Christian worldview and the Hungarian national idea and by international subversive powers criminally transplanted here from abroad." The assembled Protestants went on to declare that national salvation would only be possible if "the Christian moral worldview and the true Hungarian love of country again marches in as a driving power to every area of Hungarian public life."[4] A prominent Catholic politician, István Haller, was also present to register agreement on behalf of Hungarian Catholics. He too blamed Hungary's Jews for having pursued their own interests rather than those of the nation's and linked this subversion to the partition of the country. "Every part of the country was more Christian than the capital, and our national minorities turned away from us in the first place because of this." The country's territorial integrity was thus inextricably tied to the fortunes of Christian values in society.[5]

Such expressions of patriotic ecumenism were well-received in the right-wing nationalist press. The newspaper *New Generation*, financed by the press division of Hungary's Catholic Church and edited in these months by the well-known (Protestant) nationalist intellectual István Milotay, covered the Protestant conference and then published a front-page editorial in support of it the following day. In the opinion of the newspaper, "every true Hungarian [could] pay grateful tribute to those . . . Protestant leaders who across a horrific gulf of four hundred years . . . extended their right hands in a noble gesture towards Catholics, so that with common strength they can together build Hungary." This unity, the editors maintained, was the fulfillment of a historical promise made three and a half centuries earlier, at a moment when the nation had also teetered on the verge of extinction. Facing Turkish occupation, the poet and national leader Miklós Zrinyi had called for Catholics and Protestants alike to join in common cause against the nation's enemies. Now, Hungary again faced a struggle for national survival, and was again occupied by foreign powers. Zrinyi's call for Christian and national unity challenged "true Hungarians" to place themselves in the service of the nation. Catholics and

4. "Protestánsok a keresztény egységért," *Új Nemzedék* (5 December 1919): 4–5.
5. Ibid.

Protestants, Christians alike, might yet relieve Hungary from its agony, ensuring that Hungary might yet "remain Hungary."[6]

The belief that Hungary's Jews had weakened the nation through revolution, leaving it helpless before rapacious neighboring states, became a point of consensus around which almost all public figures could rally in the months following the collapse of the Kun regime. Conservative politicians, returned from exile in Vienna, eagerly embraced the notion of "Christian-national unity," transforming Hungary's tiny (Catholic) Christian party into a party of government that went through several changes of name, each of which proclaimed its intention to protect and restore "Christian morality" to public life in Hungary. Leaders of Hungary's Christian churches continued to hold public conferences devoted to national unity and the defense of the "Christian idea" in society.[7] Prominent Catholic politicians came to occupy key cabinet positions; István Haller, the Catholic who spoke at the December 1919 conference of Protestants, served as minister of religion and public education for several years. The idea that Jews and their "spirit" had somehow eroded the national will from within also produced unanimity around a legal measure considered unthinkable anywhere but on the radical right only a few years before. In 1920, Hungary's National Assembly began to debate a *numerus clausus* law, a legal measure designed to limit the number of Jewish students who could be admitted in any year to degree programs at universities. Although the bill was originally conceived to deal with overcrowding at universities, the discussion of the bill and its subsequent revisions soon developed into a public discussion of the threats that Hungary's Jewish citizens posed to the nation.[8] Speaker after speaker rose in Parliament to repeat arguments made so controversially in the summer of 1918 by the Catholic Bishop Ottokár Prohászka. Bishop Prohászka, heavily criticized in 1918 for his radical views but vindicated in 1920 as a principled visionary, had only to repeat the arguments he had made before the collapse of the monarchy: "The problem was that Jews did not become an integrated part of us, . . . but instead became an oppressive part." This, Prohászka argued, was leading inexorably to the "de-Christianization" of Hungary. Because universities were the "workshops of genius," adopting legal remedies to restrict the number of Jews admitted was not antisemitism; it was simply

6. "Concordia christiana," *Új Nemzedék* (6 December 1919).
7. See, e.g., the proceedings of such a conference sponsored by the United Christian National League, held on 13 January 1923. *A keresztény gondolat védelme* (Budapest: A "Hangya" házinyomdája, 1925). Among those taking part were the Calvinist bishop, László Ravasz; the Lutheran bishop, Sándor Raffay; and the Catholic bishop, Ottokár Prohászka.
8. Katalin N. Szegvári, *Numerus clausus rendelkezések az ellenforradalmi Magyarországon a zsidó és nőhallgatók főiskolai felvételéről* (Budapest: Akadémiai kiadó, 1988), 114ff.

"racial self-defense."[9] On 22 September 1920, the Hungarian National Assembly passed the *numerus clausus* law, limiting the number of Jews in any university class to 6 percent of the total. It was the first anti-Jewish law in postwar Europe.

There were some who opposed these developments.[10] Despite the shift in political climate, a number of representatives still rose to denounce the proposed bill as illiberal, and unworthy of Hungary's national traditions. Even among religious figures, there was dissent. The Catholic prelate, Sándor Giesswein, a figure who had stood at the head of the most socially progressive wing of the prewar Christian Socialist movement, declined to question the fundamental premises of the new anti-Jewish law but did publicly ask whether a discriminatory law was the best means to the desired end. He also voted against the *numerus clausus* bill, arguing that if Jewish students had had better access to higher education than Christian students, then the state should devote itself to extending equal opportunities to all, rather than discriminating against one group in society.[11] Yet another religious leader, the Calvinist bishop Dezső Baltazár, true to the nineteenth-century liberal heritage of his church, denounced the deepening antisemitic climate, arguing that if Jews had committed "sins" during the revolution, then these were human sins, and did not derive in any way from the religious and moral traditions of Judaism. Persecuting fellow citizens because they were Jews was not, he argued, the example that Jesus had set for Christians.[12] These voices were drowned out, however, by the clamor in 1919 and 1920 for the defense of the Christian nation. As the literary critic Antal Szerb wrote later of these years: "Now, after the revolution, ... religion and nationalism ... became virtually compulsory."[13]

Redemptive Violence: The White Terror

The new consensus that declared Hungary a Christian nation was broadly accepted, but remained vaguely defined. Beyond the concrete measure of the *numerus clausus* law, it was unclear what it meant to establish the "Christian idea" in all aspects of public life. For some, this meant handing out material advantages to any Hungarian who was not a Jew. For others,

9. Speech of 16 September 1920 in the National Assembly.
10. See, e.g., Zsuzsa L. Nagy, *The Liberal Opposition in Hungary, 1919–1945* (Budapest: Akadémiai Kiadó, 1983).
11. Speech of 18 September 1920 in the National Assembly.
12. Dezső Baltazár, *A probáltatások idejéből* (Debrecen 1920), 180–81.
13. Cited in Ignác Romsics, *Hungary in the Twentieth Century* (Budapest: Corvina-Osiris, 1999), 111.

the "Christian idea" was more metaphysical in nature, suggesting a thorough, if not yet fully imagined, transformation of society that would restore moral virtue in society, even as it restored the historic borders of the nation. If Hungarians were to embark on a "Christian-national course," as many public figures now demanded, what form would this take? Would the new course rely mainly on a public rhetoric of morality, crystallized in one or two carefully conceived anti-Jewish measures? Or would the "Christian-national course" take a more violent form? Already in the last months of the war, there had been some on the Hungarian Right who insisted that a concentration of Christian strength in Hungary meant quite literally arming for battle and preparing to wage war against "the other Hungary" for the nation's survival. To those who had advocated counterrevolutionary violence in September and October of 1918, the months that followed had been bitter proof that their instincts had been sound. Now, as Béla Kun fled into exile and opponents of the revolutionary government took the reins of power, there were some on Hungary's Right who believed the time had come to redeem their nation by violently cleansing it of its enemies.

The officers in Admiral Horthy's so-called National Army embodied these sentiments. Many of them were active in the numerous counterrevolutionary political societies formed in the months after the collapse of the monarchy. These groups had been banned by the Communists in March 1919, but were quickly revived after the Kun regime fell in August. In these groups, Horthy's officers were joined by refugees from the occupied territories, especially civil servants and other middle-class professionals. These social groups formed the broad base of Horthy's political support and saw in his National Army the best hope to restore the life and social status they had lost almost overnight. Some of the political societies were little more than right-wing political clubs, in which the army officers around Horthy had to compete (often unsuccessfully) with experienced politicians for control of the organization. But others grew into terrorist organizations in which military men clearly had the upper hand. The most violent of these were the Association of Awakening Magyars (ÉME) and the Hungarian National Self Defense Association (MOVE). These paramilitary squads also declared the rebirth of Christian Hungary after the infamy that had been Kun's Bolshevik regime. A pamphlet describing the aims of the Awakening Magyars put this quite clearly: "It is the unalterable will of the Association of Awakening Magyars to re-establish the reign of pure Christian morals and national feeling throughout the country and to exterminate those destructive doctrines spread by the Jews which already contaminated the Christian population of Hungary."[14] Like

14. Citation reproduced in Nathaniel Katzburg, *Hungary and the Jews: Policy and Legislation, 1920–1943* (Ramat-Gan: Bar-Ilan University Press, 1983), 43.

Horthy, the members of the Awakening Magyars also felt that the revolutions, which had emanated from Budapest, had done incalculable damage to national society and that the "Jewish spirit" which had inspired these revolutions must be beaten back at all costs.

Among the members of groups like the Awakening Magyars, "Christian" was a term understood to exclude "Jews" absolutely. In the new Christian-national consensus, it was common for nationalists to style themselves as defenders of the Hungarian race.[15] Among secular and religious figures alike, however, there was significant slippage between invocations of the Hungarian nation as a race (a *magyar faj*), as a people (a *magyar nemzet* or *nép*), and as a geographic place (a *haza*); Bishop Ottokár Prohászka had, for example, declared antisemitism to be "racial self-defense" (*faji önvédelem*). But he had also tacitly accepted the possibility of Jewish assimilation, however limited in scope, when he argued that all the nation's troubles stemmed from the fact that Jewish assimilation had been incomplete and insufficient. Very few in Hungary in 1920 rooted their discussion of "racial defense" in notions of biological destiny. However, the radical nationalists gathered in groups like the Awakening Magyars did find some similarity between their own self-appointed mission and the racial politics of radical movements elsewhere in Europe. In one article in the newspaper affiliated with the Association of Awakening Magyars, a member reported on "Christian national politics" in Germany. The author, a Dr. Konrád Weiss, reserved his Christian and national admiration, not for the Catholic Center Party in Germany, but for radical rightist groups in Germany like the *Deutschvölkischer Schutz— und Trutzbund*, part of a growing antisemitic *völkisch* movement that also included the newly formed National Socialist German Workers', or Nazi, Party.[16] In his assessment, Weiss acknowledged the differences between the Hungarian and German contexts. Yet, he concluded that the best analogue to Hungary's "Christian-national" politics could be found in the radical German groups that described themselves as *völkisch*.

The ex-military men and radical nationalist agitators in groups like the Awakening Magyars also shared with their German counterparts a sense that the battle they envisioned with their nation's enemy was absolute. References to "extermination" and "contamination" in their programmatic pamphlets were in no way incidental to their vision. Of course, the social order they felt they were restoring was decidedly conservative. Many of them came from gentry backgrounds and believed that Hungary's survival as a nation depended on the preservation of traditional so-

15. János Gyurgyák, *A zsidókérdés Magyarországon* (Budapest: Osiris, 2001), see esp. 377–440.
16. Dr. Konrád Weiss, "A keresztény lelkiismeret ébredése," *Hazánk* (19 September 1920), 1–2.

cial relations between landlords, smallholders, and peasants. Yet the military men at the center of the counterrevolution meant something more by "Christian Hungary." For the most part, they were young officers, captains and majors in their twenties who had been deeply marked by their wartime service. They tended to view the counterrevolution through the prism of their combat experience, seeing the "spirit" behind Bolshevism as a flesh and blood enemy that had to be cleansed from the nation. Indeed, these officers often framed the orders they gave to one another in the months after the collapse of the Bolshevik regime in terms of national purification: Colonel Anton Lehár recalled receiving orders to "cleanse" a particular area of "Reds." "Communists" the instructions continued, "are to be killed quietly."[17] Thus, the "Szeged idea," as it was popularly described, inspired its adherents to do more than identify, vilify, or even discriminate against those they suspected of antinational tendencies. Ultimately, it called on them to wage war against the nation's enemies and thereby eliminate them.

The Szeged officers took their mission literally. All of them shared the belief that an "international Jewry" had foisted the Bolshevik revolution on a helpless nation, and they were determined to act on this belief. Even before the collapse of the Kun regime, when the counterrevolutionary National Army was confined to the southern city of Szeged and its environs, the officers around Horthy began to terrorize those in the area whom they accused of being part of this Judeo-Bolshevik conspiracy. Captain Pál Prónay established an interrogation center, in which captured Jews and Communists were tortured and often killed. After the Kun regime had collapsed, Prónay suggested to Horthy that his army divide itself into armed detachments, which could fan out and bring the counterrevolution to the countryside. These detachments made their way through the region between Szeged and Budapest slowly, searching the towns they entered for those who had taken part in the Bolshevik revolution, and anyone (especially Jews) suspected of having sympathies for communism.[18] In some cases, they also lynched peasants who spoke out against Hungary's powerful landholders during the revolutionary months. All of these victims were understood to be agents of "Jewish terror." Pál Prónay described the arrival of his troops in the town of Simontornya thus: "I rode to Simontornya, where. . . . [a fellow officer named Captain József Rády] informed me about individuals who had

17. Anton Lehár, *Erinnerungen: Gegenrevolution und Restaurationsversuche in Ungarn, 1918–1921*, ed. Peter Broucek (München: R. Oldenbourg Verlag, 1973), 109.

18. Pál Prónay describes the course his detachment took in his diaries: Pál Prónay, *A határban a halál kaszál: Fejezetek Prónay Pál feljegyzéseiből* (Budapest: Kossuth, 1963), 101–48.

proven to be pronounced Communists during the soviet regime. As my detachment arrived, I had these people rounded up and hung from the nearest locust tree. There really were a lot of Jews and terrorists among them."[19] Those unlucky enough to be caught in these patrols were generally lynched in this way. In many villages, leaders of the detachments would assemble the community, speak to them of the wrongs they had suffered at the hands of Jews and Bolsheviks, and so incite them to mob violence.

Moreover, it is clear from reports of the atrocities committed in rural Hungary in 1919 and early 1920 that these armed detachments often targeted Jews as enemies simply because they were Jews.[20] The captains in charge of these units maintained afterward (with good reason) that their superiors knew of their actions and tacitly approved them. However, domestic and international pressures did not allow the opportunity for this campaign to develop into a more organized persecution. International humanitarian groups collected reliable accounts of the violence in the Hungarian countryside and lodged formal protests with both the Hungarian and Western governments.[21] More important, the Entente Powers determining the fate of Hungary's borders and the traditional prewar political elite, who were already reclaiming their old positions of authority, were both committed to reestablishing the rule of law within Hungary. The armed detachments were soon forced into underground terrorism. Nevertheless, while the squads had a free rein in the region west of the Danube, they sometimes targeted as enemies Jews whom no one accused of having had anything to do with either the Károlyi or Kun regimes. A report submitted by a member of the American military mission in Vienna to the inter-allied military mission to Hungary reported that companies under Anton Lehár's command had "killed all the Jews" in the village of Diszel, and had murdered Jews and looted Jewish-owned property in a number of other towns in the region.[22] In other parts of Hungary, units committed mass murders in which Jews comprised a large number of the victims. The most notorious of these were at Orgovány and Siófok, in which forty to fifty people, mostly Jews, were rounded up, taken to the woods, and

19. Ibid., 114.

20. See the reports of atrocities, prepared and submitted to government officials by the Budapest Jewish community, some of which were also published in the 18 September and 25 September issues of *Equality*. "A dunántuli zsidóüldözések aktáiból (A pesti zsidó hitközség panaszirodájának jegyzőkönyvei)," *Egyenlőség* (18 September 1919), 1–6; and (25 September 1919), 3–6.

21. See, e.g., Nathaniel Katzburg, "Louis Marshall and the White Terror in Hungary, 1919–1920," *American Jewish Archives* 45, no. 1 (1993): 1–12.

22. Excerpts of this report are reproduced in Katzburg, *Hungary and the Jews*, 39–40.

shot.[23] All told, the White Terror may have claimed as many as two thousand victims.[24]

The Szeged officers were also prominent in the political life of the new post-Bolshevik regime. As members of the newly reconstituted National Assembly, or in the councils of the secret political societies, these military men helped to shape the new regime's strongly anti-Bolshevik and antisemitic policies. Their influence was evident in the decree authorizing the creation of internment centers, camps in which political suspects could be detained without charges indefinitely. These would, the authors of the ministerial decree claimed, "ensure that communist rule, which radically shook the foundations of the Hungarian nation and which brought the country to the brink of ruin morally, culturally, and particularly economically should never again come to life."[25] At their height, some seventy thousand Hungarians were interned in these camps, of which twenty-seven thousand were brought to trial for alleged misconduct under the Károlyi and Kun regimes.[26] This system of political retribution, supervised by Gyula Gömbös, one of the Szeged captains and a rising star in postwar Hungarian politics, resulted in countless sham trials. To the same end, the new government also authorized the arrest and expulsion of foreign nationals who were considered to be threats to "public order" or practitioners of "activities damaging our economic life." These too were code words for Communists and Jews; on this authority, police deported a large number of Jewish refugees from Galicia and other parts of eastern Europe. Finally, the Szeged counterrevolutionaries, who were quickly becoming the radical right in Hungary's new political spectrum, lobbied hard for antisemitic legislation. Their efforts helped produce the 1920 *numerus clausus* law.

These decrees and laws served to legalize the cause for which the Szeged officers had fought. At the same time, they acted as restraints on their violent terrorism. Of course, the military men in organizations like the Awakening Magyars did not submit to the newly reestablished rule of law immediately. Throughout the first half of the 1920s, they continued to target prominent Jewish citizens for assassination. In a number of instances, they

23. Ibid., 40–41.
24. I take this estimate from László Kontler, *A History of Hungary: Millennium in Central Europe* (New York: Palgrave Macmillan, 2002), 339–40. Estimates for the number of victims of counterrevolutionary terror vary widely between less than a 1,000 to as many as 5,000. For an excellent discussion of the histories of these numbers, see Johnson, "Cleansing the Red Nest," 83–87, who argues that an historical consensus is forming around 1,500–2,000 victims of the White Terror.
25. Ferenc Pölöskei, *Hungary after Two Revolutions (1919–1922)* (Budapest: Akadémiai Kiadó, 1980), 49.
26. Nicholas M. Nagy-Talavera, *The Green Shirts and the Others: A History of Fascism in Hungary and Rumania* (Stanford: Hoover Institution Press, 1970), 54.

also firebombed Jewish owned shops and synagogues, and vandalized Jewish-owned property. Those charged with these crimes rarely served prison time. However, the new Hungarian government was keenly aware that rampant terrorism created a poor impression in international circles. Indeed, Captain Prónay remembered in his diaries that as he was preparing his detachment to hunt down the Judeo-Bolshevik enemy in the countryside outside Szeged, his commanding officer, General Károly Soós, told him "not to kill too many Jews since this can also cause problems."[27] Appearances were even more important after the Treaty of Trianon officially separated rump Hungary from the occupied territories, since any hope of border revision depended on the favor of Western governments. Hungary's counterrevolutionaries might have been ambivalent about this; indeed Admiral Horthy himself vacillated for years between his sympathies for his fellow Szeged officers and his more conservative instincts for the rule of law and traditional social order. Yet even he finally allied himself with conservatives intent on restoring Hungary's prewar political system and repairing their country's international reputation. Slowly, the terrorist squads found themselves marginalized, much to the chagrin of the officers on the radical right. The counterrevolution had indeed triumphed, but the officers had been forced to abandon the war they had waged in its name.

Ecclesia Militans: Counterrevolution as Counterreformation

The Szeged officers were not the only ones to proclaim the nation's redemption in the midst of revolution and postwar collapse. Catholics like Bishop Prohászka joined secular nationalists like the officers surrounding Horthy in presenting the battle against Bolshevism and the "Jewish spirit" as an apocalyptic battle between good and evil for the nation's future. Writing in 1920, as debates about substantive anti-Jewish legislation were beginning, Bishop Prohászka accused the "interpellating saviors of the rule of law, the defenders of the security of person and property" of compromising the "Christian-national course" on which Hungary so desperately needed to embark. In a tone dripping with contempt, the bishop denounced faint-hearted liberals who anxiously informed the public of a "paramilitary scourge (*tatárjárás*)" or of "secret military dictatorships," but never once asked, "What is the cause of all this?" The "Jewish spirit," Prohászka charged, still dominated public life. Though he assured his

27. Prónay, *A határban*, 102–3.

readers that "we too condemn violence" and that "we too profess the demands of security of property and person," he insisted that Hungarians
had to root out the cause of their nation's calamities. "It is not the rule of
law," he concluded, "that must be saved, but Christian Hungarians."[28]
Other Catholic clergy offered the armed detachments similar kinds of
moral or rhetorical support in their anti-Bolshevik crusade during the critical months after the collapse of the Kun regime. The Franciscan friar,
István Zadravecz, was perhaps the most zealous in this regard, joining
Horthy's national army in Szeged already at the height of the Bolshevik
revolution.[29] As a kind of de facto military chaplain, Zadravecz said mass
for the officers in the armed units and blessed their colors with much
pomp and circumstance. After the counterrevolutionary government established itself in Budapest, Zadravecz formally became military bishop, a
position he held until 1927. Of course, the friar was exceptional in his de-
votion to the counterrevolutionary military squads. But other Catholic
churchmen, among them Bishop Prohászka, also expressed their support
for the officers' detachments in the last months of 1919, precisely the period when these units launched their campaign against the nation's enemies in areas west of the Danube.[30] Catholic lay and religious leaders also
joined secular nationalists in calling for antisemitic legislation to drive
Hungary's Jews from their positions in Hungarian economic and cultural
life. Again, Bishop Prohászka was at the forefront, speaking on the assembly floor as a member of Parliament in favor of the *numerus clausus* law.

However, Catholics like Bishop Prohászka hoped for an altogether
different sort of national rebirth than did the military officers whose ban-
ners they blessed. The bishop's fears of a "de-Christianized" society revealed as much. Even as he excoriated a Jewish conspiracy for having led
Hungary to its present straits, the bishop filled the pages of his diary in
these months with thoughts on the postrevolutionary society to come, focusing on the role, not of the armed terrorist squads, but of the Catholic
Church. "We know," he wrote of his church, ". . . that only we can ensure
pure morality. On this depends the state, society, . . . order, discipline, and
happiness."[31] The nation's future, he maintained, depended on Hungarians returning to the Christian values as they were specifically embodied in
the institution of the Catholic Church. If Hungary's youth could be raised

28. Ottokár Prohászka, "A keresztény kurzus kisíklása," in *Prohászka Ottokár összegyűjtött munkái,* 22:243–45. The article first appeared in *Új Nemzedék* (20 June 1920).
29. *Páter Zadravecz titkos naplója,* ed. György Borsányi (Budapest: Kossuth könyvkiadó,
1967).
30. Thomas L. Sakmyster, *Hungary's Admiral on Horseback: Miklós Horthy, 1918–1944*
(Boulder: East European Monographs, 1994), 33.
31. Entry for 7 July 1919. Ottokár Prohászka, *Naplójegyzetek III: 1919–1927,* ed. Zoltán
Frenyó and Ferenc Szabó, S.J. (Szeged: Agapé, 1997), 31.

in a Christian Hungary led by the Catholic Church, Prohászka reasoned, they would be immune to foreign (and "Jewish") socialist agitation: if "Christian feeling lives in the family, if they are not betrayed by the schools, then there will be a Christian generation."[32] Thus the counterrevolution would rise or fall as a Catholic restoration, and its success, Prohászka claimed, depended on the Catholic Church's ability to inspire the nation with its social vision.

Other Catholic leaders made this point even more bluntly, claiming for the Catholic Church the sole right to determine what in "Christian Hungary" was truly Christian. In his 1920 book, *The Rebuilding of Hungary and Christianity*, the Jesuit publicist Béla Bangha admonished the members of Hungary's other Christian confessions for doubting the Catholic Church's unique role as the nation's redeemer. Speaking to those Protestants he claimed were nationally minded, Bangha maintained: "Protestants . . . sense very well, however much they may adhere to their confession, that Catholicism is the strongest fortress of the Christian faith and morality, the strongest bastion in the fight against liberal thought and destruction and has contributed the most value in the foundation of the country's moral powers."[33] To Bangha and Prohászka, the Catholic Church remained the paramount Christian nationalist institution. Protestants and secular nationalists could, of course, offer the Christian nation their support; indeed Bishop Prohászka often spoke of the need for concentrating all Christian forces to address the most pressing national questions. But none of this obscured the leading role that he and other Catholics imagined for their church.

For Father Bangha, facing the aftermath of revolution and defeat, the problem seemed the same as it had to an earlier generation of conservative Catholics: how could a society create a political order in which its laws and institutions were in harmony with deeper religious commitments? Bangha put the problem precisely in his examination of the role he foresaw for Christianity in the reconstruction of Hungary. For a nation to survive and flourish, it needed "not only material tools, not only laws," but also "moral factors, forces, . . . which a society or nation with its bureaucratic, legislative, and military apparatus cannot create, but can only develop, protect . . . and the creation of these . . . depends in the first instance on moral factors, among which the most valuable without a doubt is Christianity."[34] In a manner reminiscent of Cardinal Lőrinc Schlauch a generation earlier, Bangha argued that liberalism, promising

32. First entry for 14 July 1919, Ibid., 40.
33. Béla Bangha, *Magyarország újjáépítése és a kereszténység* (Budapest: St. István Társulat, 1920), 151.
34. Ibid., 126.

civic bonds based only on philosophical notions of right and equality, could not provide the enduring moral foundation on which a stable society might rest. Only Christianity, its immutable moral principles defended across the centuries most surely and most implacably by the Roman Catholic Church, could offer true moorings to a society adrift amidst the wreckage of modern war and revolution.

This version of counterrevolution was distinctly religious. Religious and secular nationalists alike could agree on the need for antisemitic legislation to provide new opportunities for Christian Hungarians in the country's social and economic life. Catholic leaders, however, understood such legislative tools to be part of a much broader religious agenda for the nation. Bishop Proházka had expressed this connection well when he accused Jews of "de-Christianizing" Hungary. The "Jewish spirit," he argued, had been so destructive, precisely because it had been more than a blueprint for revolutionary politics. Instead, it had been a precondition for revolution, a set of beliefs and values shaping opinions on economic and cultural questions in a manner inimical to national tradition. For the counterrevolution to succeed, these beliefs and values had ultimately to be overturned. This would require vigorous pastoral initiatives as much as it would tough anti-Jewish laws. The church, Catholic leaders maintained, would have to win Christian Hungarians back to Christianity, a kind of latter-day Counterreformation that joined secular and religious politics in its defense of God and country. In the aftermath of two revolutions, the counterrevolution that Catholic leaders imagined amounted to the "re-Christianization" of society under the guidance of the church militant.

Hungary's Catholic clergy often did conduct their pastoral care with renewed missionary zeal in the first years of the new counterrevolutionary regime, declaring their intention to reestablish Hungary as the Kingdom of Mary [the *Regnum Marianum*] it had once been. The image was apposite, since the Jesuits who had come to Hungary during the Counterreformation three centuries earlier had also invoked Marian imagery in support of their own battle against heresy. The Hungarian Jesuit order was particularly prominent in the years after 1919 as well, establishing scores of Marian congregations throughout Hungary in an attempt to foster a more self-consciously Catholic identity among their flock. Though their success was ultimately limited, the Hungarian Jesuits pursued their work with energy and their efforts attracted a great deal of publicity. Protestants decried this kind of militant Catholicism, protesting to the public that this was a calculated violation of the peace between confessions on which national unity rested. The leading bishop of the Lutheran Church, Sándor Raffay, demanded that Catholics declare Hungary a Kingdom of Christ [a *Regnum Christianum*] rather than the Kingdom of

Mary.[35] The former, he argued, suggested cooperation between all Christian Churches for the national good; the latter only conjured up memories of religious persecution.

Missionary zeal, however, was not without risks. Even as Hungary's Catholic leaders proclaimed their desire to "re-Christianize" Hungarian society, they worried that their explicitly religious nationalism would get lost in the din of a vague (and largely secular) Christian nationalist rhetoric. Father Bangha, the Jesuit publicist, had feared already before 1914 that the Catholic Church was not pressing its own agenda of what Christian nationalism was vigorously enough. All his efforts to create a truly Catholic media in Hungary were intended to rectify this problem. Without this, he maintained, the Christianity in nationalist politics would sooner or later became so watered down that it would lose its power to transform society. "In the final instance," he argued in a wartime report on the future of a Catholic press in Hungary, "we want a *Catholic* press for the defense of *Catholicism*." Christian politics, like Christian newspapers, had, he implied, to preserve its specifically confessional character lest it be reduced to impressive sounding slogans. "It cannot be otherwise. And I might add: understanding and sober Protestants cannot imagine it otherwise either, . . . because only here [within Catholicism and within the pages of Catholic press organs] will they see strong principles, a healthy program, a source of moral strength; they will see that only here can they build a strong defensive barrier against enemy invasions."[36]

At the same time, Bangha also worried about the potential for uncontrollable violence inherent in antisemitic politics. In his recommendations, he had proposed a moderately antisemitic course: "We cannot frighten the public with exaggerated assertions of the Catholic program in an unsuitable place or manner. . . . For this reason, antisemitism ought to be employed in a vigorous but truly refined, skillful, and gentlemanly [*uri*] tone."[37] Again, his views about what Catholic newspapers should say were emblematic of his thoughts on Christian nationalism as a whole. "The whole content of a newspaper cannot be the denigration of Jews [*zsidószidás*] alone."[38] In his programmatic book on the role of Christianity in the reconstruction of Hungary, Bangha also reiterated his belief that arresting or punishing antinational perpetrators was the least of Hungary's concerns; instead a Christian-national course must focus squarely

35. Sándor Raffay, "Regnum Christianum," *Evangélikusok Lapja* (20 December 1920), 2–4.
36. EPL. Cat. 44. 3078/1920. "Father Bangha's Report about the Catholic Press Question."
37. Ibid.
38. Ibid.

on replacing liberal or "Jewish" ideas in public life with truly Christian concepts. Bangha went on to distinguish true Christian nationalism from racial nationalism: "According to the Christian national idea, the nation is not so much a togetherness based on race or language or origin. Instead it means a higher cultural and moral unity based on these connections and on geographical and historical community formation (*egybetartozás*)."[39] For this reason, Father Bangha denounced anti-Jewish violence even before the Bolsheviks came to power, arguing that such acts were "a stain on the Christian idea" and saying that he "could not imagine a greater misfortune to the Catholic world, the Catholic idea, and the Catholic movement than a massacre of Jews. This would discredit us for ten years."[40]

Bangha's warnings seemed especially prescient in the first years after the collapse of the Bolshevik revolution. Many in the church leadership were appalled by the religious indifference of the most radical secular nationalists and were deeply suspicious of the militant officers in armed terrorist squads like the Awakening Magyars or the Hungarian National Defense Association. Some were publicly critical. In a statement given to the Catholic daily, *National News*, the bishop of Szombathely, Count János Mikes, declared that the church had long demanded of the government that it "bring an end to the red as well as the white unrest . . . if only for the reason that we saw a serious danger to the tolerant and peace-loving Christian idea when the too-radical elements of the counterrevolution abused the Christian name."[41] Even Bishop Ottokár Prohászka, hero to many of those in right-radical circles, was quickly disappointed by the predominantly secular character of Christian nationalism. "A Christian course without Christianity or Christians," he complained in his diary.[42] He too began to wonder if the nationalist fervor of his allies in the right-radical groups really had the high purpose which he envisioned for it; after one meeting with them, he wrote, "I was . . . with the Awakened [i.e., the Association of Awakening Magyars]; it seems not even they are truly awakening."[43] By 1922, Prohászka, already an old man, began to retreat ever more into his diocesan duties in Székesfehérvár.

Hungary's prince-primate, Cardinal Csernoch, tried to express these concerns in a speech he gave to the members of the Hungarian National Defense Association (MOVE), one of the most significant radical-right groups. In his remarks, he drew careful distinctions between MOVE's

39. Bangha, *Magyarország újjáépítése*, 18, 134.
40. "Lesz-e pogrom Budapesten?," *Az Újság* (11 December 1918), 3.
41. Mrs. Iván Dévényi, "Csernoch János tevékénysége az ellenforradalmi rendszer első éveiben," *Századok*, 111, no. 1 (1977): 69. Dévényi cites an article in *Nemzeti Ujság* (16 October 1923).
42. Entry for 30 June 1920. Prohászka, *Naplójegyzetek III*, 151.
43. Entry for 8 November 1921. Ibid., 185.

brand of zealotry and a more explicitly religious nationalism, even as he conceded the decisive role of the radical right in the counterrevolution. In a time of crisis, he said, they had saved the country from an organized minority under the direction of foreign (i.e., Jewish) influences. MOVE was thus a group of patriots who would never tolerate the subjection of their nation to outside powers. But their time, Csernoch seemed to be saying, was passing. Hungarians now had to turn their attention to the real meaning of the Christianity in Christian-nationalism. "We cannot permit Christianity to be compromised. Those who do not respect the holy principles should not be allowed to act in their name."[44] Despite the admiration Csernoch expressed for MOVE, his message left them little role in Hungarian politics. The task before Hungary now was to protect Christian truths. To the men in MOVE and the other radical groups who had done so much to terrorize Jews, union leaders, and socialists, Csernoch preached the power of law. "Christianity recognizes the law of just and brotherly love as binding even towards non-Christians."[45]

In his remarks, then, the cardinal walked the same fine line between admiration for and condemnation of the secular radical right that many of his colleagues in the church leadership had tried to maintain. Catholics like Bishop Prohászka had welcomed the redemptive zeal with which the officers of the armed detachments had proclaimed the triumph of Christian nationalism in Hungary, since it so closely matched their own sense of the struggle between Christianity and the "Jewish enemy" for the soul of the nation. Their fervor held out the promise that Hungarian society could transform itself, rejecting a whole set of "destructive" social and cultural values in favor of an entirely new and "Christian" social order. Yet Catholic leaders remained troubled by nationalist violence that did nothing to usher in the religious utopia they imagined and indeed distracted attention away from the pastoral initiatives that they felt were essential to the nation's redemption. Moreover, many of them worried that the continuing violence only undermined the very social order that the counterrevolution had been meant to restore. These ambiguities would define the nationalist politics of the Catholic Church in the years to come.

Facing down the Counterreformation: The Election of László Ravasz

Bishop Ottokár Prohászka was not the only one to understand the tumultuous clash between revolutionaries and counterrevolutionaries as a "cul-

44. Draft of Csernoch's speech to MOVE, filed on 15 January 1921. EPL. Cat. C: 179/1921.
45. Dévényi, "Csernoch János tevékénysége," 69.

ture war." Calvinists also saw the struggle to reconstruct "Christian Hungary" from the rubble of the Kun regime as a battle with an antinational "spirit" for the nation's destiny. Indeed, Jenő Sebestyén, the Calvinist theologian who had done so much to find a place for the Reformed Church in the Christian nationalist politics that had emerged in the decades before the war, maintained even in the weeks before Béla Kun and his fellow Bolsheviks seized power that Calvinists must remain an organized force in the coming battle over religion in public life. "A great culture war will break out, and only with absolute organization and preparation can victory go forth in hope."[46] Sebestyén also could agree in principle with his Catholic rival that a reconstruction of Christian society was only possible when Hungarians began to approach the great political and social questions of the day with a point of view shaped by religious faith. "Christianity must bring its tremendous powers into social and political life and realize itself there."[47] Yet even as Hungary's Bolsheviks prepared to take the reins of government, Sebestyén argued vehemently that the best ground on which to base this national rebirth was Calvinism and not Roman Catholicism. "Calvinism has proven to be a supreme nation-conserving and freedom-defending power in the life and battles of the Magyar nation, and it would be its historical mission in these difficult times to demonstrate these strengths again."[48] Sebestyén had argued in the last years of the monarchy's existence that Calvinism offered the Hungarian nation its best hope for confronting modernity without abandoning its national particularities. Now that the monarchy was gone, he used these same arguments to make sense of the revolutionary chaos raging in Hungary.

Calvinism had always suggested a fundamentally conservative sort of freedom to Sebestyén, a view that acquired a new relevance following the collapse of the Bolshevik regime. In the years before the war, the theologian had begun to make sharp distinctions between true Protestant liberalism, rooted in scripture and committed to social order, and "libertinism," which amounted, in his view, to a reckless moral relativism. Only by embracing a more rigorous sense of true Protestant freedom as it had been imagined by John Calvin could Hungary's Calvinists bring an energized faith into public life and thereby renew the life of the nation. For this reason, Hungarian Calvinists like Sebestyén had little patience for the close links between progressive politics, "free thought," and the most liberal of Calvinist church figures. Sebestyén had denounced progressives like Jenő Zoványi for asserting that free-thinking Protestants, especially those in

46. Jenő Sebestyén, "A kálvinista politika szükségessége," *Protestáns Egyházi és Iskolai Lap* 62, no. 9–10 (2 March 1919): 43.
47. Ibid., 42.
48. Ibid.

academic positions, ought to assume no more truth for their own faith than they would for any other moral or ethical system. To Sebestyén, the idea that a Protestant theologian might conclude that Buddhism was as valid a worldview as Calvinism was absurd and dangerous. In such a moral vacuum, Hungarian society could only descend into anarchy and revolution.[49] Progressive Protestants, on the other hand, were outraged by what they understood as a new dogmatism within their church. They also noticed the close links between theological and political conservatism. These tensions within the church had remained unresolved in the years before the war. In the aftermath of the revolutionary upheavals, however, the rifts became exposed for all to see.

In the new counterrevolutionary regime, Calvinists could no longer hope to keep their internal differences to themselves. Catholics like the Jesuit publicist, Béla Bangha, explicitly invoked prominent liberal Calvinists as evidence for their argument that the nation's redemption could only be found within the Catholic Church. Many of the figures Bangha named were those whom neoconservatives like Jenő Sebestyén had long felt to be liabilities.[50] A particular target was the liberal bishop of the Transtibiscan Church District, Dezső Baltazár. Though no theological progressive like Zoványi, Baltazár embodied the liberal nationalist traditions that had guided his church throughout the nineteenth century. In particular, Baltazár had argued in Jewish periodicals like *Equality* that emancipation and equal rights for all before the law must be regarded as a national good. "This truth," he wrote, "must be defended with solicitous care . . . because if the truth of the law should become obscured regarding the Jews, then this shadow could easily extend to the interest of [other] confessions."[51] In 1920, however, Catholics like Father Bangha could claim a privileged role for the Catholic Church, precisely because outspoken liberals like Baltazár could never be found in the ranks of the Catholic clergy. In the new "Christian national course" declared by Catholics and secular nationalists alike, it was painfully obvious to many Calvinist leaders that the church would have to address this liability.

Rival Catholics were not the only group in counterrevolutionary Christian Hungary to attack members of the Reformed Church for their supposedly "antinational" leanings. Progressive Calvinists also attracted the violent attentions of the secular radical right. Jenő Zoványi, the instructor at the seminary in Debrecen whom neoconservative Calvinists had especially criticized in the prewar years, was arrested in 1920 as part of the

49. Jenő Sebestyén, *Kálvinizmus és demokrácia* (Budapest: Kókai, 1913).
50. Bangha, *Magyarország újjáépítése*, 151.
51. Dezső Baltazár, "Az 1848: XX t.-c. és a zsidóság," *Egyenlőség* 36, no. 45 (17 November 1917), 2.

mass reprisals against anyone suspected of having supported the Bolshevik revolution. Zoványi was held in prison for several months along with many of Debrecen's most prominent politically liberal citizens, both Jewish and Christian. Many of these suffered worse, as Zoványi recalled in personal court testimony drafted several years later.[52] A good number of Debrecen's Jewish community were beaten by the members of the radical right terrorist squads. Some were also robbed outright; others were blackmailed into paying large sums of money as ransom. Zoványi himself was under no illusions about the origins of his misfortune, since he avowed in his statement that he could in no way reconcile himself with the Christian national course. Even those, he claimed, who had welcomed the Communist terror were now "first-class citizens, if they made themselves white [i.e., counterrevolutionary] and abused Jews; I, on the other hand, am a second-class citizen, deprived of my rights."[53] Zoványi was released but was stripped of his pastor's certificate by the University of Debrecen.[54]

Zoványi was not the only teacher in the Reformed Church to suffer for his intellectual and political positions. Almost immediately after the Kun regime collapsed, the church began internal reviews of many of its schoolteachers and seminary faculty.[55] Others too were accused of collaborating with the Bolshevik regime or of having prepared its seizure of power with their scholarly work. Scores were dismissed from their posts.[56] Some of these teachers had, like Zoványi, been in positions in and around Debrecen, in eastern Hungary. Conservatives like Sebestyén had apostrophized their political and intellectual tendencies as the "spirit of Debrecen" and had excoriated it in their publications since the turn-of-the-century. Though Sebestyén looked askance at the rough tactics of MOVE and the Association of Awakening Magyars, he could only approve of the housecleaning which those squads had prompted. Church leaders in Debrecen had tolerated "unchecked liberalism" and had now to reap what they had sown. "The Lord God has, in the behavior of Zoványi and his comrades, punished the entire Debrecen leadership for this spirit."[57] The punishment meted out to Zoványi was also, Sebestyén implied, a kind of divine justice.

Nevertheless, the retribution visited on the "spirit of Debrecen" and its representatives in the Reformed Church only highlighted the problem con-

52. RL. C./101, Papers of Jenő Zoványi, 25. doboz—Átvételi jegyzék #1.
53. Ibid., 2.
54. "Uj hangok Debreczenben," Kálvinista Szemle (22 August 1920), 2–3.
55. Jenő Szigeti, "Egyházaink az 1919/20–as ellenforradalmi fordulatban," Theologiai Szemle 12, no. 7–8 (1970): 221.
56. Imre Kádár lists the cases of other teachers and pastors. Imre Kádár, The Church in the Storm of Times: The History of the Hungarian Reformed Church during the Two World Wars, Revolutions, and Counter-Revolutions (Budapest: Bibliotheca, 1958), 34–41.
57. "Uj hangok Debreczenben," 2–3.

servatives like Jenő Sebestyén had identified before the war. How could the Reformed Church find a place in the politics of Christian-nationalism? To one side stood their Catholic rivals. Sebestyén's liberal opponents in the church had been quick to point out that the rise of antiliberal politics had given new life to Hungarian Catholicism. Dezső Baltazár, the liberal bishop at Debrecen and long time defender of Jewish equality in Hungary, had once said: "Protestantism only has its justification in this world so long as it remains liberal. If it loses this characteristic, then it would do better to melt back to where it came from."[58] Now, in the even more hostile postrevolutionary climate, Baltazár again accused reactionaries of serving the interests of the Catholic Church, especially when they embraced the rhetoric of antisemitism to prove their own nationalist zeal. In 1920, Baltazár argued before the National Association of Reformed Pastors that Christian-national unity could only mean Catholic hegemony: "It was not difficult for the extreme wing of the reaction to preoccupy spirits with the Jewish question and distract attention from the defense of the religious and ethical treasure which has been entrusted to the Hungarian Calvinist Church. . . . While the Jesuits . . . openly say that a faithless Catholic is worth more than a believing Protestant . . . naifs among us still hope for some kind of unity."[59] Baltazár thus rejected Christian-nationalism as a transparent effort to roll back the achievements of Hungarian liberalism.

Conservative Calvinists felt the same need as their Catholic rivals did to distinguish their own explicitly religious understanding of Christian nationalism from that proclaimed by secular nationalists. Jenő Sebestyén was particularly careful to distance himself from the radical officers in the counterrevolutionary terrorist squads. In contrast to the paramilitaries, who proclaimed that Jews remained ineluctably Jews no matter their intentions, Sebestyén maintained that Jews were simply at the epicenter of a "destructive front," which included a "host of non-Jewish elements."[60] Christian Hungarians were fighting a "Jewish spirit," the chief, but not exclusive, representatives of which were Jews. The real enemy was secularism, and he chided ardent nationalists, clearly those in the armed detachments, for forgetting this in their zeal to launch a terrible campaign against the Jews. In his understanding of antisemitism, Sebestyén emphasized the transformative power of Christian faith. Jews had, he argued,

---

58. Dezső Baltazár to László Ravasz, 6 March 1914. RL: C./141, Papers of László Ravasz, 13. doboz.
59. Dezső Baltazár, "Elnöki megnyitó az O.R.L.E. választmányi gyülésén," *Lelkészegyesület* 13, no. 25/6 (26 June 1920), 69–70.
60. Jenő Sebestyén, "Antisemitizmus és kálvinizmus," *Kálvinista Szemle* 1, no. 38 (19 December 1920): 3.

ushered in the present era of destructive cultural and economic practices. But Calvinism was its own "worldview," a vision of life extending beyond the church walls that offered salvation and renewal. It was, thus, the possibility of Jewish conversion that symbolized the hope for a new and harmonious Christian society. "Immediately, those spiritual and life energies which now pose such a threat to world Christianity would change in a new direction."[61] This was most definitely a counterrevolutionary Christianity, but one which claimed real distance from the terror practiced by the armed paramilitary squads. It remained to be seen, however, if he and his colleagues in the Reformed Church could maintain this position in the turmoil of Christian national politics.

These concerns burst into the open in 1921. Jenő Zoványi had complained in his drafted court testimony that violent squads had run loose in Debrecen throughout 1920, as they had in many other parts of Hungary. A climate of lawlessness, directed against Debrecen's liberal notables and their property, persisted for some time thereafter. In January 1921, vandals broke into the city's Great Church, Hungary's largest and architecturally and historically most important Reformed church, and desecrated it. The perpetrators were never caught, but the graffiti they left behind on the walls of the church made it clear that the attack was meant to intimidate the city's bishop, Dezső Baltazár, and his liberal allies. Undaunted, Baltazár convened a meeting of the National Association of Reformed Pastors, of which he was president, for March, declaring that the meeting would also mark the reopening of the Great Church after all traces of its desecration had been removed. Calvinists of every political persuasion looked forward to the event as a way to reassert the importance to the national interest of confessional peace between Catholics and Protestants. However, the event quickly turned sour. City policemen arrived at the meeting of the Pastors' Association to monitor it. When Baltazár declared this a calculated insult to Calvinists everywhere and demanded to speak with the chief of police, the police broke up the assembly. J. István Kováts, a prominent Calvinist and a representative in the National Assembly, tried to describe the whole affair in his parliamentary interpellation as a tactless misunderstanding between Baltazár and the police.[62] Nevertheless, the damage had been done: once again, the commitment of the Reformed Church to preserving national order had been put in doubt.

Critics were quick to place the blame on Bishop Baltazár. Dezső Szabó, a writer whose 1920 novel, *The Village Swept Away*, seemed best to cap-

---

61. Ibid.
62. Kováts's parliamentary speech of 7 March 1921 and subsequent interpellation are both reprinted. "A felekezeti béke a nemzetgyűlésen: Dr. Kováts J. István két beszéde," *Kálvinista Szemle* (20 March 1921) and (27 March 1921): 101–8.

ture the national mood of disorientation and made him into one of the most important intellectuals of the interwar period, wrote an open letter to Baltazár a few days after the Great Church in Debrecen had been desecrated. Szabó openly proclaimed his Calvinist upbringing; his criticism of his own church thus stung Calvinist leaders particularly sharply. "The good bishop," Szabó declared, "is the most typical incarnation of a spiritual form which is a deadly danger for Hungarians."[63] As Hungary fell under the sway of a "foreign imperialism," Baltazár remained blind to the new historical mission of Hungarian Protestantism to unite with Catholics in defense of European morality and cultural values. Instead, in public statements and articles written in Jewish religious publications, Baltazár had, throughout his career, rejected anti-Jewish polemics as a form of reactionary politics. "You [Baltazár] did not hear the despairing sobs of the Hungarian agony, because the Jewish *Equality*, which rewarded you as its devoted gladiator, filled your ears with its screeching applause." Szabó went on to accuse Baltazár of abdicating his clerical responsibilities and preaching a charity toward Hungary's Jewish citizens that was tantamount to "Hungarian death" and "the murder of Christianity." To Szabó, the survival of the nation thus demanded that Protestants see Catholics as comrades-in-arms against a destructive spirit, not as rivals in petty confessional disputes.

Thus even intellectuals with open sympathies for the Reformed Church seemed to be suggesting that the Reformed Church could only find a future in Christian Hungary if they embraced a more ecumenical nationalism. In response, conservative Calvinists rose in defense of their church to put some public distance between themselves and liberals like Baltazár, while trying at the same time to defend the office of Calvinist bishop that he held. The ever-resourceful publicist, Jenő Sebestyén, for example, reached out to allies at secular nationalist newspapers, chiefly the daily *Hungariandom* run by István Milotay, for help in recrafting the image of the Calvinist church.[64] Milotay was a prominent journalist and a leading intellectual of the radical right who had begun his career with the newspaper *New Generation*, funded by the Catholic Church. Soon after the collapse of the Kun regime, however, Milotay began his own newspaper. In later years, Milotay would become an ardent supporter of Hungary's fascists and an outspoken enthusiast for Nazi Germany.[65] This was still in the

---

63. Dezső Szabó, "A debreceni csufság," *Virradat* 4, no. 22 (28 January 1921): 1.

64. Imre Révész described *Magyarság* as a "capital city newspaper in good standing" with Sebestyén and a good forum for material that was not suitable for the more theologically oriented church-sponsored journals. Imre Révész to Jenő Sebestyén, 6 September 1921. RL: C./68, Papers of Jenő Sebestyén.

65. Péter Sipos, "Milotay István pályaképéhez," *Századok* (1971): 709–35.

future, however. In 1921, Milotay was very much in the mainstream as a prominent exponent of the "Szeged idea" espoused by the secular nationalists of the radical right. For this reason, his paper was an excellent forum for Sebestyén to explain his opinion of the real essence of Calvinism to a wider, nonconfessional audience.

Sebestyén took the opportunity to discuss the difference between liberalism and Christian freedom as the Reformed Church understood it, drawing a theological distinction he had often made. But he also added pointed criticism of Baltazár: "Baltazár, instead of stepping into the fight against clericalism from independent Calvinist principles, makes the mistake of going over to the other extreme and wants to oppose clericalism with radicalism!"[66] Sebestyén's comments matched Milotay's own editorial direction. *Hungariandom*, a newspaper widely read by those on the secular radical right, had run several articles, both signed and unsigned, extremely critical of Baltazár and his liberal Protestant associates. Milotay himself had advised Calvinists to "stand against the recent efforts of the bishop [Baltazár], that they might protect him from himself and also protect those values which are the common values of Protestantism and the Hungarian nation."[67] With newspapers like *Hungariandom* behind them, conservative Protestants could have more confidence that the nationalist public might see Baltazár and Calvinist liberals like him as isolated figures within their own church.

An even better opportunity to change the public image of the Calvinist church came with the death in March 1921 of Elek Petri, bishop of the Danubian Church District. The church district was a purely administrative construct comprising all the congregations in a swath of land stretching south of Budapest to Hungary's southern border, but its symbolic importance was great, for the district encompassed the city of Budapest itself. Calvinist seminaries and district seats in eastern Hungary—principally in Debrecen, in Sárospatak to the north, and in the provincial capital of Transylvania, Kolozsvár (Cluj)—may have all had much longer histories as centers of Reformed Protestant culture. But the Calvinist seminary in Budapest had grown in importance as the capital had boomed in the second half of the nineteenth century. By the turn of the century, some of the most important Calvinist theologians and teachers, including Jenő Sebestyén, had positions at the school on Ráday Street in Pest. As Sebestyén so clearly recognized in his relationship with István Milotay, church leaders in Budapest could take advantage of connections with the secular media to shape public debate much more easily than those work-

66. "A magyar kálvinisták a Baltazár mozgalma ellen," *Magyarság* (9 March 1921).
67. István Milotay, "Debrecen," *Magyarság* (30 January 1921).

ing at institutions in the provinces. The advantages of having a strong presence in the bishop's seat in Budapest, especially in a country truncated for the foreseeable future, were obvious to all Calvinists.

One name often mentioned in the discussions about possible successors to the deceased Bishop Petri was that of László Ravasz.[68] Ravasz was an instructor at the Transylvanian theological seminary in Kolozsvár (Cluj), and in the first years of the twentieth century, had made a name for himself as a publicist and editor, most notably of the Calvinist Church's *Reformed Review*, and of the interconfessional (Calvinist and Lutheran) monthly, *Protestant Review*. Ravasz was among those in the young generation of conservative Calvinists who mistrusted the secular challenges to religious values. Ravasz was also particularly outspoken in his condemnation of the "Jewish spirit" at the root of all these evils.[69] For these views, he had attracted the scorn of the prewar radical democrats; Endre Ady, Hungary's most important fin-de-siècle poet and an icon to democratic reformers of the era, derided the antisemitic tone that he found to be characteristic of the publications Ravasz edited.[70] However, the controversy only enhanced Ravasz's reputation as one of the few Calvinist figures who could play a leading role in the public debates of the day.

Calvinists in Budapest sorely wanted this quality in the first months of the "Christian national course." Aladár Szilassy, a lay leader active in the Reformed Church's inner mission program, wrote to Ravasz in 1920: "Believe me, we often talk about it, and everyone regrets that you are not here. . . . We have need here . . . of every Christian and Protestant support. The Christian course is mainly a R[oman] C[atholic] course."[71] As the discomfort about Bishop Baltazár's public defense of liberalism and Hungarian Jewry grew in the subsequent months, more conservative Calvinists began to view Ravasz as a necessary counterweight and a public demonstration of their church's real sympathies. Imre Révész, an instructor in Debrecen and later bishop there, wrote to Jenő Sebestyén in the days after the public furor surrounding Baltazár and the disrupted pastoral meeting to assure him that there were still "spiritually independent" Calvinists in Debrecen and to comment that "it might be a providential thing in many respects if he [Ravasz] became a Budapest pastor and Danubian bishop (and by the way, this would be the most radical solution to

68. There is no biography of Ravasz. István Kónya offers some information in his study of Ravasz's theology. István Kónya, *A magyar református egyház felső vezetésének politikai ideológiája a Horthy korszakban* (Budapest: Akadémiai Kiadó, 1967).

69. See his contribution to the open forum conducted by the journal *Twentieth Century* in 1917. *A zsidókérdés Magyarországon: A Huszadik Század körkérdése*, 126–29.

70. Endre Ady, "Az én kálvinistaságom," *Nyugat* 1 (1916): 378–79.

71. Aladár Szilassy to László Ravasz, 8 March 1920. RL: C./141, Papers of László Ravasz, Correspondence, 15. doboz.

the Baltazár question)."[72] Ravasz felt the pressure from these colleagues acutely, for he traveled to Budapest in April 1921, one month after Bishop Petri's death and at a time when the Romanian army was still restricting travel between occupied Transylvania and rump Hungary, to discuss the issue with prominent Budapest church leaders.[73]

However, several problems loomed over Ravasz's candidacy. As Imre Révész asked in his letter to Sebestyén, "What will happen with Transylvania then?"[74] Ravasz came from a family which had been prominent in Transylvanian politics and cultural life for generations, and he himself had spent his entire career up till that point in the province. Transylvania, scene of some of the defining events in Hungarian history, had long been portrayed by historians and poets alike as the most national of historic Hungary's many regions, and as a result, nearly every Hungarian felt its loss to the new greater Romanian state as the painful apotheosis of a national tragedy. Hungarians across the political spectrum hoped to convince the Western powers that the Treaty of Trianon was unjust. But until this diplomatic victory was assured, would it not be essential that the ablest and most talented Transylvanian Hungarians remain in the region to defend national interests? This was evidently the train of thought which moved István Bethlen, a fellow Transylvanian soon to be prime minister of Hungary, to write to Ravasz: "I absolutely do not advise you to accept either the invitation of the Budapest congregation or the candidacy for the Bishop's seat here. . . . A great mission awaits you in the near future. No one can replace you, not today and not in the future."[75] Ravasz's backers in Budapest, including Aladár Szilassy, acknowledged that this would be a wrenching decision, but maintained that he could do more important work in the capital. "We know that leaving Transylvania in the present circumstances is difficult, but believe me—from the point of view of building the church and the country of God, this position is very, but very, important; from the interest of raising our fallen Church, it is incalculable!"[76] It was crucial that Ravasz be in the capital and not elsewhere.

Campaigners for Ravasz maintained that the Calvinist church needed someone at its head who could stand up to the growing influence of the Catholic Church. One pamphlet quoted at length from Béla Bangha's book, *The Rebuilding of Hungary and Christianity*, citing passages where

---

72. Imre Révész to Jenő Sebestyén, 16 March 1921. RL: C./68, Papers of Jenő Sebestyén.
73. Ravasz, *Emlékezéseim*, 146.
74. Imre Révész to Jenő Sebestyén, 16 March 1921. RL: C./68, Papers of Jenő Sebestyén.
75. István Bethlen to R.[avasz], 23 March 1921. RL: C./141, Papers of László Ravasz, 13. doboz. The document is written on cloth, an indication, perhaps, of the shortage of paper in these years.
76. Aladár Szilassy to László Ravasz, 7 March 1921. RL: C./141, 15. doboz.

the Jesuit father suggested that truly national Hungarians were slowly drifting back to Rome. "What is this, if not Counterreformation?" the authors of the pamphlet exclaimed. "What will become of our Church, if precisely in the Danubian church district, where Catholicism is the most aggressive and developed, where most of our nobly born followers live, where the regent of the country lives, we cannot place our greatest preacher at the head of our church?"[77] The Catholic Church had learned to take advantage of the possibilities for public organization which Budapest offered. The Calvinist church would have to follow suit or risk total marginalization.

Ravasz's supporters touted his antisemitic credentials as a particular asset. They reminded the electors of Ravasz's controversial intervention some years earlier in the national debate over the "Jewish question." In 1917, the important journal of sociology, *Twentieth Century*, had conducted a poll among leading Hungarian intellectuals, asking them, among other things, to answer the question "Is there a Jewish question in Hungary?" Ravasz had replied in a long essay that indeed there was and that it was not a new phenomenon, but rather a permanent feature of Jewish history, and a marker of their inability as a people to assimilate fully. In his response, he went on to criticize those who were so beholden to Enlightenment ideas about man's absolute personal freedom that they had come to romanticize Jewish emancipation as a hallmark of a just society.[78] This last comment, though made in a general way, was clearly a response to Baltazár's public defense of the rights of Hungarian Jewry. In fact, the journal in which Baltazár had published some of his most trenchant criticisms of antisemitism, *Equality*, responded to Ravasz's 1917 essay by describing him as the "father Bangha of the Protestants" and "one of the most shameless of confessional agitators."[79] To Ravasz's supporters in 1921, this was all wonderful proof that their candidate was "to the core, a Hungarian and Christian person of faith."[80] If the Jewish editors of *Equality* could be outraged by his public statements, then who could doubt the Christian nationalist fervor of László Ravasz?

Ravasz was elected bishop of the Danubian Church District and was installed in his post on 1 October 1921. All members of the Reformed Church closed ranks around him to present a unified front to the rest of Hungary. But liberal Calvinists looked to the future with some trepida-

77. Seven-page campaign leaflet. RL: A/1.C. 1921: Az 1921–es püspökválasztással kapcsolatos levelek, nyomtatott cikkek, 3.
78. *A zsidókérdés Magyarországon: A Huszadik Század körkérdése*, 126.
79. From *Egyenlőség* 32 (18 August 1917). Cited in a seven-page campaign leaflet. RL: A/1.C. 1921: Az 1921–es püspökválasztással kapcsolatos levelek, nyomtatott cikkek, 6.
80. Ibid., in the same seven-page leaflet, 7.

tion. The "Christian national course" proclaimed by religious and secular public figures in the aftermath of the revolutions was clearly hostile to all visions of social reform. Would long-cherished hopes of a different Hungary, nurtured in the very different years before the war, now evaporate completely? One concerned Protestant wondered in the newspaper that Baltazár edited what Ravasz's election meant for the future of any sort of democratic and social reform.[81] Was it not possible, this writer asked, that Ravasz's supporters would use his considerable talents to repress the aspirations "which reside in the souls of the smallholders, of the so-called peasantry, and which they wanted to see realized in church life as well through a man of their own." More directly put, had Ravasz not been the candidate of the "magnate-gentry order"?

The writer did not go much farther than this, concluding only with the observation that Ravasz had much to do to dispel these suspicions. Nevertheless, the writer's comments were well-founded. The Reformed Church now had a champion in Budapest, the center of Hungarian public life, to defend their interests and to dispute slander against their patriotism. But in many ways, Ravasz did represent a new direction for Hungarian Calvinism. With his election, the church had successfully reoriented itself to the new demands of Christian-national politics and could present itself once more as the equal to Hungary's Catholic Church. The political gains of this strategy were great. Liberal Calvinists wondered, however, if the church had not also lost something in the process.

Retribution and Redemption

As the Bolshevik regime collapsed in Hungary, nationalists of all stripes described the work of reconstruction that faced them as a war for the nation's culture. Looking into the postrevolutionary future, they saw an enemy within as well as enemies without. To combat this threat, the secular counterrevolutionaries grouped in Szeged had formed a National Army, readying themselves literally to wreak vengeance on the nation's oppressors. Yet religious nationalists also described the coming counterrevolution in the language of retribution. All three, the secular nationalists as well as the Catholic and Protestant religious nationalists, had constructed similar visions of the Judeo-Bolshevik enemy, a composite stereotype of the "other Hungary" that did encompass real leftist revolutionaries, both Christian and Jew, but could also expand to cast all of Hungary's Jews as potentially treasonous. This image represented the motive force

---

81. "Jegyzetek," *Lelkészegyesület* 14, no. 40 (8 October 1921): 167.

behind Hungary's failed revolutions and stood as a symbolic source for all the cultural trends that had contributed to the rise of radical politics. Nationalists, both secular and religious, were determined to rid Hungary of its insidious power.

Yet Christian nationalism also spoke of redemption, and it was on this point that secular and religious understandings of the nation differed. The protofascist officers banded together into paramilitary squads understood their mission quite literally as a war. Cleansing Hungary of its enemy became for them a military objective, and the atrocities they committed in the last months of 1919 are brutal testimony to their zeal. Christian Hungary to them was a utopian vision, an image of Hungary freed at last from vestiges of an alien, Judeo-Bolshevik enemy. Of course, religious nationalists upheld a vision of Christian Hungary no less utopian. Nor were they less committed to the elimination of Jewish difference. Yet both Catholics and Protestants hoped to give real meaning to the Christianity they saw at the center of Hungarians' national identity. Religious faith, rather than violence, would transform Hungarian society, reconstructing the social bonds which the "Jewish spirit" had unraveled. Naturally, the leaders of each confession saw in their own church the finest expression of Christian nationalism. But both maintained that Christian nationalism was more than an umbrella under which all anti-Communists could gather, and more than a license to persecute Jews. Religious nationalists thus found themselves in an ambiguous position as the counterrevolutionaries triumphed in Hungary. Hungary's churchmen shared with radical secular nationalists a missionary zeal to redeem Christian Hungary of its sins and purify it of its enemies. At the same time, they found themselves struggling with their radical secular rivals to control what this meant in practice. This tension would continue to define the politics of Christian nationalism until its apotheosis in the spring of 1944.

4

The Political Culture
of Christian Hungary

Writing in the 1960s from London, the writer and critic Pál Ignotus described the prevailing sense of "discomfort," "bewilderment," and "disenchantment" he and his fellow progressives on the Hungarian Left felt in the years after the triumph of the "Christian-national course" in Hungary: "To belong to the Left in Hungary, after the victory of the 1919 counterrevolution, entailed the dual liability of being treated like a cad, or at least as incurably adolescent, for demanding social change, and of being despised, at best pitied, as incurably old-fashioned. It was to have the worst of both worlds: to look moth-eaten and yet not look virtuous."[1] Before 1914, democratic reformers had boldly envisioned an end to all forms of backwardness in Hungary, dreaming of a nation socially and culturally transformed. To them as well as to the Bolshevik commissars who took control in 1919, the postwar revolution was to have signaled Hungary's entry into a new world where equality and justice reigned. By 1920, such dreams were the object of public scorn, and the Left in Hungary had been reduced to a shadow of its former self. Many were forced into exile. Of course, the former Communist rulers had to leave. Béla Kun fled to Vienna and then to Moscow. But Oszkár Jászi left as well, taking up a professorship at Oberlin College in Ohio. So too did György Lukács and Károly Mannheim, choosing the intellectual hothouse of 1920s Berlin over the hostile political climate of "Christian Hungary." Those that stayed found their country changed indeed, the journals and debating circles formerly so vibrant with intellectual energy now consigned to a place on the margins of public de-

1. Paul Ignotus, "Radical Writers in Hungary," *Journal of Contemporary History* 1, no. 2 (1966): 149.

bate. Many of the prewar journals still appeared—*West* resumed publication, as did *Twentieth Century* under a new name—but the arguments in them no longer electrified a generation. To a nation looking for stability and order, the notion of reform or change seemed "old-fashioned" indeed.

Led by István Bethlen, the scion of an old Transylvanian noble family who became prime minister in 1921, Hungary's gentry oligarchs, eager to restore the political hegemony they had lost, aimed at nothing less than a return to a social order untroubled by hopes of revolutionary upheaval. A skilled and cunning politician, Bethlen succeeded in reconstructing the prewar political system by the mid 1920s.[2] Though the Entente powers had put pressure on Hungary's postwar governments to foster a true multiparty system, Bethlen and his allies restored much of the electoral chicanery that had characterized the Dualist era. Parliament also passed an electoral law in 1922 restricting voting eligibility; under new educational and age requirements, only 28.4 percent of the total population could vote. In 1920, twice that number (58.4 percent) had been enfranchised.[3] At the same, Bethlen was also able to reconstruct a political landscape very similar to that of the prewar era, reestablishing a liberal parliamentary system in which the independent but weakened opposition had no real chance of unseating a single, dominant "government" party. By 1926, Bethlen had even managed to recreate the Upper House of Parliament, an undemocratically selected body of notables, church leaders, and aristocrats with the right to vote on the passage of all legislation. By these means, "Christian Hungary" became once again a rigidly preserved hierarchy, one that the historian Gyula Szekfű aptly described as "neo-baroque."[4]

Prime Minister Bethlen's success rested on his ability to co-opt much of the language of Christian nationalism while at the same time containing the violence of the radical right. Those on the radical right could, for example, find nothing objectionable when Bethlen declared in late 1922 that Hungary stood "on a Christian foundation, and we define this foundation correctly if we say that Christian ideals have to be brought back into our public life. . . . We must regain for Christianity the positions we have lost in our economic and cultural life."[5] He and his ministers duly denounced the impact that the "Jewish media" had exercised (and continued to exercise) over the Hungarian public; they also defended the anti-Jewish *numerus clausus* law before international opinion, a measure one of his ministers described as necessary and "derived from our extraordinary situation, which can be set aside as

2. Ignác Romsics, *István Bethlen*.
3. On the new voting restrictions, see ibid., 172–84.
4. The phrase is Gyula Szekfű's. See the revised version, published in 1934, of *Three Generations*. Szekfű, *Három nemzedék*, 402–16.
5. Romsics, *István Bethlen*, 192.

soon as our social and economic life again returns to its normal course."[6] At the same time, Bethlen and his conservative allies insisted on a moderate course, maintaining often that their government would be a "golden mean," a "middle road," and the embodiment of "Christian liberalism."[7] The prime minister never explained exactly what he meant, but the results were plain enough to see. By 1922, the government had put an end to accelerated trials for those suspected of having supported the revolution; at the same time, Bethlen's regime drastically restricted the conditions under which political suspects could be interned. The new regime also aimed at moderation in anti-Jewish policy. In 1928, the Hungarian parliament modified the 1920 *numerus clausus* law despite opposition from the radical right, eliminating reference to racial and ethnic minorities and thereby effectively revoking it. Without overtly antagonizing the extreme right, Bethlen had succeeded in recreating a version of prewar normality.

Interwar "Christian" Hungary was thus a strange mixture of continuity and rupture, a country in which its rulers excoriated the "spirit" of the prewar years even as they hastened to rebuild the political and economic forms that had produced it. The rhetoric of Christian nationalism pervaded public culture in a way that it had never done before 1914. Yet much about the Christian nation remained vague and undefined. What exactly were Christian national values, and who defined them? Were those values Catholic? Or Protestant? Or was Christian nationalism a kind of nationalist ecumenism? Debates about these questions lay at the center of the political culture of interwar "Christian Hungary."

Confessional Peace in a Christian State: Disarming the Church Militant

Throughout the interwar period, the Hungarian government insisted that the nation's redemption depended on the unity of all Christian Hungarians. Though political leaders might invoke symbols or rituals that had a clear Catholic or Protestant history, secular officials insisted that any public manifestation of religiosity have, above all else, a unifying nationalist purpose. No state ritual embodied this spirit of nationalist ecumenism better than the annual celebration of St. István's Day, a national holiday in Hungary between the two world wars.[8] Every year on 20 Au-

---

6. Országos Levéltár (OL), K305, 1922–16–6; "Klebelsberg Kunó gróf előterjesztése a numerus claususról a Nemzetek Szövetségének," 1.

7. Romsics, *István Bethlen*, 180ff.

8. For a detailed discussion of the role of the political cult of St. István in interwar Hungary, see Klimó, *Nation, Konfession, Geschichte*, 244–89. I am grateful to Dr. Klimó for our many conversations about the historical culture of interwar Hungary.

gust, the feast day of St. István according to the customs of the Roman Catholic Church, state officials joined Catholic clergy to celebrate the life of Hungary's first Christian king and patron saint with much pomp and circumstance. The day generally began with a procession, as the country's highest clergy, clad in their richest vestments, carried the saint's embalmed right hand—Catholic Hungary's most sacred relic—from its resting place in Budapest's Basilica of St. István through the streets of the capital. Catholic clergy were also highly visible later in the day as well, when politicians and civil servants presided over an official state celebration. Yet Protestant politicians also celebrated the life of István. From daises usually erected in Heroes' Square, Regent Miklós Horthy, himself a baptized Calvinist, sat side by side with members of the Hungarian Catholic episcopate as the political elite, regardless of confession, vied with one another to express their commitment to the ideals of Christian-nationalism. Each held up St. István as a model for latter day nationalists to follow, and each claimed to be acting in the traditions set out by their first Christian king in the dimly remembered medieval past. Hungary's political leaders thus had the chance to present Hungary's conservative restoration as the timeless continuation of national traditions common to all Christian Hungarians. Catholics, who revered Hungary's first Christian king as a holy saint, and Protestants, who believed neither in Catholic saints nor in the sacred relics of their bodies, might also find other meanings in the day's religious festivities. But these differing interpretations were meant to be entirely private. In public, St. István was above all a symbol of Christian national unity.

Secular politicians also encouraged all Hungarians, regardless of their confession, to understand their nation's partition in eschatological, explicitly Christian, terms. Responding to the Treaty of Trianon, which allotted some two-thirds of historic Hungary to successor states, many, in the governing circles and beyond, placed the state at the center of a national cult of martyrdom, in which Hungary was a crucified Christ whose resurrection would come with the revision of the unjust borders.[9] Numerous commemorative albums, written and translated into other European languages to publicize the injustice done to Hungary, depicted the nation, represented pictorially as all the historic crownlands of St. István before partition, on a cross or with a crown of thorns.[10] The ministry of education also published prayer books assigning young schoolchildren the task of praying in school for an end to the nation's agony and the resurrection

---

9. Miklós Zeidler, *A reviziós gondolat* (Budapest: Osiris, 2001), 162–63ff.

10. See, e.g., Ottó Légrády, ed., *Igazságot Magyarországnak: Trianon kegyetlen tévedései* (Budapest: A Pesti Hirlap ajándéka, 1931). The book was translated into English, French, and German. More generally, see Katalin Sinkó, "A megsértett Hungária," *Néprajzi Értesítő* 77 (1995): 267–82.

of an integral or complete Hungary. At school, teacher and students began and ended classes with part of a hymn written to invoke divine assistance in restoring the nation's borders. The so-called Magyar Credo, written in 1920 by a Mrs. Elemér Papp-Váry, became a staple item at public events and religious services without regard to confession throughout the interwar period. The first and last verses of the fifteen verse poem, generally recited by themselves, ran: "I believe in one God / I believe in one home / I believe in divine, eternal justice / I believe in the resurrection of Hungary. / Amen."[11] Through countless recitations all over the country, the credo, along with the many images of the crucified nation that accompanied it, firmly established in public discourse the vision of a Hungary redeemed amidst national death. The image of Hungary on the Cross suggested, just as the celebration of St. István's Day did, that national redemption depended on the renewal of a Christian morality common to Catholics and Protestants alike. Christian national unity would thus make whole again what war, revolution, and the Treaty of Trianon had broken apart.

Religious nationalists worried, however, that these public rituals of national unity reduced Christianity to a meaningless symbol. It was all very well to speak of a state united by Christian values, they argued. But those values only had real transformative power in society if they came from religion as it was actually practiced, in the Catholic or Protestant churches of Hungary. Shorn of this confessional context, Christianity amounted mainly to a vague hope for a better future. For this reason, the Jesuit Béla Bangha had insisted in his book, *The Reconstruction of Hungary and Christianity*, that only Catholicism had the moral force necessary to redeem the devastated nation.[12] It was also common for Catholics to link the renewal of Christian morality in Hungary to the cult of Mary, reminding their flock that István had decided to convert himself and his people to Christianity only after he had seen a Marian vision. For this reason, Catholics maintained, Christian Hungary was truly the Kingdom of Mary, the *Regnum Marianum*. Indeed, the Catholic Church in Hungary even consecrated a new church in Budapest with this name. Built on the edge of the great city park, the church celebrated the expulsion of anti-Christian (i.e., "Jewish") morality and revolutionary fever from the capital city and the reconstruction of the Christian *Regnum Marianum* in Hungary. Though church leaders insisted these symbols did not exclude

---

11. Other verses only reinforced the iconography of national crucifixion, e.g., "This is my faith / This is my life / For this I bear the cross upon my shoulders / For this I would even be hanged upon it." Sinkó, "A megsértett Hungária," 276; Zeidler, *A revíziós gondolat*, 176.
12. Béla Bangha, *Magyarország újjáépítése*.

Hungarian Protestants from the work of reconstruction, symbols like those of the Marian cult certainly had more than an air of religious triumphalism.

Other Catholics tied the renewal of a particularly Catholic religious sentiment even more explicitly to government policy, arguing that only their faith had the necessary force to make possible the territorial restoration of the historic Kingdom of Hungary. The military bishop, István Zadravecz, was one of the most provocative, continually drawing the wrath of Hungary's Protestant communities with his incendiary remarks at public ceremonies.[13] On one occasion, a group of leaders of Hungary's Lutheran Church wrote a letter of complaint to the minister of defense, protesting a speech Zadravecz had given at a Catholic dinner held by a lay organization in Buda. According to newspaper reports, the bishop had declared in his remarks that "if Hungary was to be integral [that is, regain its territories lost in the peace settlement], then it must be in the first instance Catholic. Not Christian. That is such an anemic thing. Neither fish nor fowl. . . . Catholicism brought Hungarians to Christianity."[14] In a sense, the bishop made Hungary's national future contingent on the specifically Catholic fervor of its citizens. As military bishop, Zadravecz also pushed to introduce into military life the veneration of a new patron saint, arguing that the might of the Hungarian state was best symbolized by a medieval Franciscan monk, János Kapisztrán, who had served as a papal emissary to Hungary during a time of Crusade against both Hussites and Turks. Embodying the defense both of the Catholic faith and of the Hungarian state, Zadravecz argued that Kapisztrán would be the best symbol for Hungary's military of Christian national patriotism.[15]

These actions outraged Protestants, who accused Catholics like Zadravecz of exploding the national unity of all Christian Hungarians. Above all, Protestants resented the prominence of Catholic symbols in the new Christian Hungary. Amongst themselves, and in the pages of their own journals, they criticized the new state cult of St. István, arguing that Protestant Hungarians should not confuse István's towering achievements as a Christian king with Catholic idolatry of his body as a holy relic. Though Protestant church leaders refused to denounce the cult of St. István openly, they did suggest that Hungary's Protestants might better

---

13. Zadravecz describes his perpetual annoyance at Protestant criticism in *Páter Zadravecz titkos naplója*.

14. Evangélikus Országos Levéltár (EOL): Egyetemes Iroda iratai, 41/1922, Letter from the General Office of the Hungarian Lutheran Church to the Ministry of Defense, 17 February 1922.

15. Klimó, *Nation, Konfession, Geschichte*, 231–34.

spend 20 August in private reflection about the meaning of Hungary's first Christian king for Protestant Hungarians today. Above all, Protestants rejected the implication, which Father Bangha had stated so baldly, that the Catholic Church was somehow more important to Christian nationalist politics in Hungary than its Protestant counterparts were. One Calvinist, who described himself simply as a "Calvinist" in his column for *Calvinist Review*, denounced Catholics like Béla Bangha for reducing Protestants to "second-class Christians," explaining that he did indeed have a "strong opinion against [Father Bangha's] idea that the state 'should follow Christian principles mainly in a Catholic sense,' because the state in this case would simply be a confessional, Roman Catholic state, which contradicts the basic principles and the true concept of the state."[16] For similar reasons, the Lutheran bishop Sándor Raffay had denounced the Catholic practice of referring to Christian Hungary as the *Regnum Marianum*. Invoking Mary excluded Protestants from the project of rebuilding Hungary on Christian moral foundations. Instead, Christian Hungary should be a *"Regnum Christianum,"* a state that united all Christian Hungarians in their struggle for national redemption.[17] Thus, religious leaders in both camps held up the same ideal of Christian unity, only to accuse their rivals of breaking it.

To the secular conservatives who established Hungary's restorationist government in the early 1920s, a competition to identify Christian Hungary as a state with a particular confession was plainly unacceptable. In their view, Christian nationalism was above all an ideology of national unity, one that transcended any particular confessional interest. Clearly, Christian national values had their origins in religion, whether Catholic or Protestant. However, their significance in the restoration of Christian Hungary was primarily civic. For this reason, Prime Minister Bethlen's government insisted that Hungary's historic Christian churches subordinate their confessional interests to the greater national good. From his position as minister of religion and public education, Kunó Klebelsberg stood at the head of the government's campaign for "confessional peace." Klebelsberg was by all accounts a devout Catholic, yet he valued national unity above anything else. Speaking before the annual Catholic Conference in 1927, the minister reminded Catholic leaders that Hungary as a nation was still recovering from the wounds that had been dealt it. Partition was, of course, the worst of these injuries. But Klebelsberg was not insensitive to the concerns of religious leaders, also including the "religious

16. Kálvinista, "Első és másodosztályú keresztények," *Kálvinista Szemle* 2, no. 5 (30 January 1921): 34–36.
17. Sándor Raffay, "Regnum Christianum."

indifference" of the second half of the nineteenth century in his litany of injuries done to the Hungarian national body. Nevertheless, the minister insisted to his Catholic audience that recovery required the cooperation of all Hungarian patriots for the highest national good. "The nation has not yet entirely left its sick bed and so what should the doctor do with the family member or the visitor who wants to bring commotion into the recovery room?" Lest the assembled Catholics miss the point of his metaphor, Klebelsberg then went on to warn them that sympathy for religious institutions would wane "if patriots have to see the churches squander the powers entrusted to it by the state in fruitless quarrels between themselves." He went on to advise the churches to voluntarily subordinate themselves to the national interest: "every church, without waiting for the intervention of the state or of other churches, should itself silence any screeching voices of aggressiveness in its own camp." His message was clear: Christian-nationalism did not give either church the license to pursue its own confessional agenda.[18]

Faced with a government friendly to religion, but insistent on its governmental prerogatives, Hungary's Catholic leaders took care to preserve the appearance of confessional peace. The primate, Cardinal János Csernoch, and his colleagues on the episcopal bench thus kept a careful distance from Catholic activists who insisted too vigorously on a radical religious nationalism. Béla Bangha, the outspoken Jesuit publicist, was recalled to Rome for a time by the general of the order, ostensibly to help in administrative matters there. His temporary departure removed one unwelcome dissenter from the new politics of consolidation and accommodation.[19] The military bishop, István Zadravecz, also found himself out of favor. When he ran into political trouble some years later, as a result of a complicated money counterfeiting scandal, the episcopal bench seized its opportunity to remove him from his post and place him in a less public position. With figures like these removed, Csernoch and the other bishops could give their church a cooperative public face. They dutifully appeared at official state functions alongside their Protestant counterparts in a public display of national unity. Catholic priests frequently served mass or performed other liturgical services at state-sponsored events.

Even more important, the Catholic hierarchy lent their unqualified support to Prime Minister Bethlen and his conservative allies in their attempt to contain the threat of mass political upheaval in Hungary. Under episcopal pressure, Catholic oligarchs took care to ensure that Catholic political

---

18. "A katolikus nagygyűlés előtt," *Nemzeti Újság* (9 October 1927). Reproduced in Kunó Klebelsberg, *Neonacionalizmus* (Budapest: Athenaeum, 1928), 82–87.

19. Jenő Gergely, *A politikai katolicizmus Magyarországon*, 62–63.

parties remained highly aristocratic affairs with little popular support.[20] Moreover, the leaders of Catholic lay organizations abandoned any hope they had of channeling Catholic antirevolutionary zeal into some kind of mass political movement. Hungary's episcopate was so scrupulous in maintaining the appearance of confessional peace that figures in the Vatican began to question the wisdom of the strategy.[21] In an interview, the papal nuncio, Cesare Orsenigo, and Cardinal Gasparri, state secretary of the Vatican, put these doubts to Csernoch. Would such a close association with Protestants at state celebrations not lead ultimately to religious indifference? The nuncio also objected to accounts he had heard of masses in which political announcements were closely associated with church liturgy, a reference in the first place to the common practice of reciting the so-called Magyar Credo in religious services and at public events.[22] To these charges, the cardinal and his bishops replied honestly that much of this was simply advisable from the "point of view of tolerance." Later, in a letter to Vatican officials, Csernoch explained the political pressures. Put simply, "a modus vivendi," a publicly acceptable rapprochement with the other Christian confessions, "had to be found."[23]

Hungary's secular political elite made certain that Catholic leaders continued to look for this nationalist "modus vivendi." Kunó Klebelsberg was so disturbed by reports that Vatican officials might be criticizing Hungary's episcopate for their nationalist posture that he made it a subject of his annual New Year's greeting to Cardinal Csernoch. "It was most disturbing," he wrote "that the papal nuncio under pressure of Roman politics directed against nationalism, criticized the practice of singing the national anthem and the Magyar Credo and more generally the stronger manifestations of nationalism." He reminded the cardinal that he and the government he served had always worked to "strengthen the Catholic Church and, joining with your Eminence, to make it into the main source of national life." Opinions like those expressed by the papal nuncio only hindered these efforts. Moreover, he hinted darkly, such criticism would only redound ultimately to the disadvantage of the Catholic Church. "If the Church weakens nationalism here, this will in no way strengthen

20. Jenő Gergely, A keresztényszocializmus Magyarországon, 1924–1944 (Budapest: Typovent Kiadó, 1993).

21. Dévényi, "Csernoch János tevékénysége," 71–72.

22. Notes from the conference of 17 March 1926. A püspöki kar tanácskozásai: A magyar katolikus püspökök konferenciáinak jegyzőkönyveiből, 1919–1944, ed. Jenő Gergely (Budapest: Gondolat, 1984).

23. Dévényi, "Csernoch János tevékénysége," 72. Dévényi cites a draft of a letter from Csernoch to Gasparri, dated 8 November 1926. EPL: Cat. D, püspöki konferencia jegyzőkönyvei.

Catholicism."[24] Klebelsberg's words contained both an offer and a threat. Secular nationalists were willing to offer the church a high degree of public prominence, especially in the matters of education so close to Klebelsberg's heart. Yet this prominence came with a price: church leaders had to acknowledge that the state's interest in national unity took precedence. Religious activists could pursue their confessional interests only as long as these furthered the government's policy of consolidation. When these became a political distraction, Klebelsberg, and the government that stood behind him, would demand that religious nationalists yield in the name of confessional peace.

A Counterreformation by Other Means:
Gyula Szekfű and the Power of History

Hungary's secular politicians insisted that Christian nationalist icons like St. István stood for the unity of all Christian Hungarians. Yet Protestant Hungarians had reasons to be concerned. Try as one might to place the legacy of István as a Christian king in a nationalist and ecumenical context, the fact remained that 20 August was chosen as a national holiday precisely because it was already a day sacred to Catholics in Hungary. Even if they were not part of a campaign to proselytize for the Roman Catholic Church, the signs and rituals of 20 August—the mass in the Catholic Basilica of St. István and the procession of the reliquary containing the holy right hand of the saint—were undeniably Catholic. Moreover, the new emphasis on the deep continuities between contemporary Christian Hungary and the medieval Christian kingdom founded by István was a marked departure from the public historical culture of the prewar period. During the Dualist Era, politicians and historians alike had tended to emphasize Hungary's resistance to Catholic Habsburg rule. As a result, public figures most frequently invoked episodes in the nation's history in which Protestantism had marked the struggle for national independence. Above all, secular politicians of the late nineteenth century had looked to Reformation-era Hungary, presenting the Protestant leaders of that time as icons of nationalist zeal and liberal principle. After 1919, however, Hungary's political leaders were eager to disassociate the nation from any hint of liberal thought. As a result, the Reformation, formerly an age in which the Hungarian nation's yearnings for freedom and cultural progress

24. EPL: Cat. C. 1927 Kunó Klebelsberg to Cardinal János Csernoch. 10 January 1927. This letter is found in the collection of holiday greetings which Cardinal Csernoch received for the new year.

were in perfect harmony, became a much less usable past. Though secular nationalists insisted that the medieval past was broadly Christian, many Hungarian Protestants still worried about the consequences of this shift. If the origins of Christian national values were all to be found in a time before the Reformation, what guarantee was there that Protestantism would continue to have an equal place in the history of Christian Hungary?

The historian Gyula Szekfű stood at the center of this debate about the nation's Christian past. His most widely read work, *Three Generations and What Came Afterwards*, was a foundational text of Christian nationalist ideology, providing the most influential scholarly presentation of the theses that united Christian nationalists in Hungary. In it, Szekfű had argued that Hungary had severed its ties to the nation's political traditions in the nineteenth century, when its political leaders had embraced a foreign liberalism. This, in turn, had allowed alien and "Jewish" cultural and social values into Hungary, distorting the country's path to modernity. The catastrophes of war and revolution, Catholics and Protestants in postwar Hungary could and did agree, were the inevitable result. Yet Gyula Szekfű had also made a reputation for himself as a Catholic historian, one who was interested in the long continuities linking the medieval Christian state to the present. In *The Hungarian State*, published in 1918 before the end of the war, Szekfű argued, contrary to prevailing historiographical consensus, that the history of Hungary as a nation must be written as the history of the Hungarian state in all its different historical forms. That state, he maintained, had come into being on the ground of the "medieval Christian-German cultural community."[25] Throughout the interwar years, Szekfű continued to examine the political and cultural legacy that Hungary's first Christian king and founder of the state had bequeathed to later generations, achieving prominence as one of the foremost critics of liberal thought in Hungary. To many Protestants, however, Gyula Szekfű's critique of the liberal past in Hungary was shaped too powerfully by Catholicism.

The state founded by István and dedicated to Christianity was significant for Szekfű above all because it represented universal values that transcended any one people or ethnic group. As he put it in one essay devoted to exploring the concepts of state and nation, the "historical Hungarian state concept" "peacefully . . . blended together over a millennium the Hungarians with so many other non-Hungarian nationalities!"[26] "Under the transformational power of Christianity," Szekfű argued in another essay on minorities in medieval Hungary, the Hungarian state never be-

25. Gyula Szekfű, *Der Staat Ungarn: Eine Geschichtsstudie* (Stuttgart: Deutsche Verlags-Anstalt, 1918), 8.

26. Gyula Szekfű, "Népiség, nemzet és állam," in *Szekfű Gyula*, ed. Erős (Budapest, 2002), 207.

came "the oppressor of other peoples' particularities." It was not that non-Hungarians had had (or needed) carefully protected minority rights. A Christian state did not "promise minority rights," but instead "that Christian manner of dealing" which a Christian king owed to all his Christian subjects, whether long-rooted or newly arrived in the kingdom. In a Christian monarchy, "national, ethnic, racial differences . . . were unknown . . . , because these differences, in the essence of a Christian monarchy, and under its universal rule, hardly appeared in its state and political life."[27] Only under the foreign influence of liberal political thought had Hungary's political leaders abandoned this universalist Christian tradition and embraced modern nationalism. Szekfű had described this transformation in *Three Generations*, and the results, now seen in the partition of Hungary and the disadvantages suffered by Hungarians as minorities in new nation-states, had been catastrophic for Hungary and for the region. Because of this, Szekfű argued that liberalism had been out of place in multiethnic Eastern Europe. Hungarians had instead to embrace the ancient political traditions left as legacy by St. István. As a Christian state, one that stood for universalism above national conflict, Hungary might once again be made whole, and Hungarians might once again live (as first among equals, of course) in peace with the many nationalities in the old Kingdom of Hungary.

These conclusions begged the question, however, of exactly what sort of Christianity had shaped Hungarian political development most profoundly and had given Christian governance in Hungary its "universalist" quality. Gyula Szekfű continued to ponder the meaning of St. István to Hungarians throughout the interwar years. In the 1930s he had the chance to develop his historical conception more clearly on a grand scale, in the multivolume general history of Hungary he wrote together with Bálint Hóman, a fellow historian and minister of religion and education for much of the 1930s. In it, Szekfű argued that the Catholic Counterreformation of the sixteenth and seventeenth centuries had played a decisive role in transmitting the values of István's medieval Christian kingdom to the more recent past. According to Szekfű, Catholics of the seventeenth century, faced with the challenges of Turkish occupation, invoked the memory of St. István's kingdom (the *Regnum Marianum*) to understand their mission. "Old Hungarian memories and impressions of the miseries of the Turkish campaigns, refreshed daily, together produced the historical philosophy of the *Regnum Marianum*, which alongside its Catholic character, postulated an integral Great Hungary led back to its old bor-

27. Citations taken from Gyula Szekfű, "A magyarság és kisebbségei a középkorban," in *Szekfű Gyula*, ed. Erős, 459–60.

ders, under the leadership of the crowned king and his ancient patron, the Virgin of the Hungarians."[28] Gyula Szekfű was a careful historian and his interpretation is clearly situated in his discussion of sixteenth- and seventeenth-century Hungary, when the state was divided into a zone under Turkish occupation, a region under Habsburg rule, and an autonomous Transylvania, which existed uneasily between those two great powers. Yet the parallels with interwar Hungary, when the crownlands of St. István were again divided between several different powers, were not difficult to see. In effect, his history linked national fortunes to the Hungarian state and made Catholicism the essential spiritual tie between the two. The Counterreformation was thus a supremely important episode, for it was a time when Hungary rediscovered its historical origins after a century and a half of occupation and division.

Szekfű assigned much of the credit for this work of national preservation to the Catholic Habsburg state. Though liberal historians of the nineteenth century had excoriated the Catholic dynasty for snuffing the lights of liberty and intellectual progress during the Counterreformation, Szekfű argued that tyranny was not the defining feature of Habsburg rule in Hungary. Szekfű was willing to acknowledge certain excesses in the dynasty's rule. Yet he found the mediating role that the Habsburg state had played in Hungarian history of greater historical importance. Put simply, the Habsburg state had tied Hungary to broader developments in Europe at a crucial period in its history, preserving critical elements of Western civilization in a society on the borderlands of Europe. In the most sharply written discussion of Protestant rule in the East of Hungary and Catholic Habsburg rule in the West during the time of Turkish occupation and partition, Szekfű argued that:

> Of the two Hungarian state-entities . . . only the western half had possibilities for development in politics and culture. . . . The western half upheld tradition, and a connection with the ancient, and at the same time, under a king of foreign origin, in close connection with foreign territories, was much more exposed to Western influence than the Hungarian state had been before, perhaps never so much since the time of St. István. Old Hungarian traditions and European Western influence: these two powers now worked and brought to life the Habsburg state, the traditional form of the political life of the Hungarian nation through four hundred years.[29]

The Catholic Habsburg state, in other words, had been an essential frame in which Hungarians could nurture and develop their own political tradi-

28. Gyula Szekfű and Bálint Hóman. *Magyar Történet* (Budapest: Királyi magyar egyetemi nyomda, 1928–34), 5:292–93.
29. Ibid., 4:63.

tions. Without that frame, it seemed, the Hungarian nation might well have lost its place as a political community among the nations of Europe. Protestant intellectuals found this treatment of the Reformation nothing less than scandalous. Their response to another of Szekfű's studies on the era of Reformation and Counterreformation—his biography of Gábor Bethlen—is the best example of their outrage.[30] Bethlen was a sixteenth-century Transylvanian Calvinist noble who had united the Magyar gentry under one political banner and had protected Transylvania's political unity and autonomy in an age when the Habsburg and Ottoman empires were vying for hegemony in southeastern Europe. Many Calvinists looked back on this period and revered Bethlen for embodying and preserving the national will when threats abounded on all sides. Szekfű's treatment of Bethlen, though careful and well-researched, cast serious doubts on the reverence which the story of that Magyar noble inspired. Szekfű placed Bethlen in the wider context of contemporary European economic and social developments, and drew a portrait of a leader representing a very specific political interest in a situation that no one political actor could master. Szekfű's Bethlen tried to steer a course between the Habsburgs and the Turks to achieve his own political ends; the imperial powers were equally willing to view Bethlen as a piece in a larger puzzle. This approach also emphasized the cleavages between Magyars in Transylvania and those in Western, Habsburg-controlled Hungary, making it clear that Bethlen did not always speak for all Magyars.

Calvinists rejected this reassessment outright. One particularly irate Calvinist historian, István Rugonfalvi Kiss, blasted Szekfű's book in a review for the *Protestant Review*.[31] Kiss was particularly angered that Szekfű, in reconstructing the social, diplomatic, and economic context of the time, had allowed little possibility for values like love of nation or religious faith to shape Bethlen and drive him in his actions. Where Szekfű had shown divisions among Magyars, Kiss wanted to preserve the idea of a suprahistorical national loyalty that gave coherence to this complicated period. Calvinists had always argued that Bethlen had negotiated with the Ottoman Turks because he perceived the German Habsburgs to be the greater threat to national survival; the cultural renaissance which Hungarians had enjoyed within autonomous Transylvania seemed to prove the wisdom of this policy. Now, Kiss argued, Szekfű had overturned these truths. "According to Szekfű, the Turks . . . forced Bethlen on Transylvania; thus Bethlen was an instrument of Turkish interests!"[32] Calvinists took this argument for an accusation and bitterly resented the idea that

---

30. Gyula Szekfű, *Bethlen Gábor* (Budapest: Magyar Szemle Társaság, 1929).
31. István Rugonfalvi Kiss, "Szekfű Gyula: Bethlen Gábor," *Protestáns Szemle* 38 (1929): 123–32.
32. Ibid., 128.

they might have loosened Hungary's ties to Western civilization by cozying up to the infidel. Szekfű's book also suggested that Transylvania, that perfect blend of national pride and Protestant piety which took center stage in the Calvinist imagination, was perhaps not as representative of the entire nation as many had previously believed. In sum, there was much dynamite in Szekfű's scholarly treatise, and many Protestants joined Kiss in condemning Szekfű for "transvaluating" not just the history of Gábor Bethlen, but of all Hungarian history.[33]

In his response, Szekfű confined himself to a devastating critique of István Rugonfalvi Kiss's historical method, discussing source documents rather than polemics about the politics of history.[34] However, Szekfű continued to argue for long continuities in Hungarian history that linked foundational events in the Middle Ages to the present. He thus necessarily relativized the importance of the Reformation, reducing it to one of several important cultural forces that affected Magyar society, rather than the seminal period in which Magyar national consciousness was born. In addition, he argued that the real significance of the Reformation and the ensuing Counterreformation lay in the fact that both bound Hungary to European civilization inseparably: "Indeed now, as the waves of Reformation and Counterreformation flooded medieval Hungary one after the other, these waves again stopped at the eastern borders: again Hungary was Europe's furthermost border region. . . . The religious movement thus again proved that Hungary was a territory of Europe, even more its outermost region, beyond which there was no more European culture nor European development."[35] Szekfű himself tried to present this argument as unpolemically as he could, taking care to acknowledge the real achievements of Reformation-era Protestants in Hungary. Yet it was not difficult to infer from Szekfű's corpus of works that if the Catholic restoration had failed in Hungary, then Hungarian society might well have slipped beyond the pale of European civilization. Szekfű himself had described the historical ideology of the *Regnum Marianum* as "implacably anti-Turkish."[36] It was thus ultimately as a Catholic state, or at least a state in which Catholicism was predominant, that Hungary would fulfill its historical mission as the border guard of Europe.

To secular conservative politicians, this long view of Hungarian history,

33. Kiss issued his own defense of the "transvaluated" Bethlen that same year. István Rugonfalvi Kiss, *Az átértékelt Bethlen Gábor: Válaszul Szekfű Gyulának* (Debrecen 1929).
34. It is more revealing that Szekfű published this response in Béla Bangha's Jesuit-run journal, *Hungarian Culture*. Gyula Szekfű, "Kritika és terror," in two parts, *Magyar Kultura* 36, nos. 6 and 7 (20 March and 5 April 1929), 251–56 and 300–305.
35. Szekfű and Hóman, *Magyar Történet*, 4:232.
36. Ibid., 5:293.

Catholic or not, was especially attractive, since the issues central to Szekfű's project—the continuity of the Hungarian state and the role of Christianity in binding Hungary to Europe—were central as well to Hungary's political reconstruction after 1919. Political leaders embraced the idea of St. István's state because it provided a vision of a Hungarian constitution created in a distant past which would admit no serious political revision.[37] The innovations of the revolutionaries in 1918 and 1919 were thus null and void, and represented ideas truly alien to Hungarian political traditions. Moreover, Christian Hungary's historic mission to serve as a bulwark of Western Christendom against the advances of the infidel inspired Hungary's political elite in their counterrevolutionary zeal. Where once Hungary had battled against the Turks, it would now stand against the new enemies of Christian Europe—the Bolsheviks. Finally, the memory of St. István's state suggested an argument for territorial revision, since it was within the framework of a large multinational Hungarian state, ruled by Hungary's traditional nobility, that Western civilization had come to the Carpathian Basin. After World War I, then, the ideology of St. István's state, manifested in public festivities, political speech-making, and historical research, implied a profoundly conservative vision of the nation's past and future.

Back to the People! Magyar Ethnicity and the Intellectual Life of Interwar Hungary

Not all of Hungary's historians were equally enamored with Gyula Szekfű's vision of the Hungarian past. In 1931, the medieval historian Elemér Mályusz, a younger historian who became Szekfű's greatest rival within the profession, published the most thorough critique in an essay collection entitled *New Paths of Hungarian Historiography*. In it, he discussed the insufficiencies he found in Szekfű's work. The problems that Mályusz found were not so much ones of method, as ones of emphasis. Szekfű, he felt, was too concerned to understand the effects of a "universal" or pan-European spirit on cultural life in Hungary. In such an approach, Mályusz could only find the argument that "Magyars were never masters of our own destiny (and) have lived in a kind of shadow-world, . . . in an alien-inspired web of traditions, which have been with us from times immemorial."[38] Moreover, Mályusz felt that Szekfű's focus on

---

37. József Kardos discusses the importance of St. István to the debates about Hungary's constitutional arrangement following the counterrevolution in 1919. József Kardos, *A szentkorona-tan története, 1919–1944* (Budapest: Akadémiai Kiadó, 1985).

38. Citation in Vardy, *Modern Hungarian Historiography*, 108.

the history of the Hungarian state was all wrong. Modern nations inevitably outgrew the limits placed on them by premodern political elites. It was thus the historian's task, wrote one interpreter of Mályusz, "to examine and to aid the process whereby political nations are transformed into people-oriented 'ethnic nations' (*népi nemzet*), which [Mályusz] saw as the unavoidable fate of all twentieth-century nations."[39] Szekfű and his students, the young medievalist felt, ignored this truth, grossly undervaluing the creative force of the "Magyar spirit" in history. This spirit, the ethnic consciousness in which is "compressed the unconscious life and cultural activities of the people as a whole,"[40] defined Hungarians as an ethnic nation. States might come and go, but the ethnic nation, he claimed, was "untouchable and inviolable."[41] Its story, Mályusz claimed, would reveal that "notwithstanding all oppression—Turkish conquest, Mongol devastation, and alien tyranny (Habsburg rule)—they [i.e., the Hungarians] still remained Magyars (and) retained their lands, customs, and language."[42] This tale of endurance against all odds would be the stuff of a truly national history.

In his programmatic essay, then, Elemér Mályusz imagined an "ethnohistory" of Hungary to counter the "etatism" he saw in the works of Gyula Szekfű and his disciples.[43] Such a history had, in the words of the historian Steven Bela Vardy, two goals: first, to "to learn everything about the past of the people," and second, "to retain the cultural and spiritual unity of the forcibly fragmented Magyar nation."[44] Mályusz and his students were methodologically ambitious in pursuit of both these intellectual goals. Together, they imagined a multidisciplinary approach that enlisted the fields of linguistics, anthropology, sociology, folklore studies, and demography. With techniques from each of these disciplines, the members of the "ethno-historical school" hoped to uncover a level of social reality existing beneath supposedly artificial and arbitrary political units imposed on the people from outside. This approach deferred the sort of synthetic essays championed by historians like Szekfű to a later date; the first order of business was to produce detailed knowledge of Hungarians as a locally situated and unitary ethnic group in all their regional complexity. During the 1930s and 1940s, Mályusz and his students produced a number of high-quality studies of medieval social history in this spirit. They also encouraged their colleagues in related disciplines to join them in

39. Ibid., 106.
40. Ibid., 103.
41. Ibid., 106.
42. Ibid., 107.
43. See ibid., 102–20.
44. Ibid., 106.

their study of Hungarian ethnic history, urging linguists, for example, to devote their full attention to the development of local variations in vernacular Hungarian. Mályusz also imagined a role for local researchers who could, from their positions in towns and villages throughout Hungary, collect raw data on local place names, folk customs, and folklore, material that would be an invaluable source base for scholars in the academy.[45]

Like his rival, Szekfű, Elemér Mályusz was both representative of and a leading figure in a broader intellectual current in Hungary. During the interwar era, a broad spectrum of Hungarian intellectuals had turned their attention to the history and shared cultural practices of Magyars as an ethnic nation. This interest had clear irredentist motives. In an age when ethnic Magyars were arbitrarily divided among several neighboring political entities, writers and social scientists alike felt compelled to elaborate and celebrate what bound them all together. Mályusz himself had argued that Hungarian historiography should take up the "struggle for the people beyond the (current) political frontiers (of rump Hungary)."[46] Such research, deeply influenced by turn-of-the-century debates about cultural authenticity, invariably focused on the ethnic Magyar peasantry, in the belief that Hungary's national traditions could be found in their purest form among those thought to be least touched by the influences of modern culture.[47] The world economic crisis of the 1930s lent a new and heightened urgency to this intellectual interest in Magyar ethnicity. Hungary, like its neighbors in Eastern Europe, was primarily an agricultural economy, dependent for meeting its balance of payments on exporting its farm produce to foreign markets.[48] As the Depression began to wreak havoc on the economies of the wealthier Western nations, demand for Eastern European produce plummeted, helped along by new import restrictions designed to protect Western markets from further collapse. The bottom fell out of the world agricultural market, and countries like Hungary were forced to sell vast amounts of produce for a pittance; in the first years of the crisis, agricultural income in Hungary fell by nearly 36 percent.[49] Hungary's peasantry, already eking out marginal existences before the crisis began, were among the hardest hit and now faced catastrophe. Without support, most of these most "Magyar" of ethnic Magyars would soon be little more than beggars.

45. Ibid., 110.
46. Ibid.
47. For the intellectual history of populism in Hungary, see Dénes Némedi, *A népi szociográfia, 1930–1938* (Budapest: Gondolat, 1985).
48. Iván T. Berend and György Ránki, *Economic Development in East-Central Europe in the Nineteenth and Twentieth Centuries* (New York: Columbia University Press, 1974), 242–65.
49. Ibid., 245.

Intellectual interest in the "people" (*nép*),[50] and particularly in the history and culture of ethnic Magyar peasants, had strong political overtones in the 1930s. Studying the customs of rural ethnic Magyars led many observers to petition the Hungarian government for more comprehensive welfare relief. Throughout the 1930s, waves of writers traveled to remote villages in rural Hungary to gather firsthand impressions of a nation in crisis. These intellectuals, a loosely defined circle of social critics, journalists, sociographers, and novelists, produced harrowing accounts of agrarian poverty, always suggesting that the misery they uncovered was only a harbinger of a greater national decline to come. More important, those who searched for the origins of rural poverty invariably focused on one or several political or social institutions still existing in the present-day. As a result, populist writers wrote especially critically about patterns of property distribution in Hungary, excoriating large landholders and particularly the Catholic Church (as one of the largest landholding bodies), for enriching themselves while millions of landless Magyar peasants barely avoided starvation as sharecroppers and day laborers. The more historically minded of these populist critics echoed scholars like Elemér Mályusz, observing that the vast majority of the country's large latifundia had been imposed on Hungary as part of the Habsburg restoration in the eighteenth century. None of this sat well with Hungary's conservative political elite, who had fashioned the country's postrevolutionary political system precisely to recreate and preserve the prewar political hierarchy and property relations as best they could. Inevitably, studies about ethnic Hungarians spoke to more than folk history or folk customs. These works were also calls for urgent and radical reform.

Those interested in Hungarian ethnicity, however, did not necessarily find inspiration in their nation's Christian past. Focusing on those qualities that united Magyars as an ethnic nation and made them unique in Europe often led Hungarians to idealize the pagan Magyar tribes who conquered the historic Kingdom of Hungary in pre-Christian times. Many scholars interested in the history of the ethnic Magyar nation studied topics from precisely this period, hoping to learn more about the tribal people that had migrated from the Central Asian steppes into Europe. Legends about the Magyars' "conquest" of the Carpathian Basin had long occupied a prominent place in nationalist iconography.[51] In countless monuments and murals erected in the nineteenth century and after, these conquering Magyar tribesmen, and particularly their chieftain Árpád, always represented eth-

---

50. In Hungarian, *nép* is a collective singular, much like *Volk* in German.
51. Katalin Sinkó, "Árpád versus Saint István: Competing Heroes and Competing Interests in the Figurative Representation of Hungarian History," *Ethnologia Europaea* 19 (1989): 67–83.

nic uniqueness and independence. The large statue group of Árpád and the other tribal leaders, erected in 1896 in Budapest's Heroes' Square to celebrate a thousand years of Hungarian history in Europe, was only the most prominent of these. These symbols retained their meaning in the interwar period as well. In addition, a number of Hungary's right-wing radicals preferred to invoke the history of the nation's Eastern, extra-European origins, rather than its Christian character, as a sign of their militant nationalism. One of the most prominent right-wing student organizations, for example, took its name (*Turul*) from the eagle that was the pagan Magyars' totem animal. As the shadow of Nazi Germany began to loom more darkly over the lands of East-Central Europe, many right-wing radicals began to associate the symbols of Hungary's pagan past with an explicitly biological racism premised on the purity of Magyar blood. Though conservative intellectuals like Gyula Szekfű argued persistently in a variety of public forums that any notion of racial purity in a region so ethnically diverse as the Carpathian Basin was simply absurd, many on the far right looked ever more frequently to Árpád and the pagan past for a mystical transformative power that would help the Magyar nation master the growing crises of the 1930s.

At the same time, some intellectuals associated with the populist movement developed their critical examination of rural social conditions into an ideology of liberation closely resembling socialism. Indeed, a generation of Hungarian intellectuals heatedly debated the relation between populism and socialism. Some saw affinities in the common call for popular democracy; others insisted that the special focus on Magyar ethnicity distinguished the populist movement from socialism completely.[52] To be sure, a measure of antisemitism was not absent from these debates, since many populists denounced Jewish intellectuals in Budapest for advocating an alien socialism entirely divorced from the hopes and aspirations of rural ethnic Magyars. However, this was often the only way in which these often vitriolic attacks and counterattacks could be considered part of Christian nationalism. Populist intellectuals devoted most of their energies to imagining concrete social and economic reforms; few paid much attention to hopes for religious revival. Thus secular nationalists from the radical right to the left took up the rhetoric of ethnic nationalism to give shape to their political opposition. In both cases, religion and nationalism seemed utterly divorced.

Nevertheless, populist advocates for the ethnic Magyar poor still found

---

52. This was one significant aspect of the hostilities between Hungary's "urban" and "populist" intellectuals. See *A népi-urbánus vita dokumentumai, 1932–1947*, ed. Sz. Péter Nagy (Budapest: Rakéta Könyvkiadó, 1990).

tremendous power in Protestantism as a set of cultural symbols. Precisely because of its long association with struggles for national independence, Protestantism, and the Calvinist Church in particular, could suggest much more easily than could the Catholic Church an interaction with Western civilization that did not erase the nation's unique cultural identity. Dezső Szabó, a writer whose 1920 novel *A Village Swept Away* became a founding text of the interwar populist movement, tried to capture this distinction in several essays from the 1920s. On the one hand, he rejected outright everything that St. István stood for, angrily invoking Hungary's pagan past as an argument for Hungary's particular national destiny in one 1922 essay.[53] At the same time, Szabó consistently invoked the historical mission of Hungary's Protestant (and especially Calvinist) clergy. In a 1926 essay entitled "Contemporary Problems of Hungarian Protestantism," Szabó described Protestant pastors as a caste of native intellectual leaders who could adapt the cultural influences of the West to the particular needs of Hungarian society. Indeed, it was precisely because they had ceased to perform this function, Szabó argued, that Hungary's modernization had gone off course in the liberal era of the late nineteenth century.[54] Though the nation's pre-Christian past continued to fascinate ethnic nationalists like Szabó, the potential to make of Hungary's Protestant past a symbol for balancing European civilization with national identity was too great to ignore. For many of them, it was thus Protestantism, and not the Catholicism implied in the symbols of St. István and his medieval Christian Kingdom, that best represented the idea of Christian Hungary.

An Alternate Christian-Nationalism: The Reformed Church and Populist Politics

Of all Hungary's Protestant communities, Hungary's Calvinists believed their church best embodied this balance between Europe and nation. They derived this self-understanding partly from their memory of the itinerant Calvinist preachers of the Reformation who had spread the Gospel in Hungarian. Even more important, Calvinists had traditionally seen their church as advocate and champion of the national interest. Not only had the Reformed Church fought implacably for national independence during the centuries of Habsburg rule; it had also traditionally been at the forefront of debates about threats to Magyars as an ethnic nation. Unlike Lutherans, Hungary's Calvinists were almost uniformly ethnic Magyars.

53. Cited in Sinkó, "Árpád versus Saint István," 21.
54. Dezső Szabó, *A magyar protestantizmus problémái* (Budapest: Génius, 1926).

Church leaders frequently alluded to this when they described theirs as the "Magyar religion." This homogeneity had made Calvinism into a marker of ethnic stability within public culture. Before 1918, Calvinists were at the forefront of concerns about the increasingly disadvantageous ethnic balance with Magyars and Romanians in their stronghold, Transylvania. For example, one turn-of-the-century novel extremely popular in Protestant circles entitled *The Silenced Bells* by Viktor Rákosi presented the Hungarian reading public with a Calvinist preacher who receives an excellent seminary education in Utrecht, Holland, but who returns to a remote village in Transylvania, compelled by a sense of responsibility for his people. There he attempts to shepherd a flock teetering on the edge of ethnic extinction. The novel ends tragically; the final scene has the pastor dying on the steps of his church as the last Magyars in the village go to take communion in the Romanian Orthodox Church. Despite the maudlin ending, the image of a Protestant pastor, learned in the intellectual traditions of Western Europe, yet ever willing to serve his ethnic national community, was tremendously suggestive, as was his willingness in the novel to draw a sharp distinction between the uncaring state and the homeland (*haza*), home to a people proud but "in tatters, begging, and humiliated."[55] These themes made of the Hungarian Reformed Church a symbol for the salvation of the ethnic nation.

Elsewhere in Europe, in Poland or Croatia for example, the Roman Catholic Church could claim to be the champion of a homogenous ethnic nation. In Hungary, this was impossible. Though Catholic sociologists might amass statistics showing that Catholics far outnumbered Protestants in Hungary, and that Catholicism was thus the more "Magyar" of religions,[56] nothing could hide the fact that, even in a Hungary stripped of its ethnically most diverse regions, Catholicism remained a multinational faith. The majority of ethnic Germans in interwar Hungary, the country's largest ethnic minority, were Catholic. So too were many in the much smaller Slovak community along the northern border with Czechoslovakia.[57] Though the Hungarian Catholic Church did little to promote minority cultural rights in the interwar years, scrupulously following the lead of the Ministry of Religion and Public Education in making Hungarian the sole language of instruction for older children in religious schools, these

55. Viktor Rákosi, *Elnémult harangok* (Budapest: Révai, 1903), 342.
56. Antal Pezenhoffer, "Melyik a magyar vallás?" *Magyar Kultúra* 5(1918): 155–66. The article was continued in the next two issues. Roman Catholics made up almost two-thirds of the population of Hungary in 1920. Some 21 percent of Hungarians in Trianon Hungary belonged to the Reformed Church.
57. In 1930, there were just over 477,000 ethnic Germans in Hungary, about 5.5 percent of the population. 82 percent of them were Roman Catholic. There were also just over 104,000 ethnic Slovaks, 1.2 percent of the population.

minorities remained indisputably Catholic parishioners. Most important, the Hungarian Catholic Church was one of the largest landowners in Hungary, deriving a good part of its wealth from vast estates in the south and west. Given this vested material interest, the episcopate could hardly support any serious effort at land reform that might improve the lot of Hungary's ethnic Magyar peasantry and so remained skeptical of anything that smacked of populism.

Populists, in turn, considered the church's latifundia an especially black mark on Hungarian Catholicism. By the 1930s, many Hungarian social scientists had determined that patterns of land ownership in which large landed estates dominated were the cause of the staggering drop in birth rates among ethnic Magyars in certain regions of the country. Concern in the interwar years centered particularly on southern Transdanubia, a predominantly Catholic region of Hungary southwest of Budapest. In many places in Hungary, but especially here, an egregiously inequitable distribution of property concentrated much of the best arable land in the hands of a very few large landowners. Among the most prominent of these was the Roman Catholic Church. By contrast, peasants owned next to nothing and worked, for the most part, as agricultural laborers on these great estates. However, property laws often prohibited primogeniture, forcing many of them to contemplate dividing what little they had among several male children. Within a generation or two, they knew their families would be reduced to absolute destitution. Without any hope of acquiring new land, many families intentionally limited their number of children, hoping to keep their property as much as possible under one roof. The resulting "only child" (*egyke*) custom, combined with a heavy rate of prewar emigration to the United States, drained the region of a sizable portion of its population. Birth rates in the region had been falling for more than fifty years, and contemporary Hungarian demographers depicted a looming population crisis if the trends were not halted.

Throughout the 1930s, many openly denounced the Catholic Church for contributing to a looming demographic apocalypse. Among the most active was the Reformed pastor of a village (Kákics) not far from the present-day border with Croatia, Géza Kiss. In an address to a Protestant youth group in 1937, he sounded a common theme: ethnic Magyars had been dealt a great injustice by the Catholic Habsburg dynasty and the Catholic Church that served it in the years following the expulsion of the Ottoman Empire from the Carpathian Basin. Though the Magyars had survived the Turkish occupation with their cultural traditions and their communities intact, they were denied the chance to regain the land the Turks had taken from them. Kiss described what happened instead: "The Austrian ruling house saw that the time was ripe to remove the one hindrance to their plans, to wipe out weakened Hungariandom. . . . Of the old property owners, the Magyars, not a single one regained his old rights. Of the old property owners, only the Catholic ecclesiastical holdings remained."[58] The Magyar smallholders stood no chance against the combined juggernaut of the Counterreformation and the Habsburg restoration. Much of the land in Transdanubia, the region west of the Danube, was given to Catholic magnates loyal to the ruling house. To make matters worse, in Kiss's opinion, the Austrian empress, Maria Theresa, encouraged Catholic Germans from other regions of the empire to settle in southern Transdanubia. These came in sizable numbers, permanently altering the ethnic balance of the region. As Kiss told his audience of Protestant youth: "The age of Maria Theresa, which it has become customary to praise in Catholic circles, filled Transdanubia with those Swabians (*svábok*) and which such a mass of large landowners, who will stamp the fate of those already condemned to death by the only-child (*egyke*) system, if in this last hour, we do not awaken and we do not declare war against, first, our own sins and if we do not break every bond which is strangling this people and its future."[59] Kiss thus emphasized a different element of the traditional Protestant hostility to Habsburg rule. If, in the nineteenth century, Calvinist patriots had despised the ruling house in Vienna for depriving them of their political rights, Reformed Church figures like Kiss accused them in the 1930s of deliberately initiating processes that were leading inexorably to Magyar ethnic extinction.

Kiss's disdain for the state-centered and Catholic inspired narrative of national history championed by scholars like Gyula Szekfű was obvious. Like other religious activists in his church, however, he hoped to do more than rehearse the litany of tragedies that fate had dealt their nation. In Kiss's view and in the view of many pastors like him, the Reformed Church had a sacred obligation to act as advocate for the Magyar nation in crisis. In a manner reminiscent of Elemér Mályusz's call for detailed empirical study of the cultural and social particularities of the ethnic Magyar nation, Kiss and his colleagues proposed to understand the extent of the demographic crisis through careful local studies. In his own monograph on the region in which he lived, the Ormánság, Kiss wrote a comprehensive account of the regional folk customs of a dwindling community of Reformed Magyars, invaluable cultural practices of dress, speech, and sociability that would soon be lost forever.[60] At the same time, Kiss tried to publicize the extent of the problem in numerous essays published

---

58. Address to the youth of Zaláta, 1937. RL: C./231 (Papers of Géza Kiss). Box 4, undated manuscript, 4.
59. Ibid.
60. Géza Kiss, *Ormánság* (Budapest: Sylvester R.T. kiadása, 1937).

throughout the 1930s. In these, he argued that the Hungarian public needed detailed knowledge of the demographic crisis, a map of population decline that might enable policymakers to more easily target those regions and communities where the Magyar element was in greatest danger. Many of Kiss's fellow pastors in southern Transdanubia agreed. At a diocesan conference convened in early 1934 to discuss the "only-child problem," the assembled Baranya County pastors requested that every church district in Hungary should gather the natality statistics of its congregations.[61] Through these efforts, activist pastors hoped, the nation's political leaders might be spurred to action long overdue.

For Kiss and his fellow pastors, the disappearance of Reformed Magyar communities was a cause for national, not just confessional, concern. Precisely because the Calvinist Church had long served as a potent symbol of ethnic stability, Kiss, like many in the Hungarian Reformed Church, presented the decline of Calvinist communities in border regions of mixed ethnicity as a matter of the gravest national security. In his correspondence with his bishop, László Ravasz, Kiss explicitly used the Calvinist communities in particular regions of southern Hungary as a symbol of a dissolving ethnic homogeneity, arguing that villages which he knew were once purely Calvinist (*színreformátus*) were changing and that Hungarians, as an ethnic group, were slowly vanishing in these critical regions. "What is happening here? The ancient and pure Hungarian race (*az őstiszta magyarfaj*), the Reformed community, is on the verge of extinction, and an ugly (*szörnyű*) mix of peoples is coming for their place from the gypsies, Romanians (*oláh*), Serbs (*rác*), and Germans (*sváb*). . . . I know of one village in the Ormánság, where the gypsies at the edge of the village already have more children than the entire village."[62] In another letter, he wrote in a similarly apocalyptic vein: "It is my feeling, that if the rest of the Danubian District is this way . . . that your eminence can sound the death bell for Reformed Hungariandom along the Danube."[63] Without strong Calvinist congregations to imprint an ethnic national character on the region, Baranya County, situated so crucially on the border with Yugoslavia, would slide into a chaotic and unreliable mish-mash of ethnic heterogeneity.

This belief in the ethnic purity and reliability of their church inspired Calvinist activists to imagine remedies for the crisis. In particular, Reformed community leaders called for a comprehensive program of resettlement, a coordinated effort that would help Reformed Magyar families

61. Géza Kiss, "Egyke-értekezlet Baranyában," *Református Élet* 1, no. 9 (24 February 1934): 68–69.
62. Géza Kiss to László Ravasz. 12 March 1934. RL: A./1.b. 446–1934.
63. Géza Kiss to László Ravasz. 11 February 1934. RL: A./1.b. 446–1934.

move from relatively overpopulated (and ethnically secure) regions on Hungary's Great Plain to troubled areas like southern Transdanubia. Strategic resettlement of Calvinist families would serve not only to eliminate economic disparities between regions of Hungary by, in the words of church leaders from Inner Somogy County, giving a better life to landless peasants from eastern Hungary and "populating the depopulated Transdanubian congregations."[64] It would also quite literally provide reinforcements for a nation battling for ethnic control of critical border regions. Géza Kiss had himself seen this as the ultimate aim of his demographic mapping; he, like many other populist writers, hoped that the houses and farms without heirs would revert to state authorities, who could then redistribute them according to national need.[65] His colleagues in the Upper Baranya diocesan assembly agreed with him, passing a resolution that linked questions of economic assistance to vital matters of national security:

> If demographic statistics show perhaps in certain ancient Reformed communities, especially after the new settlement of peoples from the Bácska, streaming in after the Serbian occupation, a majority of a different religion, yet everywhere Reformed institutions—churches and schools—stand ready and wait with joy to welcome within their walls the solely reliable [group] from the national standpoint—the racially pure Magyar Calvinists [*fajmagyar reformátusok*], settling here from the great Hungarian Plain [Alföld].[66]

In this way, resettling Calvinists in ethnically and confessionally mixed border regions would be an explicit act of national defense.

Because of this passionate advocacy, ties of affinity between the populist reform movement and the Calvinist Church in Hungary were always closer and more numerous than they were with the Catholic Church. Certainly, the writers who stood at the forefront of Hungarian populism considered the movement to be independent, the "work" of neither church.[67] Yet the fact remained that the leaders of the Reformed Church, committed though they were to the postrevolutionary conservative restoration, were far more willing to condone the presence of young reform-minded churchmen in church organizations than were their Catholic counterparts. Spurred on by the enthusiasm of Protestant university students, resettle-

64. Minutes of the General Convent of the Reformed Church. Held 29 April 1932. Point 298.
65. Géza Kiss, "Az 'egyke,' " *Protestáns Szemle* 43, no. 1 (1934): 10–18, esp. 17–18.
66. Minutes of the General Assembly of the Upper Baranya Reformed diocese. Held in Siklós on 26 September 1935. Point 20b.
67. Jenő Gergely, "Egyházak és népi mozgalom," in *A népi mozgalom és a magyar társadalom. Tudományos tanácskozás a szárszói találkozó 50. évfordulója alkalmából*, ed. Levente Sipos and Pál Péter Tóth (Budapest: Napvilág, 1997), 391.

ment soon became one of the Reformed Church's most significant pastoral initiatives. Moreover, young Calvinists in seminaries at Sárospatak and elsewhere took the lead in organizing village seminars to educate and train Hungarian peasants. Most significantly, the Calvinist confessional youth organization, Soli Deo Gloria, became an important forum for populist debate in the 1930s and 1940s; the Soli Deo Gloria–sponsored summer workshop on the banks of Lake Balaton (at Balatonszárszó) was host, in 1943, to a seminal gathering of all populist intellectuals eager for social change in Hungary. Young Catholics, of course, also embraced populist reform enthusiastically. Catholic Church organizations, like those established to offer adult education programs in basic education and skills, aimed at improving the lives of Catholic Magyar peasants in much the same way that Protestant youth groups did. The most successful of these by far was the National Body of the Catholic Agrarian Young Men's Groups, or KALOT.[68] Nevertheless, the Catholic Church in interwar Hungary remained a powerful icon for stability and social order, an image church leaders defended scrupulously even as populist intellectuals demonized them for it. So long as the episcopate refused to contemplate land reform in particular, and social reform more generally, Catholic pastoral initiatives among Hungary's peasantry remained constrained. In the politics of ethnic nationalism, where secular and religious figures alike maneuvered to speak in the name of the ethnic people, the Reformed Church would always have pride of place.

To Hungary's secular conservative leaders, Christian nationalism was, above all, what the Italian historian of fascism, Emilio Gentile, called a "political religion," a politicized cult that governments used as a tool to legitimize power but also to transform "the people into a moral community animated by a single faith."[69] Of course, Christian nationalism never became a cult of an all-powerful state; the conservative elite ruling Hungary after 1919 imagined "neonationalist" or "Christian nationalist" renewal as the restoration of a traditional social order in which an oligarchic elite extended its paternalist care to all subjects of the state. Even so, there were parallels with other more radical right-wing regimes in interwar Europe, like Fascist Italy and even Nazi Germany. In all of them, the regime in power placed tremendous emphasis on a quasi-religious "political style" resting on set of symbols, myth-histories, and values that all patriots must revere for the sake of the nation's good and the social order.[70] Like Mussolini, for example, secular conservatives in Hungary saw Hungary's

---

68. Margit Balogh, *A KALOT és a katolikus társadalompolitika, 1935–1946* (Budapest: MTA Történettudományi Intézet, 1998).
69. Gentile, *The Sacralization of Politics*, 85.
70. Mosse, *The Nationalization of the Masses*, 1–9.

Christian churches as both useful allies and potential rivals. In "Christian Hungary," the nation's political leaders insisted that religion could not be confined to private life; nor could it exist as one organization among many others in civil society. Instead, Hungary's Christian churches were to play an important role in defining and spreading those values deemed essential to the nation's renewal. Yet Hungary's secular government insisted that those values were "Christian," not Catholic or Protestant. Despite all their solicitude toward Hungary's religious leaders at public festivities, the country's secular rulers ultimately demanded that religious leaders, regardless of confession, accept state authorities as the final arbiters of what Christian nationalism was and how it would be implemented in society.

However, Hungary's secular conservatives could not reduce the religious symbols of Christian nationalism to simple instruments of political control. Those symbols were so powerful precisely because they could embody questions to which many Hungarians desperately sought answers in the interwar era. The Christian nation symbolized a break with the liberal past and with everything that had led to the revolutionary catastrophes. It also symbolized a nation reborn from an apocalyptic death. On this much, all Hungarians could agree. Nevertheless, the fact that there were multiple and contradictory Christian traditions in Hungary meant that debates about the meaning of Christian nationalism embraced a variety of views about Hungary's place in Europe and about the relationship of the nation to the state. In popular debate, Catholicism stood as a metaphor for stability, for conservative consolidation, and for a political order that some found oppressive. It could also represent a Hungary firmly tied to a wider Europe and open (some would say, too open) to the powerful cultural influences at work there. Calvinism, on the other hand, symbolized undiluted national traditions and an ethnic purity extending back through countless generations to those Magyars who came from the East to settle in Europe. In a Hungary shaped by Calvinism, Hungarians might embrace what it needed from Europe while still preserving the essence of Hungarian uniqueness. Calvinism also suggested popular opposition. Its history in Hungary evoked a sympathy for the less privileged members of the national community. The oppositional images which these confessional traditions invoked were aspects of long-running debates about what was "truly" Hungarian. The paired oppositions—Catholic/Protestant, West/East, European/Magyar—served as orienting points around which public discussion about Hungarian national identity could focus.[71]

Of course, arguments about whether Protestants were or were not

71. Susan Gal describes how symbolic oppositions frame existential questions such as these in the Hungarian context in "Bartók's Funeral: Europe in Hungarian Political Rhetoric," *American Ethnologist* 18, no. 3 (1991): 440–58.

"second-class Christian Hungarians," at times vitriolic, only served to underscore how marginal Hungary's Jewish community was to the political culture of interwar Hungary. Throughout the nineteenth century, assimilating Jews had embraced the republican tradition of 1848, asserting their equality in a nation dedicated to the Rights of Man. After 1919, few public leaders spoke proudly of the democratic hopes raised in the revolutionary struggle of 1848. Lajos Kossuth's struggle for a free and liberal Hungary, while never forgotten, received little attention in Christian Hungary. In the sweeping narrative of Hungarian history favored by the political establishment, the decades in the late nineteenth century of Jewish assimilation and cultural efflorescence represented a dead end. Jewish intellectuals responded by resisting this passionately, looking back to 1848 as the source of "true" national traditions so different from the Christian national rhetoric of the moment.[72] Some argued that the Dualist Era (1867–1918) had not held the sum of Jewish life in Hungary. The most ambitious scholars sought to trace Jewish history in Hungary farther back than that, even to the age of St. István and the founding of the state.[73] Little came of all this effort. The politicians and historians who had crafted the long narrative of Hungary's history as a Christian state continued to see the liberal Dualist Era as quintessentially Jewish and therefore an aberrant episode in the national past. Nor could Hungarian Jews take greater comfort in the ethno-nationalist version of Christian Hungary. Here, too, Jewish intellectuals detected a tendency to deny to Hungary's Jews an unequivocal membership in the "people" or the ethnic nation about which the populists spoke so much.[74] The Jewish critic Lajos Hatvany commented that much of the ethnocentric populist literature left the country's Jews outside of the nation's history, and in a kind of "spiritual ghetto."[75]

As long as a conservative elite could guarantee political stability and social order, such exclusion remained mainly rhetorical. After the political consolidation of the mid 1920s, there were no new anti-Jewish measures for many years. But as the nation's political stability unraveled toward the end of the 1930s, however, the violent possibilities inherent in this language of exclusion became terrifyingly real.

72. Guy Miron, "History, Remembrance, and a 'Useful Past' in the Public Thought of Hungarian Jewry, 1938–1939," *Yad Vashem Studies* 32 (2004): 131–70.
73. See, e.g., Venetianer, *A magyar zsidóság története.*
74. See, e.g., the 1937 exchange between Ferenc Fejtő and Péter Veres, reproduced in *A népi-urbánus vita dokumentumai*, 339–90.
75. Lajos Hatvany, "Nyilt levél Németh Lászlóhoz," *Századunk*, no. 4 (1934): 179–82.

5

The Christian Churches and the Fascist Challenge

Despite Prime Minister István Bethlen's success in restoring conservative rule, the radical right did not disappear from Hungarian political life. For some ten years, through the 1920s and into the mid 1930s, Bethlen and his political allies had managed to marginalize the country's radical right, co-opting their rhetoric of Christian national renewal while pushing them to the sidelines and restoring the rule of law. However, the military officers and disaffected civil servants who had enthusiastically supported the White Terror were deeply disappointed. "Christian Hungary," once the banner of a conservative movement determined to purify the nation of its enemies and restore traditional moral and social order, seemed to have dissipated into a few public displays of splendid, but superficial, opulence, like the annual celebration of St. István on 20 August. Social order had been restored, but only a small elite of "Christian Hungarians" had benefited. Many of the civil servants and university-educated professionals who had come down in the world after the catastrophes of 1918–19 continued to feel their loss of social status. Increasingly, these disaffected members of Hungary's "gentlemanly middle class," as they styled themselves, took inspiration from the success and vigor of the National Socialist Party in Germany. They lamented that counterrevolutionary violence had not produced a similar political organization in Hungary. Ferenc Rajniss, a journalist of the extreme right with a good feel for the mood of the most politically radical of Hungary's ruling class, captured this bitter disappointment in some remarks from 1922: "The national Christian direction could not create a militant organization, which could maintain a closed and unified battle front against clearly determined enemies, institutions, and economic forms of income; everything became watered-down."[1] Throughout the 1920s and 1930s, radical Christian nationalists kept alive their hopes of national redemption and of a nation purified by a thorough (and violent) assault on the many manifestations of the "Judeo-Bolshevik spirit" that they believed had ruined their country.

Many on the extreme right saw a second chance to renew a radical Christian nationalism in the wake of the economic crisis in the early 1930s. When his government proved unable to master the worsening depression, István Bethlen stepped down. The regent, Miklós Horthy, replaced him first with an interim cabinet and then, in 1932, with one of his closest associates from the early counterrevolutionary days in Szeged: Captain Gyula Gömbös. Gömbös had been a prominent figure in the military detachments that had scoured the southern Hungarian countryside for national "enemies" in the autumn of 1919 and was thus an icon to the extreme political right. As Gömbös was sworn in as prime minister, expectations ran high. However, his time in office brought only more disappointment to the radical right. Gömbös found himself constrained by precisely those political and social institutions that Hungary's conservatives had reconstructed so carefully in the first years after the war. In his efforts to bolster the country's failing economy, he even toned down his own invective against "Jewish financiers," believing that he needed the help of Hungary's financial elite, many of whom were indeed Jewish, to guide the country out of its fiscal woes. Gömbös did attempt radical changes in other areas. During his tenure, for example, he promoted a new cadre of officers to command positions within the Hungarian military and gendarmerie. Largely sympathetic to the radical right, these "Gömbös men" would play a significant role in Hungarian politics after the start of the Second World War. Yet Gömbös never could transform the ruling government party into a unified fascist movement. Invariably, his ambitions ran up against resistance from traditional conservatives in the county administration, old elites who were loyal to István Bethlen and loathe to cede their political power.[2] Though Gömbös still enjoyed the support of the country's radical right, it became increasingly apparent that he was powerless to effect the political and social "changing of the guard" for which so many of them hoped.

When Gömbös died of illness in the autumn of 1936, the one figure in whom all factions of the radical right could place their trust passed from the political scene, leaving the right-wing opposition fragmented and dis-

---

1. Cited in Péter Sipos, *Imrédy Béla és a Magyar Megújulás Pártja* (Budapest: Akadémiai Kiadó, 1970), 212.
2. Sándor Kónya, *Gömbös kisérlete totális fasiszta diktatúra megteremtése* (Budapest: Akadémiai Kiadó, 1968).

contented.[3] A number of political movements vied with each other to fill the vacuum. Some, like the Scythe Cross, were short-lived movements of agrarian discontent; others were simply new variations on the secret societies of military officers that had advocated violent terrorism in the early 1920s. The most important was a movement loosely modeled on the National Socialist Party in Germany and led by a former General Staff officer with a penchant for grandiose and generally incoherent speech-making. Ferenc Szálasi's Arrow Cross Party, as the movement soon became known, grew quickly from political obscurity into the largest opposition party in the country by the end of the decade. Throughout 1937, Arrow Cross sympathizers flooded the streets of Budapest with leaflets proclaiming their imminent seizure of power. However unlikely this may have been, many began to fear a fascist putsch.[4]

Ferenc Szálasi and his Arrow Cross Party were not necessarily the ideal candidates to replace Gyula Gömbös as the leading force on the radical right. Of course, Szálasi's party demanded radical action against "Jewish forces" working in Hungary and denounced the conservative elite as agents of the nation's enemies. Moreover, Szálasi and the circle around him hoped to unite all factions of right-wing discontent into a single political party outside of and in opposition to both the state apparatus and the dominant governing party.[5] All this certainly stirred the sympathies of every Christian nationalist dissatisfied with the reigning conservative political system. Yet, the Arrow Cross Party also had ambitions to become a true mass political party, and their political rhetoric clearly promised broader social opportunities for all strata of Christian Hungarian society, not just for the relatively small number of those who thought of themselves as the "gentlemanly middle class." The party's supporters came from a broad spectrum, attracting lower-middle- and middle-class tradesmen and shopkeepers eager for the social and economic privileges enjoyed by Hungary's traditional elites.[6] Arrow Cross propaganda also included frequent paeans to the value of peasant labor, so that smallholders, despairing of any significant government-sponsored land reform, turned to the Arrow Cross for a more vigorous approach to these issues.[7] The fas-

3. Sipos, *Imrédy Béla*, and Nicholas M. Nagy-Talavera, *The Green Shirts*, 83–171.

4. Deák, "Hungary," *The European Right: A Historical Profile*, 390–91.

5. Margit Szöllösi-Janze, *Die Pfeilkreuzlerbewegung in Ungarn: Historischer Kontext, Entwicklung, und Herrschaft* (Munich: R. Oldenbourg, 1989). See also Miklós Lackó, *Arrow-Cross Men, National Socialists, 1935–44* (Budapest, 1969).

6. See especially György Ránki's analysis of Arrow Cross support in the election of 1939. "The Fascist Vote in Budapest in 1939," in *Who Were the Fascists? Social Roots of European Fascism*, ed. Stein U. Larsen, Bernt Hagtvet, and Jan P. Myklebust (Bergen: Universitetsforlaget, 1980), 401–16.

7. Szöllösi-Janze, *Die Pfeilkreuzlerbewegung in Ungarn*, 133–47.

cists made inroads into Hungary's industrial working classes, enjoying support particularly among unorganized factory and mine workers. Finally, the party enjoyed the support of disillusioned migrant day workers in urban areas, as well as university students. Some on the radical right, who felt that the long-hoped for "changing" of the social and economic "guard" should be limited in scope and should extend only to themselves, feared that the Arrow Cross was simply a vehicle to bring the rabble into public affairs. For this reason, some leading extreme right politicians kept their distance from Szálasi, preferring more exclusive antisemitic parties. Many others, however, saw in the Arrow Cross Party the only viable alternative in the historical context of the late 1930s to Hungary's conservative political establishment.[8]

Irredentism also inspired many to support the Arrow Cross. Even though Hungary's political establishment had been forced to sign the Treaty of Trianon in 1920, every Hungarian public figure continued to call for border revisions at the first opportunity. By the late 1930s, however, Hungarians had come to very different ideas about how these goals might be soonest achieved. Traditional conservatives like István Bethlen looked to Great Britain out of political conviction and temperament, seeing in the British Tories the most congenial partners in any future diplomatic negotiations. Across the extreme right a different view prevailed. Here, attention was fixed on Nazi Germany, a state that had radically altered the balance of power on the continent in only a few short years. Alliance with Germany, many hoped, would be the key to resurrecting Greater Hungary from its destruction at Trianon. Because the party enjoyed particularly close ties with the Nazi Party, the Arrow Cross stood to benefit from this widespread assumption. In pamphlets and speeches, party leaders called insistently for the restoration of Greater Hungary; Szálasi himself spoke often, if vaguely, of the "Carpatho-Danubian Great Fatherland." As in all things, the Arrow Cross leader's personal views on this issue were peculiar and often unfathomable. Szálasi, for example, often described Greater Hungary as the "landscape land," a country in which every ethnic group might have its own region within a Magyar-dominated state. The details of his vision were unimportant. What mattered was his style, consciously modeled on the Nazi German example. As Germany continued to run the diplomatic tables in the 1930s, many Hungarians believed that a fascist party of their own might be able to ride the spirit of the times and achieve similar foreign policy triumphs.[9]

In military circles, interest in the new fascist party was particularly

8. Ibid., 183–86.
9. Nagy-Talavera, *The Green Shirts*, 114–18.

strong. Most of the officers in the Hungarian army were convinced that war was coming again to Europe, and that an alliance with Nazi Germany was vital to Hungary's interests. They also believed, as Hungary's fascists did, that the army was destined to play a central role in the resurrection of the nation. Largely appointed by Gyula Gömbös in the 1930s, these military men embraced Szálasi's view that "the war of the future [would] be total" and that "only those nations will emerge successfully where the masses stand united behind the fighting army." Like Szálasi, they also insisted that Hungary must fight that "war of the future" as a Christian nation. In the coming clash with the forces of Judeo-Bolshevism and archaic liberalism, it was essential that Hungary link its struggle for Greater Hungary with the larger defense of a Christian moral order. For this reason, Szálasi's views on the role of the army in national renewal were popular in military circles: "When the Army sees that in the nation the three pillars of Religion, Patriotism, and Discipline have been shaken, then it is the Army's duty to force the nation back on these pillars." Only if it were firmly anchored in Christian national ideals would Hungary be able to achieve its diplomatic and military objectives.[10]

However, the Christian moral order as it was embraced by the extreme right clearly served nationalist politics above all else. Much as prominent Nazi leaders in Germany embraced the idea of "positive" Christianity as an ideal of Christian faith that would transcend confessional divisions and become a kind of unifying national religion, Szálasi wrote in *The Road and the Way* that it was the duty of every "Magyar priest" to be "the priest and brother of every Magyar and, according to the commands of his faith, should bring his Magyar brothers closer to God, but not as Catholics, Calvinists, Lutherans, Greek Catholics, Greek Orthodox, or Unitarians."[11] Christian Hungarians would be, first and foremost, Hungarians. In similar fashion, members of the extreme right often preferred to invoke the "God of the Hungarians" (*a magyarok Istene*) in their public statements rather than more confessionally specific intercessors like the Virgin Mary, emphasizing with this phrase the national unity proclaimed by the romantic nationalist poet Sándor Petőfi in his 1848 National Song.[12] Of course, it was

---

10. Deák, "Hungary," 393–94.
11. From Ferenc Szálasi, *Út és cél* (1935). Excerpted in *Szálasi Ferenc alapvető munkája és 3 beszéde* (Buenos Aires: Hungarista Mozgalom kiadása, 1959), 11. On the idea of "positive Christianity," see Richard Steigmann-Gall, *The Holy Reich*, esp. 13–86.
12. The phrase "God of the Hungarians" (*a magyarok Istene*) was widely used in the nineteenth century. During the late 1930s, it was typically a code word for extreme nationalism. For an example of religious dissent, see, e.g., the outraged reaction of a Calvinist writer who objected to the idea that God might be the exclusive property of the Hungarians: B. Á. (Balla Árpád), "Magyarok Istene a rádióban," *Lelkészgyesület* 33, no. 6 (10 February 1940): 21–22.

not exactly clear how these sentiments would be expressed in the church-state relations of a future fascist regime. Still, religious leaders felt they had good reason to fear for the independence of their churches and their religious schools. From everything Szálasi said and wrote, it seemed entirely possible that a fascist regime would try to reduce the Christian churches to large nationalist associations with no special status and nothing in particular to distinguish them legally from secular organizations possessed of the same nationalist zeal. Such language unnerved Hungary's religious leaders, already concerned about the way in which the Nazi Party in Germany had dealt with the Christian churches there. Catholics throughout Europe, in particular, were appalled that the German Catholic Church had been compelled to disband many of its associations and that Catholic youth groups would be dissolved in the Hitler Youth with little or no provision for their Catholic religious education.[13] Indeed, Pope Pius XI had condemned these policies in his encyclical letter *Mit brennender Sorge*, decrying the measures as a violation of the concordat that the Reich had signed with the Vatican in 1933. Of course, Szálasi himself was a devout Catholic, unlike Adolf Hitler. Even so, the Hungarian fascist leader's views on the role of religion in national politics seemed to mirror the stance taken by Nazi ideologues in Germany.

Religious leaders also had reason to wonder exactly how seriously Szálasi and his associates took the Christianity in Christian nationalist ideology. Hungary's fascists certainly celebrated the history of Christendom in Hungary without reservation, though in a way markedly different from the vision of the past embraced by the country's conservative establishment. For example, the cult of St. István was far less important to them than it was to Hungary's anti-Nazi conservatives. More often, the radical right held up another Hungarian saint, St. László, instead. Successor to István's crown after a chaotic period marked by bitter feuding and numerous rival pretenders to the throne, King László was highly regarded for deepening the nation's commitment to Christendom while at the same time resisting the political demands of the church in Rome, thereby proving himself to radical nationalists in the twentieth century to be the ideal fusion of Christianity and nationalist zeal. King László also appealed to the military, having undertaken eight successful campaigns during his lifetime, including the conquest of Croatia in 1091. Finally, László also forbade the marriage between Christians and Jews in his kingdom, an act that radical antisemites interpreted without hesitation as an act of racial self-defense to be emulated in the present. For all these reasons, portraits

---

13. Guenter Lewy, *The Catholic Church and Nazi Germany* (New York: McGraw Hill, 1964)

of St. László, rather than St. István, could often be found hanging in fascist party offices. In the fall of 1944, the first Hungarian SS division was named in his honor as well.[14]

But Hungary's fascists also celebrated the role that Hungary's original pagan leaders had played in their nation's history with open zeal, mythologizing a confused account of Hungarian origins in which racial ideology was central.[15] Like many adherents of national socialism in Germany, Hungary's fascists easily blended Christian symbolism and visions of blood and race.[16] Szálasi's views on Christian doctrine were bizarre, to say the least: in his idle moments, the Arrow Cross leader researched Jesus' racial origins, concluding that Christ had not been Jewish, but had in fact been a member of the "Godvanian race." For others in the movement, racial ideology coexisted more uneasily with Christian teaching. Many of the movement's ideologists rejected the Jewishness of Christ and called openly for a Christianity purified of Jewish influence and based on a clearly Aryan or Turanian foundation.[17] There was precedent for this. In Nazi Germany, such theories had even been taken up by Protestant theologians eager to cleanse their faith of Jewish traces.[18] In Hungary, however, Christian religious leaders, both Protestant and Catholic, rejected such proposals and worried openly about the resurgence of "neopaganism" in Christian Hungary. Indeed, prominent Catholic and Protestant figures wrote publicly about the impossibility of defining Hungarian identity on the basis of racial purity: in 1939, the Catholic historian Gyula Szekfű edited a collection of essays on this theme entitled *What Is the Hungarian?* to which László Ravasz, bishop of the Reformed Church's Danubian Church District, contributed an article.[19] At the same time, church leaders could not ignore the political support which the Arrow Cross enjoyed. Its platform of radical change—of a complete remaking of national society, however vaguely defined—inspired hope in many who did not see it in the continued rule of Hungary's conservative elites. By comparison, the Christian nationalism that religious leaders proposed

---

14. See, e.g., Pál Koltay, *Szent László a m. kir. honvédgyalogság védszentje* (kiadja a m. kir. 18. honvéd kiegészítő leventeparancsnokság, Békés: Petőfi ny., 1944).
15. János Gyurgyák discusses the most important figures in *A zsidókérdés Magyarországon*, 446–71.
16. Richard Steigmann-Gall, *The Holy Reich.*
17. Nagy-Talavera, *The Green Shirts*, 119–20. "Turanian" refers to a (supposedly) racially pure Hungarian nation's origins on the steppes of Central Asia. The "Godvanians" were entirely the product of Szálasi's odd, but ever fertile, imagination.
18. See, e.g., Susannah Heschel, "When Jesus Was an Aryan: The Protestant Church and Antisemitic Propaganda," in *Betrayal: German Churches and the Holocaust*, ed. Robert P. Ericksen and Susannah Heschel (Minneapolis: Fortress Press, 1999), 68–89.
19. *Mi a magyar?* ed. Gyula Szekfű (Budapest: Magyar Szemle Társaság, 1939).

seemed weak indeed. Their dilemma only became more vexing as Hungary's fascist movements increased in strength.

Catholic Hungary: Defense Bastion of Christian Europe

Religious and secular conservatives viewed the rising tide of Arrow Cross activism with alarm. Though István Bethlen, the former prime minister, had been out of office since 1931, he and his political allies still exerted a great deal of influence. In these years, Bethlen increasingly had the ear of the regent, Miklós Horthy, whose sympathies for the extreme right were more and more tempered by his concern for law and order. Hungary's conservatives also still controlled important branches of the government, especially the Ministry of Interior, which controlled the police. As the ranks of the Arrow Cross swelled in 1937 and 1938, police and gendarmes broke up numerous fascist rallies, imprisoning prominent Arrow Cross agitators and shutting down their newspapers. At the same time, conservatives looked for ways to undermine the tremendous appeal of fascism to so many people. In this regard, 1938 presented a heaven-sent opportunity, for that year was the nine hundredth anniversary of the death of St. István, the saint and Christian king who had come to embody a conservative vision of Christian Hungary and the legitimacy of its social order during the interwar years. For years, the Hungarian Catholic Church, supported by the Vatican, had been planning a year's worth of festivities to celebrate the legacy of Hungary's patron saint to Catholics in Hungary and around the world. The grandest event of all was to come in the spring of 1938: the International Eucharistic Congress, held in Budapest that year as a special tribute to the role Hungary's first Christian king had played in the history of Christendom in Europe. As preparations began for this Catholic celebration, conservatives could look forward to a public symbolic display of Hungary's timeless social order, vigilant against extremists on both the far left and the far right.

Hungary's Catholic leaders, joined by church officials in the Vatican, had always imagined the congress as a festive display of international opposition to Bolshevik revolution from the left. Events in Spain in the mid 1930s had given church leaders a new sense of urgency in its fight against the "godlessness" which they saw emanating from the Soviet Union. As the Spanish Civil War intensified after 1936, Catholic opinion throughout Europe was horrified by news that fighters loyal to the Republican government frequently ransacked and burnt churches, and beat and sometimes killed priests and nuns to punish the clergy for supporting Franco, the

Phalangists, and the forces of conservative restoration in Spain. To Catholics everywhere, this was proof that Bolshevism was on the march throughout Europe, presenting an imminent threat to social and moral order. Béla Bangha, editor of Hungary's foremost Catholic journal, had made the congress's anti-Bolshevist nature clear in an article written one year before the congress was to be held. The congress came, he declared, "in the middle of a world turned toward Bolshevism, at the height of social hatred and destructive anarchy. . . . The calling is ours to give joyful voice, in this darkened and alienated world, to the most beautiful ardor of belief and love of Christ!"[20] In the face of this "hatred" and "anarchy," the Catholic historical narrative of Hungary as a bastion of defense for Christendom suited organizers in the Vatican perfectly. Cardinal Eugenio Pacelli explicitly invoked this tradition at the opening ceremony. In a long speech, the Vatican state secretary, speaking in the name of the ailing Pope Pius XI, recapitulated the basic themes of Christian Hungarian history as they had been imagined by Hungary's Catholic intellectuals, praising Hungarians for their defense of "Christian civilization" in the face of the Turkish infidels. The Eucharistic Congress, he maintained, would serve to renew this defense of Christendom in an age once more troubled by unbelief, to "awaken in the hearts of those who participate therein the spirit which creates the heroes to save the world of today and the human race, to defend the Church and Christian civilization against the leaders of religious negation and of social revolution by opposing them, as did Hungary of the seventeenth century."[21] Hungary was thus a model of a Christian nation that had united to face down an enemy in defense of their faith, their Christian civilization, and their traditional social order.

By 1938, however, the Congress had also become a chance for the Catholic Church to express its concerns about Germany's Nazi regime and the rising tide of radical fascism throughout Europe. Of course, the Vatican continued to perceive Bolshevism as, by far, the greater menace to Christendom, even as the German Reich annexed Austria and as fascist movements in Hungary and elsewhere grew in strength. In a clear reference to events in Spain, Congress organizers described Bolshevik atrocities against Christian morality in the most graphic terms, citing "desecrated altars, pillaged churches . . . thousands of priests, nuns, and monks martyrized, millions of the faithful murdered and tortured to death."[22] Yet, they also mentioned "religious persecutions of another character: the inner conscience

20. Béla Bangha, "Mit várhatunk az Eucharisztikus Világkongresszustól?" *Magyar Kultúra* 24, no. 5 (5 March 1937): 131–33.

21. *Album Congressus XXXIVi Eucharistici Internationalis* (Budapest: Sumptibus et typis Societati Sancti Stephani, 1938), 135.

22. Ibid., 112.

of man violated, his religious sentiments held up to mockery, the youth of the land misled by false propaganda, the very soul of the people poisoned by brutal means." In the wake of the papal letter *Mit brennender Sorge*, these remarks were a clear, if more abstract, reference to the religious politics of Nazi Germany. Similarly, Cardinal Pacelli used the congress to discuss the church's timeless role as guardian against social upheaval from any quarter, right or left. Communism, in his evaluation, remained the greater evil, but he was also critical of those who turned to the new fascist movements. "In the face of the violent upheaval which the pioneers of atheistic communism are trying to spread through the world, it is the right, it is the duty, of the threatened nations to oppose it for their own sake, and not to allow the destroyers of Christian society to carry into other nations their incendiary torches of revolution and class war. On the other hand, no illusion could be more pitiful, nor in the long run more dangerous, than to try in this reaction to do without the spiritual strength which the faith in God and Christ gives the individual and society."[23] The church, Pacelli claimed, was indispensable in the battle to save Christian society in Europe from the perils of Communism; any movement which thought it could fight Bolsheviks without the moral authority of the church was ultimately doomed to fail.

Hungarian Catholics shared the Vatican's sense of the Budapest Eucharistic Congress as an event at once both anti-Communist and antifascist. Leading figures in the Hungarian church drew the same comparisons between Bolshevism and Nazism in Germany and at home that Cardinal Pacelli had done. In the new year's edition of the journal *Politics*, for example, the archbishop of Kalocsa, Count Gyula Zichy, wrote that "with dismay, we saw in the course of the old year that radical ideas and trends grew in our country as well, and that, under the slogan and banner of various sorts of crosses, the ever more unrestrained arrow cross agitation upset the whole country."[24] Against this, the church, Zichy vowed, remained resolute in its "battle against extremisms," no matter the quarter from which such radical trends might come. Zsigmond Mihalovics, president of the Hungarian Catholic Action's presidial committee, emphasized the importance of the congress's mission for the interests of the state, declaring the congress to be "Hungary's greatest affair and its most serious and most precious concern. All Hungarian Catholicism, the whole of Hungarian society, indeed the official state itself shares in this concern."[25]

23. Ibid., 136.
24. Count Gyula Zichy, "Küzdelem a szélsőségek ellen," *Politika* 7, no. 1 (2 January 1938): 1–2.
25. Zsigmond Mihalovics, "Az Eucharisztikus Kongresszus hajnalán," *Magyar Kultúra* 25, no. 10 (20 May 1938): 291–2.

The congress would be a formal reenactment of Hungary's thousand-year Christian traditions and a sign of their enduring power. For its defense of social stability against right-wing radicals, the church received a lot of good press from liberal, generally anticlerical papers eager to see the symbols of St. István as the basis of an explicitly antifascist front. One even concluded a printed interview with Zsigmond Mihalovics with quite uncharacteristic praise for the work of religious organizations like Catholic Action.[26]

Hungary's fascists seized on public statements such as Mihalovics's interview to expose the hypocrisy they found in the church. Had not the church formerly been among the most outspoken critics of Budapest's liberal newspapers, they asked? In their own newspaper, the Arrow Cross provocatively counterposed the church's antisemitic past with their supposed equivocations in the present. "We see with deep dismay and sorrow that they [i.e., church leaders like Mihalovics] are afraid for the Eucharistic Congress' sake of those people who, both before the war, as well as under Communism, defended the Church with their blood."[27] The reference was to the counterrevolution of 1919, in which both churchmen and secular anti-Communists had joined forces to root out the vestiges of Béla Kun's short-lived Bolshevik regime. Thus, fascists were keen to present the church as an irresolute member of a common Christian nationalist front. The authors of this particular article underscored their dismay by simply reproducing in its entirety an article that had first run in the Catholic newspaper *Constitution* more than twenty years earlier. The piece was entitled "The Jewish Press against Christianity." As the fascist paper had already claimed that the newspaper in which Mihalovics had given his interview was Jewish-owned, no further editorial comment was deemed necessary.

Despite all this, the congress concluded without disturbance. For five days in May 1938, public life in Hungary was given over to the celebration of Hungarian Catholicism. Tens of thousands of Catholic pilgrims and dozens of cardinals and archbishops from around the world gathered in Budapest for a succession of masses, conferences, and festivals. Cardinal Pacelli himself led a mass in the capital's Heroes' Square, a rite attended by Hungary's leading politicians, both Catholic and Protestant. All this was followed by special celebrations to honor St. István in Esztergom, the primatial seat, and around the country. Yet the warm feeling of unity that the congress organizers had tried to inspire did not last much

26. "Mihalovics Zsigmond kanonok nyilatkozata a vakmerő nyilas támadásról," *Társadalmunk* 9, no. 3 (21 January 1938): 5.

27. "A Társadalmunk, a Szív, és a katolikus sajtóegyesület háborúelőtti kiadványai a zsidó sajtóról," *Összetartás* (6 March 1938): 11.

beyond Pacelli's departure from Budapest. Already in the last hours of the congress weekend, Arrow Cross supporters littered Budapest's streets and tram cars with flyers depicting the message "K.U.J."[28] The acronym, Hungarian for "After the Congress, it's our turn," was an ominous sign that the social stability that the congress had symbolized had been simply a respite and not a harbinger of things to come. Indeed, Arrow Cross violence in Budapest only became more extreme during the summer months of 1938.[29] Moreover, the common front of church and state did not inspire wider reverence for the existing social order in Hungary. Populist critics continued to argue that whole communities of the Hungarian people remained impoverished in a country run by a tiny elite. Nor were all Hungarians willing to accept the national unity symbolized by reverence to St. István. The vision of Christian Hungary offered to the nation during the Eucharistic Congress may have enjoyed official sanction in May 1938. It did not, however, mask the fact that other visions existed as well.

We Are the New *Kuruc*! Protestants, Populism, and the "Third Way"

Though leaders of the Reformed Church resented the explicitly Catholic character of the St. István ideology and the Eucharistic Congress,[30] they were no less committed to social stability than were their Catholic counterparts. With the elevation of László Ravasz to the position of bishop of the Danubian Church District in 1921, the Reformed Church had clearly indicated its willingness to take a place alongside the Catholic Church within the sociopolitical order of interwar Christian Hungary. Like the Catholic episcopate, Hungary's Protestant bishops likened Arrow Cross agitation to the revolutionary demagoguery of the Bolsheviks whom they had opposed in the years after World War I. In the same issue of *Politics* in which the Catholic archbishop of Kalocsa had proclaimed his church's "battle against extremisms," the Calvinist bishop of the Transtibiscan Church District, Károly Makláry, wrote that "the Arrow Cross movement originated in chaotic and irresponsible demagogy; its rude agitation is not a political movement that runs within normal bounds, but is a revolutionary phenomenon ready for destruction, against which it is not only the right of every

28. For *Kongresszus Után Jövünk*. My thanks to Professor István Deák for sharing his memory of this with me.
29. Some particular incidents are described in Lackó, *Arrow-Cross Men, National Socialists, 1935–1944*, 47ff.
30. Klimó, *Nation, Konfession, Religion*, 274ff.

stratum of Hungarian society, but also its duty to organize as soon as possible and as thoroughly as possible." He concluded by comparing the Arrow Cross to the Communist threat: "Revolutionary destruction, whether it wears red or green rags, always comes with devastation."[31]

At the same time, Protestant churchmen openly acknowledged the tremendous inequities in Hungary's social system. Already in the mid 1930s, many pastors, especially those of a younger generation, had become active in bringing to public attention the misery in which ethnic Magyar peasants lived in many parts of Hungary. They had blamed Hungary's social and political elites for doing nothing to alleviate this dire poverty and had even raised the specter of ethnic extinction along the borders of the state. Now, Arrow Cross leaders seemed to be echoing much of their rhetoric, promising radically different prospects for the nation's peasants in a Hungary dominated by fascists. In the face of this challenge, church leaders found themselves forced to debate how to address social inequity without opening up the door to radical social upheaval. In his opening address to a 1937 meeting of the mission committee of the Reformed Church's General Synod,[32] Jenő Balogh, the synod's lay cochairman, tried to strike a balance: the church, he said, "had to examine the existing problems, injustices, and abuses which arise from the abandonment of particular social classes. The Reformed Church also has the duty to work together with others on the creation of a more just, more Christian economic and social order. But it does not want to achieve this by radical revolutionary means, but instead with gradual and continuous progress."[33] Other speakers made similar distinctions between right and wrong paths to social reform. Sándor Makkai, a prominent theological lecturer at the University of Debrecen, emphasized again that radicals, working without a proper sense of the spirit that ought to inspire a Christian nation, could have no hope of lifting their people out of misery: "Only the truly elect can carry out mission work, not amateurs and dilettantes."[34] The language was specifically Calvinist, but the political sentiment behind it was apparent. Fascists, obsessed with wild and impractical

31. Károly Makláry, "Válasz Zichy Gyula gróf kalocsai érseknek," *Politika* 7, no. 1 (2 January 1938): 3–4. Arrow Cross members wore green shirts as part of their uniform, and were often called simply "the green shirts."

32. The synod is the main legislative and executive body of Hungary's Reformed Church. It consisted of lay and clerical leaders from each of the church districts, who met to formulate policies for the entire church. The synod's mission committee was charged with establishing broad guidelines for all missionary work conducted in Hungary.

33. As reported in *Református Élet*. "Kronika: A missziói küldetése csak az egyháznak van . . . ," *Református Élet* 4, no. 40 (2 October 1937): 379. The conference was held in Budapest, 27–29 September 1937.

34. Ibid.

political schemes, would only destroy exactly those things they wanted most to save.

This fine balance threatened to alienate the younger generation of Calvinist churchmen. By the late 1930s, many Calvinists within or sympathetic to Hungary's populist movement openly rejected the unjust social system that conservative elites were so eager to defend against revolution from the left or right. For them, the traditionally pro-Habsburg and deeply Catholic "St. István idea" invoked at the 1938 Eucharistic Congress was an almost criminal ideology that only deepened the division between a wealthy elite and the real Hungarian nation of ethnic Magyar peasants teetering on the edge of starvation. For conservative politicians, a symbolic narrative in which the Catholic Counterreformation mediated the essential truths of medieval Christianity to the present might count as the most usable of histories. To populists, it was simply the story of Hungary's colonization by a foreign (and German-speaking) dynasty, a tale of humiliation and debasement that did not gain in virtue when put in the service of antifascist politics. There was no point in arguing, as one populist mockingly wrote, that "brown [i.e., Nazi] German influence is impermissible, because of worldview reasons; black [i.e., clerical] German influence is permissible and desirable, because it means the defense of an endangered worlview and self-interest."[35] In the end, there was no difference. Both were "German," foreign powers that sought to dominate the true Hungarian nation. Real national sovereignty—the hope of a socially equitable Hungary ruled by and for ethnic Hungarians—had to remain the highest social good.

As the nation's political elite embraced a profoundly conservative Catholic national history for political reasons, populists responded with the counterhistory they had already used vigorously in the natality debates of the early 1930s. In it, East countered West, and Protestantism opposed the Catholic Church. One contributor to *Hungarian Way*, a "Reformed oriented"[36] journal with close ties to the Calvinist youth group Soli Deo Gloria, spelled out these oppositions.[37] Eastern Hungary symbolized national unity, whereas Western Catholic Hungary had fractured the national community. In the West, the Catholic Habsburgs had "accomplished the Counterreformation" and had created an unjust feudal order in Hungary by parceling out land to loyal nobles. In the minds of Hungary's populist intellectuals, Catholicism, so crucial to the "St. István idea," embodied a Hungary divided socially into rich and poor, haves and have-nots. This, to

---

35. Tamás Esze, "A kuruc legitimizmus," *Magyar Út* 6, no. 46 (11 November 1937): 2–3.
36. The journal *Magyar Út* is described as a "Reformed oriented journal" in *Újszászy Kálmán emlékkönyv*, 44.
37. György Bodor, "Az új kurucokhoz," *Magyar Út* 8 (7 January 1939): 2.

men like the Calvinist pastor Béla Pap, was the crux of the issue. The opposed symbols of East and West, Protestantism and Catholicism, stood for "a Hungariandom in and for itself and the advocates of a second-class Hungariandom immobile in foreign service. The Hungary of lords and the Hungary of the people stand against each other here, a fawning and feudal Hungary afraid of itself and the new social and democratic popular (*népi*) Hungary."[38] The remedy was clear to another writer in the same journal: "We must openly and sincerely deny this [Western] past and join with that real and existing tradition of independence, which offers to all those who worry for Hungarian survival a vast strength deriving from 400 years of bitter struggle."[39] Hungarians had to become "new *kuruc*," taking up again the legacy of the early-eighteenth-century anti-Habsburg, anti-Catholic rebels. Only by turning to a more authentic (and more Protestant) national history could Hungarians find the "third way" (*a harmadik út*), a truly Hungarian path laid out neither by communists nor by a capitalist oligarchy.[40] The St. István idea, twisted by Hungary's rulers to legitimize their own rule and thus a symbol of the unjust "Hungary of lords," had no place in the national future. Rallying to its banner, even for the sake of warding off the fascist threat, would only prove Hungarians no wiser than Esau, the short-sighted son of Isaac who had "sold his birthright for a . . . mess of pottage."[41]

Such passionate advocacy of a "third way" or a uniquely "Magyar way" led many populists, including the Reformed churchmen among them, to look sympathetically on radical right-wing movements in Hungary. Of course, everyone associated with populism in Hungary, church and lay figures alike, took a firm stand against subordinating Hungarian society to foreign domination. In this sense, they were anti-Nazi (or, more precisely, opposed to Nazi German imperialism in East-Central Europe). Yet some writers left their readers with the impression that home-grown right-radicalism ought to be judged by a different standard. Opinions like these also found their way into print in those journals read by younger, politically active Protestants. One contributor to *Hungarian Way*, writing of the "messianistic expectations" he saw among poor Hungarians in the countryside, noted that just across the border (he was writing after the Nazi German annexation of Austria in March 1938) "a great empire has undergone a tremendous national and social rebirth of historical importance."[42] He left it to his readers to infer that this might in some way be a

38. Béla Pap, "A sok üres frázis . . . ," *Magyar Út* 6, no. 46 (11 November 1937).
39. Bodor, "Az új kurucokhoz."
40. The phrase is László Németh's.
41. Béla Pap, "A sok üres frázis . . ."
42. Dániel Fábián, "A zsidóság és a földkérdés," *Magyar Út* 7, no. 18 (5 May 1938): 6–7.

model for Hungarians to emulate. Another wrote that the right wing in Hungary had a valuable role to play in fighting "feudalism," and that Hungarians would do well to hear them out. Such arguments clearly compelled some Reformed pastors to support the Arrow Cross. One Arrow Cross Party member, who described himself as a "village pastor" in Somogy County, published an article in the Arrow Cross paper *Solidarity*, expressing deep disappointment that his bishop, Károly Makláry, had spoken so strongly against Hungary's fascist movements. "Does he not see," the pastor asked, "the need for a more truly social order?"[43] Inspired by similar sentiments, two of the sixty-three Arrow Cross candidates in the 1939 elections were Calvinist ministers.[44] Both won their contests and took their seats in parliament.

Reformed pastors within the populist movement also embraced the antisemitic rhetoric shared by all segments of the Christian national public. Anti-Jewish laws, they agreed with Arrow Cross party leaders, could be a way to overthrow a "feudal" social structure and reallocate wealth, taking it from "rich Jewish financiers" and transferring it to the needy millions that made up the "other Hungary." In this spirit, the Calvinist pastor and editor of *Hungarian Way*, Béla Pap, argued that "in the interest of Hungarian national organization, a government up to its high calling has not only the right but also the duty to force both large property owners and Big Business to accept sacrifices." It was unacceptable that every attempt to create a more equitable distribution of property should be condemned "with clever rabulistic arguments" as a kind of Bolshevism. Such intransigence would only produce even greater zeal for social change. Pap left no doubt who, in his mind, would be the ultimate targets of this struggle for social justice: "The lords of property should not forget . . . if they are not ready for sacrifice, or if they try to evade it, a burning reaction will not take 8 or 20 percent, but everything, indeed it will destroy not only the property but also the eternal Shylocks who own it."[45]

Older Reformed Church leaders worried that so many within and outside their church were embracing antisemitism for what they understood to be the wrong reasons. For decades, conservative Protestants had denounced both capitalism, and the social dislocation that it produced, as the product of a distinctly "Jewish spirit." They too had been concerned that Hungarians of Jewish origin seemed to wield a disproportionately large measure of power in the economic development of their country, and like their Catholic counterparts, had long hoped for a new Christian

---

43. Dezső Tánczos, "Visszhang," *Összetartás* (9 January 1938): 11.
44. Nagy-Talavera, *The Green Shirts*, 153.
45. Béla Pap, "Végre! . . . ," *Magyar Út* 7, no. 10 (10 March 1938): 1.

middle-class that might direct Hungary's economic development along a path more compatible with social harmony and traditional moral values. For these reasons, church leaders had long supported some kind of government action against the "Jewish spirit." However, they were wary of radical social upheaval and feared that excessively zealous discrimination against Hungary's Jewish minority might have unexpected and undesired consequences. Thus, leading figures in the church preferred to speak of their struggle against "Jewry" in spiritual, rather than economic, terms. Social stability, they argued, depended on the ubiquity of a Christian spirit in all political and social activities. Church leaders consistently reminded their congregations that social reform must be tempered by higher spiritual ideals; without them, radicals only tightened the grip that secular materialism held on Hungarian society. In one article, the church's leading expert on Christian-Jewish relations discussed the role of "spirit" in solving social problems like the "Jewish question:" "Without this key, every protest is but a stupid blustering and every argument is futile. Without it, it is possible to solve neither the Jewish nor any other question, because we only increase disorder and pour oil on the fire."[46] The church did not dispute the issues that many of the right wing reformers raised. Nor did they repudiate the antisemitic terms in which radicals framed those issues. Instead, arguing in explicitly anti-Jewish terms, church leaders tried to shift Hungary's "Jewish question" from the realm of concrete social policy to a more theoretical plane. In so doing, they hoped to blunt the power of the radical right.

Not all members of Hungary's Reformed Church were comfortable striking such fine balances between acceptable and unacceptable forms of antisemitism. One presbiter in Budapest, Károly Ratkai, recalled in 1946 that, after it became clear that many Calvinist churchgoers reacted negatively to openly antifascist statements, church leaders agreed that they would have to be much more circumspect. According to Ratkai, churchmen sympathetic to the Left were prevented from speaking publicly and from writing in church journals like *Reformed Life*. Although those journals never openly embraced figures like Szálasi, they did not explicitly denounce them either. Few other outlets remained for figures like Ratkai to express their concerns about what they believed to be a betrayal of the church's democratic principles.[47] Despite this, some Calvinist seminarians kept their distance from the most extreme right-wing (as well as left-wing) groups. Kálmán Újszászy, a leader among young Calvinists, recalled no "right-ward drift" among the students that he knew in Sárospatak. In-

46. Gyula Forgács, "A zsidókérdés," *Református Élet* 4, no. 17 (24 April 1937): 170–71.
47. Károly Ratkai, "A kálvinizmus örök," *Haladás* (12 January 1946): 2.

stead, he and his peers tried to keep their focus on those common social questions that linked populists across the political spectrum from the radical left to the radical right.[48] It seems, however, that these young seminarians made such political decisions on their own. In the face of an aggressive radical right, the leaders of the Reformed Church chose instead to emphasize those broad principles on which all Christian Hungarians could agree. By stressing spiritual antisemitism, rather than more disruptive plans to expropriate Jewish property, church leaders certainly drew distinctions between themselves and fascist parties like the Arrow Cross. No one, however, could mistake this for vigorous public opposition.

The Catholic Church and the Fascist Challenge

By the end of 1937, Catholic leaders began to realize that their public embrace of the conservative "St. István idea" was no guarantee that their church could remain aloof from the fascist challenge. In the spring of 1938, all Hungarian Catholics, clergy and lay, took part in the Eucharistic Congress with enthusiasm, openly avowing their nation's Catholic heritage. At the same time, however, there were signs that calls for radical social change being heard on the extreme right were not falling on deaf ears within the Catholic community. Throughout 1938, reports and rumors mounted that members of the Catholic clergy sympathized with the Arrow Cross. It is impossible to know how many priests supported Szálasi's movement in 1938. Nor can one really establish the depths of their commitment to the fascist party. Still, reports from police agents who had gone undercover to Arrow Cross meetings at party headquarters in Budapest made their way to the cardinal's desk in Esztergom. Their accounts told of a number of clergymen taking part enthusiastically. One report listed the names of ten priests who had recently joined. Another described a party dinner in a restaurant often frequented by Budapest's fascists; the informant spotted one priest in attendance despite the fact that the evening's speakers discussed their plans for an apolitical and subordinate church at some length.[49] Such reports were sometimes difficult to corroborate. In certain cases, the names proved to be wrong; on others, the priests were old and infirm and seemed unlikely to have engaged in political activity of any kind. Some priests, however, confirmed their involvement when asked. One, a chaplain in the Society of Eternal Prayer, ex-

48. *Újszászy Kálmán emlékkönyv*, 41–44.
49. Both of these reports are in the file EPL: Cat. D/C 1022/1940. The first is undated from 1938, document numbers 67–8; the second is dated 25 November 1938, document numbers 84–85.

plained that he was a close personal friend of Ferenc Szálasi, the Hungarian Nazi leader, and that only these bonds of friendship had compelled him to join the party.[50] Another, a religious instructor by the name of Lackovits, was less disingenuous.[51] He admitted to joining the party in mid April 1938, "solely on account of its anti-Jewish program." He went on to explain that his membership had only been "of theoretical character," that is, an intellectual sympathy for the party's goals without any regard for his own personal political advancement.

These and similar confessions upset church leaders, who thought it best that their clergy should display no sign of political opposition at all. The episcopal bench raised the issue at its meeting on 21 October 1937, concluding in its summary notes that "in the current politically tumultuous times, it is necessary that we protect our priests from radicalisms (e.g., the Arrow Cross movements)."[52] Though Catholic leaders had advocated public political engagement in earlier years to combat the threat to religion from left-wing progressives, the episcopate responded to the fascist threat by drawing a sharp line between religion and public politics. Cardinal Serédi emphasized this in a letter to his deputy in Budapest.

[You] know that from the beginning . . . I have tried to push the political activity of the clergy into the background. . . . Thus those reports according to which many of my young priests have recently engaged in radical political agitation and activity are all the more disconcerting. Please advise the Budapest clergy that, with the exception of those who have engaged in politics for a longer period with my express or tacit permission, they must devote their energies solely to the care of souls, putting aside any sort of political activity.[53]

The church was thus unwilling to condone even the least suggestion of political engagement. Clergymen, like Lackovits the theological instructor, got the message and quit the party. In a statement to his diocesan superiors, he promised to abstain "not only from any political connection, but also from its appearance as well."[54] In this way, the episcopate generally managed to keep its clergy from any formal political commitments.

At the same time, Catholic leaders were keenly aware that this theoretical stance had real practical drawbacks. The populist movement of the 1930s had generated great excitement among young Catholics as well, who were eager to put the institutional might of their church behind na-

50. EPL: Cat. D/C 1022/1940; letter of József Varga, 15 July 1938, document number 60.
51. EPL: Cat. D/C 1022/1940, letter of József Laczkovits, 4 August 1938
52. Reproduced in *A püspöki kar tanácskozásai*, ed. Jenő Gergely, 244.
53. EPL: Cat. D/C. 1022/1940. Cardinal Jusztinián Serédi to Deputy Archbishop János Mészáros, 11 May 1938, doc. number 69 and 71.
54. Ibid., Letter of J. Laczkovits.

tional efforts to lift Hungary's rural poor out of their poverty. By the late 1930s many of the organizations working under the umbrella of Hungary's Catholic Action had turned their attention to the social and economic problems plaguing Hungary's rural areas. For the most part, these groups directed their efforts toward cultural improvement, following Protestants in organizing adult education schools and youth groups. Some prominent figures within Catholic Action, however, also began to speak of land reform, raising the prospect of real conflict with the episcopate. Hungary's bishops never endorsed the idea of land redistribution in any guise, undermining the reformist intentions of Catholic Action organizers. Yet the dispute revealed the extent to which populist politics had affected the standing of the institutional church.

In response to the crisis, young Catholic leaders, at the behest of József Pehm, then still a parish priest in Zalaegerszeg but later to change his surname to Mindszenty as he rose in prominence, convened a conference on 19 April 1938 to clarify their position. After much deliberation, they produced a two-page document in which they warned that Catholic leaders had to take care not to be tarred with the brush of liberalism, simply because they opposed the Arrow Cross on certain issues.[55] As they put it, "The danger looms that, by a complete misunderstanding of the Church's past, we will be lumped together precisely with those / Jews, large landowners, etc. / against whom we have fought for decades."[56] To counteract this danger, reform-minded Catholics had to reaffirm explicitly their long-standing desire for a more vigorous approach to the "Jewish question" and remind the Hungarian public of their church's long history of antisemitic politics:

> We consider the Jewish question to be a social, economic, and worldview question. For fifty years, we and our predecessors, at the time of the height of the world of usury, stood on the side of Istóczy and later of the People's Party, even when practically everyone in the country was a friend of the Jews. The Christian party that we supported passed the one racial defense law, the *numerus clausus*, the odium of which we bear until this very day [i.e., within the "Jewish media"].[57]

The statement was a direct response to those who felt that the church was in some way holding to a middle-of-the-road course on anti-Jewish measures. For Pehm and his associates, the history of the church, including explicitly its legacy of antisemitic politics, made it a much better representative of the Christian nation than the Arrow Cross could ever hope to be.

55. EPL 1027/1940, copy of Pehm *mozgalom* platform
56. Ibid.
57. Ibid.

Many other Catholics, especially those in Catholic Action, the umbrella organization for all Catholic social initiatives, were equally concerned for the church's reputation as an institution committed to addressing the social and economic questions of the day. Several of them wrote letters to Cardinal Serédi, acknowledging that the church had to preserve its independence but worrying that, by categorically refusing to talk with the Arrow Cross, they could be burning bridges that they might one day need to cross.[58] Indeed, leaders of the Young Men's Agrarian League (KALOT), rural youth groups run by Catholic Action, even met with Ferenc Szálasi in April 1938 to discuss issues of mutual interest. Nothing came of the meeting beyond vague expressions of mutual respect, and the KALOT leaders soon ended their contact. However, the group continued to express its reformist zeal in terms that had much in common with secular right-radicals. In an essay written for the KALOT newspaper, József Közi-Horváth, a young priest working in the administration of Catholic Action, urged Catholic youth to support strong measures to "clean the country" of immigrant "Galician Jews," a group that by his references to large banking houses, leading newspapers, as well as village shopkeepers clearly encompassed all of Hungarian Jewry.[59] In another important series of articles, Közi-Horváth tried to find some balance between his church and the radical right: "It takes a good will . . . to say bravely that the Arrow Cross and national socialist economic and social demands are exaggerated and unrealizable, but at the same time to go [oneself] to the outermost extremes in the treatment of the problems and in the fulfillment of the demands."[60] To this end, he organized a short-lived movement of Catholic professionals interested in maintaining ties with secular radical-right movements. His efforts were in vain, as the group, which called itself the Blue Cross Movement, disbanded; its members generally joined the explicitly fascist parties.

These initiatives outraged a faction within the Catholic community deeply opposed to any dealings with fascist movements. These intellectuals gathered around the journal *Word of Our Times*, edited by the esteemed Catholic publicist, Count György Széchényi.[61] Contributors to the

58. Margit Balogh, *A KALOT*, 64–68.

59. József Közi-Horváth, "Nemzeti, szociális, és keresztény Nagymagyarország," *Dolgozó Fiatalság* 3, no. 4 (April 1938): 1–2.

60. József Közi-Horváth, "A magyarországi nemzetiszocialista pártok története, programmja, és jelenlegi állása," *Magyar Kultúra* 25, no. 4 (20 February 1938): 116–17. This is the third part of a serialized essay appearing in this journal: the first part was published in the 20 January 1938 issue, 48–52; the second in the 5 February 1938 issue, 75–78.

61. On the newspaper *Word of Our Times* (*Korunk Szava*), see the essay by Miklós Vásárhelyi, "Korunk Szava (1931–1938)," in *A bilincsbe vert beszéd: Vásárhelyi Miklós sajtótörténeti tanulmányai*, ed. Gábor Murányi (Budapest: Élet és Irodalom, 2002), 125–42.

journal, a group that included the Catholic historian Gyula Szekfű, openly chastised priests and prominent Catholic laity for speaking sympathetically of Hungarian fascist movements.[62] Nor did Széchényi shy away from controversy with more prominent figures in his church. In his most controversial article, he came very near to accusing members of the episcopate and the leaders of Catholic Action of willfully disregarding the precepts established by their pontiff in the encyclical *Mit brennender Sorge* and of lending tacit support to Hungary's Nazis. "Hitlerization," he maintained, "appeared in Hungary *expressis verbis* as a Catholic illness; since serious and consistent and suitably energetic opposition has not come from the part of the official Church, it [i.e., "Hitlerization"] has even been able to spread unchecked under the aegis of the A[ctio] C[atholica] [i.e., Catholic Action] as well."[63] In his frequent discussions of Catholic Action in Hungary, Széchényi felt that he could discern in the group's public declarations a tacit admiration for much of what the Nazi Party had achieved in Germany, especially in its "resolute" persecution of Bolshevism, Social Democracy, and the "Jewish spirit." In one article, Széchényi criticized a pamphlet written by József Közi-Horváth for this very reason, asking bluntly, "Do they [i.e., the Nazis] treat 'resolutely' and 'justly' with Jews and with Social Democracy in Germany or inhumanely and unjustly?"[64] Széchényi found such posturing to be examples of what he perceived to be moral duplicity within the church.

The leaders of Catholic Action were naturally outraged by these accusations. In a sharply worded letter to Cardinal Serédi, the organization's president, Zsigmond Mihalovics, reminded the primate that Catholic Action was a movement "which stands under the supervision of the highly esteemed Episcopal Bench and under the highest leadership of your Eminence [i.e., Serédi]."[65] Mihalovics explicitly rejected the insinuation that his organization was some kind of Trojan horse for "Hitlerism" in Hungary. He also took pains to defend his colleague, József Közi-Horváth. "[Széchényi] cannot stand Közi-Horváth. He holds him to be a Hitlerite, because Közi is an antisemite. But I can vouch for Közi before your Eminence, that he [Közi] stands far removed from Hitlerism."[66] Mihalovics concluded by informing Serédi that he had received many letters and

---

62. An example is Béla Horváth, "Levél egy plébánoshoz, aki cikket irt egy nyilas lapba," *Korunk Szava* 7, no. 20 (15 October 1937): 595.

63. Count György Széchényi, "Magyar hitleristák és az enciklika," *Korunk Szava* 7 (15 April 1937): 229–30.

64. Count György Széchényi, "Ártalmas védelem. Közi-Horváth József dr. füzete," *Korunk Szava* 7, no. 12 (15 June 1937): 357–38.

65. EPL. Cat. 21; 1613/1937; Zsigmond Mihalovics to Cardinal Jusztinián Serédi, 23 April 1937.

66. Ibid.

telegrams about this controversy from concerned Catholics throughout Hungary; the large majority, he claimed, stood behind him. The president of Catholic Action thus rejected Széchényi's argument that antisemitic rhetoric only played into the hands of the fascist movement. Cardinal Jusztinián Serédi and the rest of the episcopate were sympathetic to such arguments. Their opinion of Széchényi's activities found expression during the semiannual meeting of the episcopal bench held on 21 October 1937. At that meeting, the assembled bishops discussed the need to keep their priests from "radicalisms" and mentioned the Arrow Cross movements by name. Their interventions and inquiries after suspected Arrow Cross clergy throughout 1938 demonstrated their seriousness of purpose. Yet at that meeting, the bishops also discussed the need for Catholic papers to "exercise judgment in their criticism of the behavior of Church figures in connection with such movements."[67] In the official protocol of the meeting, the bishops listed one paper by name: György Széchényi's *Word of Our Times.*

Thus Catholic leaders took decisive measures to prevent their own clergymen from openly joining the fascist movement. However, Catholic leaders, both in and outside of Catholic Action, recognized that the extreme right had seized the initiative in pushing for anti-Jewish legislation. They made these demands in the name of Christian Hungary, an idea to which the church had committed itself for so long. Many Catholics felt that, György Széchényi's Cassandralike warnings to the contrary, the church had to meet the radical right halfway, by acting on those issues that the Arrow Cross had made their own, even as they drew careful distinctions between themselves and their fascist rivals. For many, the distinction that Zsigmond Mihalovics drew between acceptable antisemitism and "Hitlerism" was useful. The latter symbolized Nazi hostility toward the power that an independent church might wield. Catholic leaders were careful to insist on the place of religious expression in civil society and were rigorously opposed to any political movement that sought to reduce their church to some kind of association charged with preaching progovernment ethics. They thus saw in the Arrow Cross a movement that threatened to rob religion of its autonomy. Yet Catholic leaders generally answered this challenge by insisting that there was a correct way to address the menace that the "Jewish spirit" posed to society. Antisemitism, focused "rationally" on key economic and social questions and shorn of any wild myths of blood, was a necessary tool of governance. After some twenty years of Christian nationalist politics in Hungary, the rise of fascism was evidence that Christians still had unfinished business with the

67. *A püspöki kar tanácskozásai*, ed. Gergely, 244–45.

"Jewish morality" pervading their public life. The challenge for Catholics was to prove that their church remained the most qualified to speak in the name of the Christian Hungarian nation.

The First Jewish Law—1938

Faced with a rising tide of right-wing extremism, Hungary's secular political elite opted for a policy of appeasement. To preserve as much of Hungary's conservative social structure as possible, they chose to realize some of the extreme right's demands while suppressing the most disruptive of their demonstrations. In this way, they hoped to "take the wind out of the sails" of the fascists, as the popular phrase of the day had it. Even as the plans for the 1938 Eucharistic Congress were in their last stages and the festivities were about to begin, the governments of prime ministers Kálmán Darányi and then Béla Imrédy, a devout Catholic with excellent ties to Hungary's Catholic episcopate, moved ahead with preparations for Hungary's first piece of anti-Jewish legislation since the 1920 *numerus clausus* law. Introduced into Parliament in the spring of 1938, the law, subtitled the "law on the more efficient assurance of equilibrium in social and economic life," was designed to address the perceived overrepresentation of Jews in particular occupations. Given the fervor with which supporters of Hungary's extreme right parties demanded the jobs and property "usurped" from them, or so they claimed, by "alien Jews," the provisions of the law were modest. Law XV/1938, which soon became known as the First Jewish Law, set a cap of 20 percent on the ratio of Jews to non-Jews in the free professions (e.g., law and medicine) and among business employees. It has been estimated that Law XV/1938 was harsh enough to affect some fifteen thousand Hungarian Jewish citizens, depriving them of their property, their livelihood, or both.[68] To government officials, this limit seemed a generous compromise, since it exceeded by roughly fourfold the demographic ratio of Jews to non-Jews in Trianon Hungary. They then proceeded to issue a decree barring state employees from being members of political parties, a move understood to be directed against the many civil servants who had joined extreme right groups. They also arrested many prominent fascists on charges of disrupting the peace, including, in August 1938, Ferenc Szálasi himself. Despite these carrot and stick tactics, the déclassé civil servants and middle-class professionals who made up the backbone of the extreme right in Hungary, and who felt that

---

68. Randolph L. Braham, *The Politics of Genocide: The Holocaust in Hungary*, 2 vols., rev. and enl. edition (Boulder: Social Science Monographs, 1994), 128–29.

every job in a Christian nation should be reserved for Christians alone, remained unappeased. Almost as soon as the bill was made into law, the extreme right-wing press began to agitate for even harsher and more restrictive measures.

Hungary's Christian religious leaders publicly welcomed the 1938 Jewish Law. There were, of course, some voices of opposition: Count György Széchényi, an MP in parliament in addition to his other pursuits, voted against the First Jewish Law, calling it the vanguard of foreign ideas in his speech before the chamber. But his cardinal did not join him in opposition. Nor did the Reformed bishop László Ravasz, who spoke in the Upper House of Hungary's Parliament in favor of what became Law XV/1938—the First Jewish Law. In part, Ravasz said, he was motivated by a desire for the "country's peace and quiet."[69] Antisemitism had reached such a fever pitch, he maintained, that any attempt to restrain it could only lead to an unpredictable, but surely, worse situation. Yet he was also persuaded that the law was historically necessary. As a Christian minister, he could not renounce his Christian mission to spread the Gospel to all peoples, including Jews. Nor could he sit idly by while Jews as a people (*fajta*), possessed of an alien culture, a unique history, and a foreign mentality, subverted the indigenous way of life in Hungary. "Just sit," he asked his audience to imagine, "in a third class train on the way to Nyíregyháza [a town in northeastern Hungary], in which there are 60–70 Jews, with skullcaps and caftans, and Yiddish foaming on their lips, and ask yourselves: are these Hungarians?"[70] Only redeemed from their "Jewish-ness," fully assimilated and, most particularly, converted to Christianity, could Jews escape their utterly foreign culture and ever hope to find their place among Christian Hungarians. In Ravasz's view, Law XV had merit, since it was an act of discrimination tempered with charity. Even as it worked to eliminate "Jewishness" from Hungarian life, the law, as Ravasz understood it, offered Christianity to Jews as an alternate identity. "We must win over Jews, as individuals," he argued, "so that they might fight with us together against Jewry, the Jewish destiny, and humanity's Jewish complex." Exactly how Jews were supposed to find a place in a nation whose laws were explicitly antisemitic was unclear. Still, with this rousing, if contradictory, conclusion, Bishop Ravasz voted for the law.

Ravasz's Catholic counterparts followed a similar line of reasoning. Indeed, in a committee held before the debate in the Upper House to hammer out the language of the bill to be debated, Cardinal Jusztinián Serédi

---

69. Ravasz's speech is reproduced in Henrik Fisch, *Keresztény egyházfők felsőházi beszédei a zsidókérdésben* (Budapest: published by editor, 1947), 27–40.

70. Speech of László Ravasz on 24 May 1938 to the Upper House of the Hungarian Parliament. Reproduced in Fisch, *Keresztény egyházfők*, 34.

made the same kind of distinction. Justice, he said, knew no gradations or degrees; divine laws bound all men equally. Love, however, could be measured in degrees. He explained: "There can be and are degrees, because in the sense of natural law and positive divine laws we must, *ceteris paribus*, love better those who are nearest to us than those to whom more distant family, national, religious etc ties bind us." Serédi placed this remark in the context of his discussion of the proposed law's impact on converts. Like his fellow churchmen on the committee (among them the Catholic bishop of Csanád, Gyula Glattfelder), he argued strongly that all converts (and not just those who converted before 1 August 1919,[71] as the language of the bill had it) should be exempt from the law's penalties. Yet his ruminations on the degrees of love, and the ways in which national and religious ties determined them, left open the possibility that the church could support some kind of anti-Jewish discrimination. He too voted in favor of the law a few days later, even though his objections to the position of converts had not been answered.

Thus, leading figures in both the Catholic and Protestant churches sought to distance their faiths from right-wing radicalism. Hungary's Catholics could, of course, draw on a much richer set of political symbols to emphasize their church's commitment to social stability. The Eucharistic Congress, in particular, was a splendid display of the alliance between (Catholic) church and state that had opposed godlessness and unbelief in past centuries and that would continue to do so in the future. Yet, top Calvinist church leaders made their opposition to thoughtless social radicalism no less clear. Even if some younger Calvinists drifted closer to extreme right movements, propelled by their desire for real social change, the conservative elite of the Reformed Church resisted following them. Instead, they argued that there was a right way and a wrong way to carry out needed reforms. Both churches were also wary of any secular political movement that seemed hostile to independent religious life. At the same time, neither church could remain entirely aloof from right-wing politics. By the late 1930s, demands for social change were so widespread and so insistent that religious leaders could not risk seeming to oppose them. Church leaders, both Protestant and Catholic, had spent the previous two decades describing a Christian nation of Hungarians and calling for its cultural and social improvement. Now that these same leaders were faced with a mass movement seeking to make those claims a legal reality, they found their own ability to define the goals of nationalist policy and to de-

71. A date chosen because it marked the fall of Béla Kun's Bolshevik regime. The bill's sponsors maintained that any Jew who had converted to Christianity afterward, when antisemitism became a powerful political force, could only have done so from opportunistic motives. Only those who had converted before this date were judged to have done so sincerely.

termine the place of religion with the Hungarian nation-state increasingly undermined. In response, they could only draw distinctions between acceptable and unacceptable kinds of antisemitism, trying to lift the question from practical economic matters to a more rarified discussion of mentalities and spiritual qualities. For all these reasons, every church leader who stood in Parliament on 24 May 1938 spoke at length about conversion, and the immorality of racial theories, before voting in favor of the First Jewish Law. In the face of further anti-Jewish legislation, Hungary's Christian leaders pursued this strategy with ever greater desperation.

6

Race, Religion, and the Secular State

The Third Jewish Law, 1941

The triumph of the fascist Arrow Cross Party at the ballot box in May 1939 proved to be a high-water mark rather than a harbinger of things to come. Bowing to reformist pressure, the government had introduced secret balloting for the first time in a Hungarian election, allowing voters to express their preferences without fear of oversight by government officials, gendarmes, employers, or landlords. In spite of all the electoral chicanery that the government could devise, the Arrow Cross and the several other national socialist parties attracted nearly 25 percent of the popular vote, a remarkable figure in a country where mass political movements had always been discouraged. In the aftermath, many wondered if a fascist putsch were not possible. The Hungarian government was, however, determined to prevent exactly that, and successive cabinets drafted a number of ministerial ordinances in 1938 and 1939 to protect public order. Moreover, Ferenc Szálasi, the acknowledged leader of the Arrow Cross party, never succeeded in building his party into the sole voice of the Hungarian Right. Many of those who had sympathized with the party in the months before the election, especially middle- and upper-middle-class professionals, hoped to push the government to the right without toppling it in favor of something unknown and potentially chaotic. In the aftermath of the 1939 elections, such voters found that a changed government party or one of the dissident factions within it offered a much more attractive political option than the rabble-rousing of the Arrow Cross. Hungary's fascist movement thus lost support steadily in the months after the election; by the end of 1943, the party claimed less than 100,000 mainly passive members.

Only German military occupation in 1944 could revive the Arrow Cross from this moribund state.[1]

The most significant results of the 1939 elections could be seen within the ranks of the government party. This party had taken several names during the interwar period, but was usually called simply the "government party," since it had enjoyed an unbroken governing majority in parliament since the fall of the Bolshevik regime in 1919. The 182 seats (out of 260) that it took in the 1939 elections ensured the continuity of its rule. Ideologically, however, it was not the same party. Already in the 1930s, after István Bethlen had resigned and Gyula Gömbös replaced him as prime minister, the party's profile had begun to change. In part this was a generational shift, as a cadre of politicians who had come of age in World War I replaced an older set that had entered politics in the much different atmosphere of prewar Hungary. But with this "changing of the guard" came a pronounced shift to the political right. The old aristocrats and gentry landlords who had created the party to preserve a traditional social hierarchy found themselves increasingly beleaguered in their own political home. Instead, déclassé gentry nobles with much smaller holdings and no real political experience took their places alongside members of the self-styled "gentlemanly middle class," Christian (or rather, non-Jewish) civil servants and university-educated professionals who hoped a more right-wing government might create new opportunities for them.[2]

The new composition of the government party placed tremendous pressures on any cabinet that tried to lead it. In February 1939, the regent, Miklós Horthy, had asked a Transylvanian aristocrat, Count Pál Teleki, to form a government. Teleki was widely regarded as a traditional conservative in the mold of István Bethlen, the shrewd former prime minister who had engineered Hungary's conservative restoration in the 1920s. In appointing Teleki and holding him in office even after the unsettling election returns, Horthy clearly aimed at keeping Nazi German influence at arm's length and at reining in the radical right. While this was certainly Teleki's intention, it was clear that only a fraction of his majority in parliament could be counted as unconditional supporters. By 1939, the government party leaned much further to the right than its prime minister did. Only the broad constitutional powers of the regent to propose and consent to or veto any ministerial appointment kept Teleki (and his successors) immune from a vote of no confidence. The strength of the far right compelled men

---

1. See Margit Szöllösi-Janze, "Horthy-Ungarn und die Pfeilkreuzlerbewegung," *Geschichte und Gesellschaft* 12, no. 2 (1986): 178ff., and her longer study *Die Pfeilkreuzlerbewegung in Ungarn*, 250–83.
2. Sipos, *Imrédy Béla*, 118–23.

like Prime Minister Teleki to make political concessions in the hopes of "taking the wind out of their sails."

Teleki's opponents on the extreme right took inspiration from Nazi German success. With German diplomatic and military help, Hungary regained almost 40 percent of the territory lost in the treaty of Trianon in the space of three years. When Hitler marched into the Sudetenland in 1938, he also allowed Hungary to occupy a large strip of land in southern Slovakia. Months later, Hungary reoccupied Subcarpathian Ruthenia (now in the Ukraine) when Germany forced the final breakup of the Czechoslovak Republic. Close military and economic ties with the German Reich continued to bring Hungary advantages after 1939 as well. As German military and economic planners began to consider the resources necessary for waging war against the Soviet Union, they turned their attention to the rich mineral and agricultural resources of southeastern Europe. Eager to avoid any complications that might arise from Hungarian-Romanian animosity, German diplomats simply divided up the territory of Transylvania between the two countries, forcing Romania to cede roughly 43,000 square miles of territory to its rival. Although 400,000 ethnic Hungarians still remained in Romania even after this award, all Hungarians celebrated the partial restoration of their historic kingdom. Even Regent Horthy, still suspicious of the close ties between Nazi Germany and the fascist opposition in Hungary, basked in the warm glow of nationalist triumph and reveled in the opportunity to play the role of "augmenter of the nation," as he was reverently called in the nationalist press. Just as he had in Budapest in 1919, Horthy made a show of riding into important cities (like Kassa/Košice and Kolozsvár/Cluj) in the recovered territories on a white horse, symbolizing the nation's redemption with this act. Inspired by these easy diplomatic victories, many of Hungary's politicians and most of its military leaders enthusiastically supported Germany in the war and looked forward to entering the conflict on the side of their powerful ally. Nowhere was the anticipation greater than in the pages of the extreme right press, where Nazism was extolled as the leading spirit of the age and where all voices confidently predicted Germany's ultimate victory.

As Nazi influence grew, the concept of race (faj) "began to crop up" in Hungarian political and intellectual life alongside more ambiguous terms such as "nation (nemzet), people (nép), and ethnic character (népiség)."[3] Béla Imrédy, who had been prime minister during the 1938 Eucharistic Congress and who was known to be a devout Catholic, exemplified this

---

3. Gyula Juhász, Uralkodó eszmék Magyarországon, 1939–1944 (Budapest: Kossuth, 1983), 173ff.

shift well. In an article entitled "A Sincere Word about Hungarian-German Relations" that appeared in 1940, Imrédy contrasted the outdated thinking of Christian religious leaders, who saw German racial theory as "apostasy," with the many good Christians who remained faithful but who also recognized that racial ideology was the leading principle in a "New Europe" dominated by Nazi Germany. Hungarians, he argued, would have to embrace racial thinking and adapt it to their own national conditions.[4] The Nazi example also influenced social policy. By the late 1930s, political and intellectual leaders in Hungary understood national strength in biological terms and took steps that they hoped would strengthen both the quantity and quality of racial Hungarians.[5] New laws gave the state expanded powers to regulate marriages in the name of public health and provided for improved pre- and postnatal care in rural areas. In addition, the Hungarian state made its first experiments in population transfer in this period, resettling carefully chosen ethnically "pure" Magyar families from overpopulated regions into sensitive border regions of mixed ethnicity. These concerns about the quality and strength of the nation's biological stock created a consensus around ideas of race that spanned the entire breadth of "Christian Hungary," including the extreme right, many antifascist conservatives, and some radical reformers in the populist movement.

The newspapers of the extreme right reflected admiration for Nazi Germany in another area as well. In tabloids, sold for pennies to a growing number of enthusiastic readers, radical right-wing journalists inundated Hungary's public sphere with vulgar screeds against Jews, accusing them as a race of every imaginable act of treason against the Christian Hungarian nation.[6] All of them looked to Nazi Germany for inspiration, modeling their efforts on Julius Streicher's *Der Stürmer*. Some even received photographic material from German press agencies, pictures that only enhanced the salacious novelty of their "exposés" of Jewish crimes. Hungary's conservative elite pronounced themselves disgusted by the vicious coarsening of public discourse; Regent Horthy once remarked to Prime Minister Teleki that the extreme right press made him "want to vomit."[7] Indeed, the leading practitioners of this new extreme right shock-journalism were dubious figures, a parade of hustlers whose mediocre writing talents, scandalous exploits in Budapest's seamy underworld, and frequent contact with Gestapo agents did nothing to commend them to the attention of

4. Sipos, *Imrédy Béla*, 149.
5. István Hoóz, *Népesedéspolitika és népességfejlődés Magyarországon a két világháború között* (Budapest: Akadémiai Kiadó, 1970).
6. Nagy-Talavera, *The Green Shirts*, 157–60.
7. Cited in ibid., 158.

"good society." Nevertheless, the conservative elite preferred to hold its collective nose and turn the other way. Some even were able to exercise their abilities in officially sanctioned government institutes; Ferenc Rajniss, one of the most prominent of Hungary's extreme right journalists, also served as a member of the Hungarian National-Biological Institute, formed in May 1940 to "research those means by the help of which a biologically unitary and expansive Hungariandom, 20 million strong, might be created."[8] Throughout the interwar and wartime eras, nothing significant was done to counter the extreme right press, even at times when restrictions on left-wing publications were strictly enforced. This unchecked barrage of racist antisemitism was an undoubtedly crucial factor in creating a broad public consensus for increasingly radical anti-Jewish policy.[9]

Hungary's radical right was in no way content with the pace or scope of anti-Jewish legislation. Almost as soon as Law XV/1938 (the First Jewish Law) was promulgated, the extreme right began to demand stronger measures. Within months, on 23 December 1938, the government introduced a second anti-Jewish law for parliamentary consideration, one designed to appease the right still further by reducing the number of Jews engaged in the country's economic, social, and cultural life from 20 percent of the total population to 6 percent. Where the first law had primarily come to affect civil servants and government employees, the new law would explicitly extend discrimination to Jews working in the private sector. The law also included language that tied a person's legal identity as a "Jew" to the confessional affiliation of their forebears much like the Nuremberg Laws in Germany, making a Jew someone with one parent or two grandparents who had been Jews. Yet traditional conservatives, including especially Hungary's Christian religious leaders, forced extensive revisions. As they had done months earlier in debates over the First Jewish Law, secular and religious conservatives accepted without question the need to break "Jewish control" of the nation's economic life. But they also insisted that the new bill discriminated unfairly against many Jews who had indeed become "good" Hungarians. As the bill made its way through the various stages of the legislative process, exemptions were added. In addition to provisions for those who were, among other things, Olympic champions, priests and clergymen, recipients of medals for valor in war, or widows and children of those who had fallen in combat, the revised bill substantially increased the number of Jews who were legally Christian by linking exemption to the date when a person's parents or grandparents had con-

8. Juhász, *Uralkodó eszmék*, 173–74.
9. János Pelle, *A gyűlölet vetése: A zsidótörvények és a magyar közvélemény, 1938–1944* (Budapest: Európa, 2001).

verted to Christianity. Of course the new bill would have catastrophic effects on the lives and livelihoods of the majority of Jewish Hungarians. Even so, a minority of socially prominent persons widely regarded as the worst exemplars of "Jewish power" by the fascist media remained exempt from the law's strictures, primarily because they were converts, were in marriages legally defined as "mixed," or were children of such marriages—all things that marked them as "non-Jewish" under law. These individuals began administrative proceedings to prove that they qualified for exemption, an unbelievably time-consuming process that tied up the civil service in endless reviews. In addition, it soon became apparent that the process of dismissing persons legally defined as Jews from important positions in finance and industry was not as simple a matter as it seemed. While qualified replacements were sought, many Jews stayed on in their old positions with only superficial changes in their job descriptions. To the extreme right, all this seemed like so much dithering in the face of overwhelming "Jewish power." As soon as Parliament promulgated Law IV/1939 (the Second Jewish Law) on 5 May 1939, the extreme right declared it ineffective and badly in need of revision.[10]

Despite the steady drumbeat of racist invective from the extreme right "Christian national" press, Prime Minister Teleki, true to his conservative instincts, resisted drafting a third anti-Jewish law to complement the two already passed. By late 1940, however, continued Nazi military and diplomatic success convinced him that something more was needed to appease and quiet his critics on the radical right. His concession came in the form of a bill (which became Law XV/1941) "on the complement and modification of the law of marriage." Its most important provision prohibited marriages between Jews and non-Jews, addressing the legal definition of who was a Jew and who was not. Though it dealt specifically with the technical aspects of civil marriage, it was universally acknowledged to be a "racial defense law." The authors of the preamble stated clearly that the bill, which defined a Jew as a person with two or more Jewish grandparents, had been devised for "the protection of the racial purity of the Hungarian nation."[11] The only exceptions to the law would be in cases where both the individual in question and his or her parents had been born Christian (i.e., if the Jewish grandparents had converted before having children.) This definition was far clearer (and far more restrictive) than that offered in the previous anti-Jewish laws. Closing these loopholes, Law XV/1941 radically redefined the boundaries of the nation. It also directly addressed the question of mixed marriages, fundamentally affecting the lives and legal

10. Katzburg, *Hungary and the Jews.*
11. Ibid., 158–83. Citations taken from 173–74.

status of the many Hungarians who had Jewish forebears but who were Christian and who had been born into households in which at least one parent was not Jewish. By forbidding marriages between Hungarians and Jews, the new law tried to eliminate these living embodiments of the Jewish-Hungarian symbiosis, declaring Jews and Hungarians to be absolutely distinct racial communities and authorizing Hungary's government to act on this premise to defend the unity (and purity) of the Hungarian nation. Of course, prominent political figures still had the power to soften the harshest interpretations of this law. For several years, the regent Miklós Horthy and prime ministers such as Pál Teleki and his successor, Miklós Kállay, were able and willing to do exactly this. However, these would be acts of personal conscience (or calculation, or a mixture of both) that were in no way required by law. Law XV/1941 offered a much simpler vision to the nation's political leaders: the nation achieved unity as it expelled Jews from its midst. Christian Hungary was now a racial state.

The Catholic Church and the Rights of (Christian) Man

As Hungary's Parliament convened to discuss a civil marriage law based unequivocally on racial principles, Hungary's Catholic leaders once again faced a familiar problem. Just as in the 1890s, Hungary's secular legislators used the issue of civil marriage to signal a significant shift in the moral norms of public life. Certainly, the new 1941 law could not have been more different in intention from the legislation passed in the last decade of the nineteenth century. In the 1890s, lawmakers had embraced civil marriage as a way of establishing a more inclusive national society. Now, in 1941, Hungary's elected officials reaffirmed the importance of civil marriage for social unity by imposing new regulations on it, ones that effectively excluded Jews from the national community. Yet Hungary's Catholic leaders raised the same objections in both cases. Rather than affirming eternal (Catholic) Christian truths as the foundation of public life, lawmakers had turned to marriage outside the church as a way of enforcing decidedly secular moral norms. After the 1890s, the Hungarian Catholic Church had learned to live with civil marriage, a resignation made much easier after 1919, when successive governments continually proclaimed their commitment to Christian and national values. Nevertheless, Catholic leaders never abandoned the view that civil marriage forced Hungarians to divide their loyalty between secular and religious masters. Nor did they ever concede that the secular values inscribed in civil marriage law had the same truth or permanence as Christian doctrine did. The push in 1941 for a new marriage law based on race only confirmed them in their beliefs. If two versions of civil marriage could endorse such radically different visions of who was Hungarian and who was not, then this only proved that social mores divorced from Christian religious authority were too shifting and unreliable to be the ground on which to set a modern state.

Cardinal Jusztinián Serédi emphasized the absolute truth of Christian dogma when he denounced the new marriage law. Though he and his colleagues on the episcopal bench had voted in favor of the first two Jewish laws, seeing them as necessary, if flawed, economic measures, this third Jewish law was a much different matter, as it promised to give secular authorities the power to disregard (and effectively make illegal) marriages joined within the church if those unions ran afoul of certain racial criteria. The new law thus cut right to the heart of the church's vision of a Christian society founded on marriage and family. Speaking in the Upper House of Hungary's Parliament on 18 July 1941, Serédi declared to the assembled lawmakers that the church could never renounce its right to administer the sacraments of marriage according to its own lights and without the interference of civil authorities. As Serédi reminded his audience, "The sacraments belong to the jurisdiction of the Church . . . according to the ordering of Christ and thus on the basis of positive divine law." No manmade law had the power to put asunder what God had joined. Thus "the Church . . . can never recognize that states or others might have the right to prohibit or to dispose, even in an intermediate way, with regard to the binding of sacred marriages." Fashionable racial theories to the contrary, marriage within the Christian community remained sacred, whether or not husband and wife had been born into the church or had converted to Christianity later in their lives. "For this reason, [the church] denounces that form of civil marriage which prevents the joining of holy marriage, because every convert can marry according to the laws of the Church."[12] Cardinal Serédi and Archbishop Gyula Glattfelder, the two members of the Catholic episcopate in the Upper House, stood on this position and voted against the proposed racial marriage law. They were joined in this by their Protestant counterparts. Nothing these churchmen said or did, however, could change the political atmosphere in the chamber. Law XV/1941, the "Third Jewish Law," passed in the Upper House by a majority of 65 votes in favor to 53 against.

Cardinal Serédi's remarks to Parliament reflected the Vatican's thinking about the relationship between church and secular state in the modern era.

---

12. Citation taken from László T. László, *Szellemi honvédelem: Katolikus demokrata mozgalmak és az egyházak ellenállása a második világháború idején Magyarországon* (Rome, 1980), 59–60.

On several occasions in the interwar years, the pope and other Vatican officials had confirmed the absolute right of the individual to practice the (Catholic) Christian faith in the face of state repression. Repeatedly, the church had denounced Communist antichurch policy around the world, particularly in the Soviet Union, and after the mid 1930s, in Spain as well. But Catholic officials had emphasized their vision of individual rights in the German context too. Responding to the increasing state interference in church affairs in Germany, Pope Pius XI took up this issue in his 1937 encyclical, *Mit brennender Sorge*. "Man, as a person," he told Germany's bishops, and through them all Catholic Germans, "possesses rights that he holds from God and which must remain, with regard to the collectivity, beyond the reach of anything that would tend to deny them, to abolish them, or to neglect them." Foremost among these was the right to practice the Catholic faith according to the doctrines of the church: "The believer has an inalienable right to profess his faith and to live it as it is intended to be lived. Laws that stifle or make difficult the profession and practice of this faith are in contradiction with natural law."[13] In issuing this encyclical, Pope Pius XI was most immediately concerned with registering his disapproval of the way in which the Nazi German regime banned or otherwise constrained the organizational activity of Catholic associations. He was particularly critical, for example, of the way in which the Nazi regime abolished Catholic youth groups and folded them all into the Hitler Youth. Nevertheless, the principles proclaimed in the encyclical seemed to have broader application as well. If racial law prohibited converted Christians from practicing and living their faith "as it [was] intended to be lived," did this then mean that the church was declaring Nazi racial law to be "in contradiction" with Christian teaching and natural law? If it was, how willing were Catholic bishops around Europe to see practical opposition as the logical consequence of these theological premises?

Hungary's Catholic episcopate proclaimed the rights of the believer to practice his or her faith in the face of racial law even more forcefully than did their pontiff. Both Cardinal Serédi and Bishop Gyula Glattfelder worried openly already during the preliminary discussions leading to Hungary's first 1938 anti-Jewish law about the threat that antisemitic legislation posed to the rights of believers. In committee meetings prior to the general debate of the 1938 law on the floor of Parliament, Bishop Glattfelder argued vehemently (but ultimately in vain) against any state-imposed cutoff date after which the state would not recognize conversion

13. Citations taken from the translated excerpts in Georges Passelecq and Bernard Suchecky, *The Hidden Encyclical of Pius XI*, trans. Steven Rendall (New York: Harcourt Brace, 1997), 105–6.

to Christianity. "It is unacceptable," he maintained, "that the establishment of a racial character should wrongly give baptism different degrees of validity."[14] Baptism, he argued, had a transformative power that no state could deny to any of its citizens. Cardinal Serédi took up this argument again during the debates in 1939 over the Second Jewish Law. "We espouse simply that someone who takes up the sacrament of the Cross according to the ordering of Christ, be he Aryan, be he Mongol, . . . or a member of any other race, becomes Christian."[15] Despite these misgivings, both Serédi and Glattfelder found it wisest politically to vote in favor of the first two anti-Jewish laws. However, Hungary's bishops never abandoned the position in principle. In an address given on 13 December 1942 to a Catholic lay association, Cardinal Serédi reiterated the equality of all believers before God: "There are no master races. . . . There is no people less worthy than another. The same star of epiphany shines over all of them."[16] In such proclamations, the stance of the church seemed clear enough. A state that declared itself to be Christian had no right or authority to distinguish between believers on the basis of race.

Catholic religious leaders knew full well, however, that these declarations of principle were by no means abstract to the great number of baptized Christians defined as "Jewish" under the new laws. In a letter written in November 1940 to Prime Minister Pál Teleki, Cardinal Serédi argued that "aside from those who had themselves baptized from indisputable self-interest, a truly great number of sincere converts are suffering from this situation [i.e., the situation created by the anti-Jewish laws]."[17] Of course, the reasons for which Hungarian Jews turned to Christianity were far more complex than Cardinal Serédi would admit; his distinction between "sincere" and "insincere" conversion bore little resemblance to the social reality of converts' lives. Some sought acceptance in one or another of Hungary's Christian churches because they saw opportunities for themselves and their children to climb the social ladder; others hoped, more personally, for a clearer, less troubled sense of identity and belonging.[18] In many cases, conversion accompanied mixed marriages. Rates of interfaith

14. "Serédi hercegprímás, Glattfelder püspök, és Imrédy miniszterelnök," *Nemzeti Újság* (21 May 1938): 1–2.

15. Address of 15 April 1939, reprinted in Fisch, *Keresztény egyházfők*, 38.

16. Citation taken from an article in *Schweizerische Republikanische Blätter*, 16 January 1943, reproduced in Gabriel Adriányi, *Fünfzig Jahre Ungarische Kirchengeschichte, 1895–1945* (Mainz: v. Hase u. Koehler, 1974), 159–61. See also 101–6.

17. EPL: Cat. D/C: 6802/1940. Draft of a letter from Cardinal Jusztinián Serédi to Prime Minister Pál Teleki, 26 November 1940.

18. William O. McCagg, Jr., "Jewish Conversion in Hungary in Modern Times," in *Jewish Apostasy in the Modern World*, ed. Todd M. Endelman (New York: Holmes and Meier, 1987), 158. See also Zsuzsanna Ozsváth, *In the Footsteps of Orpheus*, 34–40.

marriages were especially high in Budapest, where statistics suggest that roughly 10–15 percent of all marriages contracted by Jews between 1918 and 1938 were with a non-Jewish partner.[19] After 1918, some Jews hoped to evade antisemitic persecution by converting. The postrevolutionary White Terror in 1919 and 1920 produced a huge increase in the number of conversions (from 527 in 1915–17 to 7,146 in 1919). The impending antisemitic legislation of 1938 had the same effect; conversions shot up from 1,598 in 1937 to 8,584 one year later.[20] The sum of these individual decisions, each made for complicated reasons, made the number of "Christians of Jewish ancestry" a sizable minority of those considered "Jewish" by Hungarian civil authorities. Absolute numbers are difficult to determine; one figure, based on 1941 census statistics (which included the large Jewish communities in recaptured northern Transylvania and Subcarpathian Ruthenia) estimated that roughly 10 percent of Hungary's 725,000 Jews were converts or the children of converts.[21] Other studies placed the number as high as 100,000.[22]

As the antisemitic legislation grew in scope and severity, Catholics affected by the new laws turned to their church for guidance and protection. Many wrote desperate letters to their bishops, assuring them of the deep sincerity of their faith and describing the terrible impact that the racial laws had on their families and their livelihoods. The most politically well-connected Catholics "of Jewish origin" lobbied the church at the highest level for a more aggressive response. One of the most prominent and wealthiest converts to Catholicism, Baron Móric Kornfeld, proposed to Cardinal Serédi a "forum at the highest level, which would strike a blow for Catholic beliefs so clearly that the Church's members of Jewish origin would feel that they do not stand alone in a hostile world, but that they can count on the leaders of the Church and on its members not yet infected by the spirit of the times."[23] Cardinal Serédi agreed that the church should offer Catholics "of Jewish origin" some kind of "moral defense"; in its meeting of 3 October 1939, Hungary's Catholic episcopate approved the creation of an association for the legal and social protection of converts, called the Holy Cross Society.[24] Very soon thereafter, the society was established and at work, battling civil administrative officials over the precise boundaries of the racial laws and the growing number of ministerial decrees that derived their legal authority from them. Committee mem-

19. Nathaniel Katzburg, *Hungary and the Jews*, 171.
20. William O. McCagg, Jr., "Jewish Conversion," 158.
21. Ibid., 143.
22. Katzburg, *Hungary and the Jews*, 170.
23. EPL: Cat. D/C: 1254/1940. Letter of Baron Móric Kornfeld to Cardinal Jusztinián Serédi, 15 September 1939.
24. *A püspöki kar tanácskozásai*, ed. Jenő Gergely, 265–66.

bers filed countless petitions with various government ministries on behalf of individuals who felt the law had been unfairly or too severely applied in their cases. Those affected by the anti-Jewish laws also turned to the group for help when they could not adequately prove their family's confessional history. Some even sought material assistance. The Holy Cross Society met these requests when it could, though the stipulations within the racial legislation very often limited the help it could give to individuals.[25]

Even after the Catholic episcopate failed to stop the passage of Law XV/1941 (the Third Jewish Law), the Holy Cross Society still tried to defend the rights of Catholics "of Jewish origin." Church officials were particularly concerned about the position of converts within Hungary's labor battalions. These work groups were part of a broader policy of national defense (outlined in a 1939 law), which required all able-bodied men between the ages of fourteen and seventy to perform service in the national interest. However, the same anti-Jewish laws (and, in particular, Law IV/1939) that forced Hungary's Jews from civilian professions also banned them from armed service. As a result, Jewish men were organized into noncombatant work details under military authority. Throughout the war, labor servicemen were often poorly fed and supplied, put to work in brutal conditions, and always kept unarmed in the midst of battle. Though more fair-minded officials in the Defense Ministry did sometimes improve conditions for the servicemen temporarily, no one could deny that the policy was exploitative, humiliating, and, too often, deadly. Appalled, the members of the Holy Cross Society led the church in petitioning the Defense Ministry, asking that converts be treated with the dignity due to Christian citizens of Hungary. Their efforts did meet with some success. Christian labor servicemen typically served in separate "Christian Labor Service Companies" and were distinguished by a white armband instead of the yellow armband that Jewish labor servicemen were required to wear. Depending on the attitudes of a company's guards and officers, this could result in better treatment. But this was by no means always the case, and Christian labor service wearing white armbands often received the same abuse as those wearing yellow armbands. This was especially true for those serving on the front in the Ukraine or those assigned to murderously brutal work detail in the German copper mines at Bor, Serbia.[26]

Given the Hungarian political context in the early 1940s, these efforts

---

25. EPL: Cat. D/C: 1254/1940. Jelentés az 1939. IV. t.c. érintette katolikusok bizottságának munkájáról, 11 March 1940. Also Jenő Gergely, "A katolikus püspöki kar és a konvertiták mentése (Dokumentumok)," *Történelmi Szemle* 27, no. 4 (1984): 580–616; Leslie Laszlo, "Fighting Evil with Weapons of the Spirit: The Christian Churches in Wartime Hungary," *Hungarian Studies Review* 10, nos. 1–2 (1983): 125–43.

26. Braham, *The Politics of Genocide*, condensed edition, 37–42, esp. 42. For a more extensive analysis of Hungary's labor service battalions, see Randolph L. Braham, *The Hungarian Labor Service System, 1939–1945* (Boulder: East European Quarterly, 1977).

to defend the rights of converts were widely perceived as anti-Nazi. Since the mid 1930s, many Hungarians had enthusiastically supported the deepening relationship between their government and Nazi Germany. In 1941, Hungary entered World War II as an ally of the German Reich. Though there was no overt censorship of more liberal publications during this period, the authorities used suggestion and harassment (such as special licensing fees) to create an atmosphere in which journalists felt they had to watch what they said. As a result, many writers generally avoided overt political critique, fearing a backlash similar to the terror-filled years of the early 1920s. Instead, they approached political questions indirectly, "smuggling," as the progressive writer Béla Zsolt put it, "honest asides and clauses" into their self-censored writing. In this context, political opposition could be found in seemingly innocuous articles; an essay on the nineteenth-century nationalist poet Sándor Petőfi, printed in the newspaper *Hungarian Nation*, might be widely read and discussed (among friends) as a call for national independence from growing Nazi German hegemony.[27] Similarly, the church's defense of converts, even if divorced from any broader toleration of Jews, suggested an independent approach to antisemitism, different and less radical than that favored by the Nazis and their Hungarian allies. German diplomats certainly paid close attention to the speeches that Cardinal Serédi and his bishops gave on the subject of converts and racial law, recognizing it as criticism of their government's policies. In correspondence between the German embassy in Budapest and the Foreign Ministry in Berlin, German officials wondered aloud how Serédi might be kept silent.[28]

Even more important, defending converts led some Catholics to take a much stronger position against the extreme right in Hungary than did any of the Hungarian bishops. For example, Count György Széchényi, the maverick newspaper publisher who criticized his church for its silence in the face of the fascist threat, opposed the entire wave of antisemitic legislation. Arguing that antisemitic laws were unacceptable because they "quite simply suspended the possibility of conversion," Széchényi (also an MP) voted against the first 1938 anti-Jewish law, even when his cardinal did not.[29] After Széchényi died in 1938, a small but intellectually prominent group of Catholics, many of whom were active in the Holy Cross Society, continued to argue that the church's opposition to racial theories should compel Catholics to speak out more clearly against all forms of extreme right politics. These intellectuals, the historian Gyula Szekfű among

27. "'Olvassa el a Magyar Nemzet minden sorát!' Fejezetek a lap múltjából (1938–1944)," in *A bilincsbe vért beszéd*, 143–228. Citation of Béla Zsolt on 165.
28. Adriányi, *Ungarische Kirchengeschichte*, 104–6.
29. "A képviselő ház ülése," *Nemzeti Újság* (12 May 1938), 5.

them, published a number of important articles and essay collections during the war years that placed Catholic thinking about converts and race within a context clearly opposed to Nazi German ideology.[30] Of course, the audience in wartime Hungary for liberal, explicitly antifascist Catholic publications was miniscule when compared to the vast numbers of Hungarians who read the antisemitic tabloids published by the extreme right. In the popular fascist press, pro-Nazi journalists portrayed these liberal Catholics as "Jew-lovers" and antinational agitators whose writings were undermining Hungary's essential alliance with the German Reich.

However, the church's defense of converts had political significance beyond the extreme right. By 1939, church officials had numerous reports of unruly and chaotic scenes outside rabbis' offices involving Hungarians legally categorized as Jews who were trying desperately to document their departure from the Jewish confession. Conversions made in this way technically had no legal force; the new law clearly made an individual's racial status as a Jew or Christian dependent on the confessional affiliation of his or her grandparents. Still, some Hungarian Jews clearly hoped that conversion to Christianity, even in these circumstances, might provide some practical insurance against the worst effects of the antisemitic laws. The historian Gábor Vermes remembered that the German occupation in 1944 only heightened these wild expectations: "During the German occupation of Hungary, the news that your life could be saved if you converted to Christianity spread among the Jews of Budapest."[31] By defending the rights of converts in parliamentary debates and through the advocacy work of the Holy Cross Society, Catholic leaders gave desperate hope to thousands of Hungarians defined by law as Jews. Would the church provide refuge for the persecuted if the political situation in Hungary worsened? Some clearly hoped it might.

This possibility clearly worried the episcopate. If the church seemed a refuge to at least some of Hungary's Jews, then priests could expect even more applicants for conversion if the political climate worsened and the extreme right demanded even greater anti-Jewish measures. Officials turned to the primatial seat in Esztergom for advice.[32] How should clergy respond if, for example, Jews wanting to convert appeared with notarized

30. For example, *Katolikus írók új magyar kalauza*, ed. József Almásy (Budapest: Ardói irodalmi és könyvkiadó vállalat, 1940). See also Miklós Vásárhelyi's 1978 interview with Jenő Katona, one of the most important of these anti-Nazi Catholic intellectuals. "Katolikusok a szellemi ellenállásban: Beszélgetés Katona Jenővel," in *A bilincsbe vert beszéd*, 101–24.

31. Gábor Vermes, "A Personal Account," in *In God's Name: Genocide and Religion in the Twentieth Century*, ed. Omer Bartov and Phyllis Mack (New York: Berghahn, 2001), 260.

32. EPL. Cat. 25: 946/1939 Letter of Deputy Archbishop János Mészáros to Cardinal Jusztinián Serédi, 6 February 1939.

statements saying that they had tried to follow the legal procedure for conversion, as outlined by the civil code, but had been prevented by secular officials? Should the church accept them into the community of Christians, as the applicants requested? Or should the church respect the decisions that civil authorities were making in matters of faith? The response from the cardinal's office in Esztergom was categorical. Converts had to follow the letter of the law in filing for conversion. The cardinal's secretary, who issued the response, reminded Archbishop Mészáros that "it is not in our interest to make the conversion of Jews any easier." Any difficulties in the conversion process should be considered a "test of the convert's intentions."[33] The effect of this position was to make conversion to Christianity increasingly difficult, even as the government increased the social and economic pressure on those legally defined as Jews.

Cardinal Serédi's secretary left the church's "interests" undefined. But no one could ignore the fact that they were, in part, political. At a time when demagogues on the extreme right denounced the church for failing to keep up with the new spirit of the age, and as increasing numbers of Hungarian Jews wondered if conversion might offer protection from their persecutors, the Catholic Church was rapidly losing its power to define the difference between Christian and Jew. Throughout the interwar era and even before, Catholic churchmen had claimed to understand and define what made Hungary a "Christian" nation more ably than secular officials. The episcopate had opposed civil marriage precisely because it felt that such marriages curtailed their power to define the public mores essential to a Christian society at odds with an alien "Jewish spirit." Now, state bureaucrats, acting on the basis of civil law alone, were deciding who was "Jewish" and where the "Jewish spirit" still lurked. Religion, it seemed, was fast becoming little more than a point of view, a personal belief that was absolutely irrelevant to the authorities. To be a Christian Hungarian, one might belong to any church or none. The important thing was not to be a "Jew."

Faced with civil officials intent on seeing Hungarian identity in racial terms, Catholic leaders reminded the public that they had been among the first to describe the danger that the "Jewish spirit" posed to Christian Hungarian society. Father József Közi-Horváth, a leading figure in the Catholic Action organization, and a member of parliament, prefaced his opposition to the 1941 racial law by reminding the Hungarian parliament that "the Catholic clergy and those who first unfurled the banner of Chris-

---

33. EPL. Cat. 25: 946/1939 Letter of General Deputy Archbishop János Dráhos to Deputy Archbishop János Mészáros, 20 February 1939.

tian politics have stood for decades for preventing Jewish spiritual and material expansion." He went on to affirm that "we, faithful to the example of our predecessors, readily serve any action which has as its goal ending Jewish spiritual and material power and strengthening Christian Hungariandom." Though the church opposed the 1941 law because it made "persecution" of Christians legal, Közi-Horváth pleaded with his fellow members of parliament not to misunderstand this position. No one, he argued, should "treat the Christian Church during these proceedings as if it wanted to defend the Jews."[34] Bishop Gyula Glattfelder made this point even more bluntly in a private conversation with Minister of Defense Károly Bartha, about the converts in labor service battalions. Glattfelder assured the minister that the church acted "solely on the basis of eternal divine laws, which explains why we [i.e., the church] are not defending the Jews, but instead are raising our voices when our believers are stripped of their rights."[35] Though some Hungarians might want to read the church's defense of converts in a broader political sense, finding in it public opposition to the antisemitic politics of the day, leaders like Bishop Glattfelder and József Közi-Horváth insisted that their opposition must be understood in a much narrower sense. Converts had rights worth defending precisely because they were not Jews. Baptism washed away the stigma of race, but nothing could cleanse Jews as a community of its antinational taint.

Thus the church's opposition to Hungary's racial law rested on an exclusionary logic they shared with their fascist opponents. Even the most committed critics of the Nazi regime rarely transcended this contradiction. Members of the Holy Cross Society were undeniably anti-Nazi in their politics. Yet they too emphasized the cultural and mental difference between converted Jews and "real" Jews, deriving the civil rights of converts from the fact that they were no longer "Jewish." In their petitions, members of the Holy Cross Society emphasized that converts had purged all traces of "Jewishness," becoming, as they put it in one memorandum submitted to the office of the prime minister, "a class in which we find the characteristic mental and spiritual peculiarities of Jewry in the least measure and who are most similar to the country's indigenous population (*törzslakosság*) in spirit and opinion." One might criticize Jews for their inability to "Magyarize" (*elmagyarosodni*) in "culture" and "spirit." But one could not deny that converted Jews had in fact slipped the mental

---

34. Speech of József Közi-Horváth in the 204th session of the House of Representatives of the Hungarian Parliament, 1 July 1941.
35. EPL. 7770/1942. Letter of Bishop Gyula Glattfelder to Cardinal Jusztinián Serédi, 15 July 1942

bonds of Jewishness and become true Christian Hungarians.[36] By arguing in this way, even those Catholics with the best political intentions ultimately weakened their opposition, justifying antisemitic politics in principle even as they opposed its most extreme form in practice.

Between Race and Ethnic Nation: Converts and the Reformed Church

Law XV/1941 posed an even greater challenge to the Reformed Church. Like their Catholic counterparts, leading Calvinists tried to strike a balance between acceptable and excessive antisemitism in their approach to the nation's "Jewish question." As Cardinal Serédi had done, Bishop László Ravasz denounced the 1941 racial law as a dangerous concession to extremism. As a Protestant, however, his argument was somewhat different. Whereas the Catholic primate had seen in the law an attack on the holy sacrament of marriage, a particularly Catholic understanding of the institution, Bishop Ravasz opposed the law because it presumed to set secular limits on the transcendent power of the "Holy Spirit" to transform souls. A marriage between Christians, even if one or both partners were converted Jews, could not, he argued "be deemed harmful from a national point of view solely on the basis of blood" if "the spiritual and moral superiority of the Christian spirit appears guaranteed from a human standpoint."[37] God's grace always triumphed over an individual's racial qualities. Yet Ravasz's careful attempts to balance the "human" and the "national" points of view in his parliamentary address revealed a significant dilemma. Hungarian Protestants had always been far more willing than the Catholic bishops had been to share the burden of defining public mores with secular politicians. After all, Hungary's Protestants had supported the idea of civil marriage in the 1890s precisely because it promised a counterbalance to the overwhelming social power that the Catholic Church enjoyed. However, the new racial law passed in 1941 threatened to upset this fine balance between secular and religious authority, granting civil administrators the sole right to determine the public meaning of Christianity. Hungarian Calvinists sensed this shift and began to wonder about the future of their church. Would they still be able to maintain that theirs was the "Magyar religion," if the Calvinist Church had been demoted from partner to spectator in the politics of Christian nationalism?

36. EPL. 7770/1942 "A magyar szent kereszt egyesület memoranduma Dr. Kállay Miklós m. kir. Miniszterelnök urhoz a kivételes jogrend alá helyezett zsidó származású *katolikusok* jogi helyzete ügyében," dated 2 June 1942.
37. Ravasz's speech is cited at length in László T. László, *Szellemi honvédelem*, 60–61.

In their own church publications, Calvinist church leaders tried to explain why Bishop Ravasz had taken the stance that he had during the parliamentary deliberations of Law XV/1941. Gyula Muraközy, editor of the semiofficial church organ *Reformed Life*, presented one of the most important statements of the church's position in an article entitled "Marriage and the Magyar Reformed Idea." In it, Muraközy argued that marriage law was central to the life of a Christian nation. "God," Muraközy argued, "gave to the state and to the family spheres of their own. . . . The trouble always begins when the one wants to be entirely free and independent from the other or when one wants entirely to subjugate the other." The "Magyar Reformed idea," in Muraközy's understanding, embodied the harmony that could exist between secular and religious power, a union of faith and nation that resolved all conflicts both public and private. For legislators to consider a Calvinist as racially Hungarian in public and as a believing Christian in private was nonsense. "We, Magyar Calvinists, can no more separate our Magyarness from our Calvinist natures than an ear of wheat could live with only sunshine and not earth or with the productive powers of the earth but without sunlight." Calvinists stood ready as always to place their church in the service of the national good. However, it was incumbent on secular lawmakers not to push away or belittle so crucial an ally in the life of the nation.[38]

Not all Calvinists agreed with Gyula Muraközy that the "Magyar Reformed idea" commanded the members of the Hungarian Calvinist Church to oppose Law XV/1941. After all, Muraközy had called for a balance between civil and religious authority, but had said nothing about how exactly that balance should be struck. Many Calvinists insisted that state officials had a much greater power to intervene in family affairs than Gyula Muraközy seemed to allow. In angry letters to Bishop László Ravasz and others, some readers of *Reformed Life* insisted that civil authorities had a duty to elevate the national interest above all considerations of individual right. When considering any question, be it family policy, land reform, or military action, Parliament, as one letter writer argued, had an absolute right to defend the "Magyar future." If they believed it essential to the health of the nation, secular legislators had the right and the power to intervene in and ban certain kinds of marriages, even if the partners in question were converts to Christianity. One letter writer illustrated the claims that state power had over individual rights by drawing an analogy with military conscription: state officials did not "individually" ask soldiers sent to the front whether they wanted to "fight,

perhaps suffer, and maybe even die for a more healthy Hungary." Why,
then, should the church see the racial marriage law any differently? If the
latest social and scientific research suggested that certain marriages would
undermine "a more healthy Hungary," then legislators had the right and
the duty to set aside individual right—the "points of view of individual
persons"—and act in the national interest.[39]

Throughout the 1930s, social activists within the Reformed Church had
taken precisely this view of state and individual rights. Horrified by visions of ethnic extinction, young and socially active churchmen had demanded vigorous state intervention in all matters connected to national
survival, but especially in the sphere of family policy. To combat declining
birth rates, they argued, the state had to assume a greater role in regulat-
ing both the quality and quantity of ethnic Magyar families. In this, they
had been joined by their bishops, who lent their moral authority to organizations that promoted healthy and expanding natality rates.[40] Of course,
most of these activists had not described their nation as a biological race;
ethnic nationalists far more frequently invoked vaguer notions of "mentality," "culture," and "destiny." Even so, it was clear to them that Magyars, Jews, and Germans were all separate nations, whether or not one
wanted to see the differences in scientific racial terms or not. Each had
unique characteristics and particular interests, making it the duty of Hungarian lawmakers to look after their own Magyar nation first. Populist activists in the church urged government officials to intervene forcefully in
the most intimate spheres of family life, since "national defense" rested on
strong and healthy families. Supported by their church, these activists had
lobbied lawmakers to devise public health and social policies that would
promote higher birth rates and more prosperous Magyar peasant families.
They had also called for tough measures against "family-destroying" influences like prostitution, abortion, and pornography. All these initiatives,
transforming the lives of individual families in different ways, would,
many populist Calvinists argued, have a cumulative effect, producing a
healthier, more nationally "secure" demographic map of Hungarians
throughout the former Kingdom of Hungary. Thus, Muraközy's critics
had a point. Despite the theologian's careful opposition to the racial law,
no one could deny that the Hungarian Reformed Church, as an institu-

39. RL: C./141 Papers of László Ravasz. Box 16. Letter entitled "A magyar-zsidó
házasság az egész magyarság szemével," dated July 1941.
40. See, for example, Bishop László Ravasz's foreword in Gábor Doros, *Családvédelem:
Küzdelem a születéscsökkenés ellen* (Budapest: Magyar Családvédelmi Szövetség, 1938). The
book was published by the National Association for Family Defense, a government sponsored agency established to coordinate pronatality propaganda.

tion, had already endorsed a greatly expanded state role in the family "sphere."

But could the "Magyar Reformed idea" extend to Jews? For Calvinists, who had invested so much of their religious identity in the idea of "national defense," this question was even more politically vexing than it was for Catholics. If the Reformed Church clearly acknowledged that state officials had the right to regulate marriages according to the national interest, then it faced an even greater challenge in defining how Jews should be excluded from the national community. What could be done if state officials relied solely on secular racial theories to define the national interest? Bishop László Ravasz had set the church's official position, insisting on the transformative power of the Holy Spirit in his address to parliament opposing Law XV/1941. After the law had passed, Ravasz speculated openly about ways in which the national reliability of converted Jews might be proven. In a letter to world Protestant leaders in Geneva, for example, Ravasz proposed an "areopagus," some kind of supreme tribunal that might review every convert's life history and determine its value to the nation.[41] But such ideas were a practical absurdity and did nothing to help Reformed Church leaders solve their political dilemma. It did not help that even those who shared Bishop Ravasz's opposition to the racial law spoke of the "Magyar Reformed idea" in terms almost as exclusive in practice as the idea of race itself. In his article on marriage and Law XV/1941, Gyula Muraközy proclaimed that "Magyarness for us is a peculiar, unteachable, and irreproducible spirit."[42] Such reasoning was riddled with contradictions. In opposing the racial law, Bishop Ravasz and Muraközy confirmed that real conversion was possible, if rare. But conversion and assimilation into the community of Christian Hungarians seemed impossible, if "Magyarness" could not be taught or reproduced. Reformed Church leaders seemed of two minds. Their opposition to the 1941 racial law was principled and clear. But they remained unable to say how their vision of Christian Hungary differed in real and concrete terms from the racial state advocated by the extreme right.

This indecision did not go unnoticed. Already in 1938, in the weeks prior to the parliamentary debate of the First Jewish Law, some Calvinists had discussed their church's response to the confused tangle of race and religion. Debate was particularly lively in *Hungarian Way*, the populist journal published by the Calvinist youth group, Soli Deo Gloria. In one issue, a self-described child of Jewish converts to the Reformed faith elicited a

41. RL: C./141. Box 16, folder marked "1943." Letter to Dr. Visser't Hooft.
42. Muraközy, "A házasság és a magyar református gondolat."

strong response. The author, a certain Dr. Miklós Halász, had described his own faith and his family's long love of the Hungarian nation, a patriotism that extended back to the Revolution of 1848 and even earlier. If Jews were collectively guilty of sins against the nation, then surely, he argued, his own history, and the deep patriotic spirit of his family, proved that there were exceptions. The truly guilty, he suggested, were undoubtedly those Jews who had recently immigrated and thus did not have roots in Hungary stretching back over many generations.[43] The editor of *Hungarian Way*, the pastor Béla Pap, disagreed. Race, he insisted, was a truth independent of religion or even patriotic sentiment. "Racial character" remained "even in the case of the most complete assimilation." Because Magyars and Jews were entirely separate peoples, true Magyars found no reflection of themselves in Jews and so felt no particular sympathy when Jews experienced discrimination. Pap commended moral indifference to "Calvinist Jews" like Dr. Halász: "When even the most radical Jewish bill no longer raises feelings of discomfort in you—because you feel no connection whatsoever with Jewry—then you will be in truth Magyar and Calvinist."[44] It is impossible to say how Dr. Miklós Halász took this advice.

Béla Pap was not alone among Calvinists in arguing that "Hungarianness" was a racial identity. The same letter writer who had responded to Gyula Muraközy by drawing an analogy between the state's right to draft soldiers and its duty to ban "unhealthy" marriages justified his views by arguing that Jews and Magyars were two separate races. According to the latest scientific research, he claimed, "Magyarness" was a biological inheritance. Thus, church leaders who described "Magyarness" as a spirit, even one that was irreproducible and unteachable, only confused a complex issue unnecessarily. "A Jew," this Calvinist reminded his bishop, "might become a good Christian, could well change into an upright, decent and useful state citizen, but a Jew can never become a Magyar."[45] By the late 1930s, this distinction had wide currency in the Hungarian Reformed Church. "We do not share the belief," wrote one essayist in 1938 in *Hungarian Way*, "that a Jew cannot become a Christian by conviction; if we believed that we would not believe in the conquering power of Christianity." However, the church as an institution could not remain blind to the reality of race. The answer was clear: "We believe that an organized body of Jewish-Christians would be the only solution which would . . . solve the internal contradictions which the false alternatives of 'race or re-

43. Miklós Halász, "Igy látják ők! . . . Egy 'református zsidó' válasza mult számunk vezércikkére," *Magyar Út* 7, no. 18 (5 May 1938): 3.
44. Béla Pap, "Mi igy látjuk!," *Magyar Út* 7, no. 18 (5 May 1938): 3–4.
45. RL: C./141 Papers of László Ravasz. Box 16. Letter entitled "A magyar zsidó házasság az egész magyarság szemével," dated July 1941.

ligion' cause."[46] Two churches, Magyar and "Jewish," united by doctrine but separated by race, would neatly solve the church's ambiguous position on the "Jewish question," this author claimed. Jews could convert to Christianity if their consciences demanded it. Yet the truth of their racial difference would remain plain for all to see.

Such a proposal was not without precedent. Germany's Protestant church governments had split over precisely these kinds of issues. A majority of German Protestant churchmen, worried about the control that the Nazi Party was exercising in the life of their church, created the strictly nonpolitical Confessing Church in protest. However, a large minority in the so-called "German Christian" movement advocated a close partnership between church and Nazi state. These "German Christians" accepted Nazi racial ideology without reservation and hoped to cleanse all "Jewish" elements from their church and their theology. Some approved so-called "Aryan paragraphs," clauses in their church bylaws that restricted non-Aryans from pastoral office and segregated those Christians classified by law as Jews.[47] With the passage in 1941 of a racial law in Hungary modeled on Germany's Nuremberg Laws, some Hungarian Calvinists were eager to take similar measures. One pastor from a Budapest suburb proposed a number of related measures to the elders of his diocese a few months after Law XV/1941 was passed.[48] "Jewish-Christians," he argued, should be placed in a separate church. Moreover, the Reformed Church should also suspend those pastors affected by the Jewish Laws and bar those members legally determined as Jews from service in any church administrative or instructional position. Committees of clergy and lay leaders debated this proposal at the diocesan level and then at the church district level; both quickly decided that the matter was far too sensitive for them to determine.[49] The synodal committee recorded its conclusions in its minutes: "Considering that its political nature as well as the existential interests bound up in it has transformed the question into such a sensitive, even explosive problem, it would be the most dangerous course possible if different church bodies debated and voted on this or that proposal in open session."[50] The committee conceded that the matter was complex, encompassing "theological, historical, legal, and political" aspects, and referred the matter to the General Synod for an authoritative ruling.

In the end, Hungary's Reformed Church did not adopt any racial mea-

46. Dezső Fónyad, "Faj vagy vallás?," *Magyar Út* 7, no. 17 (28 April 1938): 3.
47. Doris L. Bergen, *Twisted Cross*, esp. 82–100.
48. RL: A./1/b 5806–1941.
49. Ibid. The file contains summaries of the minutes from both meetings.
50. Ibid., excerpt from minutes of the Dunamelléki református egyházkerület esperesi és gondnoki értekezlete, held on 19 November 1941.

sure similar to the "Aryan paragraph" of the German Protestant churches. Despite demands for some kind of racial distinction between Christians and "Jewish-Christians" within the church, Calvinist leaders at the highest level continued to be wary of such a step. Gyula Muraközy ultimately concluded that "if [the church] fulfills its serious and conscientious duties towards those who cross its threshold, and if it stamps them with the mark of the blood of Christ, then the Church itself can make no further distinction between its own peoples."[51] Within the church, then, there could be no distinctions between Christians. Other Calvinist leaders took an even stronger position. One of these was Imre Révész, who had become bishop of the Transtibiscan Church District in 1938. One year after taking this high office, he published one of the more strongly worded statements of church doctrine in the journal of the pastors' association, writing that his church had a duty "even at the price of serious disadvantage," he declared, "to protect from terror and brutality those Jews who had truly turned toward Christ and who professed it with their words, their lives, their actions, and their suffering." Révész went on to declare that "the Hungarian Reformed conscience must also protest against injustices and inhumanities . . . when they are committed against members of Jewish families who had not yet turned to Christ, but who were adhering honorably to the ten commandments of the Lord anyway, who were doing useful service for the nation . . . , and who had tried for generations to assimilate in good faith."[52] If violence was done to Jews, Révész argued, no Magyar should watch with indifference. Jews and Hungarians might be different, but the barriers between them were not absolute.

Emboldened by these declarations, a small group of Calvinists followed the Catholic example and created an association to protect the rights of converts. Taking the Holy Cross Society as a model, the Good Pastor Committee began work in 1942, offering legal advice, material assistance (especially blankets and warm clothes for labor servicemen), and employment counseling to those who came seeking it in the years before 1944. The Calvinists working in the Good Pastor Committee enjoyed good relations with the Holy Cross Society throughout the war years, sharing a common opposition to Nazi German hegemony in Hungary far stronger than many in their respective churches. By spring of 1943, both groups worked together on behalf of converts in the labor service battalions, sharing information and lodging joint petitions with various ministerial officials. The two groups maintained these close relations after the German occupation of Hungary in March 1944. Indeed, the director of the Good Pastor Committee, József

51. Muraközy, "A házasság és a magyar református gondolat."
52. Imre Révész, "A zsidókérdés," *Lelkészegyesület* 32, no. 2 (14 January 1939): 10–11.

Éliás, remembered that he first received detailed information about the death camp at Auschwitz in late April or early May 1944 from József Cavallier, a leading figure in the Holy Cross Society and a well-known opponent of the extreme right.[53] Éliás also recalled that after March 1944 both groups collected certificates of baptism and issued them carefully to people who could not prove their confessional/"racial" status. Neither, he claimed, asked the desperate recipients for evidence of "sincere" conversion.[54]

Such assistance, however, greatly exceeded the publicly stated intentions of the Reformed Church leaders. Throughout the war, the church generally made it more, rather than less, difficult for Jews to convert to Christianity. Calvinist theologians insisted that pastors, and not civil servants, had the final authority to determine whether or not a convert was truly converted. Even if someone had followed all the legal procedures, the church might still hesitate before accepting him or her as a sincere Christian. Jews, one theologian argued in a memorandum to Bishop Ravasz, ought legally to remain Jews until the church had accepted them and baptized them.[55] In practice, this meant that the waiting period for catechumens to become members of the Reformed Church increased dramatically during the early 1940s, something that inevitably cast suspicion on those converts who were already church members. József Éliás remembered that the Good Pastor Committee's relations with Bishop Ravasz and the church leadership were always ambiguous.[56] The church had indeed established the organization as a subcommittee of its well-established mission committee (the body that oversaw efforts to proselytize and evangelize). Moreover, the General Synod of the church printed and distributed pamphlets describing the activities of the Good Pastor group to congregations throughout Hungary.[57] Yet Ravasz, Éliás later claimed, was careful to say that this was all the church was willing to do for the committee, and even seemed to hedge on his promise not to discipline committee members if their actions attracted unwelcome public attention. Throughout the war years, the committee struggled with a lack of funds and office space.

Without a doubt, the Calvinist Church's commitment to Christian nationalist politics undermined the efforts of men like Éliás to oppose the growing power of the extreme right in Hungary. Nationalist zeal within the church made a deep impression on Karl Barth, the towering figure in European Protestant thought and an outspoken opponent of the Nazi

---

53. See the interview with József Éliás in *Befejezetlen múlt: keresztények, és zsidók, sorsok: beszélgetések*, ed. Sándor Szenes (Budapest, 1986).
54. Ibid., 19–20.
55. RL: A./1.c. 2408/1942
56. *Befejezetlen múlt*, 8–9.
57. One such pamphlet is filed in RL: A./1.b. 5772/1943.

Party, when he visited in 1936. Writing after the war, Barth recalled that he had found the Hungarian Reformed Church "in a condition of feverish nationalism next to which even that which I had till then experienced in Germany seemed pale and artificial to me."[58] Károly Rátkai, a presbiter in Bishop Ravasz's church district who was deported to Mauthausen after the German occupation in 1944, had a similar impression. Writing in 1946 in a leading newspaper of the postwar progressive left, Rátkai asserted that church leaders like Gyula Muraközy and László Ravasz had consciously decided to tone down their criticism of the Nazi regime out of "sensitivity" to those parishioners whose extreme right wing views made them more sympathetic to Nazi-style politics.[59] Moreover, leading figures of the church like Bishop Ravasz continued to call for solutions to Hungary's "Jewish question," even as they opposed the 1941 racial law on theological grounds. In a 1943 letter to the general secretary of the World Council of Churches in Geneva, Ravasz asserted that Jews in Hungary represented a "worldview" and a "value-system" that "always manifested itself as a collective unity." Resolving Hungary's "Jewish question" demanded a similar collective response, one that treated Jews "in the entire community" and not just "in individual persons."[60] Individual converts might merit exemptions; Jews as a group most certainly did not.

Torn between supporting state intervention in the "Jewish question" and opposing the 1941 racial law because it threatened to make their church irrelevant, Calvinist Church leaders generally refrained from any explicit criticism of political developments in Hungary. The World Council of Churches was not wrong at all when they chastised Bishop Ravasz and the Hungarian Reformed Church for taking positions that prevented them from "pronouncing prejudice-free criticism of national socialism."[61] Church leaders seemed to confirm this in many of their public sermons and address. In a 1939 radio address on the "Jewish question" in Hungary, Bishop László Ravasz tried to strike a fine balance on the issues that bedeviled his church. Conversion, if sincere, could transform a man's soul, he argued. It could not, however, prevent him from suffering financial loss or social ruin. If the state found it necessary to discriminate against those of Jewish origin for the national good, then converts should endure the

58. Karl Barth, *Christliche Gemeinde im Wechsel der Staatsordnungen: Dokumente einer Ungarnreise 1948* (Zürich: Evangelischer Verlag A.G. Zollikon, 1948), 56.
59. Károly Rátkai, "A kálvinizmus örök," *Haladás* (12 January 1946): 2.
60. A draft of the letter to General Secretary Willem Adolf Visser't Hooft is contained in RL: C./141 Papers of László Ravasz. Box 16; folder marked "1943." More generally, Tamás Majsai, "A magyarországi református egyház és a 'svájci' ökumené a Soáh idején. Egy lehetőség lehetetlenségének története," in *The Holocaust in Hungary: Fifty Years Later*, ed. Randolph L. Braham and Attila Pók (Boulder: Social Science Monographs, 1997), 457–512.
61. Majsai, "A magyarországi református egyház," 468.

suffering with humility and patience. "Christianity does not exist to take care of political, financial, or social inconveniences." To emphasize this point, he went on: "Christ did not call on the Jew to assimilate so that he could keep his job, his dividends, or his commission fees, nor to insure his business."[62] Conversion was a spiritual transformation that stood apart and above all these things. But this seemed to concede the very point that Ravasz and his fellow Reformed leaders had been trying to deny. If Christianity was a "spiritual institution" and not an "instrument of this world," as Ravasz, argued that it was, then the Reformed Church had no political power to oppose secular authorities who grounded public mores in racial ideology. Christians might know in private that all people could embrace Christ equally. In public, however, Calvinists must accept that Christian Hungary was a nation defined by race.

Converts, Jews, and the Inexorable Logic of Exclusion

Most of those affected by the three Jewish Laws were not converts. Jews considered "Jewish" by law had to bear the pressures of legalized racism without powerful institutions like the Christian churches lobbying on their behalf. The wealthiest and socially best connected could sometimes use contacts to ease their personal circumstances. Some Jewish business owners, for example, were able to comply with the letter of the Jewish Laws by placing a trusted "Christian" employee in positions of nominal leadership within their firms. These so-called "strawmen" acted as the legal owners, even if effective control remained entirely in the hands of the former "Jewish" owners. But these loopholes were only open to a very few. By 1942, the three antisemitic laws, and the ever growing number of administrative decrees which they authorized, had begun to place terrible strains on middle- and lower-middle-class Jewish Hungarians throughout the country. White-collar workers were often summarily dismissed from their jobs because they were Jews and forced to seek other positions that might pay even a fraction of the salary they had lost. Unskilled workers faced even greater challenges. Those with professional training also found doors slammed in their face. For example, more than half of the applicants to the Hungarian Press Chamber, an organization that gave necessary credentials to anyone working in the publishing industry, were rejected out of

62. László Ravasz, "Mit kerestek ti a keresztyénségben? Részletek dr. Ravasz László rádióprédikációjából," *Református Élet* 5, no. 51 (17 December 1938): 498–99.

hand as "Jews" according to the race laws. At the same time, thousands of Jewish men between the ages of eighteen and forty-nine were called up for harsh and degrading labor service: some fifty thousand unarmed labor servicemen accompanied the Hungarian Second Army to the Ukrainian front in 1942. The complicated racial laws also made it extremely difficult for Jews living in the territories regained in the German-brokered territorial adjustments of 1938 and 1939 to prove their citizenship. Many Jews in formerly Czechoslovak territory (southern Slovakia and Subcarpathian Ruthenia) suddenly found in 1939 that they were "resident aliens" in Hungary, even when they had never moved from their homes. Two years later, approximately eighteen thousand Jews, some of them long-time residents of Subcarpathian Ruthenia and some of them refugees from Poland, were deported to Ukraine because Hungarian civil administrators considered all of them to be stateless aliens. There, German mobile killing squads murdered all but several hundred.[63]

"By far the most devastating effect of the [1941 racial] law was psychological and propagandistic."[64] Members of Hungary's extreme right-wing movements used the debates about the anti-Jewish marriage law to raise fears of racial pollution in parliament and in the wider press. By attributing moral degeneracy and all sorts of sexual depravity to Jews in the most vicious and sensationalistic terms, they heightened public hysteria about the Jewish menace, building popular support for "necessary" solutions to Hungary's "Jewish question." The law also came into existence only weeks after Hungary declared war against the Soviet Union. As extreme right politicians argued that Jews and Hungarians were completely separate and hostile races, they also insisted that Jews, for this very reason, posed a security risk now that the nation was at war. László Endre, the fascist deputy lord lieutenant of Pest County (a position similar to a kind of lieutenant governor) who would become a state secretary in the Ministry of Interior after the Germans occupied Hungary in 1944, raised the specter of the "Judeo-Bolshevik menace" explicitly in his addresses to the public. To him, all Jews were potential spies and subversives, foreigners who rejoiced at the prospect of a Soviet victory. Endre even went so far as to demand the confiscation of radios and telephones from the most particularly suspect Jews, believing they would use these devices to pass secrets to the enemy and to spread Allied propaganda at home.[65] Given this public climate, it was entirely irrelevant to the vast majority of Hungarians persecuted as Jews under the racial laws that the Christian churches spoke out in defense of "Christians of Jewish origin."

63. Braham, *Politics of Genocide*, 159–60, 205–13, 319–22.
64. Ibid., 201.
65. Pelle, *A gyűlölet vetése*, 160–206; on Endre, see 173ff.

For the politics of Christian nationalism, however, the passage of Law XV/1941 was a watershed. Hungary's Christian churches had fought secular nationalists and each other to control the content of Hungarian national identity throughout the interwar period. Hungary, they had declared, was a Christian nation, and all their efforts to define what exactly that meant depended for coherence on a well-developed vision of an insidious and antinational "Jewish spirit" at work in Hungary. Reacting to this menace, secular and religious nationalists alike had looked to civil authorities to exercise the power of the state on behalf of the endangered nation. Yet Hungary's religious leaders had also imagined that the power of the secular state had bounds that it could not cross. As the extreme right in Hungary increasingly defined "Christian Hungary" in racial terms, they claimed the right to intervene in marriages and in baptismal practices for the good of the whole (racial) Christian nation. These were incursions into social spaces that church leaders considered to be the purview of religious, not secular, authority. By 1941, the position of converts under civil law had become the single most important location for this struggle. If secular nationalists could say who was a Jew and who was a Christian solely on the basis of secular racial law, then religion, and the social authority of Hungary's Christian churches, simply did not matter. The nature of Christian nationalism in Hungary hung in the balance.

In resisting state encroachment, both churches insisted that Jews were a hostile cultural force, not a racial enemy. However, this position was not nearly as clear-cut as Christian religious leaders liked to think, even if it did seem to promise a different attitude to antisemitic politics. Like the fascists whom they opposed, Hungary's religious nationalists based their understanding of "Christian Hungary" on a logic of exclusion that defined Jews and Christians as groups forever apart. Exactly how Christian Hungary would exclude the Jews in its midst was never clear. In the face of growing anti-Jewish hysteria, church leaders tried to keep their distance from the most radical secular nationalists. Bishops from all Christian confessions issued vague statements requesting that discriminatory laws be carried out humanely. Like secular conservatives, they found the rhetoric and tactics of Hungary's extreme right distasteful in the extreme. Some Catholics and Calvinists did even more than this, acting on their own, in defiance of the public position their superiors had taken. But the churches as public institutions, and as critical players in the politics of Christian-nationalism, did little else. As later events demonstrated, opposing racism by favoring exclusion on other grounds would prove, after 1941, to be no real political opposition at all.

7

Genocide and Religion

The Christian Churches and
the Holocaust in Hungary

Hungary declared war on the Soviet Union on 27 June 1941. Within days, Hungarian army and gendarme units had occupied large sections of Subcarpathian Ruthenia, territory in present-day Ukraine that had been part of the Kingdom of Hungary before 1918. As military and gendarme forces secured the area, the newly created National Central Alien Control Office (KEOKH) began to identify and isolate alien nationals who might be security risks. They found many likely targets. As Nazi German troops had advanced eastward first into Poland in 1939 and then into the Soviet Union in 1941, thousands of Polish and Soviet Jews had fled southward into Hungary. By the summer of 1941, there were between fifteen thousand and thirty-five thousand Jewish refugees within Hungary's borders, all registered as aliens with KEOKH. Officials responsible for controlling illegal immigration, enthusiastically supported by the extreme right press, were eager to deport all of them back into German-held territory. Using government policy against illegal immigration as a pretext, gendarmes in Subcarpathian Ruthenia began to round up any Jews who could not clearly prove their residency status. Many of those they arrested were Jewish Hungarians who were unable to produce all the proper documentation; in some cases, police simply ignored the documents presented to them and arrested Jewish citizens whose residency status was absolutely clear. In addition, KEOKH authorities rounded up resident aliens in Budapest as well. All told, some eighteen thousand Jews, many of them refugees from Poland but a large number of them Hungarian Jews, were apprehended and transported to an internment camp at Kőrösmező on the Hungarian-Ukrainian border. As Hungarian military and gendarme authorities transported roughly one thousand a day in open cattle cars across the border and into German-held territory, the rest of the internees waited with little food and water in tents pitched in a muddy, rain-soaked field. By the end of August 1941, the operation was complete. Nearly all of the eighteen thousand deported Jews were massacred by German SS units on 27–28 August 1941 at Kamenets-Podol'sk (Kamianets'-Podil's'kyi) in the Ukraine.[1]

As rumors of the massacres were confirmed, Hungary's minister of interior, Ferenc Keresztes-Fischer, ordered an immediate end to the deportations. Unlike many of his colleagues in the ministry of defense and within the gendarmerie, Keresztes-Fischer resisted the growing power of the extreme right and insisted that Hungary was a nation of laws. But he was not alone in his outrage. News of the roundups, internment, and deportation of the "alien" Jews at Kőrösmező moved a number of Hungarians to lodge formal protests at the highest levels. One of the leaders of the protest was a Catholic nun, Sister Margit Slachta, the founder of the Society of the Sisters of Social Service.[2] Almost as soon as gendarmes began to round up "alien" Jews in Subcarpathian Ruthenia, Sister Slachta wrote to Nándor Batizfalvy, an officer in the KEOKH, to protest things being done "in the name of Christianity, but against the spirit of Christianity." Justice, she reminded Batizfalvy, demanded that people be judged "as individuals. . . . It is not possible to excuse somebody simply because he is, let's say, of the Turanian race [i.e., racially Hungarian], or to condemn him simply because he is a Jew." On 5 August 1941, she traveled to Subcarpathian Ruthenia with three companions to verify what she had heard. Despite harassment and obstruction by gendarme authorities, Slachta and her companions were able to see the internment camp, discovering that many of those held captive were Hungarians and not Polish refugees, as had been widely reported. Appalled by the wretched and degrading conditions in which the internees were kept, the four eyewitnesses prepared a report describing what they had seen, concluding that "in a civilized state that calls itself Christian, the way in which these people, the majority of them entirely innocent, are being treated is simply an outrage against those principles that it proclaims so pompously." The four distributed this report to a wide circle of acquaintances in positions of social and political power. During these weeks in the summer of 1941, Sister Slachta also wrote a number of letters to acquaintances who were socially well-connected, in-

---

1. Tamás Majsai, "A kőrösmezei zsidódeportálás 1941-ben," in *A Ráday-gyüjtemény évkönyve* 4–5 (1984–85), 59–89, as well as the collection of documents reproduced in the same volume, 197–237. See also Judit Fejes, "On the History of the Mass Deportations from Carpatho-Ruthenia in 1941," in *The Holocaust in Hungary: Fifty Years Later*, ed. Braham and Pók, 305–28.

2. Majsai, "A kőrösmezei zsidódeportálás 1941-ben," 73.

cluding two to Regent Horthy's wife, impressing on them the urgency of the situation.[3]

There is no evidence that Slachta's efforts directly influenced Ferenc Keresztes-Fischer's decision to end the 1941 deportations immediately. Even so, Sister Slachta's actions called attention to the moral crisis of Christian nationalism in Hungary. Compelled by conscience, Slachta traveled to Kőrösmező to see the deportations at firsthand. There, at the border, she saw stateless Jews kept in quarantine apart from all society while they awaited deportation. As Slachta and her companions wrote in their eyewitness report, the sight was devastating: "Anyone who has truly seen the despair which sits on the faces of these people . . . anyone who has been witness to that still and hopeless quiet that says more than any word . . . will remember this until the end of their lives."[4] Stripped of citizenship, legal personhood, and nationality, the internees at Kőrösmező had lost everything save what Hannah Arendt called "the abstract nakedness of being human and nothing but human."[5] Their misery stirred compassion and outrage in a few like Margit Slachta, who lobbied desperately on their behalf. But this alone was not enough. Most were indifferent to the treatment of "illegal aliens." Some asked for more details before they would act. A few, whom Sister Slachta described as "creatures who called themselves human," enthusiastically "engaged in these atrocities and even talked about them proudly."[6] Within days, Hungarian gendarmes deported the interned "alien" Jews into Nazi-occupied territory, where all but a few were murdered. To Slachta, this violated all the moral norms of her Christian faith. In the face of such undeniable and elemental human suffering, how, she asked, could a state that openly declared itself to be Christian either undertake or condone such criminal actions?

Hungary's Christian churches remained silent on this question. Though some in both the Catholic and Protestant churches, especially those active in the defense of convert rights, actively opposed the 1941 deportations as Slachta had done, none of them enjoyed the open and public support of the leaders of their churches. Those who could have spoken with the weight and authority of high church office chose neither to support the deportations nor to condemn them openly. No doubt, many of them reasoned that the actions in Subcarpathian Ruthenia were an anomaly. Despite cries for a radical solution to Hungary's Jewish question, the Hun-

3. "Iratok a kőrösmezei zsidódeportálás történetéhez," in *A Ráday-gyüjtemény évkönyve* 4–5 (1984–85), ed. Tamás Majsai and Ilona Mona, 195–237. See esp. 197–88, 203–6, 217–26. Citations from 197 and 226.

4. Ibid., 221.

5. Hannah Arendt, *The Origins of Totalitarianism* (New York: Harcourt Brace, 1973), 290–304; citation on 297.

6. "Iratok," ed. Majsai and Mona, 221.

garian conservative ruling elite maintained a strange semblance of normality and the rule of law, in which Jewish Hungarians lived precariously, but remained alive nonetheless. The three antisemitic laws remained in effect. However, Hungarian authorities undertook no more deportations. The regime continued to call up Jewish men of draft age for brutal and often deadly work in labor service companies. Yet, between 1942 and 1943, the anti-Nazi general Vilmos Nagy, who commanded those labor service companies, did much to improve the conditions of the Jewish men who worked in them. In early 1942, army and gendarme units committed other isolated atrocities in the region around Novi Sad (Újvidék) in present-day Serbia. Again, however, conservative politicians reacted strongly, recalling the officers in charge of those massacres and ordering them to stand trial for their actions. See-sawing in this way between the extreme right and a more compassionate conservatism, Hungary's ruling elite gambled on remaining Nazi German allies just long enough for the British and the United States to win the war in Europe and keep the Soviets from occupying Hungary.

No one shared these surreal diplomatic hopes more strongly than the 750,000 Jews still alive within Hungary's borders at the beginning of 1944. In March 1944, however, the government's diplomatic fortunes collapsed. Anticipating Hungary's attempt to withdraw from their alliance and eager to mobilize Hungarian resources for the war effort, the German high command ordered Hungary to be occupied.[7] Unchecked by anti-Nazi conservatives, pro-Nazi Hungarian state officials began once more to deport Hungary's Jews, this time working in coordination with Adolf Eichmann and his team of SS men. The murderous potential inherent in Christian nationalism that Margit Slachta had glimpsed in the internment camp on the Ukrainian border in 1941 emerged again with brutal clarity. Knowing full well that deportation entailed death for many of those deported, Hungary's Christian religious leaders were forced to ask themselves how they should speak and act in the name of their churches and their faith. Could the churches, as institutions in society, remain committed to the idea of Christian nationalism, even when the definition of Hungary as a Christian nation had become a "politics of genocide?"[8]

From Exclusion to Genocide

The German army occupied Hungary on 19 March 1944. Within three days, Hungary had a new government. The new cabinet was the product

7. Christian Gerlach and Götz Aly, *Das letzte Kapitel: Der Mord an den ungarischen Juden* (Stuttgart: Deutsche Verlags-Anstalt, 2002), 98ff.
8. Braham, *The Politics of Genocide.*

of intense negotiations between Reich officials and the regent, Miklós Horthy, and was viewed by all parties as a compromise. Though German authorities had initially hoped for a cabinet with no ties to the former "government party," they were also keen to have a constitutional solution, sanctioned by Horthy and established without the use of force. As a result, the new government had several "government party" members, all highly esteemed as technical experts in their fields, which only enhanced the cabinet's legitimacy. However, the new regime was in other respects a significant change of direction. Three of the new ministers, including the deputy prime minister, were members of a radical right opposition party led by the former prime minister, Béla Imrédy. Most significantly, the Interior Ministry changed hands. Throughout the political crises of the late 1930s and early 1940s, when radical right sympathizers had begun to make their presence felt throughout the Hungarian civil and especially military administration, the upper echelon of this ministry had been widely regarded as a bastion of Hungary's traditional conservatives. In the wake of the German occupation, however, a coterie of new faces took over important positions. Andor Jaross, another of Béla Imrédy's adherents and a virulent antisemite from reoccupied Slovakia, became interior minister. The sole representative in the new government from Hungary's native National Socialist Party, László Baky, worked under Jaross as a high-ranking secretary of state in charge of the gendarmerie. Finally, a second secretaryship of state went to László Endre, another well-known radical right politician; Endre was given special competence over "Jewish affairs." The three men (Jaross, Baky, and Endre) would work closely in the coming months to coordinate anti-Jewish policy. No Arrow Cross members were included in the new government, a point on which Horthy had insisted. The regent also succeeded in installing a fellow military officer, General Döme Sztójay, as prime minister of the new cabinet. Satisfied that this arrangement was the best solution for the country given the circumstances, Horthy swore in the new cabinet on 22 March 1944.[9]

Thereafter, Miklós Horthy withdrew from politics for several months, hoping with this gesture to distance himself as much as possible from a government about which he still had misgivings. A number of other government officials stepped down for similar reasons. The new regime also dismissed some officials outright and compelled many more to tender their resignations. Within the space of a week, twenty-nine of Hungary's forty

9. A detailed account of the negotiations that brought this cabinet into being is Carlile A. Macartney, October Fifteenth: *A History of Modern Hungary, 1929–1945* (Edinburgh: University Press, 1956–57), 2:248ff.

county lord lieutenants had left office. They were followed by the lord mayor, mayor, and deputy mayor of Budapest, as well as the mayors of some two-thirds of Hungary's larger towns. New directors also took charge at institutions like the National Bank and the National Radio. All their replacements came from the farthest right wing of the government party, from Béla Imrédy's radical right opposition, or from the Hungarian national socialists; the latter became especially prominent in security positions. In many cases, the new minister of the interior, Andor Jaross, was able simply to appoint the new officials on his own authority, often choosing colleagues from Béla Imrédy's far right party to fill the vacant posts.[10] But not all political and administrative desks changed hands. A number of those in political or civil service before the German occupation continued to serve after 19 March as well. Nor did these holdovers need to be retrained in the policy aims of the new regime. Hungary's civil servants had proven themselves entirely willing to execute legally promulgated anti-Jewish decrees since the inception of the First Jewish Law in 1938.[11] The new cadre of civil administrators appointed after 22 March 1944 thus represented a decisive push in a direction many had already been leaning. The new appointments silenced voices of opposition or even of restraint in the state bureaucracy, shifting the entire political structure, from the cabinet at the top down to the county seats, markedly to the right.

The new government also took steps to give voices on Hungary's far right a monopoly in the public sphere. On 28 March 1944, both the Social Democratic Party and the Independent Smallholders, an agrarian reform party, were dissolved, silencing the most significant voices of political opposition on the Left. Shortly thereafter, the several tiny liberal parties based primarily in Budapest were shut down as well. In addition, a committee was organized to review the membership of the old government party, and several of its members were expelled or forced to resign on the recommendation of this board. State officials also closed centrist and left-leaning newspapers, leaving in operation only the official papers of the government party (under new editorial direction), the papers of the radical right parties, the two newspapers operated by the Catholic Church, and the ethnic German press. At the same time, government policy promoted the public prominence of racial antisemitism. The prime minister's new press chief made anti-Jewish propaganda a central feature in the government publications now under his control. On his authority, the works of Jewish authors were banned, and all publishing houses determined to be

10. Again, Macartney describes these political shifts. See *October Fifteenth*, 2:269ff.

11. A point emphasized by: Ágnes Ságvári, "Parancsra tették? Közigazgatás, őrségváltás, törvénytisztelő állampolgárok 1944-ben," in *The Holocaust in Hungary: Fifty Years Later*, ed. Braham and Pók, 405–24.

under "Jewish control" were closed. Government agents also organized book burnings of works by Jewish authors. Other newly founded institutions likewise encouraged public discussion of racial matters. Zoltán Bosnyák's Hungarian Institute for Research on the Jewish Question, for example, published a newspaper (*Struggle*) very similar to *Der Stürmer* as well as numerous other texts borrowed and translated from German propaganda agencies.

From the first days of its existence, the new Hungarian government pressed ahead with new and expansive anti-Jewish measures. As they occupied the country, German officials, especially those in the SS, were eager to begin the organized murder of Hungary's Jewish community as they had done throughout the rest of Europe. Adolf Eichmann, at the head of a small planning group, entered Hungary with the German army and quickly set up an office. But they did not need to coerce the new regime into adopting a policy of anti-Jewish persecution. To the contrary, the Hungarian radical right found that the German occupation had removed all the political obstacles to the antisemitic course they had long contemplated. Officials at Andor Jaross's Interior Ministry developed many of the new anti-Jewish measures on their own initiative. Across a broad spectrum of policy matters, the Hungarian government's zeal in stripping its Jewish citizens of their last remaining liberties and then organizing their deportation functioned as a complement to Nazi genocidal policy. Eager to redistribute wealth to "Christian" Hungarians, and to finance long-needed social reforms, the new Hungarian government began to expropriate Jewish property. At the same time, German authorities demanded forced laborers and material resources for their own war economy. Both governments were eager to whip up support for the war effort by rooting out "traitors" and "alien subversives" among the Hungarian population. All these factors combined to create a political dynamic in which German and Hungarian authorities cooperated to persecute, segregate, and then deport Hungary's Jews into German controlled territory, where Germans could decide who would work and who would die.[12]

The details of this process, however, should not obscure the main point. As the historian Randolph Braham has written, "The joint, concerted, and single-minded drive by these two groups made the effectuation of the Final Solution in Hungary possible: neither could have succeeded without the other."[13] For years, the radical right in Hungary had demanded that a renewed and resurrected nation violently expel Jews from its midst. But the

---

12. Gerlach and Aly, *Das letzte Kapitel.*
13. Randolph L. Braham, "The Holocaust in Hungary: A Retrospective View," in *The Holocaust in Hungary*, ed. Braham and Pók, 285–304. See 296.

persecution of Jews had also been at the center of the Nazi's own vision of German national renewal. Though this vision evolved into genocide only incrementally, by 1941 it stood at the "center of the Nazi war effort," a "strategic imperative" that connected a war of extermination against the Jews to the catastrophic war that Nazi Germany was waging against the Allies.[14] In 1944, these different visions of national redemption became one. In the days following the German occupation, radical Christian nationalists in Hungary fatally linked their country to Nazi Germany's war of annihilation.

The government's new anti-Jewish decrees came in the form of orders issued by the Ministry of the Interior. Each followed the last with breathtaking speed; taken together, the decrees stripped Jewish Hungarians of their last remaining liberties, denied them any kind of public representation apart from a state-sanctioned Jewish Council, and authorized the plunder of their property. Police arrested and interned some on false charges. In many professions, Jews were dismissed from their jobs outright. State officials received license to requisition Jewish property; in other cases, Jews were forced to register their property with government authorities, the first step toward its ultimate confiscation. Jews were prohibited from traveling and denied access to telephone communication. Most ominously, order number 1240/1944 made it compulsory for all those legally described as Jews to wear a yellow star prominently on their persons. The decree derived its definition of Jewish status from the formula given in Law XV/1941, though exemptions were granted in certain instances, as in the case of certain, highly decorated war veterans. A supplementary order (no. 1450/1944) also exempted practicing and retired clergy, members of religious orders, and deacons and deaconesses. These few exceptions notwithstanding, the series of ministerial decrees demonstrated the triumph of racist policy in Christian Hungary.

"Cast Back into Jewry": The Defense of Converts, Again

Faced with a steady onslaught of new anti-Jewish measures, the Catholic Holy Cross Society prepared a memorandum, which Cardinal Serédi forwarded to Prime Minister Sztójay a few days later, on 31 March. In the statement, Bishop Vilmos Apor, speaking on behalf of the society's direc-

---

14. Konrad H. Jarausch and Michael Geyer, *Shattered Past: Reconstructing German Histories* (Princeton: Princeton University Press), 133.

200 Genocide and Religion

tors, repeated the church's claim that religious sincerity made converts to Christianity national as well.

> The Christians of Jewish origin . . . feel themselves to be real Magyars and good Christians. In large part they were born and raised in the Christian religion; truly many of them are racially mixed, and it is natural that in Hungary it is not the Jewish, but rather the Christian origin, education, and view of life which exercises its influence in complete measure in their spiritual cast of mind. Counting or conscripting these Christians as Jews has caused real psychic pain; however, it could not destroy them in their faith to the Hungarian homeland and their Catholic faith.[15]

The society's memorandum was thus an affirmation of the power of Christian national culture to shape a personality. The children of converts, they asserted, were raised in a Christian, not a Jewish, family; moreover, the lessons they learned at home were only reinforced by Christian Hungarian society at large. The church was thus omnipresent in the public and private life of a convert, linking home and world and providing a constant formative pressure on the individual. In this way, (Catholic) Christian religion produced national identity. Converts (or at least their children), shaped by a religious nationalist milieu, could in time become "good Hungarians."

Bishop Ravasz expressed similar concerns about the treatment of converts under the decree of 30 March. He too addressed a letter to Prime Minister Sztójay, and another to Minister of the Interior Jaross. In the former, the bishop reminded the prime minister of Paul's Epistle to the Galatians, in which it was written that Jews and Greeks were "all one in Christ Jesus." Ravasz explained that "it follows from this that the burdens which punish Jews because they are Jews cannot be imposed on members of the Christian Church." But the bishop recognized that he was swimming against the tide. Government decree had made the definition of "Jewish status" given in the text of Law XV/1941 authoritative for all anti-Jewish measures, and the bishop could only add that "we cannot do otherwise than ask for sympathetic treatment within the framework of the law for those members of our church judged to be Jews." In addition to this correspondence, Ravasz met privately with a number of other prominent public figures to discuss the anti-Jewish measures. During the month of April, the bishop met twice with Regent Horthy, as well as with Gyula

---

15. Memorandum of the Holy Cross Society to the government, 29 March 1944. Reprinted in Jenő Gergely, "A katolikus püspöki kar és a konvertiták mentése," *Történelmi Szemle* 27, no. 4 (1984): 580–616. Document 4/b., 590–1. Serédi's letter of 31 March forwarding the memorandum to Prime Minister Sztójay is also reproduced. Document 4/c., 591.

Ambrózy (the head of the regent's Cabinet Office), András Tasnádi Nagy (president of the Lower House of Parliament and a lay leader in the government of the Reformed Church), and Zsigmond Perényi (president of the Upper House of Parliament). In each of these meetings, Ravasz discussed possible legal exemptions for converts.[16]

Prime Minister Sztójay responded similarly to both of these requests, insisting that his government's anti-Jewish measures had been created to solve what was a racial, not a religious nor even a cultural, problem. In a letter to Cardinal Serédi of 3 May 1944, Sztójay argued that the Hungarian government had to proceed within a racial framework in order to show that it could "adapt itself to the European order being built on new foundations."[17] One week later, Sztójay wrote also to Bishop Ravasz. In this letter, he expanded on his government's racial policy.

> The ... government ... cannot veer from its principled point of departure, according to which Jews are a race and thus the regulation of the Jewish question is a racial and not a religious problem. All members of the Hungarian Royal government believe and profess the transformative power of the sanctity of baptism on the inner religious lives of baptized individuals; this power, according to the natural order, does not, however, radically alter given racial qualities.[18]

With these two letters, the prime minister thus rejected the larger claim which the Hungarian churches had been trying to make for some time. National identity, he claimed, was primarily a racial category, and Jews, whatever their religious convictions, were therefore excluded as a separate race.

Despite these differences, leaders in both the Catholic and Protestant churches continued to seek exemptions for their followers who were affected by the new antisemitic ordinances. Their strategies were similar, though it seems that the Catholic Cardinal Serédi rejected offers of official

16. Ravasz's letter of 6 April 1944 to Prime Minister Sztójay is reproduced in a Pro Memoria, entitled "A református egyház vezetőségének állásfoglalása a zsidókérdés ügyében. (Egy fejezet Ravasz László készülő püspöki jelentéséből.)," which Ravasz began preparing already in December 1944 or January 1945. There are several drafts of this document of varying lengths, clearly composed at different points in: RL: C./141 Papers of László Ravasz, 16. doboz. I am using a copy marked "1945." Randolph Braham bases his account of the actions taken by the Protestant churches on a copy of this document, as did Albert Bereczky in his translated account from the immediate postwar period. See Braham, *Politics of Genocide*, 1185–86 and Albert Bereczky, *Hungarian Protestantism and the Persecution of the Jews* (Budapest: Sylvester, 1945).

17. Cardinal Serédi included excerpts from Sztójay's letter of 3 May 1944 in his circular letter to Hungary's bishops, dated 17 May 1944. This document is reproduced in Gergely, "A püspöki kar és a konvertiták," Document 12, 603.

18. This letter is reproduced in Ravasz's Pro Memoria, 8–9.

cooperation between the confessions on several occasions. Their efforts produced only a few modest results. The government did promise Cardinal Serédi and Bishop Ravasz alike that they had no objections to a subcommittee for "Christians of Jewish origin" being established within the framework of the Jewish Council. The prime minister, in an effort to distinguish racial from religious policy, also professed himself indifferent to whatever marker converts chose to wear to declare themselves as baptized, so long as they also wore the yellow star as the decree demanded. The government also granted some further exemptions to families defined as mixed marriages, including the right of these families to continue to employ household servants. (The antisemitic decrees had forbidden Christians from working in any capacity for Jews.) Finally, Bishop Ravasz did win the verbal, though not the written, consent of the interior minister for issuing official certificates to Reformed church elders affected by the anti-Jewish laws. With this encouragement, the bishops of the Reformed Church issued such certificates to the elders in their church districts. Writing after the war, Albert Bereczky observed that civil authorities had often honored these as proof of non-Jewish status.[19]

Church leaders were, however, acutely aware that even these modest achievements only goaded Hungary's radical right into ever greater paroxysms of anticlerical rage. Fascist newspapers lashed out even at the pastoral newsletters of the Catholic Church, simply for advising converts to wear a white cross beside their yellow star.[20] Moreover, the churches' ardent defense of converts' rights had persuaded many of Hungary's Jews to file for conversion. In Pest alone, there were 2,260 registered conversions in 1940. Available statistics show a similarly high rate for the following years: 1,463 in 1941; 1,858 in 1942; and 994 in the first nine months of 1943.[21] An equally great number prepared to convert in the days following the German occupation. Within the first month, 788 Jews in Pest had filed for conversion; this contrasted with the 176 individuals in the capital who had converted in the three months before Germany had occupied Hungary.[22] Both churches continued to insist on an instructional period of at least several months (generally one year, in the case of the Reformed Church); in addition, the newly converted often found their act brought them little good as Hungary's gendarmes rounded up Jew and convert

19. Bereczky, *Hungarian Protestantism*, 18.
20. U.S. National Archives. RG 208 Box 275 NC 148/E.367 File "E: Balkans (Hungary)—6." Report "The Attitude of the Hungarian Churches toward the New Regime" prepared by the Office of War Information; Bureau of Overseas Intelligence. Central Files 1941–45. My thanks to David Frey for sharing this source with me.
21. Braham, *Politics of Genocide*, 896–97.
22. Ibid., 935 n. 90.

alike with little or no attempt at discrimination. Even so, the perception that Hungary's churches offered some sanctuary, however uncertain, to Hungary's Jews angered many on the radical right. László Endre, the state secretary in the Ministry of the Interior with special responsibilities for "Jewish affairs" complained in a public speech: "After the order had been issued to crowd them into ghettos, the Jews tried everything to get out of there. . . . In the saving of Jews, unfortunately—and I must say this honestly—the pastors of all kinds and ranks of the Christian confessions stand in the first place."[23] Even after the deportations had ceased, the director of Catholic Action, Zsigmond Mihalovics, could report to Cardinal Serédi that the "mass baptism of Jews" had resulted in waves of "anti-priest and anti-Catholic agitation" in Budapest.[24]

None of this slowed the pace of the anti-Jewish campaign. On 26 April 1944, the Sztójay government decreed the compulsory roundup of Hungary's Jews into ghettos. This came ten days after authorities in reoccupied Subcarpathian Ruthenia and northern Transylvania had already proceeded on their own authority to round up the Jews in their jurisdictions. Leaders of both churches responded by asking that Christians forced by law into the ghettos be placed separately. Cardinal Serédi wrote to Prime Minister Sztójay on 10 May asking that the precedent of special treatment established within the labor service battalions be extended to the ghetto administration as well. Serédi was particularly concerned that clergy be allowed into the ghetto to minister to their followers within.[25] Nine days later, the directors of the Reformed Church's General Synod made a similar request, though they prefaced it by declaring that they "decidedly disapproved of" the government's policy of forced resettlement and that they believed such a measure from the ancient past of Christendom "could not be renewed."[26] Catholic bishops were equally concerned by the measure. Bishop Endre Hamvas of Csanád described atrocities committed against the Jews in his diocese and recounted reports that he had heard of far worse in northeastern Hungary. Yet, he also reserved his greatest concern for "Christians of Jewish origin," claiming that his clergy were doing what they could "to exempt the converts from ghettoization."[27] But these efforts were in vain. By mid April, Hungarian authorities had begun to round up Jews and converts alike in ghettos. Only a few weeks later, the

23. Citation in Károly Hetényi Varga, "A magyar katolikus egyház az üldözöttekért (1944–1945)," in *Magyarország 1944: Üldöztetés—Embermentés*, ed. Szabolcs Szita (Budapest: Nemzeti tankönyvkiadó, 1994).
24. EPL: 6647/1944. Zsigmond Mihalovics to Cardinal Jusztinián Serédi, 5 August 1944.
25. Gergely, "A katolikus püspöki kar," Document 12, 604.
26. Ravasz, Pro Memoria, 10; Directors of the General Synod to Prime Minister Döme Sztójay, 19 May 1944.
27. Cited in Braham, *Politics of Genocide*, 1178.

government issued orders for all those "of Jewish origin" to be deported. From mid May until early July, transport trains ran constantly from entrainment centers throughout Hungary to Auschwitz.

The Politics of Public Protest

The systematic mass deportation of Hungary's Jews began on 15 May 1944. For several weeks prior to this date, representatives from Hungary's Interior Ministry had met, joined on several occasions by members of Adolf Eichmann's special planning group, to arrange the expulsion of all of Hungary's Jews from Hungarian territory. These experts had divided Hungary up into a number of gendarmerie districts and coordinated a timetable with Reich officials to eliminate bottlenecks in the transport system. During the period of systematic deportations (slightly less than two months), transport trains brought some twelve thousand to fourteen thousand Hungarian Jews to Auschwitz per day. Hungary's gendarmerie working closely with local civilian and police officials began deporting the Jews of Subcarpathian Ruthenia and northern Transylvania first. When this was completed some three weeks later, officials in northern Hungary began deportations. This was followed in turn by the deportations from southeastern, western, and southwestern Hungary. According to the schedule developed by Interior Ministry planners, the Jews of Budapest were to be the last group deported. But as police began relocating Jews in the capital city into specially designated "yellow-star" houses, a group of advisors around Regent Miklós Horthy began to consider halting deportations, a decision the regent finally took on 7 July. Several days later the Interior Minister dismissed both László Baky, chief of the gendarmerie, and László Endre, secretary of state with special authority in "Jewish affairs," at Horthy's request. By this time, however, nearly 440,000 had been deported to Auschwitz, where the vast majority of them would be murdered or worked to death as slave labor.[28] Only the Jews of Budapest (and the Jewish men who had been conscripted into the labor battalions) remained in Hungary.

Official propaganda maintained that the deportees were being sent to Germany to work. However, leaders in both the Catholic and Reformed Churches, like many in Hungary's political elite, had a good, and in some cases detailed, understanding of all that these deportations entailed.[29] The office of Angelo Rotta, the papal nuncio in Budapest, was one source of

---

28. Randolph Braham discusses the sources on which such estimates can be made in *Politics of Genocide*, 1296–1300. See also his tabulated statistics on the deportations, 674.
   29. Ibid., 832–34.

information. By 1942, Vatican officials had begun to receive detailed reports about the systematic mass murder of Europe's Jews.[30] Papal diplomats in Rome shared this information with their nuncios and representatives throughout Europe. Indeed, József Éliás, the director of the Reformed Church's Good Pastor Committee, a group established to protect Calvinists "of Jewish origin," remembered after the war that he had learnt "almost everything that was important" through Catholic channels already as the Germans occupied Hungary.[31] In his interview, he mentioned József Cavallier, the director of the Holy Cross Society for Catholic converts, as a source of particularly detailed information. Cavallier, relying on information he had received at the Budapest nunciate, could share with Éliás the "entire German schedule concerning Hungarian Jewry," by which he meant the process of segregation and ghettoization which led ultimately to deportation and murder.[32] Gennaro Verolino, *uditore* (a kind of first secretary) at the nunciate in Budapest, acknowledged this when he recalled after the war that "by then we knew they were being taken to Auschwitz. We knew that those found unfit for work were being murdered right upon arrival."[33]

In addition, both Cardinal Serédi and the Calvinist bishop László Ravasz had received a detailed description of the camp at Auschwitz by the end of May 1944. The report in their possession, commonly called the Auschwitz Protocols, had been prepared by two escapees, who took the pseudonyms Rudolf Vrba and Josef Lanik. Both had held positions in the camp and so were able, after their escape to Slovakia, to prepare an accurate description of the layout and operations at Auschwitz. One copy of the report came into the hands of Géza Soós, head of a Hungarian resistance organization and prominent figure in the youth organizations run by Hungary's Reformed Church.[34] Soós in turn gave the report to József Éliás, the director of the Good Pastor Committee, for translation. Éliás and his secretary prepared five copies: one was given to Bishop Ravasz; another to Cardinal Serédi (delivered by József Cavallier of the Holy Cross Society); a third to Bishop Sándor Raffay of the Lutheran Church; a fourth

30. John F. Morley, *Vatican Diplomacy and the Jews during the Holocaust, 1939–1943* (New York: Ktav, 1980), 202–3. On Rotta's role, see 80 and 153.
31. Sándor Szenes, "'Saving People Was Our Main Task . . .': An Interview with Reverend József Éliás," in *Studies on the Holocaust in Hungary*, ed. Randolph L. Braham (Boulder: Social Science Monographs, 1990), 1–64. See 26.
32. Ibid.
33. Péter Bokor, "Fifty Years Ago, The Darkest Year: Conversation with Archbishop Gennaro Verolino on the Siege of Budapest," *The Hungarian Quarterly* 35, no. 136 (1994): 82–89; see 84.
34. Szenes, "'Saving People Was Our Main Task." See also Braham, *Politics of Genocide*, 824–32.

to Ottó Komoly, head of the Hungarian Zionist League; and the fifth (passing through several people) to Mrs. István Horthy, the regent's daughter-in-law.[35] Éliás maintained in a postwar interview that both Ravasz and Serédi had received their copies by mid May, roughly around the time when systematic deportations began. Cardinal Serédi's secretary in 1944, András Zakár, confirmed this, recalling that he remembered reading a copy of the report toward the end of May 1944.[36]

These were not the only sources of information available to Hungary's political elite. In addition there were Western radio broadcasts. Hungarian soldiers who returned from the Eastern front talked of what they had seen. Jewish labor servicemen also served as witness to the murders in Ukraine. Of course, none of this guaranteed that those who possessed such information were willing to believe it. Still, by this late date in the war when so much was known about Nazi policy toward the Jews of Europe, it was obvious that deportations would be deadly for many of Hungary's Jews. This was certainly apparent to Jewish Hungarians themselves: the historian Richard Breitman notes that "despite postwar accusations that Hungarian Jewish activists had concealed essential information, it now appears that much information was available by spring of 1944."[37] The same conclusion can be drawn for the leaders in the Catholic and Protestant churches. Key figures in Hungary's two largest Christian churches were well aware of the fundamental shift that had taken place: Christian nationalism had become a state policy of physical exclusion that they knew would certainly lead to the deaths of many, if not most, of those deported. The ministerial order to deport Hungary's Jews thus placed a great burden on both the Hungarian Catholic and Protestant churches to respond. Throughout the late spring and early summer of 1944, as the deportations proceeded apace, leaders of all of Hungary's Christian confessions debated what kind of public statement would be most appropriate.

The Catholic Church

Jews had figured ambiguously in Catholic discussions of human rights, both in specific legislative debates in Hungary (as in the debate over Law XV/1941) and in the broader condemnations of racism issuing from the

35. In addition to Szenes, " 'Saving People Was Our Main Task," see also the interview with Éliás's secretary, Mária Székely, in *Befejezetlen múlt*, ed. Sándor Szenes, 107–26.

36. András Zakár, secretary to Cardinal Serédi in 1944, remembered reading a copy of the report toward the end of May 1944. See the interview with him in *Befejezetlen múlt*, ed. Szenes, 127–86, esp. 138ff.

37. Richard Breitman, *Official Secrets: What the Nazis Planned, What the British and Americans Knew* (New York: Hill and Wang, 1998), 204.

Vatican during the years before the outbreak of war. Both the Hungarian episcopate and its pontiff in Rome proclaimed a set of natural rights inherently held by all individuals regardless of their origins; the individual person, they declared, stood immediate to God and his or her interests could therefore never be subsumed into the interests of the state. At the same time, however, Hungary's bishops, like many in the church's hierarchy, continued to speak of Jews as a collective, an unindividuated group possessed of an essential "spirit" that was by its nature hostile to Christian morality.[38] It was thus unclear to what extent Jews, as Jews, were understood to possess those natural rights the church believed all men and women possessed by divine right. Hungary's bishops only compounded this uncertainty with their adamant defense of baptized Jews, who, they claimed, had thoroughly distinguished themselves through their conversion from the Jewish community whence they came. Church leaders had voted against Law XV/1941 on this basis and had maintained this position in the face of the anti-Jewish decrees drawn up by the Sztójay government in 1944.

Not all within the Hungarian church presented this distinction so starkly. Áron Marton, the bishop whose diocese encompassed all of Hungarian-held and Romanian-held Transylvania, condemned the anti-Jewish decrees of 1944 in striking terms in a sermon he gave in the provincial capital of Kolozsvár (Cluj) when the Jews of the area were still interned in the ghetto there. Like his fellow bishops, he too spoke of "an order built on justice, on laws that are equally applied to all" and condemned racial theories. However, his sermon was perhaps the clearest statement made by any high cleric in the Hungarian church, explicitly extending this vision of a just order to unbaptized Jews. He and his parishioners, he claimed, had thus been "shocked by news of the restriction of freedom and uncertain fate of certain persons, and [had] followed with great concern the measures that [had] lately been carried out against the Jews." For this, the bishop was publicly condemned by Interior Minister Jaross.[39]

Cardinal Serédi's correspondence with Prime Minister Sztójay before and immediately after the start of deportations contained none of this clarity. In one of his first letters (dated 23 April) to the prime minister written on behalf of the whole church, Serédi had condemned the notion of collective guilt, arguing that neither the church nor the government could deprive fellow citizens (*polgártársaink*) of their rights "to life, to personal freedom, to religious freedom, to the freedom to work, . . . to private property, to human dignity" without "sufficient reason and with-

38. Passelecq and Suchecky, *The Hidden Encyclical*, 163.
39. A large excerpt of this sermon is reproduced in Braham, *Politics of Genocide*, 1192.

out the judgment of a legally empowered judicial body." However, Serédi then went on to request exemptions for "Christians of Jewish origin" on this basis, a deduction which seemed to qualify the universality of the rights that he had only just proclaimed. Similar ambiguities marked a later letter, dated 10 May, one written after gendarmes had begun forcing Hungary's Jews into ghettos. In this appeal too, the cardinal made special mention of converts, asking that "Christians of Jewish origin" be interned separately and that they have access to Catholic pastoral care.[40]

After the Hungarian government had issued the deportation order on 15 May 1944, officials in the Vatican, speaking through the nunciate in Budapest, began urging the Hungarian episcopate to take a more vigorous stand. The nuncio, Angelo Rotta, had himself submitted a formal letter of protest to Sztójay's government, charging that the "whole world knows what the deportation means in practice," and requesting that the Hungarian government "not . . . continue its war against the Jews beyond the limits prescribed by the laws of nature and God's commandments, and to avoid any action" against which either the Vatican or international public opinion would inevitably protest. He too requested that Hungarian authorities distinguish between the baptized and the unbaptized in executing the other anti-Jewish decrees.[41] At the same time, however, Rotta contacted Serédi on several occasions, urging him and the whole Hungarian episcopate to take a firmer stand. In a letter written toward the end of June 1944, the nuncio asked the episcopal bench to "stand up for Christian principles, in defense of our fellow patriots (*honfitársaink*) unjustly punished by the racial decrees, but especially in defense of Christians, so that our compliance has no share in the unfavorable judgment which falls to the detriment of ourselves and of Hungarian Catholicism." In his reply, Serédi rejected the charge that the Hungarian church was compliant, citing only the possibility of still greater dangers which prevented his episcopate from speaking out more strongly.[42]

Saul Friedländer has noted that Rotta's note of protest to Prime Minister Sztójay was important for being "the first official protest against the deportation of Jews made by a representative of the Holy See."[43] It was, with its mention of what deportations "meant in practice," also a remarkably frank acknowledgement that expulsion was tantamount to murder.

40. Gergely, "A katolikus püspöki kar," Document 12, 601–5.
41. Braham, *Politics of Genocide*, 1216–17.
42. Serédi included excerpts from Rotta's letter of 27 June 1944 in a second circular letter to the episcopate, dated 9 July. See Gergely, "A katolikus püspöki kar," Document 18, 615. See also Braham, *Politics of Genocide*, 1178.
43. Saul Friedländer, *Pius XII and the Third Reich*, trans. Charles Fullman (New York: Knopf, 1966), 218.

Some members of the Hungarian episcopate urged their cardinal to follow Rotta's example more closely, touching off a debate over what sort of intervention the church should make. Vilmos Apor, bishop of Győr was the most insistent. As president of the Holy Cross Society, he too had urged Cardinal Serédi throughout the month of April to be more energetic in defending all members of the Catholic Church from the force of the racial decrees. After deportations began, Apor delivered a sermon similar in tone to that of Bishop Marton's, stating that "he who . . . asserts that there are people and groups and races one is permitted to hate, and advocates that there are men whom one may torture, be they either Negros or Jews, . . . is in fact a pagan and clearly guilty."[44] Bishop Apor urged his cardinal to issue a pastoral letter, to be read publicly in parishes throughout Hungary, in response. Deportations gave other prelates pause as well. The bishop of Székesfehérvár, Lajos Shvoy, wrote to Esztergom in late June, saying that the roundup of Jews and their subsequent deportation had left his diocese unsettled and uncertain. He too urged Serédi to issue a pastoral letter that might provide guidance to the faithful.[45]

By late June, Cardinal Serédi began working on a draft of a pastoral letter. However, his assistant, Archbishop Gyula Czapik of Eger, saw fit to remind him of the popular reaction that any statement on behalf of Hungary's Jews would arouse. The church had, after all, virtually been accused of treason by the radical right even for insisting on certain minimal exemptions for converts. "We must choose a mode and a text for this pronouncement," he advised the cardinal, "which, alongside its principled decisiveness, gives as little unnecessary pretext as possible to the expected anti-Church attacks . . . which . . . would turn to the Church's detriment." Czapik included with his letter drafts of two texts which he thought suitable: the first, a short declaration; the second, a longer pastoral letter. The plans for a pastoral letter, a document addressed specifically to the faithful and thus more than a simple statement of principle, concerned Czapik especially. In his view, the cardinal needed to strike the right balance between compassion for Hungary's Jews and concern for the Hungarian nation. It "should not refer only to the Jewish matter, because we could rightly be criticized if only this caused us pain when the life of the whole homeland and nation is at stake."[46]

However, Czapik's prescription was not simply reactive. Certainly, he had a good sense of the virulently antisemitic mood prevalent in Hungary.

44. Excerpts of this sermon are reproduced in Braham, *Politics of Genocide*, 1190–91. A number of Bishop Apor's letters to Cardinal Serédi are reproduced in Gergely, "A katolikus püspöki kar"; see Documents 9/a, 11/a and b, and 15/a.
45. Gergely, "A katolikus püspöki kar," Document 15/b, dated 24 June 1944, 608.
46. Ibid., Document 16/a, dated 24 June 1944, 608–9.

Yet he also believed that the church could use this public intervention to reassert its own vision of Christian nationalism. In both his proposed texts, Archbishop Czapik placed the note of protest in an explicitly national context. To this end, he began his draft of a circular letter with an extended paean to the love of nation which was every Hungarian's sacred duty. He also proposed separating the suffering caused to Hungarians by Allied bombing runs from the "ordering of the Jewish question." Regardless of the form Cardinal Serédi ultimately chose for the public statement, Czapik felt that the church should openly review the history of the "Jewish question" in national life. He suggested: "Without a doubt, many with origins in Jewry have been complicit in the experienced destruction of Hungary's economic, social, and moral life." Czapik went on to place much of the blame for this on Jewish leaders, who had proven unable to restrain "the destructive spirit, harmful to the life of the Magyar nation" which came from within their community. The archbishop also thought it wise to remind the public of the Catholic Church's long history of struggle against this "Jewish spirit" in defense of "our Christian Hungarian national culture and life."[47]

In the end, Cardinal Serédi opted for a pastoral letter to be read during mass in all of Hungary's parishes. Both Bishop Apor and Archbishop Czapik advised Serédi on the final drafts of the text; indeed many of Archbishop Czapik's proposals found expression in the letter that was prepared for distribution. Thus Serédi condemned the damage caused by Allied bombing raids over Hungary. More significantly, the letter contained echoes of Archbishop Czapik's own indecision on the "Jewish question." The church, Serédi declared, deplored the new anti-Jewish measures as an affront to divine law. "To you, our dear believers, we need not list in detail the measures which are well known to you along with the manner of their execution, and which violate or even deny the inherent rights of some of our fellow citizens [*magyar polgártársaink egy része*], even some who are together with us, members of our holy faith, only because of their origin. . . . You could only understand all this, if the same deprivation of rights happened to you."[48] However, the cardinal also conceded, much as Archbishop Czapik had advised, that the state was undeniably responsible for addressing the "Jewish question," since "a part of Jewry has had a guilty subversive influence on the Hungarian economic, social, and moral life." Jewish leaders, he maintained, had not restrained the offending members of their community, and so it was now necessary for the state to

47. Ibid., Documents 16/b and 16/c.
48. The entire text of the letter is reproduced in the original in Gergely, "A katolikus püspöki kar," Document 17 and in translation in Braham, *Politics of Genocide*, 1179–82. I take my citations from Braham's translation.

resolve matters "in a legal and just manner." At the same time, though, it was the church's responsibility to "make very certain that the just shall not suffer, and our Hungarian fellow citizens and Catholic believers not be offended merely because of their origins." On this basis, the church had asked the government to cease deportations to no avail. The cardinal concluded the letter by advising his clergy that the church "disavowed [its] responsibility" for the measures and urging them to pray "for all our Hungarian co-citizens without exception, mainly for our Catholic brethren," for the church and for Hungary.

The letter was dated 29 June 1944, by which date most of Hungary's Jews living outside of Budapest had already been deported. The text was reprinted in sufficient number for every parish priest to receive a copy. Ultimately, the cardinal withdrew it.[49] As officials in Esztergom were sending shipments of the letter to each of Hungary's dioceses, the minister of justice, István Antal, learned of the action and ordered the letter confiscated. Both Antal and Prime Minister Sztójay then met with Cardinal Serédi, warning him particularly of an Arrow Cross coup if the government's legitimacy were undermined. After some negotiation (held on 6 July), in which the cardinal insisted particularly on the exemption of Christians from the anti-Jewish measures, Serédi agreed to withdraw the letter. In return, Prime Minister Sztójay produced a letter that spoke to many of the church's concerns.[50] By this time, the regime had decided to halt deportations, a fact which Sztójay could announce to the episcopate. In addition, the government established an Organization of Christian Jews, separate from the Jewish Council. It also promised to exempt "Christian Jews" if it became necessary to deport the Jews of Budapest, though it gave no guarantee for this. Cardinal Serédi summarized these events in a circular letter sent to each of Hungary's bishops.[51]

In the end, a few archdioceses received the letter before the ministry officials could prevent it. There were reports that the letter was even read in some parishes. In most, however, it was not. Many priests never got a copy; those that did were instructed by their cardinal on state radio (broadcast on 8 and 9 July) that the letter was for the information of clergy and church officials only. In its place, Serédi commanded parish priests to read a short and pointless statement, to the effect that the episcopate continued to negotiate with state officials "in connection with the decrees relating to the Jews and especially the converts." This was done throughout the country on 16 July 1944.

49. Braham describes the letter's fate in *Politics of Genocide*, 1182–85.
50. This letter is reproduced in ibid., 1182–83.
51. Gergely, "A katolikus püspöki kar," Document 18.

The Protestant Churches

Two days after Hungarian officials began systematic deportations, the General Synod of the Reformed Church produced a draft resolution that all were willing to sign. The lay and pastoral presidents of the synod, Jenő Balogh and Bishop László Ravasz respectively, forwarded the text to Prime Minister Sztójay shortly after that. The bulk of the letter dealt with concerns church leaders had been raising since the beginning of the German occupation in March: in the letter, the synod as a body thanked the government for the few exemptions it had been willing to grant and continued to press for further exemptions in the case of Christians with mixed, but largely non-Jewish background. (Specifically, it asked that individuals who had been younger than six when their parents had converted to Christianity be regarded as fully Christian.) It also requested that converts be treated separately as they were relocated in ghettos. However, the church leadership also broached the question of deportations in their letter: "We would like to draw [Prime Minister Sztójay's] attention to those tragic events which have brought the similar deportations of the Jewry of other countries to their final conclusion [*végső befejezés*] and we ask [Sztójay] to do everything to avoid such events and to deflect the responsibility for this from the . . . government and with this the entire Hungarian nation."[52]

The director of the Reformed Church's Good Pastor Society, József Éliás, claimed after the war that by the time the General Synod agreed to this formal statement, Bishop Ravasz, the synod's religious president, had already received and studied a copy of the so-called Auschwitz Protocols. Indeed Éliás suggested that this passage reflected Ravasz's reaction to what he had learned from the document.[53] This may well be true. However, the letter, and its decidedly oblique reference to Auschwitz, if reference it was, did not mark a new approach to the "Jewish question" in Hungary or a reevaluation of the consequences of antisemitic rhetoric. Indeed, a month or so later, Ravasz again defended his church's long-held position on anti-Jewish policy to the World Council of Churches in Switzerland. After deportations of Jews from Hungary had begun, the council again urged the Hungarian Reformed Church to adopt a more critical stance against the Hungarian government and, in particular, its anti-Jewish policies. Ravasz responded with an extended apology for the church's actions since the occupation.

He began with the question "How have Jews behaved during this pe-

---

52. Ravasz, Pro Memoria, 10.
53. Interview with József Éliás in *Befejezetlen múlt*, ed. Sándor Szenes, 61.

riod?" and answered it with an extended criticism of Jewish greed and self-interest. As he had done in 1941, during the debates over Law XV/1941, he reserved particular scorn for those seeking to convert to escape the penalties of antisemtic laws, especially for those who had tried to convert in the period after the German occupation. Ravasz accused these of considering conversion "as if they were taking out life insurance with a company of the first rank, a company which would cheaply undertake to see that not one hair of their heads should be harmed in the case of threatening Jewish persecutions." The church, he claimed, was not called to convert Jews so that "they could keep their millions, their social rank, their political and human rights." In recent months, Ravasz claimed, he had received numerous letters from people affected by the new ordinances, asking for some kind of help or protection. Not one of them had asked simply for "the Word, the Holy Spirit." Nevertheless, the church, he maintained, had not been inactive. If it had not done more, this was precisely because it wished to avoid a *Kulturkampf*, a war with Hungary's fascists over religion that would force the Reformed Church to "burn every bridge" and drive the "life of the Church to partisan warfare." Ravasz concluded on a resentful note, protesting against those foreign countries not yet tested by war and those churches living in comfort who sought to sit in judgment over others. Hungary, Ravasz noted, was suffering greatly because of the war. As a result, his church "cannot accept it when the churches of those nations which have sent these dangers to us nevertheless hold the Hungarian Reformed Church in their bad graces because in the Jewish question it hasn't begun a war of street barricades under the leadership of cardinals and bishops."[54] In the note, then, Ravasz reiterated nearly every prejudice about the "Jewish spirit" that he and the leaders of his church had so richly developed throughout the interwar period. Even at a time when their exclusion from the nation meant murder rather than slander for Jewish Hungarians, leaders of Hungary's Reformed Church refused to abandon this basic tenet of Christian nationalism. Insistence on absolute Jewish difference stifled Protestant efforts to mount a public protest against the deportations just as surely as it had silenced the Catholic Church.

Nevertheless, Hungary's Protestant leaders were keenly aware of the criticism from international groups like the World Council of Churches. All Hungarians knew by the summer of 1944 that the war was nearing an

54. The document, titled "Ravasz László általános tájékoztatója arról, hogy a magyar evangéliumi egyházak mit tettek a legújabb időkben a zsidókérdéssel kapcsolatban," is reproduced in *Budapesti Negyed* 3, no. 2 (1995): 169–80, along with an accompanying commentary written by Tamás Majsai, entitled "Biborosok és püspökök a zsidómentés barikádharcában." Both can be retrieved at: http:// www.bparchiv.hu/magyar/ kiadvany/bpn/08/.

end, however bloody the denouement. Moreover, politicians and public figures alike were desperate to secure better terms of peace after this conflict than those under which Hungarians had chafed since 1918. Faced with these pressures, Protestant leaders began to explore the possibility of a public statement in mid June (by which time deportations had been underway for over a month.) Their first thought had been to win the Catholic Cardinal Serédi's support for a joint statement. The cardinal, however, rejected this idea out of hand.[55] Left to their own devices, several of Hungary's Protestant bishops, both Calvinist and Lutheran, then prepared yet another letter of protest intended for Prime Minister Sztójay.

This letter, dated 20 June 1944, was indeed more explicit in its condemnation of the deportations than anything that had preceded it. In it, the committee of bishops discussed reports of trains carrying Jews across the border on a road which both they and their family members knew "ended in ultimate destruction." The bishops acknowledged that the "Jewish question" was a political question, and thus inherently not in their sphere of competence. However, the "eternal laws of God" compelled them, they claimed, to protest against the "manner" in which the issue was being handled. At the same time, however, the bishops also made special mention of converts, observing once more the essential differences that separated them from other Jews. Converts, they said, "had given proof with their individual lives of their Christian spirit and morality" and were being punished for a " 'Jewish mentality' [*zsidó szellemiség*] with which they had ceremonially broken, and from which not only they, but in many cases their forebears also, had closed themselves off." The letter ended with a warning. The Protestant churches had no desire to increase the many difficulties facing the government. However, if the regime persisted in ignoring their legitimate complaints, then Protestant leaders would feel bound to issue a statement "before the public opinion of our church as well as world Protestantism."[56]

Shortly thereafter, Bishop Ravasz drafted such a statement. The text he envisioned was short, instructing every pastor in both the Reformed and Lutheran Churches to announce to his congregation that numerous appeals to the government regarding the ghettoization and deportations of Hungary's Jews, "be they Christian or not" had gone unanswered. Ravasz also included excerpts from the letter delivered to Sztójay on 21 June, passages in which the committee of bishops had emphasized the inviolability of God's laws. In response, Ravasz claimed, government officials had

55. Ravasz, Pro Memoria, and Éliás interview in *Befejezetlen múlt*, ed. Sándor Szenes.
56. Letter to Prime Minister Sztójay of 20 June 1944, reproduced in Ravasz, Pro Memoria, 19.

promised on several occasions to investigate reports of atrocities, but had each time reneged on their vow to put an end to them. This statement was to be read from every Calvinist and Lutheran pulpit in Hungary on the last Sunday in June. To meet this deadline, Bishop Ravasz immediately began trying to win support for the draft among Hungary's other Protestant bishops.[57]

Without a governmental hierarchy, Hungary's Protestant bishops had to reach a consensus before they could issue any official statement in the name of their churches. It soon became clear, however, that no such agreement existed. Bishop Ravasz, along with several of his colleagues in Budapest, met or corresponded with prominent leaders in every church district more than once in the weeks that followed. Many of those with whom he spoke admitted candidly that such a statement would not be universally popular in their congregations. At one conference, Bishop Andor Enyedy offered his support for the draft but worried about the way in which it would be made public. In his view, many followers would see a political statement in the proclamation, and would be incapable of separating this misapprehension from the content of the letter.[58] Other bishops echoed this worry at a later conference held on 3 July; in the minutes of the meeting it was noted that "more than one raised the difficulty that there would be many pastors who would not read such a protest, and that moreover it would raise great opposition in the congregations."[59] Church leaders in Transylvania shared these concerns. One lay leader noted simply that there was no agreement about condemning the deportations among the district's churchgoers; another noted that the letter would cause arguments in many villages.[60]

Many Protestant leaders also objected to a public statement that only discussed the situation of Hungary's Jews. This was a particular concern among Reformed Church leaders in Transylvania, a region that was, by the summer of 1944, on the front lines in the war against the advancing Red Army. Several prominent members of the regional church government voiced their concerns in a meeting held in the provincial capital of Kolozsvár (Cluj) on 29 June 1944. As noted in the minutes of the meeting,[61] one lay leader criticized Ravasz's proposed public statement, saying that it should "not only emphasize the suffering of the Jews, but the gen-

57. The text of the draft is reproduced in: Tamás Majsai, "A magyarországi református egyház és a holocaust. A nyilvános tiltakozás története," *Világosság* 36, no. 5 (1995): 50–80; see 56–57 (Document 3).

58. Ibid., Document 4, 58.

59. Ibid., Document 8, 62–63.

60. Ibid., Document 7, 59.

61. "Az erdélyi egyházkerület állásfoglalása" (29 June 1944). Reproduced in ibid., Document 7, 60–61.

eral suffering, the bombings, and the damage as well." Indeed, a number of the assembled leaders found it unacceptable that the letter drew attention only to the responsibilities of the Hungarian Protestant churches without also finding fault with the military tactics of the Allied powers, an issue that Bishop Ravasz himself had raised in his defensive letter to the World Council of Churches in Geneva. At the conclusion of the meeting in Kolozsvár (Cluj), Bishop János Vásárhelyi summarized the mood of the session: "He found [the letter] wanting, since it only judges us, but has no word for the awful actions of others. . . . It is impossible that we should speak only of Jewish suffering and be silent about the suffering of our own Magyar people." In the name of the church district, the bishop promised to ask László Ravasz in Budapest to delay issuing the letter until all church leaders had a chance to address these concerns. The most prominent lay leader in Transylvania, Count Miklós Bánffy, repeated this request in a private letter to Ravasz written two days later. In Bánffy's view, the pastoral letter would be a historical document and thus must judge "not only the Jewish matter, but also that inhumanity with which English and Russian bombers murder women and children as well."[62]

Four days after this meeting in Transylvania, Bishop Ravasz himself met with several Calvinist and Lutheran bishops at a home outside Budapest where he was convalescing.[63] There too some of the participants, like Bishop Andor Enyedy, maintained that the churches could not issue a statement about the Jews without also speaking out against the Allied bombing attacks. Others also worried that any critical statement they made would only compel civil officials to take strong punitive measures against the churches. Bishop Dezső Kuthy speculated that the government might cease issuing financial subventions to Christian churches or close parochial schools; it might even intern or imprison the churches' bishops. Some like the Lutheran bishop Béla Kapi wondered if it might not be better to issue a statement informative, rather than critical, in tone. All this, László Ravasz concluded, put church leaders "farther than ever from consensus." Nevertheless, the participants closed the meeting resolved to draft a new resolution "in which, next to the criticism of the atrocities involving the Jewish question, the bombing attacks would also be discussed."

Bishop Ravasz did indeed prepare a draft of a new letter that day, which he was able to distribute in the days that followed to his colleagues throughout Hungary. The new statement differed significantly from the original in two aspects. First, there was a far more explicit discussion of

62. Miklós Bánffy to László Ravasz, 1 July 1944. Ibid., Document 7, 61–62.
63. Bishop Ravasz was chronically ill during these critical months. Report of Meeting held 3 July 1944 in Leányfalu. Ibid., Document 8, 62–63.

converts, whose plight was described alongside the more general "events surrounding the solution of the Jewish question." Second, Ravasz included a lengthy passage about the bombing attacks "against the entire Magyar nation," listing in particular detail the defenseless women and children who had died in hospitals or schools or even churches when bombs had fallen on those buildings. Both the "Jewish question" and bombing attacks received equal weight in the new statement. The letter was to be read throughout the country on 9 July.

Most of Hungary's Protestant bishops found the new text acceptable. However, the letter was never read. By this time, government ministers could share with Protestant leaders the results of their negotiations with Cardinal Serédi; they could also inform Bishop Ravasz and his colleagues that the Regent Horthy had ordered an end to deportations. High-ranking civil officials, including the minister of religion and education, met with several Protestant bishops some days later, repeating many of the promises they had previously made to Catholic leaders, including (unguaranteed) assurances that converts would remain in Hungary if deportations ever resumed. These officials also emphasized the seriousness of Hungary's political situation, and urged church leaders to do nothing which might undermine the regime's stability and propel the nation into even more dire straits. He also warned the assembled Protestant representatives that the government would feel compelled to react to any criticism with strong antichurch measures, or else be forced to step down, an action which could only lead to a cabinet even less sympathetic to the demands of religious leaders. In the end, Bishop Ravasz and his colleagues insisted only on a short, six-line statement, very similar to the statement released by the Catholic Church. Pastors throughout Hungary advised their congregations on 12 July 1944 that leaders of both Protestant churches continued to hold talks with the government regarding the Jewish question, "and particularly in the interests of baptized Jews."[64]

Thus the plans of Protestant leaders to take a public stand on the deportation and mass murder of Hungary's Jews came to nothing. Bishop Ravasz and his colleagues were slow to address the issue; once they began, their disagreements on the content and purpose of the pastoral letter delayed their efforts again and again until they no longer mattered. One particular issue caused much of the delay: few leaders in the governments of the various Protestant church districts could imagine making any public statement about the "Jewish question" in Hungary without at the same time insisting on Jewish difference, a belief that Jews as a group were alien

64. For accounts of these negotiations, see Documents 12 and 13 and Tamás Majsai's explanatory note, ibid., 64–69.

to the Hungarian nation. If the churches were to comment on inhuman suffering, then their church had to decry Magyar suffering and Jewish suffering in separate and equal terms. Moreover, church leaders plainly recognized that many of their followers would misunderstand any objection made to the government's handling of the "Jewish question." Through several drafts of their pastoral letter, Bishop Ravasz had tried to strike a balance: the churches would confirm the need to solve the "Jewish question," but would criticize the means the Sztójay government had adopted. This was a subtle argument. But Hungary in the summer of 1944 was no place for fine distinctions. Worried that their criticism might be misconstrued as "softness" on the "Jewish question" and concerned that the government might retaliate against their churches, Hungary's Protestant leaders debated while deportations continued. By the time Reformed pastors were instructed to read a few meaningless lines during services, nearly 440,000 Jews had been deported to Auschwitz.

Regent Miklós Horthy's decision to suspend the deportation of Hungary's Jews on 7 July 1944 did not end their persecution. His order came too late to save Jews in the farthest-most Budapest suburbs. In addition, Adolf Eichmann managed to arrange two further deportations of interned Jews even after Horthy's order was in force.[65] In the months between the order and the German-sponsored Arrow Cross coup on 15 October, all those in Hungary still subject to the anti-Jewish ordinances knew their safety depended ultimately on the whims of a hostile civil administration. Moreover, the brutal and degrading anti-Jewish decrees remained in effect. In particular, government ordinance continued to require those legally designated as Jews to live in overcrowded "yellow star houses" throughout the city, specially designated and clearly marked apartment buildings intended for Jews only. The government's antisemitic propaganda also continued unabated, further terrorizing the city's Jewish population.

By late September 1944, Soviet troops had reached the eastern border of interwar Hungary. Desperate to avoid the devastation of a total war fought on Hungarian soil, Regent Horthy authorized diplomats to travel to the front and begin secretly to sue for peace. On 15 October, Horthy announced in a radio address that Hungary was withdrawing from the war. The Nazi occupation forces were, however, well informed about these maneuvers by their sources within the Hungarian military and gendarmerie. Almost immediately, they launched a well-prepared plan to topple Horthy and replace him with an Arrow Cross government led by Ferenc Szálasi. In the last months of the war, Hungary's fascists seized their

65. Braham, *Politics of Genocide*, 890–92.

chance to plunder and kill indiscriminately. While Nazi officials arranged with their Hungarian counterparts to send many of Hungary's remaining Jews on death marches to the western border, police rounded the Jewish population of Budapest into an ever more crowded ghetto. There, the helpless population was subject to arbitrary raids and massacres. Liberation came only with the military advance of the Soviet Red Army.

Still the regent's decision to suspend deportations demonstrated how much Nazi officials had to depend on Hungarian cooperation by 1944 in order to carry out their genocidal program. As German military units struggled to hold an eastern front against the Red Army, a small group of SS planners, led by Adolf Eichmann, had organized the deportation of Hungary's Jews in concert with high-ranking ministerial officials in Budapest. However, it had been the Hungarian gendarmerie, supported by Hungarian civil authorities, who had executed these plans from Munkács (Mukachevo) in Subcarpathian Ruthenia to Sopron on the Austrian border. Nazi genocide depended on this cooperation. As the effect of Horthy's 7 July order shows, noncooperation or hesitation hindered the campaign of mass murder tremendously. A public questioning of deportation policy would have been an even greater complication.

In this lies the significance of the churches' failure to respond. Hungary's bishops lodged several private protests with government officials, however equivocal those may have been. Undoubtedly, their concerns, along with those of a number of other prominent figures in Hungarian political society, such as the former prime minister István Bethlen, carried some weight with Regent Horthy as he debated whether to halt the deportations. However, the protests of the international media, relief agencies such as the International Red Cross, and the (soon-to-be) victorious Allied powers, as well as the generally deteriorating military situation, most likely played a greater role.[66] These efforts notwithstanding, it must be said that leaders of both the Catholic and Protestant churches in Hungary took the greatest pains to preserve their Christian national public face. In part, they feared government retaliation and, both at the time and later, justified their refusal to voice public opposition to the deportation with this. Church leaders were also aware that many of their flock supported the anti-Jewish campaign and would have been puzzled to find their pastors and priests speaking words against a policy that expelled all the Jews from Hungary. But the very terms in which church leaders spoke about the Hungarian na-

66. Leslie Laszlo argues for the impact of the Hungarian churches' actions in "The Role of the Christian Churches in the Rescue of the Budapest Jews," *Hungarian Studies Review* 9, no. 1 (1984): 23–42. Both Randolph Braham and Thomas Sakmyster assign the greatest weight to international protests from the Vatican and the Allied powers. See Braham, *Politics of Genocide*, 861–82, and Sakmyster, *Hungary's Admiral*, 349–50.

tion presented an even greater obstacle to their moral outrage. Both the Hungarian Catholic and Reformed Churches, each in their own ways, had presented themselves as the best guarantors of Christian Hungary and had offered a fusion of religion and nationalism as the most suitable means to liberate Hungary from "Jewish" cultural and social power. In 1944, church leaders held fast to this position, even when they knew that exclusion—an insistence on essential Jewish difference—carried with it radically altered and far graver consequences than before. The bishops of both churches tried as they could to preserve some possibility for a true religious nationalism in Christian Hungary. In the end, their efforts drove them to fall silent as the deportations continued.

This silence contrasts sharply with the individual efforts of a number of men and women in each of Hungary's Christian churches, all of whom saw the conflict between "Christian principle" and what was "being done in the name of Christianity" in much the same way that Sister Margit Slachta had seen it in the internment camp in Subcarpathian Ruthenia in 1941. Certainly, Slachta was an exceptional figure. Not only did she vigorously protest the 1941 deportations, she also tried to rouse her church to protest against the deportation of Jews from neighboring Catholic Slovakia. To this end, she even had an audience in the Vatican with Pope Pius XII. But Slachta was not alone in her concern. There are many accounts of religious figures (clergymen, nuns, and lay members, acting singly or in small groups) who extended some kind of assistance to persecuted Jews in Hungary, primarily in Budapest after the deportations had ended, and especially after the Arrow Cross takeover on 15 October 1944.[67] Often this involved supplying those affected by the Jewish laws with false papers, either forged (and suitably backdated) conversion papers or so-called Christian (not conversion) certificates, forged identity papers stating that the bearer was a member of a Christian church. In a number of cases, men and women in Catholic religious orders as well as those Catholics and Protestants in charge of church hospitals also illegally sheltered Jews and labor servicemen in their hospitals or convents, hiding them from ruthless and arbitrary police raids. Convert defense associations were especially active, rarely asking about the religious background of those they helped. Until November 1944, when its leader, József Cavallier, was shot and arrested by the Arrow Cross, the Holy Cross Society helped hundreds of Jews to get special protective passes from the papal nunciate. After Cavallier's arrest, much of the society's activity was merged into the efforts of the Good

---

67. See Varga, "A magyar katolikus egyház az üldözöttekért" and Tamás Majsai, "A protestáns egyházak az üldözés ellen." Both offer a good introduction into the literature on such figures and are in *Magyarország 1944*, ed. Szabolcs Szita. See also Braham, *Politics of Genocide*, 1170–1204.

Pastor Society, with which the Hungarian Lutheran Church had also associated itself in May 1944. Led first by József Éliás, and then by the Lutheran pastor Gábor Sztéhló, the Good Pastor Society also helped many get protective passes with the diplomatic legations of neutral states like Sweden, coordinating their work with diplomats like Raoul Wallenberg and the Swiss envoy, Carl Lutz. At tremendous risk, Sztéhló and the Good Pastor Society also cared for hundreds of Jewish children, many of them orphaned by the atrocities of Arrow Cross rule. Sztéhló spent the final days of the siege of Budapest huddled in the basement of his apartment building with some thirty Jewish children he had hidden.

These acts of resistance are rightly honored and some of these figures, like Sister Margit Slachta, have justly found a place among the "righteous gentiles" distinguished at Yad Vashem. They do not however alter the larger picture of the Holocaust in Hungary. When Slachta and her three companions wrote their report about the men, women, and children deported into certain death in Ukraine in 1941, they concluded their memorandum with these words:

> We raise our voices to protest that in our country such mass official atrocities can happen and we do this as human beings, as Christians, and as Hungarians. As human beings, our every human feeling and healthy natural instinct revolts against it. As Christians, we see in it the most serious violation of the commands of God and our religion. As Hungarians, we cannot let the stain on our Hungarian honor that these terrible outrages represent pass without a word. . . . We know that right now we do not represent a popular view. But we consider it our responsibility to raise our voices in those matters where silence would be a sin according to our consciences.[68]

Three years later, none of Hungary's Christian churches issued any public statement like this. Whatever their personal reservations about the manner in which the government was proceeding, leading figures in Hungary's Christian churches held to a well-established vision of their Christian nation and called for the state to defend Christian Hungarians against harmful "Jewish influence." In the eyes of the Christian state, Hungarians and Jews were separate peoples. Hungary's Christian religious leaders might have disagreed with secular authorities over what exactly this meant. There had been many such disagreements throughout the interwar era. But Hungary's churches, as institutions with public moral authority, never used that authority to question the central tenet of Christian national ideology: Hungary was to be a Christian nation, a nation in which Jews had no place.

---

68. "Iratok," ed. Majsai and Mona, 226.

8

Christian Hungary as History

During the German occupation of Hungary, roughly 564,500 Jewish Hungarians lost their lives.[1] The majority (440,000) were deported to Auschwitz and were murdered there or died in labor camps throughout the rapidly shrinking German Reich. Others died of illness or disease in the Budapest ghetto, were murdered by Arrow Cross thugs in the winter of 1944–45, or perished as the fascist government mobilized Jewish labor in forced marches to western Hungary. The German occupation shattered Hungarian society in other ways as well. After October 1944, when the Germans deposed Regent Miklós Horthy and put the Arrow Cross in power, Hungary had a government only in the loosest sense of the word. For the next four months, central Hungary became the battleground on which the German army fought its doomed terminal battle. Destroying infrastructure and forcing mass evacuations, as they had everywhere in their war of annihilation with the Soviet Union, German forces retreated to a fortified position in Budapest, which they held against Soviet siege until 13 February 1945. Tens of thousands of civilians died, and the entire city was devastated during the fighting.[2] Some 1 million Hungarians fled westward as the Red Army advanced. Fighting lasted on Hungarian soil until 12 April 1945, when the Soviets finally drove the last German units across the western border. Amidst the ruins of Christian Hungary, all Hungarians now had to face the task of remaking society anew in a land occupied by the Soviets.

---

1. Randolph L. Braham, *The Politics of Genocide: The Holocaust in Hungary: Condensed Edition* (Detroit: Wayne State University Press, 2000), 252.
2. Krisztián Ungváry, *Budapest ostroma* (Budapest: Corvina, 1998).

To Jewish Hungarians, the arrival of the Red Army in Hungary was without question a liberation. When Soviet troops drove the last German units from the capital, they dismantled the Budapest ghetto and put an end to the Arrow Cross reign of terror there. Soon, survivors from the concentration camps that the Nazi regime had established all over Europe began to trickle back into Hungary, destitute, brutalized, and desperate to know which of their loved ones still lived. In many cases, these survivors returned only to find that others had seized their homes and property while they had been in the concentration camps. Their faith in the inclusiveness of Hungarian national society utterly shattered, some turned to Zionism, giving energy to a movement that, until 1945, had never been very strong in Hungary. Within months, Zionist groups in Hungary had begun working with organizations in Palestine to help tens of thousands of Jewish Hungarians emigrate. Others turned to the Communist Party, believing it to be their best and only champion after 1945. Soon the number of Jewish Hungarians in prominent positions within the party apparatus, the judicial system, and the political police was noticeable to all. Of course, not all Jewish Hungarians found Communism so enticing. Many had been solidly bourgeois in outlook and politics before the war and were only anxious to restore as much as possible of prewar normality. Even so, it is fair to say that all Jewish Hungarians, whatever their political orientation, could not but recognize the critical role that the Red Army had played in destroying a genocidal regime once and for all. Whatever came next would undoubtedly be better than what had just been.

For those whom Christian nationalist ideology did not mark as "Jews," Soviet occupation came as a far more mixed blessing. Soviet victory meant the definite end to a war in which hundreds of thousands of Hungarian soldiers had died fighting on the side of the German Reich. It also meant that civilians could begin to rebuild from the devastation caused by the fighting on Hungarian soil. Those whom the Arrow Cross had persecuted as "enemies of the state" were now released from prison. Soviet occupation also sounded the death knell for Hungary's traditional social structure. Although no one could be certain in 1945 what the future held, it was clear that Hungary would no longer be dominated by a tiny oligarchy. Within a year, a new government supported by the Soviets had pushed through a far-reaching land reform that promised greater social equality and broke once and for all the power of Hungary's traditional gentry elite. But occupying Soviet troops pillaged and looted indiscriminately, taking their own measure of revenge on a country that had been an enemy combatant until April 1945. The Red Army also deported to Siberia about half of the 600,000 Hungarian captives it had taken in the course of fighting; these prisoners were held for at least several years (and sometimes many more.) Throughout Hungary, women lived in fear of rape by Soviet soldiers.[3] Moreover, the new regime soon established people's courts to try war criminals, enemies of the state, and other "enemies of the people." Without a doubt, these courts sentenced to prison or death many people who richly deserved their punishment. Among those executed were Ferenc Szálasi, the "deportation trio" of László Endre, László Baky, and Andor Jaross, and the leader of the extreme right, Béla Imrédy. For this reason, Hungary's Jewish citizens looked to the courts for some measure of justice, however rough. But not everyone convicted by these courts was equally guilty, nor did all those executed deserve the maximum punishment. Soon, a feeling began to spread among Hungary's non-Jewish citizens that justice was not blind, but was, in fact, a thinly veiled form of retribution.[4]

Because they had experienced Christian nationalist ideology, German occupation, and Soviet victory so differently, Hungarians could find no easy consensus about what should (or ought) to be salvaged from the ruins of "Christian Hungary." Some insisted that Hungary's Christian churches must be rescued from the rubble of war. As an institution and as a cultural and moral force, they argued, religion was vital to reconstructing society in the aftermath of war and the anarchy of Arrow Cross rule. Tens of thousands of Hungarians took part in the celebration of St. István between 1945 and 1948, even as Communists condemned the practice as reactionary and antidemocratic.[5] For some, this may have been a political statement; for others, the expression of a need for faith and moral certainty amidst destruction. For most, it was probably a mix of both.

Even as they did this, however, others remembered how the churches had competed to define Christian nationalist ideology, sanctioning the exclusion of Jews from national society, and thereby linking themselves fatefully to a "politics of genocide."[6] One survivor, Rabbi Henrik Fisch of Kápolnásnyék, published the complete texts of parliamentary speeches that prominent Christian leaders (Catholic cardinal Jusztinián Serédi, the Calvinist bishop László Ravasz, and the Lutheran bishop Sándor Raffay) gave in 1938 and 1939 in favor of Hungary's First and Second Jewish Laws. In the preface to the volume, published in 1947, he argued that

3. Andrea Pető, "Memory and the Narrative of Rape in Budapest and Vienna in 1945," in *Life after Death: Approaches to a Cultural and Social History of Europe during the 1940s and 1950s*, ed. Richard Bessel and Dirk Schumann (New York: Cambridge University Press, 2003), 129–49.

4. László Karsai, "The People's Courts and Revolutionary Justice in Hungary, 1945–46," in *The Politics of Retribution in Europe: World War II and Its Aftermath*, ed. István Deák, Jan T. Gross, and Tony Judt (Princeton: Princeton University Press, 2000), 233–51, esp. 246–47.

5. Klimó, *Nation, Konfession, Geschichte*, 365–80.

6. Braham, *Politics of Genocide*.

"there was a causal connection between Auschwitz" and the antisemitic speeches made by Hungary's most prominent bishops.[7] These issues of historical memory would only become more contested, as they became entangled in the tense struggle for the political future of Hungary.

Religion, Memory, and a Reignited Culture War

In his 1948 book-length essay on *The Jewish Question in Hungary after 1944*, the writer and social critic István Bibó tried to understand the causes for the failure of civil society in 1944. Scrupulously balanced and carefully reasoned, the essay remains even today the single most important critical analysis of antisemitism and the Holocaust in Hungary. In the pages he devoted to religion, Bibó focused on what might be called the churches' sins of omission, acknowledging that Hungary's Catholic and Protestant churches both shared in a certain "religious antisemitism." However, he insisted that this be kept analytically distinct from "modern, mass murderous antisemitism, of which religious antisemitism is a historical precursor, but with which however it cannot be identified sociologically or morally without going further." For Bibó, the churches' principle failure lay in the inability of religious leaders to understand that the political situation in the late 1930s and early 1940s had begun to change radically. Rather than using their moral authority to "engage with special sharpness against the moral nihilism of Hitlerism and racial thinking," Christian religious leaders continued to insist on the theological and doctrinal differences between Christians and Jews. Even after the German occupation in March 1944, Bibó argued, the Catholic and Protestant leaders generally continued to act and speak as if the moral stakes had not dramatically changed. By failing to see the political situation clearly, Hungary's Christian leaders, Bibó concluded, must bear a share of responsibility for the catastrophe of 1944.[8]

However, the presence of the Red Army in Hungary after 1945 inevitably made such sober analysis very rare. Between 1945 and 1948, a coalition government dominated by the Communist Party ruled in Hungary. Supporters of the new regime, both Communist and non-Communist, eagerly used every accusation against the political system they had replaced to highlight their own commitment to social and economic justice. In many ways, the culture war that had dominated Hungarian political and cultural life in the years before 1918, long "settled" by the post-1919 conservative

7. Fisch, *Keresztény egyházfők,* 16–18.
8. István Bibó, *Zsidókérdés Magyarországon 1944 után* (Budapest: Múlt és Jövő kiadó, 2001), 25–29.

restoration, resurfaced after 1945 in a new and far more ominous struggle of beliefs. Inheritors of Hungary's radical democratic tradition consciously recalled the battle between progress and reaction that an earlier generation had fought with such zeal.[9] In numerous publications, progressive democrats and socialists set their memories of the horrors of war, and especially of the mass murder of Hungary's Jews, within a much broader critique of Hungary's interwar social and political system. A good deal of their invective was directed against Hungary's churches, and especially the Catholic Church, much as it had been at the turn of the century. The churches, they argued, had helped Hungary's political leaders to demolish the nation's liberal and progressive traditions after World War I by preaching "proto-fascist" demagoguery.[10] Across the Left, public intellectuals asserted that "Christian Hungary" had been a society hostile in every way to modern and progressive ideas of justice and equality.[11] The fact that pogroms occurred in several places in 1946 only confirmed for them that "reactionary clericalism" was not dead in Hungary, even after the mass murder of 1944.

Hungary's Communist Party also joined non-Communist progressives in attacking "clericalism" as the spirit of counterrevolution and in branding the Catholic Church a pillar of "Horthy-fascism" in the emerging Communist-written history of Hungary's past.[12] Although the Communist Party saw Hungary's institutional Christian churches, and especially the Catholic Church, as significant obstacles to their long-term goal of creating a Soviet-style one-party state in Hungary, pragmatic considerations dictated that the party proceed cautiously in removing those obstacles. Much as Zsigmond Kunfi, minister of religion and public education in Béla Kun's Bolshevik regime, had done in 1919, leading members of the Communist Party initially drew a sharp distinction after 1945 between private faith and the public institutions of the churches. Thus, Mátyás Rákosi, leader of the Hungarian Communist Party, told a gathering of party members in 1947, "The majority of the working people are religious, and the Hungarian Communist Party (MKP) is the guardian of all types of freedom, including freedom of conscience. As long as the MKP has a role in the government, we can assure people that they can safely attend church, and we will assure that no sacrilegious hand will disturb

9. Gyula Mérei, *Polgári radikalizmus Magyarországon.*
10. See, e.g., the many articles of Béla Zsolt in his newspaper, *Haladás.* Among others, "Emberi és politikai hála," *Haladás* (27 October 1945), 1–2.
11. Again, this is the tone in newspapers like *Haladás.* See, e.g., Béla Zsolt "Lipótváros," *Haladás* (11 September 1947).
12. See, e.g., Béla Balázs, *A klerikális reakció: A Horthy fasizmus támasza* (Budapest: Művelt Nép könyvkiadó, 1953), and Erzsébet Andics, *Az egyházi reakció 1848–1849-ben* (Budapest: Szikra, 1949).

them." As they made these assurances, the party sought ways to dismantle the churches' formidable network of civic associations, combating "reactionary clericalism" by removing religious life from the public sphere. Much of their attention was focused on youth and youth organizations, since the Communist Party presented itself as the vanguard of the future Hungarian democracy. In 1946, the party used the assassination of two Soviet soldiers and a Hungarian girl by a man whom they claimed was a member of the Catholic youth group KALOT as the pretext for the destruction of Catholic youth groups.[13]

In place of "backward" religion, Communist ideologues hoped to instill faith in a utopian future. In every aspect of public life, the party emphasized that all of Hungary's "working people" were now freed from the social and economic shackles that had bound them until their "liberation" by the Red Army. Led by the party, workers and peasants would build a "people's republic," one in which social justice would be the cornerstone of a new moral order. To symbolize this change of epochs, party ideologues replaced the holidays and historical symbols of the interwar era with entirely new public festivities. As the Communist Party attacked the Catholic Church as a "reactionary" institution, it also tried to discredit the cult of St. István that had linked the history of Christian Hungary so closely to Catholicism. Though Hungarian Catholics continued to celebrate their patron saint publicly until 1948, party ideologues immediately began to offer alternative holidays. The traditional feast day of St. István, 20 August, became the "day of the new bread," an explicitly nonreligious holiday when party committees urged all Hungarians to celebrate their own labor. After 1948, 20 August was more formally converted into a secular holiday, becoming Constitution Day. Most important, Communists revived 15 March, the day that marked the beginning of Hungary's 1848 revolution against the Habsburgs, as the state holiday that best embodied the democratic aspirations of the working people of Hungary. By investing national history and public symbols with new meaning, the Communist Party dramatized their intention to transform society completely, replacing Christian Hungary with a new and resolutely secular utopia.[14]

In the face of these withering attacks against "reactionary clericalism," Hungary's Christian religious leaders struggled to defend their churches. After 1945, a new cardinal in Esztergom, József Mindszenty, stood at the

---

13. Peter Kenez, "The Hungarian Communist Party and the Catholic Church, 1945–1948," *Journal of Modern History* 75 (December 2003): 864–89, esp. 878–82. Citation of Mátyás Rákosi on 879. It seems the young man, István Pénzes, had once been a member of KALOT in 1943, but had had nothing to do with the organization for years at the time of the incident.

14. Klimó, *Nation, Konfession, Geschichte*, 390–413.

head of Hungary's Roman Catholic Church. In March 1945, the ailing Cardinal Jusztinián Serédi had died, leaving the church in Hungary without a head. At first glance, Mindszenty was an unlikely replacement. For many years a parish priest in Zalaegerszeg, he had only been a bishop since 1944, in a diocese (Veszprém) that was not historically among the more significant in Hungary. Nevertheless, Mindszenty's intransigent anti-Communism was well-known to influential figures within the Vatican. In addition, Mindszenty had been arrested in 1944 by the Arrow Cross while he was bishop of Veszprém for protesting the continuation of the war on Hungarian soil, a fact that established his anti-Nazi credentials. These factors may have convinced Pope Pius XII to pass over other figures in the Hungarian Church and select Mindszenty in August 1945 to be cardinal at Esztergom and thus prince-primate of Hungary.[15] From the very first, Mindszenty openly disparaged the new regime and dismissed the very idea of a republic as something alien to Hungary's national traditions as well as the tenets of the Catholic faith. He insisted that the church and the Catholic faith stood as something good and true that had endured the cataclysm of war, a moral center that should and could not simply be made into a matter of personal opinion. Echoing leading Hungarian Catholic figures of an earlier generation, Cardinal Mindszenty argued in 1946 that "societies which regard religion as a personal matter, unrelated to the conduct of public life, will soon be swallowed up in corruption, violence, and sin."[16] In his view, it was precisely this catastrophe that had befallen Hungary in 1944–45, when anti-Christian politics, not exclusionary antisemitism, reactionary ideology, or mass murder, had destroyed a humane social order in Hungary.

Led by Cardinal Mindszenty, the Hungarian Catholic Church as a body denied any connection between their efforts to address Hungary's "Jewish Question" before the war and the murderous events of 1944. In making sense of the recent past, church leaders typically interpreted the German occupation of Hungary and the months of Arrow Cross rule as a reign of terror over the country unconnected to anything that had come before it, a totalitarian dictatorship aimed at destroying all independent organizations and beliefs. Faced with radical evil, Catholic churchmen maintained that they had stood in opposition.[17] They had defended freedom of conscience and the right to worship and they had continued to deny that racial laws

15. Kenez, "The Hungarian Communist Party and the Catholic Church," 867–71.
16. "Address of October 20, 1946." Reproduced in József Cardinal Mindszenty, *Memoirs*, trans. Richard Winston, Clara Winston, and Jan van Heurck (New York: Macmillan, 1974), 289–90.
17. See, e.g., the various essays in *A magyar katolikus egyház és az emberi jogok védelme*, ed. Antal Meszlényi (Budapest: Szent István Társulat, 1947).

had the power to negate sincere conversion. Some men and women of the church had also tried to the best of their abilities to assist persecuted Jews. Moreover, a number of church figures, including Mindszenty himself, had been imprisoned by the Arrow Cross. Now, after 1945, in a Hungary occupied by the Soviet army, the church stood ready to oppose new violations of "human rights" and "Christian morality," such as unfair trials before the People's Courts, the expulsion of Hungary's ethnic Germans, and above all, Communist harassment of Hungarian Catholics in the public practice of their religious faith.[18] All of these, Cardinal Mindszenty and the Hungarian Catholic Church maintained, were equally grave attacks against the norms of Christian civilization.

Because of this, Catholic leaders resented what they considered to be the excessive attention paid to the persecution of Jews during World War II. Jewish suffering might be undeniable, but, the church's defenders argued, it was far from being the whole story of Hungary's battle against totalitarian terror.[19] Nazism and communism threatened Christian civilization equally, they argued, because both movements aimed at driving religion from social life and setting up an all-powerful state ruled according to a secular and materialist ideology. In an address in Pécs on 20 October 1946, Cardinal Mindszenty explained: "Hitler and his followers regarded religion as a private matter which should be kept in the home. We have seen the results of this attitude: Dachau, Auschwitz, a nation of prisons and gas chambers, ruled by the Gestapo. . . . Now other people have come to seize his [i.e. Hitler's] bankrupt estate."[20] In this ongoing war between belief and unbelief, the church remained even more committed to defending the values of Christian civilization and Christian Europe against nihilistic radicals.[21]

Hungary's Protestant churches found their position in this "culture war" somewhat ambiguous. Obviously, they had been no less committed to Christian nationalist ideology than the Catholic Church had been. Nor had they been less enmeshed in the sociopolitical structure of interwar "Christian" Hungary. Even so, the Hungarian Communist Party saw Protestantism as much less of an ideological threat. As the party searched for symbols to legitimize its rule, its ideologues seized on the anti-Austrian and anti-Catholic elements of Hungarian history in which Protestantism

---

18. Margit Balogh, *Mindszenty József* (Budapest: Elektra kiadóház, 2002), 111–17.
19. Balduin Pénzes, "Amit a zsidóknak el kell mondanunk," *Új Ember* 2, no. 41 (13 October 1946): 1–2.
20. "Address of October 20, 1946," in Mindszenty, *Memoirs*, 289–90.
21. This view was shared by Catholic episcopates throughout Europe. Damian van Melis, " 'Strengthened and Purified through Ordeal by Fire': Ecclesiastical Triumphalism in the Ruins of Europe," in *Life after Death*, ed. Bessel and Schumann, 231–42.

as a cultural force had played so important a role.[22] In addition, Protestants, and especially Calvinists, were divided about the need for social revolution. Although the generation of leaders who had guided the Reformed church since 1919 remained conservative and were eager to present their church as a stabilizing force in an age of upheaval, a younger generation of Calvinists were much more eager for change. Many of them felt the time had come for new leadership in the church, just as it had come for new and more progressive leadership in the nation's government.

These divisions were particularly apparent when Hungary's Calvinists debated each other about whether and how strongly to repent for the sins they had committed in the past. Within the Calvinist tradition, penitence and reflection on one's sins was closely linked to renewal, both of the individual and of society. For this reason, Hungarian Calvinists argued, with a language very different from that used by Cardinal Mindszenty's Catholic Church, that a society trying to rebuild from a devastating war had to acknowledge and repent its sins. Only days after the Soviet army had finally driven the Germans from Budapest, László Ravasz, Calvinist bishop of the Danubian church district and the leading figure in Hungary's Reformed Church, preached his first sermon of the postwar era on the subject of sin and repentance. Speaking in the famous church on Calvin Square in Pest, Ravasz found meaning in the devastation and suffering by seeing it as a sign of divine anger at the worldly obsessions of men. Violence had been repaid with more violence. Only by profound reflection on one's sins—a duty incumbent on everyone individually—could men hope to knit together the bonds of civility and reconstruct their society.[23]

However, this call for penitence was not as clear as it might seem at first glance. The sins of men had led to the horrible devastation of war, and leaders like Bishop Ravasz did discuss the particular suffering that Jews had endured during that war. Protestant leaders were also more willing than Catholic bishops were to concede that they might have done more or said more on behalf of Jews, even if they also maintained that they had spoken out against persecution clearly.[24] But Hungary's Protestant bishops typically marginalized the mass murder of Jews in their nation's collective memory by finding similarities or even equivalences between the persecution of Jews and the suffering to which (Christian) Hungarians had been subjected during the war. For example, Bishop Ravasz remembered the last year of the war in Budapest thus: "While we were still our own

22. Árpád von Klimó, *Nation, Konfession, Geschichte,* 355–90.

23. Sermon of 11 February 1945, ("Amit vet az ember, azt aratja."), in *Ravasz László: Válogatott írások, 1945–1968,* ed. Gyula Barczay (Bern: Európai Protestáns Magyar Szabadegyetem kiadása, 1988), 24.

24. Bereczky, *Hungarian Protestantism.*

masters, whole groups of people were slaughtered in Budapest like harmful beasts of prey and were closed inside a ghetto like some kind of infectious herd, and it only took a few months before every human life in Budapest became absolutely uncertain, and everyone lived for weeks like the most oppressed victims of the ghetto."[25] A specific memory of genocide was clouded still further by the broad list of sins for which the nation had to repent, according to Calvinist and Lutheran church leaders. In his February 1945 sermon, the Reformed Bishop Ravasz offered a long litany of transgressions, reminiscent of the Catholic Church's invective against modernity: Hungarians had been too individualistic, had embraced rampant capitalism, had indulged in vain pleasures and superficial pursuits like playing bridge.[26] Calvinist and Lutheran leaders had typically described these vices as "Jewish" up until 1945. What made them different from anti-Jewish violence was generally unclear.

However, some members of the Calvinist Church wanted public penitence to cut more deeply and to contribute to the transformation of Hungarian society. Writing in leftist journals like Béla Zsolt's *Progress* as well as in their own church journals, they described how right-wing attitudes had dominated church debate in the late 1930s and early 1940s.[27] They also remembered that their church had consistently tried to make it harder for Jews to convert to Christianity, even as the anti-Jewish decrees became harsher and more numerous. These reformers believed that Calvinism could only reclaim its moral authority in the new Hungary if it broke completely with its past, and if they, as Calvinists and as Christians, examined the part they had played in the ruin of their country. A group of these reform-minded Calvinists met in August 1946 in the northeastern city of Nyíregyháza to imagine how their church, under new leadership, might lead the way in Hungary's moral rebirth.[28] Calling themselves the Free Council (*Szabad Tanács*), the assembled churchmen argued that the Hungarian nation, led by the Reformed Church, had to act on its own without reference to others when it begged forgiveness for all its sins. Most particularly, they acknowledged that the segregation and deportation of Hungary's Jews had torn society apart: "Under the burden of the responsibility that falls on us," they declared, "and suffering together with our people because of the sins and omissions we committed against the

25. Ravasz, sermon of 11 February 1945, in *Ravasz László*, ed. Barczay, 25.
26. Ibid., 24.
27. See, e.g., Rátkai, "A kálvinizmus örök."
28. The most important speeches and declarations were reprinted. See *Országos Református Szabad Tanács. Nyiregyháza, 1946. Augusztus 14.-17: Határozatai, deklarációi, kérelmei és az ott elhangzott közérdekű beszédek*, ed. Benő Békefi (Budapest: Schlitt Henrik, 1946).

Jews—conscious of the horrible pain which the surviving Jews bear on account of the inhumane carrying off and horrible extermination of their loved ones—and though it comes late, we ask Hungary's Jews before God for forgiveness."[29] By accepting responsibility, the council declared, Hungarians could find sense in their own suffering and could thus renew themselves, finding their way amidst the wreckage to the new and just society so many hoped for in those days.

The Free Council's declaration was not well received. Almost immediately, it touched off a storm of outrage among Hungarian Protestants, Calvinists and Lutherans alike.[30] In direct response to the council's declaration, Calvinist Bishop László Ravasz stated emphatically that the Reformed Church had no need to ask Jews for forgiveness.[31] He publicly chastised the council for presuming to do penance for the collective sins of a whole people. He asserted, as he had done many times, that totalitarian terror and racial violence, unconnected to anything before and which Ravasz called "Hitlerism," had descended on Hungary in 1944–45.[32] In the face of this challenge, Ravasz insisted, no less forcefully than did Hungary's Catholic episcopate, that his church had spoken out against evil when so many good people had been terrorized into silence. He also reminded critics that many men and women in the Protestant churches had risked their lives to help Jews in those months. The church, he said, had always sought only rational ways to solve Hungary's undeniable "Jewish question."[33] It had always repudiated the "soul-destroying danger of anti-semitism" and "every kind of blood libel or mad legend which evil men invent and stupid men believe."[34] Ravasz also accused the men of the Free Council of political irresponsibility. True democracy, he argued, required self-discipline, restraint, and moral character only to be found in the Gospels. Without these checks, reconstruction would be in vain and democracy would become "dictatorship."[35] At a time when the Communist Party was trying to establish itself as the chief political and moral arbiter in Hungary, the meaning of these remarks, however generally phrased, were clear. It was counterproductive and even dangerous, Ravasz seemed

29. Ibid., 73.
30. Tamás Majsai, "Szempontok a Soá 1945 utáni (Magyarországi) evangélikus és református egyházi recepciójához," in *Magyar megfontolások a Soáról*, ed. Gábor Hamp, Özséb Horányi, and László Rábai (Budapest: Balassi, 1999), 190–91.
31. See his opening presidential address to the National Association of Reformed Clergymen of 25 September 1946, "ORLE elnöki megnyitó beszéd," in *Ravasz László*, ed. Barczay, 69–86, esp. 76–77.
32. Ravasz explained these views to the progressive media in "Védőbeszéd és vádirat: Interju Ravasz László ref. püspökkel," *Haladás* (22 December 1945), 5.
33. Ibid.
34. ORLE elnöki megnyitó beszéd, *Ravasz László*, ed. Barczay, 77.
35. Ibid., 69–70.

to suggest, to undermine the position of the church with ill-considered blanket statements about collective responsibility. Such criticism only gave ammunition to the churches' enemies. In the weeks and months that followed, conservative allies of Ravasz expanded on this response by addressing the charges that leftist churchmen made in progressive newspapers with rebuttals of their own.[36] Through their articles, it was clear that the Free Council's approach to mastering the past remained marginal within Hungary's Reformed Church. In this way, the most ambitious attempt to acknowledge the role that Hungary's Christian Churches had played in the exclusion of Jewish Hungarians from national society came to nothing.

In the tense political climate of post-1945 Hungary, it proved impossible to discuss the ways in which Hungarian society had become bound up in the Nazi genocidal project without taking part, willing or unwillingly, in a debate about a future under Communist rule as well. Even as the Communist Party endorsed public trials of prominent figures involved in the deportation of Hungarian Jews in 1944, party leaders were entirely willing to manipulate antisemitic rhetoric in order to consolidate power, hoping thereby to distract attention from the fact that so many of them (including all four of the most powerful and prominent leaders of the party: Mátyás Rákosi, Ernő Gerő, Mihály Farkas, and József Révai) were in fact Jewish. Just as Communist parties throughout the Soviet zone of occupation did, the Hungarian Communist Party frequently turned a blind eye to crimes committed by "little Arrow Cross men," suggesting that these petty fascists had been misled by ideologues who preyed upon their desire for social equality. Party leaders also played with antisemitic stereotypes as they encouraged "popular judgment" (*népítélet*) against black marketeers and other speculators who profited from the inflation crippling Hungary in the immediate postwar years. In late July 1946, the party leader, Mátyás Rákosi, denounced these enemies of the people in a speech in Miskolc, a town in which antisemitic graffiti calling Rákosi the "king of the Jews," among other things, had appeared on factory walls only days earlier. Three "speculators," two of whom were Jews, were arrested, but a mob of factory workers, probably informed of the arrests, lynched the two Jews. The police did nothing to intervene. In other cases, the Communist Party manipulated pogroms to its political advantage. In the wake of the anti-Jewish violence in Kiskunmadaras in May 1946, in which two Jews were killed and fifteen injured, party leaders pushed for public investigations into these instances of "political reaction." In the

---

36. See, e.g., "Muraközy Gyula válasza Rátkai Károlynak a 'Haladás' c. lapban megjelent cikkére," *Élet és Jövő* (19 January 1946), 5.

4567890126789

end, the trials only served Communist interests, as the party invoked the need to defend democracy from fascists as pretext for attacking their political rivals in the Smallholders Party. All this only discredited any open and honest appraisal of antisemitic politics in Hungary and its role in genocide.[37]

Instead, the Communist Party rigidly enforced its vision of a utopian future. Declaring the victory of revolutionary progress over the forces of reaction, the party crushed the independence of the Christian churches in Hungary as it completed Hungary's transformation into a one-party state. In 1948, the party began a campaign to nationalize the country's schools, a clearly anticlerical measure in a country where over half of all primary school students attended church-run schools and where some of the best high schools (gymnasiums) in the country were administered by one or another Christian confession. Despite vehement protestations by Cardinal Mindszenty and the Catholic episcopal bench, as well as widespread popular opposition, particularly in rural areas, nationalization was complete by the end of the year. In 1950, the regime liquidated all religious orders, and established a State Office of Church Matters in 1951 to assist existing state security offices in the surveillance of religious life in Hungary. In these years, the police also arrested hundreds of priests as "reactionaries," including Cardinal Mindszenty himself, whom they tried, convicted, and sentenced to life imprisonment in 1949 on trumped up charges of treason, conspiracy, and misuse of foreign currency. Only in the 1960s did the Communist regime begin to take a more conciliatory attitude toward the Catholic Church, a shift made possible only after hardliners like Cardinal Mindszenty were clearly removed from power. The party's approach to the country's Protestant churches was much less dramatic. Bowing to political pressure, Protestant leaders like Bishop László Ravasz, who had guided the churches through the interwar years, found themselves forced to step down and retreat into private life. They were replaced by a new generation far more willing to accept the dominance of the party in all public matters. Some of the men who participated in the 1946 Free Council continued to write about the role that Protestant church leaders like Ravasz had played in the antisemitic politics of interwar and wartime Hungary. Their work, however, supported, and sometimes was explicitly

37. On these issues, see Peter Kenez, "Antisemitism in Post World War II Hungary," *Judaism* 50, no. 2 (spring 2001): 144–57, esp. 151–57. Also, Péter Apor, "A népi demokrácia építése: Kunmadaras, 1946," *Századok* 132, no. 3 (1998): 601–32; Éva Standeisky, "Antiszemita megmozdulások Magyarországon a koalíciós időszakban," *Századok* 126, no. 2 (1992): 284–308; Robert Győri Szabó, *A kommunista párt és a zsidóság* (Budapest: Windsor, 1997).

intended to legitimize, Communist rule after 1948 and after 1956.[38] Through these actions, the Communist regime hoped to exorcise the ghost of Christian nationalism from public memory once and for all.

_____

Since 1989, old notions of "Horthy-fascism" and "clerical reaction," advanced in the 1950s to legitimate the Communist regime, have long since been discredited. But the legacy of exclusion and genocide remains difficult to assess, since public opinion and professional historians alike must find the place for these ruptures within a history of the twentieth century that now includes the Communist past as well. One new museum in Budapest, the House of Terror, remembers the terror of Arrow Cross and Communist rule together, much in the way that Catholic Church leaders did in the months and years after 1945. In its galleries, visitors learn about the death camp at Auschwitz, and particularly about the period in 1944–45 of Ferenc Szálasi's rule, before moving along to a far more extensive exhibition on Communist tyranny. There is little in the museum about the deportations and nothing at all about the years that preceded 1944 and German occupation. To some, this is as it should be. By focusing excessive attention on the resurgence after 1989 of antisemitism and other unsavory aspects of the interwar years, it is argued that ex-Communists and their left-liberal sympathizers have constructed a bogeyman that they have used to discredit conservatives, cling to power, and retard the transition to liberal democracy.[39] But many others argue that it is the House of Terror museum that is using history for political ends, marginalizing the Holocaust by conflating two very different national tragedies under the rubric of totalitarian terror. As if in response, an even newer museum has recently opened in Budapest, the Holocaust Documentation Center and Memorial Collection. Completed in 2004, this institution claims as its mission the promotion and publication of research into all aspects of the exclusion, deportation, and murder of Jewish Hungarians during World War II. Here, visitors can see a small permanent exhibition that presents the entrainment, deportation, and arrival at Auschwitz of Hungarian Jews without any mention of the Communist era that followed. As the two museums show, there is still no consensus about how to remember the Holo-

38. See, e.g., Imre Kádár, *The Church in the Storm of Time*. For a critical appraisal of the post-1948 church and men like Imre Kádár, see Gyula Gombos, *The Lean Years: A Study of Hungarian Calvinism in Crisis* (New York: Kossuth Foundation, 1960).

39. Mária Schmidt, "The Role of the 'Fight Against Anti-Semitism' during the Years of Transition," in *From Totalitarian to Democratic Hungary: Evolution and Transformation, 1990–2000*, ed. Mária Schmidt and László Gy. Tóth (Boulder, CO: Social Science Monographs, 2000), 339–85.

236 Christian Hungary as History

caust in Hungary, nor about how to fit "Christian nationalism" into a history of the twentieth century.

These questions are all the more pressing since Hungarians have again taken up the task of remaking their society. Just as in 1945, many ask what can and should be rescued from the detritus of a collapsed system. Many remember Cardinal Mindszenty's intransigence in the face of Communist repression and argue that religion must play a prominent role in reconstructing the networks of civil society. In the last fifteen years, the Hungarian state government has restituted property to the churches, and spent public monies to strengthen the place of religious institutions in post-Communist society. Having inspired men and women of faith to speak truth to power during the darkest days of totalitarian tyranny, it is argued, religious teachings on matters such as abortion, education, or social policy now provide the antidote to four decades of Communist rule. As a new pope, Benedict XVI, speaks about the historical place of Christian faith in the development of European civilization, old arguments about Hungary's place within Christian Europe acquire a new resonance. But others worry about reviving too much of the "Christian-national" past. At a time when Christianity and Christian religious practice are in decline across Western Europe, many on the center-left argue that Hungarians should embrace a different vision of "Europe," one characterized instead by values of secularism and multiculturalism. They recall that Christian national ideology once inspired a poisonous antisemitism and wonder if those eager to restore religion are not breathing new life into something very dangerous.[40] The present is a time of optimism, but also of tense debate about what kinds of public mores a society must embrace to create a truly civil society.

As Nazi Germany exerted its power throughout East-Central Europe, Christian religious leaders in Hungary hoped to defend a place for religion against an increasingly powerful state, arguing that their view of "Jewish morality" was not at all the same as that held by fascist "neopagans." Some individuals went even further, transforming this position into acts of profound moral courage during the "age of catastrophe" in 1944 [*vészkorszak*], offering various kinds of assistance to those defined as Jews by a racist state. In our present day, it is inspiring, but also easier, to remember this opposition. As this book has shown, the history of Christian Hungary is also profoundly unsettling, especially at a time when the relationship between religion and society is the subject of such widespread debate in Eu-

---

40. See, e.g., Miklós Szabó, "A 'Prohászka-ügy,'" *Magyar Nemzet* (6 August 1992). This is reprinted in M. Szabó, *Múmiák öröksége: Politikai és történeti esszék* (Budapest: Új Mandátum, 1995), 84–86.

rope, North America, and beyond. In the decades before and after World War I, Christian religious leaders in Hungary helped to create a public culture in which the nation was imagined as a Christian community. By engaging in debates about Hungary's "Jewish question" and by seeking ways to make nationalist politics more "Christian," these religious leaders set their churches within the political and cultural environment around them, hoping thereby to adapt to it, to shape it, and perhaps even to master it. Christian religious leaders may have had their own reasons for opposing "Jews" to "Christian Hungarians," reasons not held by their opponents on the extreme right. But they shared in the common Christian nationalist consensus that some form of exclusionary policy was necessary. As deportation trains carried some 440,000 Hungarian Jews to Auschwitz, Hungary's Christian churches were silent. This too is the history of Christian national politics, a history that must be faced squarely in the present.

Sixty-two years ago, a humane society came apart. Today, a democracy now seventeen years old must make sense of the destruction. "Joining Europe," as many in Hungary describe accession to the European Union, will provide no relief from painful national debate, for Europe too is "reconstituting itself from the effects of a shattered past."[41] In this way, the history of Christian nationalism in Hungary is very much a European history as well.

41. Jarausch and Geyer, *Shattered Past*, 1–4, citation on 3.

Bibliography

Archival Materials

Esztergomi Prímási Levéltár (EPL), Esztergom, Hungary
  Collection
Evangélikus Országos Levéltár (EOL), Budapest, Hungary
  Collection
Országos Levéltár (OL), Budapest, Hungary
  Collection: K305
Politisches Archiv des Auswärtigen Amtes (PAAA), Center for Research Libraries, Chicago, IL
  Collection: Österreich 92/Bd. 2
Ráday Levéltár (RL), Budapest, Hungary
  Papers of Géza Kiss
  Papers of László Ravasz
  Papers of Jenő Sebestyén
  Papers of Jenő Zoványi
  Collections: A./1.b.; A./1.c

Newspapers/Journals

Alkotmány (Constitution)
Az Est (The Evening)
Az Újság (The News)
Dolgozó Fiatalság (Working Youth)
Egyenlőség (Equality)
Élet és Jövő (Life and Future)
Evangélikusok Lapja (Newspaper of the Lutherans)
Haladás (Progress)
Hazánk (Our Home)
Huszadik Század (Twentieth Century)
Kálvinista Szemle (Calvinist Review)
Keresztény Szocializmus (Christian Socialism)
Korunk Szava (Word of Our Times)

Lelkészegyesület (Pastors' Association)
Magyar Kultúra (Hungarian Culture)
Magyarság (Hungariandom)
Magyar Út (Hungarian Way)
Nemzeti Újság (National News)
Nyugat (West)
Összetartás (Solidarity)
Politika (Politics)
Protestáns Egyházi és Iskolai Lap (PEIL) (Protestant Church and School Paper)
Protestáns Szemle (Protestant Review)
Református Élet (Reformed Life)
Református Jövő (Reformed Future)
Századunk (Our Century)
Társadalmunk (Our Society)
Új Ember (New Man)
Új Nemzedék (New Generation)
Világ (World)
Virradat (Dawn)

Printed Sources

A zsidókérdés Magyarországon: A Huszadik Század körkérdése. Budapest: Társadalomtudományi Társaság kiadása, 1917.

A katolikus nagygyűlés Budapesten 1894: Január 16–ikán. Budapest: Athenaeum, 1894.

A keresztény gondolat védelme. Budapest: A "Hangya" házinyomdája, 1925.

Aczél, Gáspár. *A szabadkőművesség titkai.* Budapest: Márkus S. Könyvnyomda, 1911.

Album Congressus XXXIVi Eucharistici Internationalis. Budapest: Sumptibus et typis Societati Sancti Stephani, 1938.

Almásy, József, ed. *Katolikus írók új magyar kalauza.* Budapest: Ardói irodalmi és könyvkiadó vállalat, 1940.

Ady Endre összes prózai művei. Újságcikkek, tanulmányok. 11 vols. (Budapest: Akadémiai Kiadó, 1955–82).

Baltazár, Dezső. *A probáltatások idejéből.* Debrecen, 1920.

Bangha, Béla. *Magyarország újjáépítése és a kereszténység.* Budapest: St. István Társulat, 1920.

Barczay, Gyula, ed. *Ravasz László: Válogatott írások, 1945–1968.* Bern: Európai Protestáns Magyar Szabadegyetem kiadása, 1988.

Barth, Karl. *Christliche Gemeinde im Wechsel der Staatsordnungen: Dokumente einer Ungarnreise, 1948.* Zürich: Evangelischer Verlag A. G. Zollikon, 1948.

Békefi, Benő, ed. *Országos Református Szabad Tanács: Nyiregyháza, 1946. Augusztus 14.-17: Határozatai, deklarációi, kérelmei és az ott elhangzott közérdekű beszédek.* Budapest: Schlitt Henrik, 1946.

Benson, Timothy O., and Éva Forgács, eds. *Between Worlds: A Sourcebook of Central European Avant-Gardes, 1910–1930.* Cambridge: MIT Press, 2002.

Bereczky, Albert. *Hungarian Protestantism and the Persecution of the Jews.* Budapest: Sylvester, 1945.

Bernát, István. *Das verpfändete Ungarn.* Budapest: Patria, 1896.

Csergó, Hugó, and József Balassa, ed. *Vázsonyi Vilmos beszédei és írásai.* 2 vols. Budapest: Az Országos Vázsonyi-Emlékbizottság kiadása, 1927.

Czeglédy, Emánuel. *Dr. Baltazár Dezső református püspök életrajza.* Debrecen: Debrecen szabad királyi város és a tiszántúli református egyházkerület könyvnyomda-vállalata, 1931.

Doros, Gábor. *Családvédelem: Küzdelem a születéscsökkenés ellen.* Budapest: Magyar Családvédelmi Szövetség, 1938.

Erős, Vilmos, ed. *Szekfű Gyula: Nép, nemzet, állam: Válogatott tanulmányok.* Budapest: Osiris, 2002.

Fáber, Oszkár. *A keresztényszocializmus.* Budapest: Népszava, 1907.

Fisch, Henrik, ed. *Keresztény egyházfők felsőházi beszédei a zsidókérdésben.* Budapest: published by editor, 1947.

Habsburg, József. *A világháború amilyennek én láttam.* Vol. 7. *Tirol védelme és összeomlás.* Budapest: Magyar Tudományos Akadémia, 1934.

Huszár, Károly, ed. *A proletárdiktatúra Magyarországon.* Budapest: Újságüzem könyvkiadó és nyomda rt., 1920.

József, Farkas, ed. *Álmok és tények: Magyar írók a demokráciáról és a nemzeti kérdésről a monarchia felbomlása idején.* Budapest: Argumentum, 2001.

Kiss, Géza. *Ormányság.* Budapest: Sylvester R. T. kiadása, 1937.

Kiss, István Rugonfalvi. *Az átértékelt Bethlen Gábor: Válaszul Szekfű Gyulának.* Debrecen, 1929.

Klebelsberg, Kunó. *Neonacionalizmus.* Budapest: Athenaeum, 1928.

Koltay, Pál. *Szent László a m. kir. honvédgyalogság védszentje.* Békés: Petőfiny., 1944.

Légrády, Ottó, ed. *Igazságot Magyarországnak: Trianon kegyetlen tévedései.* Budapest: A Pesti Hirlap ajándéka, 1931.

Lehár, Anton. *Erinnerungen: Gegenrevolution und Restaurationsversuche in Ungarn 1918–1921.* Edited by Peter Broucek. Munich: R. Oldenbourg Verlag, 1973

Márki, Sándor, and Gusztáv Beksics. *A Modern Magyarország (1848–1896).* Vol. 10. *A magyar nemzet története,* ed. Sándor Szilágyi. Budapest: Athenaeum, 1898.

Mindszenty, József Cardinal. *Memoirs.* Translated by Richard Winston, Clara Winston, and Jan van Heurck. New York: Macmillan, 1974.

Nyisztor, Zoltán. *Vallomás magamról és kortársaimról.* Rome, 1969.

Páter Zadravecz titkos naplója. Edited by György Borsányi. Budapest: Kossuth könyvkiadó, 1967.

Pokoly, József. *A protestantizmus hatása a magyar állami életre.* Budapest: Magyar Protestáns Irodalmi Társság, 1910.

Prohászka, Ottokár. *Naplójegyzetek III: 1919–1927.* Edited by Zoltán Frenyó and Ferenc Szabó. S. J. Szeged: Agapé, 1997.

Prónay, Pál. *A határban a halál kaszál: Fejezetek Prónay Pál feljegyzéseiből.* Budapest: Kossuth, 1963.

Rákosi, Viktor. *Elnémult harangok.* Budapest: Révai, 1903.

Ravasz, László. *Emlékezéseim.* Budapest: A református egyház zsinati irodájának sajtóosztálya, 1992.

Schlauch Lőrinc bibornok-püspök beszédei és dolgozatai. Budapest: Franklin, 1899.

Schütz, Antal, ed. *Prohászka Ottokár összegyüjtött munkái.* Budapest: St. István Társulat, 1927.

Sebestyén, Jenő. *Kálvinizmus és demokrácia* Budapest: Kókai, 1913.

———. *Kálvin és Nietzsche.* Budapest: Kókai, 1917.

Szabó, Dezső. *A magyar protestantizmus problémái.* Budapest: Génius, 1926.

Szabolcsi, Lajos. *Két emberöltő: Az Egyenlőség évtizedei (1881–1931): Emlékezések, dokumentumok.* Budapest: MTA Judaisztikai Kutatócsoport, 1993.

Szálasi, Ferenc. *Szálasi Ferenc alapvető munkája és 3 beszéde.* Buenos Aires: Hungarista Mozgalom kiadása, 1959.

Szekeres, József, ed. *Források Budapest Történetéhez, 1919–1945.* Budapest: Budapest Főváros Levéltárának Kiadványa, 1972.

Szekfű, Gyula. *Der Staat Ungarn: Eine Geschichtsstudie.* Stuttgart: Deutsche Verlags-Anstalt, 1918.

——. *Bethlen Gábor*. Budapest: Magyar Szemle Társaság, 1929.

——. *Három nemzedék és ami utána következik*. Budapest: ÁKV-Maecenas Reprint, 1989.

——, ed. *Mi a magyar?* Budapest: Magyar Szemle Társaság, 1939.

Szekfű, Gyula, and Bálint Hóman. *Magyar Történet*. Vols. 4 and 5. Budapest: Királyi magyar egyetemi nyomda, 1928–34.

Szenes, Sándor, ed. *Befejezetlen múlt: Keresztények és zsidók, sorsok: Beszélgetések*. Budapest, 1986.

Szíj, Rezső, ed. *Prohászka Ottokár: Kultúra és terror*. Budapest: Szenci Molnár Társaság, 1997.

Timoleon (Gusztáv Beksics). *Legújabb politikai divat*. Budapest: Zilahy Sámuel, 1884.

Váry, Albert. *A vörös uralom áldozatai Magyarországon*. 3d ed. Szeged: Szegedi Nyomda, 1993.

Vihar, Béla, ed. *Szilágyi Dezső beszédei*. Budapest: Athenaeum, 1909.

Venetianer, Lajos. *A magyar zsidóság története: A honfoglalástól a világháború kitöréseig: Különös tekintettel gazdasági és művelődési fejlődésre*. Budapest: Fővárosi könyvkiadó, 1922.

Secondary Literature

Adriányi, Gabriel. *Fünfzig Jahre Ungarischer Kirchengeschichte, 1895–1945*. Mainz: v. Hase and Koehler Verlag, 1974.

Andics, Erzsébet. *Az egyházi reakció 1848–1849-ben*. Budapest: Szikra, 1948.

Andics, Hellmut. *Der Staat, den keiner wollte: Österreich 1918–1938*. Vienna: Herder, 1962.

Apor, Péter. "A népi demokrácia építése: Kunmadaras, 1946." *Századok* 132, no. 3 (1998): 601–32.

Arendt, Hannah. *The Origins of Totalitarianism*. New York: Harcourt Brace, 1973.

Asad, Talal. *Genealogies of Religion: Discipline and Reasons of Power in Christianity and Islam*. Baltimore: Johns Hopkins University Press, 1993.

——. *Formations of the Secular: Christianity, Islam, Modernity*. Stanford: Stanford University Press, 2003.

Balázs, Béla. *A klerikális reakció szerepe a Horthy-fasizmus uralomrajutásában és konszolidálásában*. Budapest: Szikra, 1954.

Balogh, Margit. *A KALOT és a katolikus társadalompolitika, 1935–1946*. Budapest: MTA történettudományi intézete, 1998.

——. *Mindszenty József*. Budapest: Elektra kiadóház, 2002.

Balogh, Margit, and Jenő Gergely. *Egyházak az újkori Magyarországon, 1790–1992: Adattár*. Budapest: História. MTA Történettudományi Intézete, 1996.

Bartha, Tibor, and László Makkai, ed. *Tanulmányok a magyarországi református egyház történetéből: 1867–1978*. Budapest: A magyarországi református egyház zsinati irodájának sajtóosztálya, 1983.

Bartov, Omer, and Phyllis Mack, ed. *In God's Name: Genocide and Religion in the Twentieth Century*. New York: Berghahn, 2001.

Berend, Iván T., and György Ránki. *Economic Development in East-Central Europe in the Nineteenth and Twentieth Centuries*. New York: Columbia University Press, 1974.

Bergen, Doris. *Twisted Cross: The German Christian Movement in the Third Reich*. Chapel Hill: University of North Carolina Press, 1996.

Bernstein, Béla. *A negyvennyolcas magyar szabadságharc és a zsidók: a zsidó honvédek négy névjegyzékével*. Budapest: Múlt és Jövő kiadó, 1998.

Bessel, Richard, and Dirk Schumann, eds. *Life after Death: Approaches to a Cultural and Social History of Europe during the 1940s and 1950s.* New York: Cambridge University Press, 2003.

Bibó, István. *Zsidókérdés Magyarországon 1944 után.* Budapest: Múlt és Jövő kiadó, 2001.

Bokor, Péter. "Fifty Years Ago, The Darkest Year: Conversation with Archbishop Gennaro Verolino on the Siege of Budapest." *Hungarian Quarterly* 35 (1994): 82–89.

Borbándi, Gyula. *Der ungarische Populismus.* Mainz: v. Hase u. Koehler, 1976.

Borsányi, György, ed. *Páter Zadravecz titkos naplója.* Budapest: Kossuth Könyvkiadó, 1967.

Boyer, John W. *Political Radicalism in Late Imperial Vienna: Origins of the Christian Social Movement, 1848–1897.* Chicago: University of Chicago Press, 1981.

——. *Culture and Political Crisis in Vienna: Christian Socialism in Power, 1897–1918.* Chicago: University of Chicago Press, 1995.

Braham, Randolph L. *The Hungarian Labor Service System, 1939–1945.* Boulder, CO: East European Quarterly, 1977.

——. *The Politics of Genocide: The Holocaust in Hungary.* 2 vols. Revised and enlarged edition. Boulder, CO: Social Science Monographs, 1994.

——. *The Politics of Genocide: The Holocaust in Hungary.* Condensed ed. Detroit: Wayne State University Press, 2000.

——. "The Christian Churches of Hungary and the Holocaust." *Yad Vashem Studies* 29 (2001): 241–80.

——, ed. *Studies on the Holocaust in Hungary.* Boulder, CO: Social Science Monographs, 1990.

Braham, Randolph L., and Attila Pók, ed. *The Holocaust in Hungary: Fifty Years Later.* Boulder, CO: Social Science Monographs, 1997.

Brandt, Juliane. "Protestantismus und Gesellschaft im dualistischen Ungarn." *Südostforschungen* 55 (1996): 179–240.

Breitman, Richard. *Official Secrets: What the Nazis Planned, What the British and Americans Knew.* New York: Hill and Wang, 1998.

Bucur, Maria, and Nancy M. Wingfield, ed. *Staging the Past: The Politics of Commemoration in Habsburg Central Europe, 1848 to the Present.* West Lafayette, IN: Purdue University Press, 2001.

Carroll, James. *Constantine's Sword: The Church and the Jews. A History.* Boston: Houghton Mifflin, 2001.

Casanova, Jose. *Public Religions in the Modern World.* Chicago: University of Chicago Press, 1994.

Clark, Christopher, and Wolfram Kaiser, ed. *Culture Wars: Secular-Catholic Conflict in Nineteenth-Century Europe.* Cambridge: Cambridge University Press, 2003.

Cohn, Norman. *Cosmos, Chaos, and the World to Come: The Ancient Roots of Apocalyptic Faith.* New Haven: Yale University Press, 2001.

Congdon, Lee. "Endre Ady's Summons to National Regeneration in Hungary, 1900–1919." *Slavic Review* 33, no. 2 (1974): 302–22.

Cornwell, John. *Hitler's Pope: The Secret History of Pius XII.* New York: Viking, 1999.

Csáky, Moritz. *Der Kulturkampf in Ungarn: Die kirchenpolitische Gesetzgebung der Jahre 1894/95.* Graz: Verlag Böhlau, 1967.

Deák, István. "Hungary." In *The European Right: A Historical Profile,* edited by Hans Rogger and Eugen Weber, 364–407. Berkeley: University of California Press, 1966.

——. "Budapest and the Hungarian Revolutions of 1918–1919." *Slavonic and East European Review* 46, no. 106 (1968): 129–41.

——. *The Lawful Revolution: Louis Kossuth and the Hungarians, 1848–1849.* New York: Columbia University Press, 1979.

——. "Historiography of the Countries of Eastern Europe: Hungary." *American Historical Review* 97, no. 4 (October 1992): 1041–1063.

Deák, István, Jan T. Gross, and Tony Judt, ed. *The Politics of Retribution in Europe: World War II and Its Aftermath.* Princeton: Princeton University Press, 2000.

Dersi, Tamás. *A századvég katolikus sajtója.* Budapest: Akadémiai kiadó, 1973.

Dévényi, Ivánné. "Csernoch János tevékénysége az ellenforradalmi rendszer első éveiben." *Századok,* 111, no. 1 (1977): 48–78.

de Vries, Hent. *Religion and Violence: Philosophical Perspectives from Kant to Derrida.* Baltimore: Johns Hopkins University Press, 2002.

Epstein, Irene Raab. "Gyula Szekfű: A Study in the Political Basis of Hungarian Historiography." Ph.D. diss., University of Indiana, 1974.

Ericksen, Robert P., and Susannah Heschel, ed. *Betrayal: German Churches and the Holocaust.* Minneapolis: Fortress Press, 1999.

Feinberg, Melissa. *Elusive Equality: Gender, Citizenship, and the Limits of Democracy in Czechoslovakia, 1918–1950.* Pittsburgh: University of Pittsburgh Press, 2006.

Fischer, Rolf. *Entwicklungsstufen des Antisemitismus in Ungarn, 1867–1939: Die Zerstörung der magyarisch-jüdischen Symbiose.* Munich: R. Oldenbourg Verlag, 1988.

Friedländer, Saul. *Pius XII and the Third Reich.* Translated by Charles Fullman. New York: Alfred A. Knopf, 1966.

——. *Nazi Germany and the Jews: The Years of Persecution, 1933–1939.* New York: HarperCollins, 1997.

Frigyesi, Judit. *Béla Bartók and Turn-of-the-Century Budapest.* Berkeley: University of California Press, 1998.

Gal, Susan. "Bartók's Funeral: Representations of Europe in Hungarian Political Rhetoric." *American Ethnologist* 18, no. 3 (1991): 440–58.

Galántai, József. *Egyház és politika, 1890–1918: Katholikus egyházi körök politikai szervezkedései Magyarországon, 1890–1950.* Budapest: Kossuth, 1960.

——. *Hungary in the First World War.* Translated by Éva Grusz and Judit Pokoly. Budapest: Akadémiai Kiadó, 1989.

Gati, Charles. "The Populist Current in Hungarian Politics, 1935–1944." Ph.D. diss., Indiana University, 1965.

Gentile, Emilio. *The Sacralization of Politics in Fascist Italy.* Cambridge: Harvard University Press, 1996.

Gergely, Jenő. "Keresztényszocialisták az 1918–as magyarországi polgári demokratikus forradalomban." *Történelmi Szemle* 12, no. 1–2 (1969): 26–65.

——. *A keresztényszocializmus Magyarországon, 1903–1923.* Budapest: Akadémiai Kiadó, 1977.

——. *A politikai katolicizmus Magyarországon, 1890–1950.* Budapest: Kossuth Könyvkiadó, 1977.

——. "A katolikus püspöki kar és a konvertiták mentése. (Dokumentumok)." *Történelmi Szemle* 27, no. 4 (1984): 580–616.

——. "A magyarországi katolikus egyház és a fasizmus." *Századok* 121, no. 1 (1987): 3–48.

——. *Eucharisztikus világkongresszus Budapesten, 1938.* Budapest: Kossuth könyvkiadó, 1988.

——. *A keresztényszocializmus Magyarországon (1924–1944).* Budapest: Typovent Kiadó, 1993.

——. *Prohászka Ottokár: "A napbaöltözözött ember."* Budapest: Gondolat, 1994.

——, ed. *A püspöki kar tanácskozásai: A magyar katolikus püspökök konferenciáinak jegyzőkönyveiből, 1919–1944.* Budapest: Gondolat Könyvkiadó, 1984.

Gerlach, Christian, and Götz Aly. *Das letzte Kapitel: Der Mord an den ungarischen Juden.* Stuttgart: Deutsche Verlags-Anstalt, 2002.

Gerő, András. *The Hungarian Parliament (1867–1918): A Mirage of Power.* Translated by James Patterson and Eniko Koncz. Boulder, CO: Social Science Monographs, 1997.

Geyer, Michael. "Insurrectionary Warfare: The German Debate about a *Levée en Masse* in October 1918." *Journal of Modern History* 73 (September 2001): 459–527.

Gluck, Mary. *Georg Lukács and His Generation, 1900–1918.* Cambridge, MA: Harvard University Press, 1985.

——. "In Search of 'That Semi-Mythical Waif: Hungarian Liberalism': The Culture of Political Radicalism in 1918–1919." *Austrian History Yearbook* 22 (1991): 96–109.

Goldhagen, Daniel Jonah. *A Moral Reckoning: The Role of the Catholic Church in the Holocaust and Its Unfulfilled Duty of Repair.* New York: Alfred A. Knopf, 2002.

Gombos, Gyula. *The Lean Years: A Study of Hungarian Calvinism in Crisis.* New York: Kossuth Foundation, 1960.

Gottas, Friedrich. *Die Frage der Protestanten in Ungarn in der Ära des Neoabsolutismus.* Munich: Verlag R. Oldenbourg, 1965.

Gyurgyák, János. *A zsidókérdés Magyarországon.* Budapest: Osiris, 2001.

Hajdu, Tibor. *Az 1918–as magyarországi polgári demokratikus forradalom.* Budapest: Kossuth, 1968.

——. *A magyarországi tanácsköztársaság.* Budapest: Kossuth, 1969.

Hanák, Péter. *The Garden and the Workshop: Essays on the Cultural History of Vienna and Budapest.* Princeton: Princeton University Press, 1998.

Handler, Andrew. *An Early Blueprint for Zionism: Győző Istóczy's Political Anti-Semitism.* Boulder, CO: East European Monographs, 1976.

——. *Blood Libel at Tiszaeszlár.* Boulder, CO: East European Monographs, 1980.

Herczl, Moshe Y. *Christianity and the Holocaust of Hungarian Jewry.* Translated by Joel Lerner. New York: New York University Press, 1993.

Hermann, Egyed. *A katolikus egyház története Magyarországon 1914–ig.* Munich: Aurora, 1973.

Heslam, Peter. *Creating a Christian Worldview: Abraham Kuyper's Lectures on Calvinism.* Grand Rapids: Eerdmans, 1998.

Heverdle, László. "A Martinovics-páholy antiklerikális sajtópolitikája." *Magyar Könyvszemle* 99, no. 2 (1983): 138–53.

Hoffmann, Christhard. "Christlicher Antijudaismus und moderner Antisemitismus. Zusammenhänge und Differenzen als Problem der historischen Antisemitismusforschung." In *Christlicher Antijudaismus und Antisemitismus: Theologische und kirchliche Programme Deutscher Christen*, edited by Leonore Siegele-Wenschkewitz. Frankfurt a.M.: Haag und Hercken, 1994, 293–317.

Hoóz, István. *Népesedéspolitika és népességfejlődés Magyarországon a két világháború között.* Budapest: Akadémiai kiadó, 1970.

Horváth, Zoltán. *Magyar századforduló: A második reformnemzedék története (1896–1914).* Budapest: Gondolat, 1961.

Ignotus, Paul. "Radical Writers in Hungary." *Journal of Contemporary History* 1, no. 2 (1966): 149–67.

Jarausch, Konrad H., and Michael Geyer. *Shattered Past: Reconstructing German Histories.* Princeton: Princeton University Press, 2003.

Jodock, Darrell, ed. *Catholicism Contending with Modernity: Roman Catholic Modernism and Anti-Modernism in Historical Context.* Cambridge: Cambridge University Press, 2000.

Johnson, Eliza Ablovatski. "'Cleansing the Red Nest': Counterrevolution and White Terror in Munich and Budapest, 1919." Ph.D. diss., Columbia University, 2004.

Juergensmeyer, Mark. *The New Cold War? Religious Nationalism Confronts the Secular State.* Berkeley: University of California Press, 1993.

——. *Terror in the Mind of God: The Global Rise of Religious Violence.* Berkeley: University of California Press, 2000.

Juhász, Gyula. *Uralkodó eszmék Magyarországon, 1939–1944.* Budapest: Kossuth, 1983.

Kádár, Imre. *The Church in the Storm of Times: The History of the Hungarian Reformed Church during the Two World Wars, Revolutions, and Counter-Revolutions.* Budapest: Bibliotheca, 1958.

Kaplan, Marion A. *Between Dignity and Despair: Jewish Life in Nazi Germany.* New York: Oxford University Press, 1998.

Kardos, József. *A szentkorona-tan története, 1919–1944.* Budapest: Akadémiai Kiadó, 1985.

Katz, Jacob. *From Prejudice to Destruction: Anti-Semitism, 1700–1933.* Cambridge: Harvard University Press, 1980.

——. *A végzetes szakadás: Az ortodoxia kiválása a zsidóhitközségekből Magyarországon és Németországban.* Budapest: Múlt és Jövő kiadó, 1999.

Katzburg, Nathaniel. *Hungary and the Jews: Policy and Legislation, 1920–1943.* Ramat-Gan: Bar-Ilan University Press, 1981.

——. "Louis Marshall and the White Terror in Hungary, 1919–1920." *American Jewish Archives 45, no. 1* (1993): 1–12

Kenez, Peter. "Antisemitism in Post World War II Hungary." *Judaism 50*, no. 2 (spring 2001): 149–57.

——. "The Hungarian Communist Party and the Catholic Church, 1945–48." *Journal of Modern History 75* (December 2003): 864–89.

Kertzer, David I. *The Popes against the Jews: The Vatican's Role in the Rise of Modern Anti-Semitism.* New York: Alfred A. Knopf, 2001.

Klein, Bernard. "Anti-Jewish Demonstrations in Hungarian Universities, 1932–1936: István Bethlen vs. Gyula Gömbös." *Jewish Social Studies 44* (1982): 113–24.

Klimó, Árpád von. "Die gespaltene Vergangenheit: Die grossen christlichen Kirchen im Kampf um die Nationalgeschichte Ungarns 1920–1948." *Zeitschrift für Geschichtswissenschaft 47*, no. 10 (1999): 874–91.

——. *Nation, Konfession, Geschichte: Zur nationalen Geschichtskultur Ungarns im europäischen Kontext (1860–1948).* Munich: R. Oldenbourg, 2003.

Kontler, László. *A History of Hungary: Millennium in Central Europe.* New York: Palgrave Macmillan, 2002.

Kónya, István. *A magyar református egyház felső vezetésének politikai ideológiája a Horthy korszakban.* Budapest: Akadémiai Kiadó, 1967.

Kónya, Sándor. *Gömbös kísérlete totális fasiszta diktatúra megteremtésére.* Budapest: Akadémiai kiadó, 1968.

Kooi, Cornelis van der, and Jan de Bruijn, eds. *Kuyper Reconsidered: Aspects of His Life and Work.* Amsterdam: VU Uitgeverij, 1999.

Kósa, László. "A református egyház az egyházpolitikai küzdelmek idején." *Protestáns Szemle 1* (1996/1): 52–62.

Kubinszky, Judit. *Politikai antiszemitizmus Magyarországon, 1875–1890.* Budapest: Kossuth, 1976.

Lackó, Miklós. *Arrow-Cross Men, National Socialists: 1935–44.* Budapest: Akadémiai kiadó, 1969.

——. *Válságok, választások: Történeti tanulmányok a két háború közötti Magyarországról.* Budapest: Gondolat, 1975.

Ladányi, Sándor, ed. *Emlékkönyv Sebestyén Jenő születésének 100. évfordulójára.* Budapest: Református Egyház Zsinati Irodájának Sajtóosztálya, 1984.

László, László T. *Szellemi honvédelem: Katolikus demokrata mozgalmak és az egyház ellenállása a második világháború idején Magyarországon.* Rome: Katolikus Szemle, 1980.

László, Leslie. "Church and State in Hungary, 1919–1945." Ph.D. diss., Columbia University, 1973.

——. "Fighting Evil with Weapons of the Spirit: The Christian Churches in Wartime Hungary." *Hungarian Studies Review* 10, no. 1/2 (1983): 125–44.

Lendvai, Ferenc L., ed. *A magyar protestantizmus, 1918–1948: Tanulmányok.* Budapest: Kossuth, 1987.

Lendvai, Paul. *The Hungarians: A Thousand Years of Victory in Defeat.* Princeton: Princeton University Press, 2003.

Lewy, Guenter. *The Catholic Church and Nazi Germany.* New York: McGraw-Hill, 1964.

Litván, György. *Októberek üzenete.* Budapest: Osiris, 1996.

Lukacs, John. *Budapest 1900: A Historical Portrait of a City and its Culture.* New York: Grove Weidenfeld, 1988.

Macartney, Carlile A. *October Fifteenth: A History of Hungary, 1929–1945.* 2 vols. Edinburgh: University Press, 1956–57.

Majsai, Tamás. "A kőrösmezei zsidódeportálás 1941-ben." *A Ráday-gyűjtemény évkönyve* 4–5 (1984–85): 59–86.

——. "A magyarországi református egyház és a holocaust. A nyilvános tiltakozás története." *Világosság* 36, no. 5 (1995): 50–80.

——. "Biborosok és püspökök a zsidómentés barikádharcában." *Budapesti Negyed* 3, no. 2 (1995): 169–80.

——. "Szempontok a Soá 1945 utáni (Magyarországi) evangélikus és református egyházi recepciójához." In *Magyar megfontolások a Soáról,* edited by Gábor Hamp, Özséb Horányi, and László Rábai, 179–211. Budapest: Balassi, 1999.

Majsai, Tamás, and Ilona Mona, ed. "Iratok a kőrösmezei zsidódeportálás történetéhez." *A Ráday-gyűjtemény évkönyve* 4–5 (1984–85): 195–237.

Mayer, Arno J. *The Furies: Violence and Terror in the French and Russian Revolutions.* Princeton: Princeton University Press, 2000.

McCagg, William O., Jr. *Jewish Nobles and Geniuses in Modern Hungary.* Boulder, CO: East European Quarterly, 1972.

——. "Jewish Conversion in Hungary in Modern Times." In *Jewish Apostasy in the Modern World,* edited by Todd M. Endelman. New York: Holmes and Meier, 1987: 142–64.

Mérei, Gyula. *Polgári radikalizmus Magyarországon, 1900–1919.* Budapest: Karpinszky Aladár könyvnyomda, 1947.

Meszlényi, Antal, ed. *A magyar katolikus egyház és az emberi jogok védelme.* Budapest: Szent István Társulat, 1947.

Miron, Guy. "History, Remembrance, and a 'Useful Past' in the Public Thought of Hungarian Jewry, 1938–1939." *Yad Vashem Studies* 32 (2004): 131–70.

Morley, John F. *Vatican Diplomacy and the Jews during the Holocaust, 1939–1943.* New York: KTAV, 1980.

Mosse, George L. *The Nationalization of the Masses: Political Symbolism and Mass Movements in Germany from the Napoleonic Wars through the Third Reich.* New York: H. Fertig, 1975.

Murányi, Gábor, ed. *A bilincsbe vert beszéd: Vásárhelyi Miklós sajtótörténeti tanulmányai.* Budapest: Élet és Irodalom, 2002.

Nagy, Sz. Péter, ed. *A népi-urbánus vita dokumentumai, 1932–1947.* Budapest: Rakéta Könyvkiadó, 1990.

Nagy, Zsuzsa L. "A 'nemzeti állam' eszméje Beksics Gusztávnál." *Századok* 97, no. 6 (1963): 1242–78.

——. *The Liberal Opposition in Hungary, 1919–1945.* Budapest: Akadémiai Kiadó, 1983.

Nagy-Talavera, Nicholas M. *The Green Shirts and the Others: A History of Fascism in Hungary and Rumania.* Stanford: Hoover Institution Press, 1970.

Némedi, Dénes. *A népi szociográfia, 1930–1938.* Budapest: Gondolat, 1985.

Nemes, Dezső. *Iratok az ellenforradalom történetéhez, 1919–1945.* Budapest: Szikra, 1956.

Nirenberg, David. *Communities of Violence: Persecution of Minorities in the Middle Ages.* Princeton: Princeton University Press, 1996.

Nyisztor, Zoltán. *Bangha Béla élete és műve.* Budapest: Pázmány Péter Irodalmi Társaság, 1941.

———. *Ötven esztendő: Századunk magyar katolikus megújhodása.* Vienna: Opus mystici corporis, 1962.

Ozsváth, Zsuzsanna. *In the Footsteps of Orpheus: The Life and Times of Miklós Radnóti.* Bloomington: Indiana University Press, 2000.

Paces, Cynthia J. "The Czech Nation Must Be Catholic! An Alternative Version of Czech Nationalism during the First Republic." *Nationalities Papers* 27, no. 3 (1999): 407–28.

Passelecq, Georges, and Bernard Suchecky. *The Hidden Encyclical of Pius XI.* Translated by Steven Rendall. New York: Harcourt Brace, 1997.

Pastor, Peter, ed. *Revolutions and Interventions in Hungary and its Neighbor States, 1918–1919.* Boulder, CO: Social Science Monographs, 1988.

Phayer, Michael. *The Catholic Church and the Holocaust, 1930–1965.* Bloomington: Indiana University Press, 2000.

Porter, Brian. *When Nationalism Began to Hate: Imagining Politics in Nineteenth Century Poland.* New York: Oxford University Press, 2000.

———. "The Catholic Nation: Religion, Identity, and the Narratives of Polish History." *Slavic and East European Journal* 45, no. 2 (March 2001): 289–99.

Pelle, János. *A gyűlölet vetése: A zsidótörvények és a magyar közvélemény, 1938–1944.* Budapest: Európa, 2001.

Péter, László. "Hungarian Liberals and Church-State Relations (1867–1900)." In *Hungary and European Civilization*, edited by György Ránki and Attila Pók. Budapest: Akadémiai kiadó, 1989.

Pók, Attila. "Rankes Einfluß auf Geschichtsschreibung und Geschichtsdenken in Ungarn—ein historisierter Historiker." In *Leopold von Ranke und die moderne Geschichtswissenschaft*, edited by Wolfgang J. Mommsen. Stuttgart: Klett-Cotta, 1988.

Pölöskei, Ferenc. *Hungary after Two Revolutions (1919–1922).* Budapest: Akadémiai kiadó, 1980.

Prepuk, Anikó. "Miért éppen recepció? Az izraelita vallás egyenjogúsítása az 1890–es években." In *Emlékkönyv L. Nagy Zsuzsa 70. születésnapjára*, edited by János Angi. Debrecen: Multiplex Media-DUP, 2000.

Rahden, Till van. *Juden und andere Breslauer: Die Beziehungen zwischen Juden, Protestanten, und Katholiken in einer deutschen Grossstadt.* Göttingen: Vandenhoeck u. Ruprecht, 2000.

Ránki, György. "The Fascist Vote in Budapest in 1939." In *Who Were the Fascists? Social Roots of European Fascism*, edited by Stein U. Larsen et al. Bergen: Universitetsforlaget, 1980: 401–16.

Rengstorff, Karl-Heinrich, and Siegfried v. Kortzfleisch, ed. *Kirche und Synagoge: Handbuch zur Geschichte von Christen und Juden.* Stuttgart: Ernst Klett Verlag, 1970.

Rogalla von Bieberstein, Johannes. *Die These von der Verschwörung, 1776–1945: Philosophen, Freimaurer, Juden, Liberale und Sozialisten als Verschwörer gegen die Sozialordnung.* Bern and Frankfurt a.M.: Herbert Lang and P. Lang, 1976.

Romsics, Ignác. *István Bethlen: A Great Conservative Statesman of Hungary,*

1874–1946. Translated by Mario D. Fenyo. Boulder, CO: Social Science Monographs, 1995.

——. *Hungary in the Twentieth Century.* Budapest: Corvina-Osiris, 1999.

Sakmyster, Thomas L. *Hungary's Admiral on Horseback: Miklós Horthy, 1918–1944.* Boulder, CO: East European Monographs, 1994.

Salacz, Gábor. *A magyar kultúrharc története, 1890–1895.* Pécs: Dunántúl Pécsi Egyetemi Könyvkiadó, 1938.

——. *Egyház és állam Magyarországon a dualizmus korában, 1867–1918.* Munich: Aurora, 1974.

Schmidt, Mária, and László Gy. Tóth, ed. *From Totalitarian to Democratic Hungary: Evolution and Transformation, 1990–2000.* Boulder, CO: Social Science Monographs, 2000.

Sells, Michael A. *The Bridge Betrayed: Religion and Genocide in Bosnia.* Berkeley: University of California Press, 1996.

Sinkó, Katalin. "Árpád vs. St. István: Competing Heroes and Competing Interests in the Figurative Representation of Hungarian History." In *Hungarians Between "East" and "West": National Myths and Symbols,* edited by Tamás Hofer. Budapest: Museum of Ethnography, 1994: 9–26.

——. "A megsértett Hungária." *Néprajzi Értesítő* 77 (1995): 267–82.

Sipos, Péter. *Imrédy Béla és a Magyar Megújulás Pártja.* Budapest: Akadémiai Kiadó, 1970.

——. "Milotay István pályaképéhez." *Századok* 105 (1971): 709–35.

Sipos, Levente, and Pál Péter Tóth, ed. *A népi mozgalom és a magyar társadalom: Tudományos tanácskozás a szárszói találkozó 50. évfordulója alkalmából.* Budapest: Napvilág, 1997.

Smith, Helmut Walser. *German Nationalism and Religious Conflict: Culture, Ideology, Politics, 1870–1914.* Princeton: Princeton University Press, 1995.

Standeisky, Éva. "Antiszemita megmozdulások Magyarországon a koalíciós időszakban." *Századok* 126, no. 2 (1992): 284–308.

Steigmann-Gall, Richard. *The Holy Reich: Nazi Conceptions of Christianity, 1919–1945.* New York: Cambridge University Press, 2003.

Szabó, Dániel. "A Néppárt megalakulása." *Történelmi Szemle* 20, no. 2 (1977): 169–208.

——. "A Néppárt az 1896. évi országgyűlési választásokon." *Századok* 112, no. 4 (1978): 730–56.

Szabó, Ferenc, S.J. *Keresztény gondolkodók a XX. században.* Szeged: Agapé, 2004.

Szabó, Miklós. "Új vonások a századfordulói magyar konzervatív politikai gondolkodásban." *Századok* 108 (1974): 1–65.

——. *Múmiák öröksége: Politikai és történeti esszék.* Budapest: Új Mandátum, 1995.

——. *Az újkonzervativizmus és a jobboldali radikalizmus története (1867–1918).* Budapest: Új Mandátum, 2003.

Szabó, Robert Győri. *A kommunista párt és a zsidóság.* Budapest: Windsor, 1997.

Szegvári, Katalin N. *Numerus clausus rendelkezések az ellenforradalmi Magyarországon a zsidó és nőhallgatók főiskolai felvételéről.* Budapest: Akadémiai kiadó, 1988.

Szigeti, Jenő. "Egyházaink az 1919/20-as ellenforradalmi fordulatban." *Theologiai Szemle* 12, nos. 7–8 (1970): 220–26.

Szita, Szabolcs, ed. *Magyarország 1944. Üldöztetés—Embermentés.* Budapest: Nemzeti tankönyvkiadó, 1994.

Szöllösi-Janze, Margit. "Horthy-Ungarn und die Pfeilkreuzlerbewegung." *Geschichte und Gesellschaft* 12, no. 2 (1986): 163–82.

——. *Die Pfeilkreuzlerbewegung in Ungarn: Historische Kontext, Entwicklung, und Herrschaft.* München: R. Oldenbourg Verlag, 1989.

Tocqueville, Alexis de. *Democracy in America*. New York: Knopf, 1956.

Tőkés, Rudolf L. *Béla Kun and the Hungarian Soviet Republic: The Origins and Role of the Communist Party of Hungary in the Revolutions of 1918–1919*. New York: Praeger, 1967.

Ungvári, Tamás. "A parvenü és a pária. A kulturális antiszemitizmus arcai." *Világosság* 32, no. 7–8 (1991): 492–508.

Ungváry, Krisztián. *Budapest ostroma*. Budapest: Corvina, 1998.

Vandenburg, Frank. *Abraham Kuyper*. Grand Rapids: Eerdmans, 1960.

Vardy, Steven Bela. *Modern Hungarian Historiography*. Boulder, CO: East European Quarterly, 1976.

Várkonyi, Ágnes R. *Thaly Kálmán és történetírása*. Budapest: Akadémiai kiadó, 1961.

Veer, Peter van der. *Religious Nationalism: Hindus and Muslims in India*. Berkeley: University of California Press, 1994.

——. *Imperial Encounters: Religion and Modernity in India and Britain*. Princeton: Princeton University Press, 2001.

Veer, Peter van der, and Hartmut Lehmann, ed. *Nation and Religion: Perspectives on Europe and Asia*. Princeton: Princeton University Press, 1999.

Vermes, Gábor. *István Tisza: The Liberal Vision and Conservative Statecraft of a Magyar Nationalist*. Boulder, CO: East European Monographs.

Völgyes, Iván, ed. *Hungary in Revolution, 1918–19: Nine Essays*. Lincoln: University of Nebraska Press, 1971.

Volkov, Shulamit. "Antisemitism as a Cultural Code: Reflections on the History and Historiography of Antisemitism in Imperial Germany." *Leo Baeck Yearbook* 23 (1978): 25–46.

Wandruszka, Adam, and Peter Urbanitsch, eds. *Die Habsburger Monarchie, 1848–1918. Bd. 4. Die Konfessionen*. Vienna: Verlag der österreichischen Akademie der Wissenschaften, 1985.

Weber, Eugen. *Apocalypses: Prophecies, Cults, and Millennial Beliefs through the Ages*. Cambridge: Harvard University Press, 1999.

Wistrich, Robert S. *Antisemitism: The Longest Hatred*. New York: Methuen, 1991.

Wolff, Richard J., and Jörg K. Hoensch, eds. *Catholics, the State, and the European Radical Right, 1919–1945*. Boulder, CO: Social Science Monographs, 1987.

Zeidler, Miklós. *A revíziós gondolat*. Budapest: Osiris, 2001.

Zimmerman, Susan. *Die bessere Hälfte? Frauenbewegungen und Frauenbestrebungen im Ungarn der Habsburgermonarchie 1848 bis 1918*. Vienna: Promedia, 1999.

Zinner, Tibor. *Az ébredők fénykora, 1919–1923*. Budapest: Akadémiai kiadó, 1989.

Zuccotti, Susan. *Under His Very Windows: The Vatican and the Holocaust in Italy*. New Haven: Yale University Press, 2000.

Index